Gray's New Book of Roads. the Tourist and Traveller's Guide to the Roads of England and Wales, and Part of Scotland

GRAY'S BOOK OF ROADS.

On an entirely New Plan.

PRICE SEVEN SHILLINGS BOUND;

OR, WITH A SERIES OF MAPS, FORMING A COMPLETE COUNTY ATLAS.

TWELVE SHILLINGS BOUND.

Topographical Works of Popular Interest,

PUBLISHED BY SHERWOOD AND CO.

I.

The BEAUTIES of ENGLAND and WALES; being Delineations, Topographical, Historical, and Biographical, of their several Counties. In twenty-five volumes, illustrated with upwards of seven hundred copper-plate engravings, price 30*l.* 2*s.* 6*d.* in boards, or may be had in separate Counties, as follows:—

	s.	*d.*		*s.*	*d.*		*s.*	*d.*		*s.*	*d.*
Bedfordshire	4	9	Essex	12	0	Monmouthshire	8	0	Suffolk	12	0
Berkshire	9	0	Gloucestershire	10	0	Norfolk	15	0	Surrey	10	6
Buckinghamshire	6	0	Hampshire	14	0	Northamptonshire	9	0	Sussex	8	0
Cambridgeshire	9	0	Herefordshire	10	0	Northumberland	9	0	Warwickshire	12	0
Cheshire	6	0	Hertfordshire	12	0	Nottinghamshire	12	0	Westmoreland	8	0
Cornwall	9	0	Huntingdonshire	9	0	Oxfordshire	18	0	Wiltshire	24	0
Cumberland	10	0	Kent	30	0	Rutlandshire	5	0	Worcestershire	15	0
Derbyshire	12	0	Lancashire	10	0	Shropshire	14	0	Wales, North	24	0
Devonshire	12	0	Leicestershire	10	0	Somersetshire	12	0	—— South	24	0
Dorsetshire	10	0	Lincolnshire	10	0	Staffordshire	16	0	Yorkshire	30	0
Durham	9	0									

Each County illustrated by a Map and several copper-plate Views.

II.

NEALE'S VIEWS of NOBLEMEN and GENTLEMEN'S SEATS, in England, Wales, Scotland, and Ireland; comprehending 432 elegantly engraved Views of some of the most splendid Mansions in the United Kingdom; accompanied with descriptions of the Mansions, and a genealogical Account of their Possessors. In 6 volumes royal 8vo. price 2*l.* 10*s.* each, or in royal 4to. with proof impressions of the plates on India paper, 5*l.* each.

III.

A NEW GUIDE to BLENHEIM, the Seat of his Grace the Duke of Marlborough; comprising six elegantly engraved Views from the Drawings of J. P. NEALE, with an historical description of the Mansion, and a Catalogue of the Pictures, including those lately removed from Marlborough House. In royal 8vo. price 6*s.*

IV.

A NEW PICTURE of the ISLE of WIGHT; illustrated with a Map, and twenty-six Plates of the most beautiful and interesting Views throughout the Island, in imitation of the original Sketches; by WILLIAM COOKE. To which is prefixed an introductory Account of the Island, and a Voyage round its Coast. Price 12*s.* in boards; or, in 8vo. with 10 additional Views, price 21*s.* boards.

V.

DELINEATIONS, Historical and Topographical, of THANET, and the CINQUE PORTS, (Margate, Ramsgate, Dover, &c.) comprehending 106 elegantly engraved Views by DEEBLE, of all the Churches, Castles, Vestiges of Antiquity, &c. &c. in the above districts, with appropriate Historical and Topographical descriptions. In 2 volumes, price 1*l.* 17*s.* 6*d.* in boards.

VI.

The TOPOGRAPHY of GREAT BRITAIN; or British Traveller's Pocket Directory, by G. A. COOKE; being an accurate and comprehensive Topographical and Statistical description of all the Counties in England, Wales, and Scotland, containing a minute detail of their Situation, Extent, Towns, Rivers, Lakes, Mines, Manufactures, Commerce, Agriculture, Curiosities, Natural History, Civil and Ecclesiastical Jurisdiction, &c. &c. complete in 26 pocket volumes, price 6*l.* in boards; or either County separately at the prices affixed.—

	s.	*d.*		*s.*	*d.*		*s.*	*d.*		*s.*	*d.*
Bedfordshire	2	0	Essex	2	0	Middlesex (2 parts)	4	0	South Wales	2	6
Berkshire	2	0	Gloucestershire	2	0	Monmouthshire	2	0	Staffordshire	2	0
Buckinghamshire	2	0	Hampshire	2	0	Norfolk	2	0	Suffolk	2	0
Cambridgeshire	2	0	Herefordshire	2	0	Northamptonshire	2	0	Surrey	2	0
Cheshire	2	0	Huntingdonshire and Rutlandshire	2	0	North Wales	2	6	Sussex	2	0
Cornwall	2	0	Hertfordshire	2	0	Northumberland	2	0	Warwickshire	2	0
Cumberland and the Lakes	4	0	Kent (2 parts)	4	0	Nottinghamshire	2	0	Westmoreland	2	0
Derbyshire	2	0	Lancashire (do.)	4	0	Oxfordshire	2	0	Wiltshire	2	0
Devonshire	4	0	Leicestershire	2	0	Scotland (6 parts)	12	0	Worcestershire	2	0
Dorsetshire	2	0	Lincolnshire	2	0	Shropshire	2	6	Yorkshire (2 parts)	4	6
Durham	2	0				Somersetshire	2	0	Isles of Wight, &c.	2	6

*** To Tourists and Travellers, this Work will be found a very useful guide and companion: its plan has received particular approbation, from each County being divided into easy Journeys, by which means Persons, either riding, or on foot, have the opportunity of viewing many Beauties, which might not otherwise be noticed.

GRAY'S NEW BOOK OF ROADS.

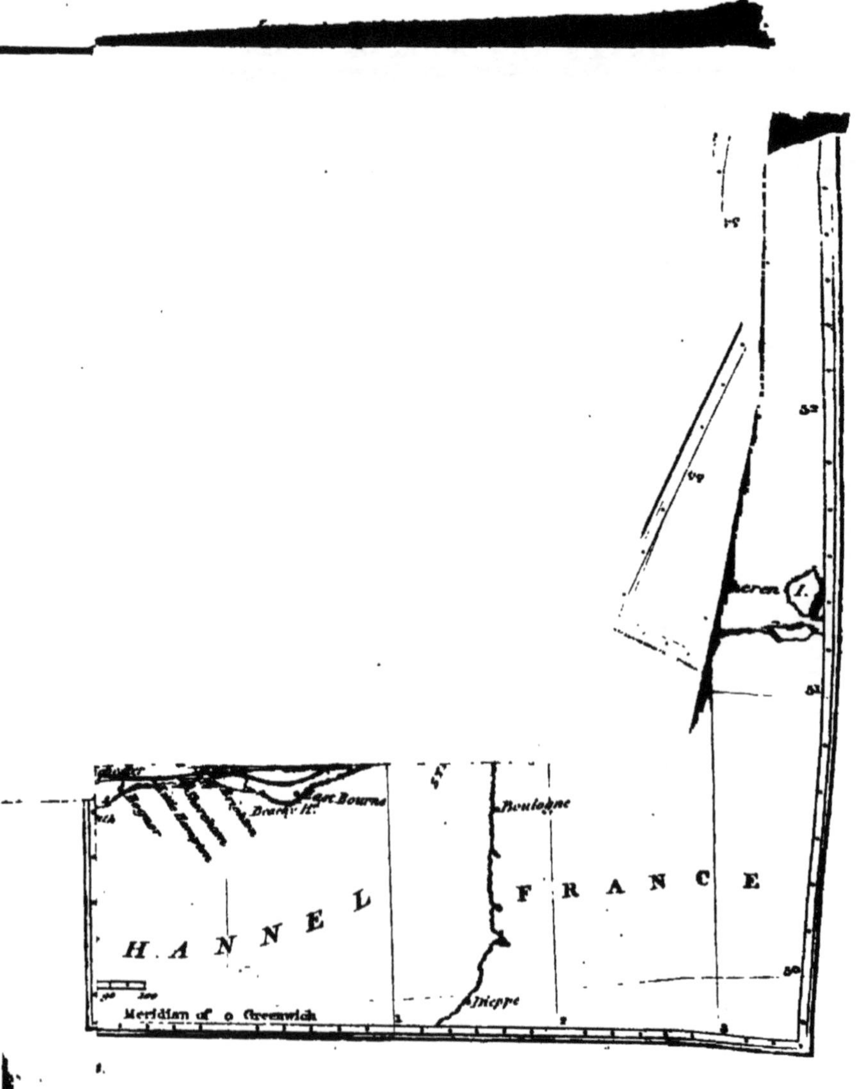

easy sou
viewing many Beauties, which might not otherwise be noticed.

GRAY'S NEW BOOK OF ROADS.

THE

TOURIST AND TRAVELLER'S

GUIDE TO THE ROADS

OF

ENGLAND AND WALES, AND PART OF SCOTLAND,

ON AN ENTIRELY NEW PLAN,

WHEREBY

THE DIFFERENT LINES OF ROUTE LEADING TO ANY REQUIRED POINT OF DISTANCE ARE BROUGHT UNDER NOTICE AT ONE REFERENCE, AND THE VARIATIONS SHEWN IN THE MARGIN:

THE GREAT ROADS,

EACH DISTINCTLY GIVEN, IN A CONTINUOUS LINE, FROM ONE EXTREME POINT TO ANOTHER, AND THE

CROSS ROADS

SO ARRANGED THAT THE ROUTE FROM ANY ONE PART OF THE KINGDOM TO ANOTHER MAY BE TRACED WITH THE GREATEST FACILITY:

WITH A VERY COPIOUS GENERAL INDEX,

AND SEPARATE LOCAL INDICES TO THE PRINCIPAL TOWNS AND WATERING PLACES: FORMING, ALTOGETHER, A COMPREHENSIVE, USEFUL, AND PERSPICUOUS

ITINERARY.

BY GEORGE CARRINGTON GRAY.

LONDON:

PRINTED FOR SHERWOOD, JONES, AND CO. PATERNOSTER ROW.

1824.

☞ This Work may be had bound up either with or without a Set of Maps forming a complete County Atlas.

The Direct Roads are explained and illustrated page viii; the Cross Roads, page 87.

In the General Map of England and Wales, opposite the Title-page, the Cross Roads are drawn in blue lines, in contradistinction to the Direct Roads in red. The points d'appui, where the roads join, being thus rendered prominently distinct, the Route from any one part of the kingdom to another may be easily traced, and referred to.

J. G. Barnard, Skinner Street, London.

PREFACE.

ON publishing a New Book of Roads, it is incumbent on the Compiler to state the grounds on which he rests his claims to the notice of the public; particularly as they are already in possession of two books of established reputation on the subject, those of Paterson and Carey, both of them works of great merit, and each of them distinguished by some particular advantage.

It is, in fact, on the principle implied by these very circumstances, that the present work has been undertaken; for, that a third book, as well on this as on any other subject, may also possess advantages, *exclusively its own*, will readily be admitted when the extreme intricacy of the subject is duly considered, as also that all knowledge being progressive, no limits can possibly be assigned to human improvement.

The grounds, then, on which this work rests its pretensions to public approbation, are, 1st, the novelty and perspicuity of its arrangement; and, 2dly, the various advantages arising out of such arrangement.

The principal of these advantages are, that we are enabled to concentrate and bring under the immediate notice of the traveller, at one reference from the General Index, the various lines of route leading to any required point of distance; and to shew the variations, not only to the ultimate point, but to all the intermediate points on the line, as exemplified and illustrated in Route I. where, at Gloucester, for instance (page 4), it will be seen that there are no less than ten variations of route to that ancient city. To Hereford, the variations are more numerous, inasmuch as the route thither is not only subject to the variations to Gloucester, but may be made through Worcester, whence it may be continued either through Malvern, or by way of Bromyard, or Stifford's Bridge. The direct line of route being given in a continuative sequence to the ultimate point of distance, and the aberrations from that line being shewn in the margin, the connecting lines of route are thus brought under the notice of the traveller in a manner which the Compiler trusts will be found as perspicuous as it is novel and hitherto unattempted.

The Cross Roads are also arranged on an entirely new plan, so as to obviate much of the intricacy which appears almost inherent in works of this description, and inseparable therefrom, and thereby enable the traveller to connect the several Roads with each other, with the greatest facility; the general index, in subserviency thereto, having been formed on such a plan as also to include distinct local indices to the principal places.

Other advantages will be found in the facilities afforded for the computation of distances, as shewn in the general explanation of the plan, p. viii.

Besides the above, another, and not the least advantage, in the estimation of many persons, will be found in the compression of this work within the limits of a pocket volume, so as to render it a most useful companion on horseback, or on pedestrian excursions, its bulk having been so far reduced by means of a compact and purposely adapted type. If what has been frequently observed of books generally be admitted, and the observation applies here with peculiar force, that a great book is a great evil, the advantages arising out of the converse proposition must be too obvious to need further notice, particularly as, in reference to a Book of Roads, the convenience of portability is so indispensable an object of consideration.

In furtherance of this object, the Compiler has of necessity been obliged to exclude all topographical information, except where it could be conveniently introduced, and also to limit his notice of the noblemen and gentlemen's seats to such as most prominently engage the attention of the traveller, or are otherwise celebrated. This deficiency is, however, the less to be regretted, in the accomplishment of the undertaking, since the requisite information is easily attainable in a multiplicity of topographical works of popular interest, some of which he has frequently taken occasion to refer to. As a pocket companion in this particular, Cooke's Topography is perhaps the most compendious, each county forming a separate and distinct volume, and comprehending (multum in parvo) much useful and interesting information.

But, though the Guide to the Roads has been thus compressed into the pocket size in which it appears, it will, nevertheless, be found to contain several lines of route, and much information relative to the roads, *exclusively its own*. We may here particularize Route 36, containing the Devonshire coast, and Route 53, containing a line of communication from the west end of the Metropolis to the Chester, Holyhead, and Manchester roads, not in any other book, as well as several lines of Cross Roads, an abstract of the new line now forming from Cheltenham to Hereford, &c. &c.*

A novel feature in this Compendium, besides what are more appositely noticed in the general explanation of the plan, will be found in the introduction of the village churches, as seen on the right and left of the road. What traveller can ride over the hills of Worcestershire and Herefordshire, for instance, without wishing to know (by way of reminiscence of the places which so pleasingly arrest the attention, and call into action a variety of latent feelings) the names of the villages which are occasionally seen to embellish the neighbouring eminences, and add so much to the beautiful picturesque scenery of those fertile counties? Many places are thus brought under the notice of the traveller, the names of which do not usually make their appearance in books of roads, in consequence of their being out of the direct line of road.

In the general execution of the work, it is hoped that it will prove satisfactory. Every care has been taken to render it as correct as possible, but in a work so abounding in figures it is too much to expect that it should be entirely faultless. The candid reader, however, appreciating the difficulties of the undertaking, will doubtless make due allowance for such errors as may have escaped notice. Any corrections, as well as suggestions for the improvement of the work, addressed to the Compiler, at the publishers, will be gratefully received, and duly noticed.

London, July, 1824.

* Since the sheet, containing the route to Cheltenham, has been printed off, the Compiler has been favoured with the following account of a further improvement on that line of road, in avoidance of Dowdeswell Hill:

"The new line of road, now forming under the direction of Mr. Baker, will totally avoid the dangerous acclivity called Dowdeswell Hill, by branching out of the present road at the bottom of the hill, and extending therefrom, leaving Dowdeswell Wood on the left hand, and the Hill on the right. It will pass by Sandywell Park and Andover's Ford, and rejoin the present road about 200 yards above Frogmill Inn. The new road will form a very beautiful drive, and the distance will not be increased more than 200 yards. It is expected to be completed within the present year, and opened to the public next spring."

THE MAIL COACH ROUTES FROM LONDON.

***Bath, Exeter, and Plymouth*, through** Reading, Marlborough, Devizes, Bath, Wells, Glastonbury, Bridgewater, Taunton, Wellington, Exeter. Thence to Plymouth; and through Liskeard, to Falmouth and Penzance.—*See page 72 to Bath; thence p 64.* [From Swan with Two Necks, Lad Lane.]

***Birmingham*, through Aylesbury, Bi-**cester, Banbury, Southam, Leamington, and Warwick.—pp 14,16. [King's Arms, Snow H.]

***Boston and Louth*, through Cambridge,** Stilton, Peterborough, Deeping, Spalding, and Spilsby—pp51,52. [Saracen's Head, do.]

***Brighton*, through Croydon, Reigate,** Crawley, and Cuckfield.—p 78. [Blossoms, Lawrence Lane.]

***Bristol*, through Reading, Marlborough,** Calne, Chippenham, Bath, Bristol. Thence to Newport, Cardiff, Swansea, Caermarthen, and Milford Haven.—p73. [Swan, Lad La.]

***Carlisle and Glasgow*, through Barnet,** Hatfield, Baldock, Eaton Socon, Stilton, Stamford, Grantham, Newark, Ollerton, Worksop, Tickhill, Doncaster, Ferrybridge, Wetherby, Boroughbridge, Greta Bridge, Appleby, Penrith, Carlisle. Thence to Glasgow, and to Dumfries and Portpatrick.—p 41, *to Boroughbridge; thence* p 46. [Bull and Mouth.]

***Chester*, through Northampton, Hinck-**ley, Lichfield, and Stafford.—p 24. [Golden Cross, Charing Cross.]

***Dover*, through Dartford, Rochester,** Sittingbourne, Feversham, and Canterbury. —p 82. [Angel, St. Clement's.]

***Exeter and Falmouth*, through Basing-**stoke, Andover, Salisbury, Blandford, Dorchester, Bridport, Axminster, Honiton, Exeter. Thence, thro' Launceston, to Falmouth and Penzance.—p 61. [Swan, Lad Lane.]

***Gloucester and Caermarthen*, through** Hounslow, Maidenhead, Henley, Oxford, Witney, Cheltenham, Gloucester, Ross, Monmouth, Abergavenny, Llandovery, Caermarthen. Thence to Haverfordwest and Milford Haven.—*Page 1 to Gloucester; thence p 75.* [Golden Cross, and Angel, St. Clement's, alternately.]

***Harwich*. See p. 56. [Spread Eagle,** Gracechurch Street.]

***Hastings*, through Farnborough, Tun-**bridge, and Lamberhurst.—p 80. [Bolt-in-Tun, Fleet Street.]

***Holyhead*, through Dunstable, Coventry,** Birmingham, Shrewsbury, Oswestry, and Bangor.—p 18. [Swan, Lad Lane.]

***Ipswich and Yarmouth*, through Chelms-**ford, Colchester, Ipswich, Saxmundham, Lowestoft, Yarmouth.—p 57. [White Horse, Fetter Lane.]

***Leeds*, through Barnet, Bedford, Ketter-**ing, Melton Mowbray, Nottingham, Sheffield; and to Huddersfield and Halifax.—p 35. [Bull and Mouth.]

***Liverpool*, through Barnet, St. Alban's,** Stoney Stratford, Daventry, Coventry, Lichfield, Newcastle under Line, Congleton, Knutsford, Warrington, Liverpool. Thence to Lancaster and Carlisle.—p 27. [Swan, Lad Lane.]

***Manchester and Carlisle*, through St. Al-**ban's, Dunstable, Northampton, Harborough, Leicester, Loughborough, Derby, Manchester, Preston, Lancaster, Carlisle.—p 30. [Swan, Lad Lane.]

***Norwich, by Ipswich*, through Rumford,** Chelmsford, and Colchester.—p 56. [Ditto.]

***Norwich, by Newmarket and Thetford*.—** p 55. [Golden Cross, and Cross Keys.]

***Portsmouth*, through Kingston, Guild-**ford, (thence to Chichester) Godalming and Petersfield.—pp 59,77. [Angel, St. Clement's.]

***Southampton and Poole*, through Staines,** Alton, Winchester, and Wimbourn.—p 60. [Bell and Crown, Holborn.]

***Worcester and Ludlow*, through Ux-**bridge, Beaconsfield, High Wycombe, Oxford, Woodstock, Chipping Norton, Worcester. Thence to Ludlow and Hereford, and to Leominster. *See p 9, to Worcester; thence to Ludlow*, p 12. [Bull and Mouth.]

***York, Edinburgh, Aberdeen, Inverness, and Thurso*, through** Ware, Royston, Huntingdon, Stamford, Grantham, Newark, Bawtry, Doncaster, Ferrybridge, York, Northallerton, Darlington, Durham, Newcastle, Alnwick, Berwick, Dunbar, Haddington, Edinburgh. Also to Aberdeen, Inverness, and Banff. Thence to Thurso.—*See p. 44.* [Bull and Mouth.]

ROUTE I.

LONDON TO OXFORD, BY HENLEY ON THAMES;

Continued to CHELTENHAM and GLOUCESTER, and thence to HEREFORD and ABERYSTWITH. The Mail Route to Gloucester.

Variations of Route, and Branch Routes.

[A] M.

London to Windsor:

By Slough to Eton, 22

Cross the Thames.

[Berks] WINDSOR 22¾

Another R. is by Staines, as follows:

HOUNSLOW 9¾

Through the Town,

L. to BELFONT 13¼

STAINES 16½

Cross the Thames.

[Surrey] EGHAM .. 17¾

[Berks] Old Windsor 20

WINDSOR 22¾

Thence to Reading:

Pass Windsor G. Park.

On R. St. Leonard's Hill 25

On L. Cranbourne Lodge.

North Street 26¼

Winkfield 28

Holly Green 29

L. *to Wokingham 7m.*

Warfield 30¼

Binfield Bridge 31½

1½ m. farther,

On R. Billingsbear Park, Lord Braybrooke.

L. *to Wokingham 3m.*

Bill Hill 35

Merry Hill Green .. 36¼

Loddon Bridge 37½

READING 41

(*a*) At Hyde Park Corner, left to Vauxhall Bridge 1½ mile, & thence to Kennington and New Cross, connecting, by the shortest line of communication, the South and South-Eastern environs of London, with the West and North-West roads.

LINE OF ROUTE.

LOC. DIST.

M. *from Hyde Park Corner.* (*a*)

Middlesex.

½ Knightsbridge.

1½ Kensington.

4 Hammersmith.

5 Turnham Green.

L. *to Chiswick, ¾m.*

6¼ *On* L. *over Kew Bridge to Richmond 3m.; thence to Twickenham 2m.*

6½ On L. Kew Palace.

7 BRENTFORD.

Cross the river Brent and the Grand Junction Canal.

7½ On L. Sion House, D. of Northumberland.

8 L. *to Twickenham thro' Isleworth, 2½m.*

9 Smallberry Green, T.G.

9½ HOUNSLOW.

L. *to Twickenham 2¼m.; thence to Kingston 3m.*

Through Hounslow, L. *to Staines;* R. *to*

12¼ CRANFORD BRIDGE.

On R. Cranford Park, Countess of Berkeley.

LOC. DIST.

M. *from Hyde Park Corner.*

13¾ SIPSON GREEN.

15¼ Longford.

17 Cross the river Coln.

Buckinghamshire.

41 17¼ COLNBROOK.

18½ Langley Broom.

L. *to Windsor by Datchet 3¼m.*

20½ SLOUGH.

L. *to Eton and Windsor* [A].

37 21¼ SALT HILL.

On R. Stoke Park, J. Penn, Esq. & Farnham Royal

On L. Windsor Castle.

23 Turn of the road to Burnham.

25 R. *to Taplow ½m.* (*b*)

33 25¼ MAIDENHEAD BRIDGE.

Cross the river Thames.

(*b*) At Taplow, and in its vicinity, are several very elegant seats. The ruins of Cliefden, which are seen from Maidenhead Bridge, add greatly to the picturesque beauties of the adjoining scenery, and are associated with much historic reminiscence. This once splendid palace (originally erected by Villiers, Duke of Buckingham) was destroyed by fire in 1795. See Britton and Brayley's Topography of Buckinghamshire.

Variations of Route, and Branch Routes.

M.

[B]

Another R. to Great Marlow, & thence to Henley:

To Burnham, (p.1.) 24
Hedsor 27
Bone End 28
Little Marlow 30
GREAT MARLOW, 31½
Medmenham 35
Mill End 36
Fawley Court...... 38
[Oxon] HENLEY on THAMES 39¼

(c) On approaching Oxford, the most prominent objects are, on the left, the dome of the Radcliffe library, and the tapering spires of St. Mary's and All Saints' churches, in contrast with the intervening Gothic pinnacles of Merton College. Next, the Cathedral spire, and the magnificent tower of Christ Church. Amidst the numerous adjoining spires and pinnacles may be distinguished those of the public schools and the two towers of All Souls. On the right Magdalen tower and grove terminate a series of objects, which, on approaching this celebrated University, impresses the traveller with corresponding ideas of its architectural grandeur and its munificent endowments. —Good views of the colleges and public buildings are given in a work entitled, *The Oxford Visitor.*

L.D. | M. *from Hyde Park Corner.*

Berkshire.

22 | 26 MAIDENHEAD.

[*Prospective Distances:*
Henley on T. .. 9 *m.*
Benson 20
Oxford 32
Cheltenham 72¼
Gloucester 81½
Ross 98
Hereford 112¼
Aberystwith .... 188]

R. *to Gt. Marlow* 5*m.* [B]

31 | 26¾ GOLDEN FLEECE INN.

L. *to Reading* 12¼*m.*

Through Maidenhead Thicket.

30 On L. Hall Place, Sir G. East, Bart.

27 | 30¾ Hurley Bottom.

33 Rose Hill.

On R. Medmenham

34 On L. Park Place, H. P. Sperling, Esq.

34¾ Henley Bridge.

Cross the Thames.

Oxfordshire. (d)

23 | 35 HENLEY ON THAMES.

[*Prospective Distances:*
Oxford .... 23 *m.*
Cheltenham .... 63¼]

L. *to Reading* 8*m.*

R. *to Great Marlow* 7½*m.*

36½ Assington Cross.

20 | 37¾ Bix (Bixgibwen) T. G.

18 | 40 Nettlebed.

R. *to Watlington* 5½*m.*

L.D. | M. *from Hyde Park Corner.*

41½ Nuffield Heath.

L. *to Wallingford* 4½*m.*

42 On R. Swynecombe

44 Beggar's Bush.

12 | 46 BENSON (Bensington).

10 | 47½ Shillingford.

49¼ Dorchester.

L. *to Abingdon* 6½*m.*

5 | 52¾ Nuneham Courtenay.

On L. Nuneham Courtenay Park, Earl Harcourt.

54½ Sandford.

55½ Little Moor.

1 | 57 Approach to Oxford (c).

57¼ St. Clement's, T. G.

Cross the river Charwell at Magdalen Bridge, and enter

* | 57¾ OXFORD.

Another route to Oxford is by High Wycombe, (See R. 3.) which is 4 miles shorter than by Henley. Consequently, in travelling the Wycombe route to Cheltenham and Gloucester, and onwards to Aberystwith, all the distances beyond Oxford will be 4 miles less from London than in the annexed route by Henley. Making these deductions, the route here given from Oxford will serve equally, whether the route to that city be by Wycombe or by Henley.

[*Prospective Distances:*
Witney .... 11½*m.*
Northleach 27½
Cheltenham 40½
Tewkesbury ... 49½
Malvern 56

* OXFORD.

Variations of Route, and Branch Routes.

[C] M.

To Banbury:

OXFORD 58
Kidlington Green, 63
Hopcroft's Holt .. 70½
DEDDINGTON.. 74¾
Adderbury 77½
BANBURY...... 81

[D]

To Cirencester:

OXFORD 58
Botley 59¾
Chorley.......... 61½
Besselsleigh 63¾
Tubney 66¼
CIRENCESTER, as in R. 2...... 95

[E]

At the junction of the roads....... 93¼
L. to Seven Wells, 96¼
Little Whitcombe, 100
Brockworth 101¼
GLOUCESTER .. 105½
By High Wycombe 101½ *m.*

(*d*) The Isis forms the southern boundary of the county, separating it from Berkshire, until its confluence with the Thame, a little above Shillingford Bridge, whence the Thames derives its name, Thame-isis. The serpentine course of the Thames to Reading, and thence to Henley, is very picturesque and diversified.—Park Place, H. P. Sperling, Esq. near Henley, is situated on the brow of a range of hills, which accompanies the windings of the river for several miles. The grounds of this elegant mansion, whose site is nearly 300 feet above the level of the water, are pre-eminently grand and beautiful.

L.D. M. *from Hyde Park Corner.*

Gloucester 49¼
Ross 66
Hereford 80½
Aberystwith 156

On Return Route:

Benson 12
Henley 23
Maidenhead 32
Hounslow....... 48

ENTERING OXFORD,
On R. Magdalen Coll.
Along the High Street,
58 On R. Queen's College.
On L. University College (*e*).
58¼ Carfax [C]
On L. Christ Church College.
Cross the river Isis.
58½ Folly Bridge.

Berkshire.

59¾ Botley.
L. *to Cirencester* [D].
61½ On R. Wytham..
26 63 Eynsham Bridge.
Cross the Isis again.

Oxfordshire.

64 Eynsham.
68¾ Newland T. G.
20 69¾ WITNEY.
[*By High Wycombe* 65½*m.*]
71 On R. Minster Lovell ......
75 L. *to Northleach*, R. *to*

L.D. M. *from Hyde Park Corner.*

76½ BURFORD (*f*).
R. *to Stow on the W.* 10*m.*
—*to Chip. Norton* 11*m.*
L. *to Farringdon* 10½*m.*
—*to Cirencester* 16½*m.*

Gloucestershire.

19 79½ Little Barrington.
80½ On R. Barrington Park, L. Dynevor.
82½ On R. Dutton Park.
On L. Sherborne House, Lord Sherborne.
13 85½ NORTHLEACH.
R. *to Stow on the W.* 10*m.*
L. *to Cirencester* 9*m.*
On L. Stowell Park, Lord Stowell.
11 87½ Compton Abdale, and Compton Park, on L.

(*e*) The University of Oxford contains 25 colleges and halls, of which a very copious and satisfactory account will be found in Cooke's Topography of the county, our limits precluding any other than a transient notice of the sites of such as present themselves on the direct line of road through the city.

(*f*) By taking the left hand road to Northleach, and leaving Burford out of the route, the traveller saves some distance, besides the relief afforded to his horses, by avoiding the valley in which Burford is situate.

Variations of Route, and Branch Routes.

M.

[F]

STOW ON THE W.
as in p. 10...... 81½
Lower Swell 82½
Thence to the junction of the roads near Dowdeswell 92
Charlton Kings .. 95¾
CHELTENHAM, 96¾

This route enables the tourist to take a view of Blenheim.

[G]

CIRENCESTER, (p. 8)........... 88½
Birdlip 102
LeckhamptonCourt 106
CHELTENHAM .. 108½

[H]

To Hereford by Gloucester and Ledbury:

GLOUCESTER, by High Wycombe. 103½
Alney Island...... 104
Maizemore Bridge. 106
Cross the Severn.
Woolridge Hill ... 109½
Turn on L. to
Staunton Swan.... 112
[Worc.] Red Marley 115½
[Heref.] Little London............ 117¼
On R. Eastnor Castle, Lord Somers.
LEDBURY 120
Wall Hills........ 123
Trumpets 124¼
Poolend 125¼
Torrington 127½
Stoke Edith 128½
Dormington 130
Barlestree........ 131
Lugwardine 132½
Cross the river Lugg.
Tupsley 133½
HEREFORD 135½

Thence to Brecon:

[See next page.

L.D. M. *from Hyde Park Corner.*

88½ On R. Hasleton
(6) 92¼ FROGMILL Inn.
(5) 93¼ Junction of the roads.
R. *to Stow on the Wold* 11½m.
L. *to Glouc. by Whitcombe* [E].
(4) 94 Dowdeswell.
(2) 96 Charlton Kings.
97¼ Cadnall.
* 98¼ CHELTENHAM.

[*By High Wycombe* 94½m.]

Other routes to Cheltenham, are by Stow on the Wold [F], or by Cirencester [G].

[*Prospective Distances:*

Gloucester	9 m.
Malvern	26
Ross	26
Hereford	40
Aberystwith	116

On Return Route:

Northleach	13
Witney	29
Oxford	40½]

(2) 100½ Division of the road.
Forward to Tewkesbury.
On R. Swindon
Turn on the left to
(3) 101½ Heydon Elm.
(5) 103 Staverton Bridge.
On R. Staverton
105½ Churchdown, on L.
(9) 107½ GLOUCESTER

[*By High Wycombe* 103½m.]

Other routes to Gloucester are as follows:

1. By High Wycombe to Oxford, and thence as in the mail route.

2, 3. By either of the above routes to Oxford, and thence by Northleach to the turn of the road leading to Whitcomb; thence to Gloucester, as in Note [E].

4, 5. By either of the routes to Oxford, and thence through Woodstock and Chip. Norton to Cheltenham, as in Note [F].

6, 7. By either of the two last routes, but quitting the Cheltenham road at the turn of the road to Whitcomb, and thence as in Note [E].

8, 9, 10. By Cirencester, and by a diversion from that route. See R. 2.

[*Prospective Distances:*

Ross	17 m.
Hereford	31
Kington	51½
New Radnor ..	58½
Rhayadergwy ..	77½
Aberystwith	106½

On Return Route:

Cheltenham	9
Northleach	22
Witney	38½
Oxford	49½]

Cross the river Severn.
108 Alney Island [H].
(28) 110 Highnam.
R. *to Newent* 6½m.
On R. Highnam Park, Sir B. W. Guise, Bt.
112 Churcham.
(23) 115 Huntley, T. G.
L. *to Mitchel Dean* 4¾m.
116½ Durley Cross.
(20) 118 Longhope.
119½ Lea.
R. *to Hereford by Hampton Bishop* 17m.

* HEREFORD.

Variations of Route, and Branch Routes.

M.

[H 2]

HEREFORD	135½
White Cross	136¾
King's Acre	138
Sugwas Pool	139½
Ware	140½
Bridge Sollers	142
Garnons	143½
Portway	144¼
On L. Monington ⛪, the reputed burial place of Owen Glendower.	
Stanton	144¾
On L. Moccas Court.	
Hanmer's Cross ..	146
Cross the Wye on L. to	
Bredwardine	147¾
Clockmill	151
Hardwick	153
On L. the Cusop and Black Mountains.	
[Brecon] HAY	155
Glasbury	159
Brynllys	162¼
Velinvach	165¾
BRECON	170
OR,	
Hanmer's Cross ..	146
Letton	147¼
Willersley	149
Winforton	149¾
Whitney	151¾
Cross the river Wye.	
Clifford	154
HAY	156½

[I]

Prospective Distances from Hereford:

Kington	20½m.
Rhayadergwy ..	46
Aberystwith	75½
On Return Route:	
Ross	14¼
Gloucester	31
Cheltenham	40
Oxford	80½

L.D.	M. from Hyde Park Corner.	
	Herefordshire.	
	122	Weston.
14	124	ROSS. *[By High Wycombe 120m.]* R. *to Ledbury 13m.* Cross the river Wye.
13	125	Wilton. On R. Bridstow .. ⛪ L. *to Monmouth 9½m.*
11	127	Peterstow.
	128½	Pengethley. On R. Rev. T. P. Symonds.
8	130	Harewood End Inn. ⛪ Pencoyd, on L. On R. Harewood, Sir H. Hoskins, Bart.

L.D.	M. from Hyde Park Corner.	
	131	Landinabo.
	132½	Great Birch.
4	134	Cross in Hand T. G. ⛪ Dewsall, on L.
3	135	Callow. On R. Holme Lacey, Duke of Norfolk.
	137	Red Hill. Cross the river Wye.
*	138¼	HEREFORD [I]. *[By High Wycombe 134¼m.]* Other R. to Hereford are by Gloucester and Ledbury, as in Note H; or through Worcester as in Route III. referred to below.¶
	139½	White Cross.

¶ Since this work has been arranged for the press, an act has passed the Legislature for the erection of a bridge over the river Severn at the Haw Passage, and for the formation of a new line of road from the Swan Inn, Comb Hill, on the Tewkesbury road, to Staunton Swan, on the Ledbury road, which will shorten the line of communication between Cheltenham and Hereford, and consequently between London and Hereford, and great part of the principality of Wales, nearly six miles, as shewn in the following abstract.

LONDON TO HEREFORD.

	By Henley.		By High Wycombe.
Through Gloucester and Ross (as above)	138¼	..	134¼
——— Ledbury, as in Note [H] ..	139½	..	135½
——— Worcester and Ledbury (p. 7)	147	..	143
——— Bromyard (p. 11)	143	..	139
——— Stifford's Bridge (p. 7, B) ..	141½	..	137½

By the proposed New Line of Road.

Through CHELTENHAM to the Swan Inn, Comb Hill, as in page 7	103¼	..	99¼
Intended Bridge over the Severn at the Haw Passage,	106	..	102
Staunton Swan (here join the Ledbury road from Gloucester)	109	..	105
L. *to Gloucester 8 miles.*			
R. *to Upton on Severn 7¾ miles.*			
Forward to HEREFORD through Ledbury, as in Note [H]	132½	..	128½

Variations of Route, and Branch Routes.

M.

[K]
Another R. to Kington:

HEREFORD 138½
Willersley (N).... 151½
Eardisley 154
On L. the Brilleys Mountain.
Bullingham Chapel 155
Sponn Moor...... 155½
KINGTON 159
R. *to Presteign 7m.*
OR, HEREFORD 138½
White Cross...... 139½
Three Elms 140¾
Tillington 143¼
Brinsop Court 144¾
Wormesley 146¾
WEOBLEY 149¾
Bond's Green 153¾
Lionel's Hall 155¼
KINGTON 158¾

[L]
To Builth and Tregarron:

NEW RADNOR. 165¾
Llanvihangel Nant Mellan 168½
Boilybachan...... 172¾
Pencross 174½
Cross the river Wye.
R. *to Llandrindod Wells 5½m.*
Brecon] BUILTH, or BUALT 177½
Llanavon 182½
Llangammarch.... 185¼
Bringwyn 189½
Llanvihangel Abergwesin 192
Card.] Dole Goch 198
TREGARRON... 209
Or, *by Hay:*
HAY (p. 5) 155
Glasbury 159½
BUILTH 174½
Tregarron, as above 206

L.D.	M. *from Hyde Park Corner.*
	Breynton, on L.
	140¾ King's Acre.
	L. *to Hay and Brecon, as in* Note [H].
	142 Stretton.
	143½ Credenhill (*g*).
	144 On R. Brinsop....
68	146 Mansell Lacy.
	147 On R. Foxley, Uvedale Price, Esq.
	Mansel Grange, on L.
	147½ Yazor.
	148¾ Norton (*h*).
	149½ Eccles Green.
	On R. Garnston Castle.
63	150¾ Sarnsfield.
	152¼ Wonton.
	153½ Wonton's Ash.
58	156 Lionel's (Lion's) Hall.
	157½ Pentress.
55	159 KINGTON [K].
	[*By High Wycombe* 155*m.*]

Radnorshire.

L.D.	M.
48	166 NEW RADNOR [L].
	[*By High Wycombe* 162*m. By Worcester* 159*m.*]
	168½ Llanvihangel Nant Mellan.
	Over the Llanhilling Hills to
41	173 Llandegley.
	174¾ Penybont.

L.D.	M. *from Hyde Park Corner.*
	180½ Nantmell.
29	185 RHAYADERGWY.
	[*By High Wycombe* 181*m. By Worcester* 178*m.*]
	R. *to Llanydloes* 12*m.*
	L. *to Bualt* 14*m.*
	Cross the river Wye.

Cardiganshire.

L.D.	M.
18	196 Cwm Ystwith.
15	199 Pentrebrunant.
12	202 DEVIL'S BRIDGE.
9	205 Eskynald.
2	212 Piccadilly T. G.
*	214 ABERYSTWITH.
	[*By High Wycombe* 210*m. By Worcester & Leominster, as in* R. 3. 207 *miles.*]

[*Prospective Distances on Return Route:*

Rhayadergwy ..	29 *m.*
New Radnor ..	48
Kington........	55
Hereford	75½
Ross	90
Gloucester	106½
Cheltenham	116
Oxford	156]

(*g*) On R. of Credenhill, the Magna Castra of the Romans; and on L. the village of Kenchester, the site of a Roman station. This village disputes with Monington (H 2) the reputation of being the place of interment of Owen Glendower.

(*h*) On R. Lady Lift Hill, from the summit of which is a very diversified prospect of the rich surrounding district, bounded by the lofty mountains on the west.

* ABERYSTWITH.

LONDON TO MALVERN.

Variations of Route, and Branch Routes.

[A]

Another Route to Tewkesbury is by Chipping Norton to

	M.
STOW on the W. (as in p. 10)	81½
Upper Swell	82¾
Condicote........	84¾
Ford	89½
Coscombe Cross ..	91
Stanway	92¼
Toddington	94¾
Aston Carrant	101½
TEWKESBURY.	103½

[A 2]

To Winchcombe:

	M.
STOW on the W.	81½
Lower Swell	82½
Lower Gniting....	88
WINCHCOMBE-	94¼

[B]

Another Route to Hereford, through Worcester:

	M.
WORCESTER ..	111
St. John's.........	112
Bransford Bridge -	114½
Leigh Senton	117
Stifford's Bridge ..	120½
[Heref.] Ridgeway Cross...........	121½
Frome's Hill	124¾
Five Bridges	126¼
Eggleton	128¼
Shucknell........	131½
Lugg Mills	135½
Cross the river Lugg.	
HEREFORD	137½

(*a*) An Act has passed the Legislature for the erection of a bridge over the Severn, at Mythe, which will conduce to great improvements in the lines of road through this district.

L.D.	M. *from Tyburn Turnpike.*
	Gloucestershire.
26	94¼ CHELTENHAM (p. 4). [*By High Wycombe to Oxford.*]
	96 Bedlam.
	97 Uckington.
21	99¼ Swan Inn, Comb Hill. L. *to Gloucester* 7*m.*
17	103¼ TEWKESBURY [A]. R. *to Pershore* 9½*m.* — *to Evesham* 13*m.* Cross the river Avon near its confluence with the Severn (*a*).
16	104 Mythe.
14	105½ Twining.
	107½ Ripple, on L.
	Worcestershire.
12	108¼ Stratford Bridge.
11	109¼ Naunton.
	109½ *Forward to Worcester* 10*m.* L. *to*
9	111 UPTON on SEVERN.
	116½ Little Malvern. L. *to Hereford* 20¼*m.*
2	118 MALVERN WELLS.
*	120 GREAT MALVERN.
	OR,
	111 UPTON on SEVERN.
	112 Hanley. *Forward to Worcester.* L. to Malvern Wells, &
	118 GREAT MALVERN.

ANOTHER ROUTE TO

MALVERN,

and thence to Hereford, through Worcester.

L.D.	M. *from Tyburn Turnpike.*
	111 WORCESTER. (p. 10) Cross the river Severn R. *to Tenbury & Ludlow*
	112 St. John's. *Forward to Bromyard* L. *to*
29	114 Powick.
	117½ Newland's Green.
	119¼ GREAT MALVERN.
	121½ MALVERN WELLS.
20	123 Little Malvern. On L. Eastnor Castle Lord Somers.
	Herefordshire.
17	126 Lower Mitchel.
	127½ LEDBURY.
	130½ Wall Hills.
11	131¾ Trumpets.
10	132¾ Poolend.
8	135 Torrington.
7	136 Stoke Edith. On L. E. Foley, Esq.
	137½ Dormington.
	138½ Barlestree.
3	140 Lugwardine. Cross the river Lugg.
2	141 Tupsley.
*	143 HEREFORD [B].

LONDON TO CIRENCESTER;

And thence to GLOUCESTER.

Variations of Route, and Branch Routes.

	M.
[A]	
Nuffield Heath (p. 3)	41½
Crowmarsh Gifford	45
[Berks] WALLINGFORD	45½
R. *to Oxford* 13m.	
L. *to Reading* 15¼m.	
Brightwell	47¼
Harwell	53¼
Ardington........	56¼
WANTAGE	59½
R. *to Oxford* 15½m.	
L. *to Hungerford* 14m.	
East Charlow	60¼
Stanford	64½
FARRINGDON..	68
[B]	
FARRINGDON..	69¾
Coleshill	73½
[Wilts] HIGHWORTH	76
Cold Harbour	79¾
CRICKLADE ..	83¾
[C]	
To Gloucester by Barnsley:	
FAIRFORD	79½
Barnsley	85½
Perrott's Bridge ..	89¼
Birdlip	99½
GLOUCESTER ..	107
[D]	
To Gloucester by Painswick:	
CIRENCESTER.	88½
Pass Oakley Park on L.	
Westwood Tinley -	94½
L. *to Stroud 5m.*	
Painswick	99¾
GLOUCESTER ..	106½

L.D.	M. *from Hyde Park Corner.*	
		Oxfordshire.
5	49¼	Dorchester (p. 3.)
	50¾	Burcot.
	52	Clifton.
1	54¾	Culham Bridge. Cross the Isis.
		Berkshire.
*	55¾	ABINGDON. [*Prospective Distances:* Farringdon .... 14 *m.* Lechlade ...... 20 Cirencester .... 33 Gloucester .... 50½] R. *to Oxford* 6½ *m.*
1	56¾	Shippon.
	59	Shipstead.
-	60	Tubney. *Junction of the road from Oxford to Farringdon.*
5	61	Fifield.
6	62	KINGSTON INN.
	65	Pusey Furze.
	67	R. *to Bampton* 4*m.*
	68	Littleworth.
14	69¾	FARRINGDON. Another Route is by Wallingford [A]. [*Prospective Distances:* Cirencester .... 19 *m.* Gloucester .... 36¼] L. *to Highworth* [B].
	73½	Buscot.
19	74¾	St. John's Bridge. Cross the Isis.

L.D.	M. *from Hyde Park Corner.*	
		Gloucestershire.
13	75½	LECHLADE.
9	79½	FAIRFORD [C].
	83¼	Poulton (Wilts).
4	84¼	Easington.
	85½	Ampney Crucis.
*	88½	CIRENCESTER [D]. [*Prospective Distances:* Gloucester .... 17½ *m.* Ross .... 34 Hereford...... 48½ Aberystwith ..124] *On Return Route:* Lechlade...... 13 Farringdon .... 19 Abingdon .... 33 Henley on T... 53½]
	98½	Birdlip.
5	101	Whitcombe.
4	102	Brockworth.
3	103	Hucclecote.
2	104	Barnwood.
*	106	GLOUCESTER. *Thence to Hereford and Aberystwith*, as in R. 1.

To Stroud:

88½ CIRENCESTER, as above.
Pass Oakley Park on R.
98¼ MINCHING HAMPTON.
101½ RODBOROUGH.
102½ STROUD.
By Westwood Tinley, [D] 99½*m.*

LONDON TO WORCESTER;

The Mail Route by HIGH WYCOMBE. Continued to ABERYSTWITH by LEOMINSTER and PRESTEIGN.

Variations of Route, and Branch Routes.

[A] M.

Bayswater ...... ¾
Kensington Gravel Pits 1½
Shepherd's Bush .. 3
Acton 5
Ealing 6
Hanwell 7½
Cross the river Brent 8¼
On L. Osterley Park, Earl of Jersey.
SOUTHALL 9½
HAYES END 12¼
Hillingdon 13¼
UXBRIDGE 15

[B]

Another Route:
H. WYCOMBE.. 29
Bradenham 33
RISBOROUGH.. 37
Kingsey 42½
Cross the Thame.
[Oxon] THAME.. 45½

[C]

At Oxford,
Prospec. Distances:
Woodstock...... 8
Chip. Norton.... 19
Morton in M..... 27½
Worcester 57
Leominster...... 83
Aberystwith 153
On Return Route:
High Wycombe.. 25
Beaconsfield 31
Uxbridge 39
See also page 3.

(*a*) A monumental inscription in Beaconsfield church records the death of Edmund Burke, therein interred, who resided at Butler's Court, in this parish. The estate is now the property of Mr. Dupre: the house was burnt down a few years past.

L.D. M. *from Tyburn Turnpike.*

Middlesex.

39 15 UXBRIDGE, as in the margin [A].
Cross the river Coln and the Grand Junction Canal.

Buckinghamshire.

38 15¾ Neals.
17½ Red Hill.
On R. Denham..
36 18 Tatling End.
R. *to Amersham and Aylesbury* (p. 15.)
34 20 GERARD'S CROSS.
On L. Bulstrode, Duke of Somerset. Near Beaconsfield, on R. Wilton Park, J. Dupre, Esq.
31 23¼ BEACONSFIELD.
On L. Hall Barns, Rev. H. Waller; formerly the residence of Waller, the poet, whose remains are interred in Beaconsfield church yard (*a*).
24½ Hotspur Heath.
26½ Loudwater.
27½ Wycombe Marsh.
25 29 HIGH WYCOMBE.
On L. Wycombe Abbey, Lord Carrington.

L.D. M. *from Tyburn Turnpike.*

31½ West Wycombe (*b*).
On L. Wycombe Park, Sir J.D. King, Bt.
22 32¼ Ham Farm.

Oxfordshire.

36½ STOKEN CHURCH.
16 38 On R. Aston Rowant
L. *to Watlington* 3½*m.*
14 40¼ Postcombe.
R. *to Thame*, 4*m.* [B].
12 42 TETSWORTH.
44½ Three Pigeons.
47½ WHEATLEY BRIDGE.
L. *to Oxford* 6*m.* the old road over Shotover Hill.
Cross the river Thame.
50 On R. Forest Hill
2 52¼ Headington.
53¾ St. Clement's T. G.
* 54 OXFORD [C].
[*By Henley on Thames* (page 3) 58 *miles.*]

(*b*) The church of West Wycombe, as well as the adjoining mansion of Sir J.D. King, are well worthy of observation. Storer's "Portfolio" contains some pleasing views of both. The orders, which have been stated in some topographical works, as operating to the exclusion of strangers from a view of the stately mansion and grounds, we are happy to say, no longer exist.

* OXFORD.

Variations of Route, and Branch Routes.

	M.
[D]	
At Wheatley......	48½
R. to Forest Hill..	50
Stanton St. John's.	51½
Islip	56
Bletchington......	58¼
Enslow Bridge....	60¼
Glympton........	64¼
Kiddington T. G...	65¾
ENSTONE........	68¼
CH. NORTON ..	72¾
Another R. is by Bicester (p. 16).	
[E]	
At BENGEWORTH	95
Cross the Avon on R.	
EVESHAM......	95½
Thence to Worcester:	
Wyre Piddle	101
Spetchley	107½
On L. R. Berkeley, Esq.	
Red Hill	108½
WORCESTER ..	110
[F]	
ALCESTER (R. 9)	97
Arrow	98
[Worc.] Stony Morton	101½
Radford	103
Kington	103¾
Grafton Flyford ..	105¼
R. *to Droitwich 7m.*	
Upton Snodsbury,	106¾
Spetchley	110¼
WORCESTER ..	112¾
[F 2]	
CHELTENHAM..	94½
Thence (p. 7) to WORCESTER ...	119½

(*c*) See Neale's Guide to Blenheim, for a copious account of this splendid mansion, accompanied with several very beautiful views.

L. D.	M. *from Tyburn Turnpike.*
	Along High Street into St. Giles's Street.
	On R. St. John's College.
	Through the City, on L. the Observatory.
	55 R. *to Deddington;* L. *to*
	56½ Wolvercot.
	58 Yarnton T. G.
	59½ Begbrook.
49	62 WOODSTOCK.
	On L. Blenheim, Duke of Marlborough (c).
	64 L. *to Charlbury 4m.*
	66½ Kiddington T. G.
	On L. Ditchley Park, Earl of Normanton.
42	69 ENSTONE.
	71 On R. Heythorpe, Duke of Beaufort.
	72 R. *to Chapel House ¾m. and thence into the present line of road again at Salford.*
36	73¾ CHIPPING NORTON.
	Another Route is by Islip [D].
	74½ Salford.
	76½ Salford Hill.
	[79¼ Oddington, Glouc. 81¼ STOW ON THE WOLD. Or, by Churchill from Chipping Norton, 82¼m.]
31	80 Four Shire Stone;
	At the junction of the Counties of Oxford, Gloucester, Worcester, and Warwick.

L. D.	M. *from Tyburn Turnpike.*
	On R. Northwick, Lord Northwick.
	R. *to Campden 6½m.*
	Gloucestershire.
30	81½ MORTON in MARSH.
28	83½ Bourton on the Hill.
	Worcestershire.
	89 Broadway Hill.
	On L. Spring Hill, Hon. J. Coventry.
21	90 BROADWAY.
	93 Wickhamford Bridge.
16	95 BENGEWORTH.
	R. *to Evesham* [E].
15	96 Little Hampton.
	101¾ Cross the river Avon.
9	102 PERSHORE.
	L. *to Tewkesbury 10½m.*
	106½ Stoulton.
2	108¾ Whittington.
	109½ Red Hill.
*	111 WORCESTER.

Other routes are by Henley on Thames to Oxford (R. 1), 115m; Or by Aylesbury and Alcester [F]. Or by Cheltenham.

[*Prospective Distances:*

Bromyard......	14 m.
Leominster	20
Presteign	40
Rhayader	67
Aberystwith....	96
On Return Route:	
Evesham	16½
Broadway......	21
Morton in M. ..	29½
Chip. Norton ...	38
Woodstock	48
Oxford	57]

* WORCESTER.

Variations of Route, and Branch Routes.

M.

[G]
BROMYARD.... 125
Stoke Lacy 129
Burley T. G. 131¼
¾m. further, on L.
Ocle Prichard
Withington Marsh, 134¾
Ewe Withington.. 135½
Lugg Mills 137
Cross the river Lugg.
Aylstone Hill 138½
HEREFORD.... 139

[H]
HEREFORD, by High Wycombe & Gloucester (p. 5) 135
White Cross....... 136½
Three Elms 137¼
Portway 139¾
New Inn 142
West Hope 144
Stretford Bridge.. 146½
Perryditch 147½
Eardsland......... 149
Pembridge 150½
Clear Brook....... 151
Staple Barr 154½
Comb 156
[Radnor] PRESTEIGN......... 158
KNIGHTON 165

[I]
Prospective Distances from Aberystwith, on Return Route:
Rhayadergwy .... 29 m.
New Radnor 48
Presteign......... 56
Leominster 70
Bromyard 82
Worcester 96
Oxford 153

Thence,
By Wycombe, p. 9.
— Henley, p. 3.

L.D.	M. from Tyburn Turnpike.	
		R. to *Kidderminster* 14m.
		—— *Bewdley* 13½m.
		—— *Stourport* 10¼m.
		Cross the riv. Severn to
	112	St. John's.
		R. to *Ludlow*, see R. 4.
		L. to *Malvern*, *Ledbury*, and *Hereford*.
22	115	Cotheridge.
	117½	Broadwas.
17	119¾	Knightsford Bridge.
		Cross the river Teme.
		Herefordshire.
	122	Brinkstee Common.
	123	Bromyard Down.
12	125	BROMYARD.
		L. to *Hereford* [G].
10	127	Munderfield.
	128½	Bridenbury.
	129½	Batchley Green.
		Grendon Bishop, on L.
5	132	Docklow.
4	133	Steen's Bridge.
3	134	Fair Mile.
	136	Eaton Bridge.
		Cross the river Lugg.
*	137	LEOMINSTER.
	139¼	Cholcestre.
	141½	Kingsland.
8	143	Mortimer's Cross.
6	145	Shobdon T. G.
		On R. Shobdon Court.

L.D.	M. from Tyburn Turnpike.	
	147½	Staple Barr.
		On R. Byton ....
	149	Combe Moor.
		Cross the riv. Endwell.
		Radnorshire.
56	151	PRESTEIGN.
		Another R. is by Gloucester and Hereford [H].
		R. to *Knighton* 7m.
		L. to *Kington* 6½m.
	153	Beggar's Bush.
	156	Kinnerton.
48	159	NEW RADNOR.
46	161¼	Llanvihangel Nant Mellan.
		Over the Llanhilling Hills to
41	165¾	Llandegley.
	167½	Penybont.
	173¼	Nantmell.
29	178	RHAYADERGWY.
		Cross the river Wye.
		Cardiganshire.
18	189	Cwm Ystwith.
15	192	Pentrebrunant.
12	195	DEVIL'S BRIDGE.
9	198	Eskynald.
2	205	Piccadilly T. G.
*	207	ABERYSTWITH [I]

LONDON TO LUDLOW;

Continued to MONTGOMERY and CAERNARVON; and thence to HOLYHEAD.

Variations of Route, and Branch Routes.

[A]

At Tenbury,
R. *to Cleobury Mortimer* 7*m.*
L. *to Leominster* 11*m.*
— *to Bromyard* 12*m.*

[B]

At Newton Green,
R. *to Church Stretton* 8*m.*
L. *to Clun* 7¾*m.*

Another R. from Newton Green to Bishop's Castle is by Walcot Park (Earl of Powis) which is less hilly than by Basford, but one mile longer.

[C]

	M.
BISHOP'S CASTLE	159
Churchstoke......	164½
Chirbury	167½
Forden Heath	170
L. *to Montgomery* 4*m.*	
Kilkewydd Bridge	172
Cross the Severn.	
WELSH POOL -	174
Another Route:	
SHREWSBURY (R. 8.)	153¼
Frankwell	153¾
Cross Gates	158½
Rowton	160¼
Trevenant	165
[Montg.] Uppington	168
Buttington	170¼
Cross the Severn.	
WELSHPOOL ..	171½

Or, to Westbury, as in Note [E], and thence over the hill to Buttington, whereby a most picturesque view will be obtained of the subjacent vale, and of Powis castle and park. But the hill is too steep for a carriage.

L.D.	M. from Tyburn Turnpike.	
		Worcestershire.
*	111	WORCESTER, p. 10. [*Prospective Distances:* Tenbury ...... 22 *m.* Ludlow........ 30½ Bishop's Castle - 48 Montgomery .. 57 Dolgelly ...... 97 Caernarvon .....136]
		Cross the river Severn.
	112¾	Henwick Hill.
3	114	Hallow.
	117½	Holt Heath.
10	121	Great Witley. On L. Witley Court, Lord Foley.
11	122	HUNDRED HOUSE INN. R. *to Kidderminster* 10*m.* — *to Bewdley* 7½*m.* L. *to Bromyard* 13*m.*
	123	Apostle's Oak T. G.
14	125	Stockton. On L. Stanford Court, Sir T. Winnington, Bart.
	126	Orleton, on L.
	126¾	Eardiston.
17	128	Lyndridge.
	129	Eastham, on L.
19	130	Newnham.
22	132¾	L. *across the river Teme to* TENBURY ¼*m.* [A], *and rejoin the road beyond the Swan Inn.*
		Shropshire.
	133	SWAN INN.
	134	Burford.
6	135¼	L. Hereford. [Heref.]
	139	Ashford.
*	141½	LUDLOW. Another R. is by Kidderminster. [*Prospective Distances:* Bishop's Castle - 17½*m.* Montgomery .. 26½ Cann's Office Inn 45 Dolgelly ...... 67 Caernarvon ....105½ Holyhead ......136 *On Return Route:* Tenbury ...... 8½ Worcester .... 30½ Oxford .... 87½]
		Cross the river Corve.
3	144½	Bromfield. On L. Oakley Park, Hon. R. Clive.
	147	Onibury.
8	149½	Newton Green [B].
	153	Basford T. G.
14	155½	Red House.
	159	BISHOP'S CASTLE. R. *to Welsh Pool* [C].
		Montgomeryshire.
7	161	Bishop's Moat.
4	164	Court House. L. *to Newtown and Llanydloes* [D].
*	168	MONTGOMERY [E].

Variations of Route, and Branch Routes.

[D]

To Towyn:	M.
At Court House ..	164½
L. to Kerry	172¼
NEWTOWN	175¾
Penystrywad	178¾
Llandinam	183
LLANYDLOES..	189
Rhyd y Porthman	194½
MACHYNLLETH	208
Penallt	212
[Merion.] TOWYN	220
Or,	
MONTGOMERY -	168
Llandyssil........	170
NEWTOWN	177
Aberhavesp	180
Llanwnog	183½
Carno	187½
Llanbrynmair	194
Penegos	203½
MACHYNLLETH	205½
TOWYN	217½
Another Route:	
RHAYADER (p. 11)............	178
St. Harmons	181
LLANYDLOES..	189½
Thence as above.	

[E]

Another Route:	
SHREWSBURY (R. 8)	153¼
Cruckton	157¾
Yockleton........	159¼
Stretton	160½
Westbury	162
Worthin	166
Brocton	166¾
Marton	168¾
Hockleton	170½
Chirbury	172¼
MONTGOMERY -	175¼

Or, from Shrewsbury through Hanwood and Minsterley to Brocton; the distance nearly the same.

L.D.	M. *from Tyburn Turnpike.*	
	172½	Berriew.
	175½	Castell Caer Einion.
28	180	LLANFAIR.
	185	Llanerfil.
22	186½	CANN'S OFFICE INN.
	191½	Dollymain.

Merionethshire.

L.D.	M.	
14	194	Nantyrhedyd.
11	197	MALLWYD.
10	198½	Tavernewyd.
8	199	DINAS Y MOWDDY
	200	Fachell.
*	208½	DOLGELLY.
	209½	Llaneltyd.
12	220½	Trawsfynd.
	225½	Maentwrog.
		L. *to Crickieth* 12*m.; thence to Newin* 15*m.*
18	226½	TAN Y BWLCH INN.
25	233	Pont Aberglasslyn.

Caernarvonshire.

L.D.	M.	
27	235	BEDDGELERT.
	241½	Bettws.
		R. *to Capel Cerrig* 12*m.*
39	247	CAERNARVON.
		(See next col.)
	250	Llanfair.
48	256	Menai Bridge.
		Thence as in R. 8, to
	277½	HOLYHEAD.

ANOTHER ROUTE TO

CAERNARVON,

by Shrewsbury.

L.D.	M. *from Hicks's Hall.*	
83	153¼	SHREWSBURY, R. 8.
	161½	Nescliff.
71	165½	Knuckin.
	171	Llanyblodwel.

Merionethshire.

L.D.	M.	
	176	Llangedwin.
	185	Llangnnog.
42	194½	BALA.
	203	Bwlch y Buarth.
24	212½	Festiniog.
	215	Maentwrog.
	216	TAN Y BWLCH INN.
14	222½	Pont Aberglasslyn (*a*).

Caernarvonshire.

L.D.	M.	
12	224½	BEDDGELERT.
	231	Bettws.
*	236½	CAERNARVON.

(*a*) This bridge across the torrent of the Colwyn, connecting two perpendicular precipices, is of 30 feet diameter, and the crown of the arch about 40 feet above the water. The altitude of the impending cliff is at least 800 feet. See Thomas Evans's Walks through Wales, in which the tourist will find much interesting topographical information, and also a glossary, illustrative of the etymology of towns and places.

LONDON TO LEAMINGTON AND WARWICK;

And thence to BIRMINGHAM. The Mail Route by Aylesbury and Buckingham.

Variations of Route, and Branch Routes.

M.

[A]

To Harrow:

At Paddington,
Cross the Grand Junction Canal to
Westborn Green .. 1½
Kensell Green 3
Holsden Green .. 4¾
Stone Bridge 5¾
Cross the riv. Brent.
Wembley Green .. 7
HARROW ON THE HILL.......... 10
Pinner 13
North Wood 15½
[Herts] Bacher Heath 16¾
RICKMANSWORTH 18

Another R. to Rickmansworth:

At Stanmore 10¼
L. to Hatch End .. 12¼
Pinner Green 14¼
Across Ruislip Com.
North Wood 16¼
Bacher Heath 17¾
RICKMANSWORTH 18¾
Or, WATFORD .. 14¾
Thence, leaving Cashiobury Pk. on R.
RICKMANSWORTH 17¾

Thence to Chesham:

Chorley Wood.... 19¾
[Bucks] Cheynies.. 21¼
L. *to Amersham 5m.*
CHESHAM...... 26¼

[B]

To Hemel Hempstead and Ivingho:

Upper Highway .. 18
Belswains........ 21½
Corner Hall...... 22¼
HEMEL HEMPSTEAD........ 23¼
[Bucks] IVINGHO 33¾

L.D. M. *from Tyburn Turnpike.*

Middlesex.

½ Paddington T.G. [A].
2½ Kilburn.
4 Cricklewood.
4¾ Brent Bridge.
6¾ Hyde.
8 EDGWARE.
On L. Canons, Sir T. Plumer.
9½ R. *to St. Albans;* L. *to*
10¼ Stanmore.
11½ Bushey Heath.
On L. Bentley Priory, Marq. of Abercorn.

Hertfordshire.

13¼ Bushey.
24 14¾ WATFORD.
R. *to St. Alban's 8m.*
On L. Cashiobury Park, Earl of Essex.
17 On L. Grove Park, Earl of Clarendon.
On R. Russell's Farm, Mrs. Biddulph.
21 18 Upper Highway.
R. *to Hemel Hempstead* [B].
18¼ Hunton Bridge.
On L. Langley Bury, Rev. Sir John Filmer, Bart.
19¾ King's Langley.

L.D. M. *from Tyburn Turnpike.*

17 22 Two Waters.
Cross G. Junc. Canal.
R. *to Hemel Hempstead 2m.*
23¼ Boxmoor.
14 24½ Bourn End.
12 26¼ BERKHAMPSTEAD
11 27¾ North Church.
R. *to Dunstable* 11*m.* by a new road, formed at the expence of the Earl of Bridgewater.
On R. Ashridge Park, E. of Bridgewater.
7 31½ TRING.

Buckinghamshire.

4 34¼ Aston Clinton.
* 38¾ AYLESBURY.
Another route is by Uxbridge [C].

[*Prospective Distances:*
Buckingham .. 17½m.
Brackley 25
Banbury 33½
Southam 47
Warwick 56
Birmingham.... 76½]

L. *to Thame 9½m.*
Cross the river Thame.
42¼ Hardwick.
5 43½ Whitchurch.
49¼ WINSLOW.
53¼ Padbury.
Cross the river Ouse.

* AYLESBURY.

Variations of Route, and Branch Routes.

[C]

	M.
Tatling End (R. 3.)	18
Chalfont St. Peter's	20½
Chalfont St. Giles	22½
AMERSHAM....	26
Little Missenden ..	28½
GREAT MISSENDEN	31
WENDOVER ..	35½
Walton T. G.	40
AYLESBURY ..	40½

[D]

DAVENTRY, (R. 8)	72½
Staverton	74½
[Warw.] Shuckburgh	77½
Napton	79½
SOUTHAM	82½
Ufton............	85
Radford	87½
LEAMINGTON	89½
WARWICK	91½

[E]

Other routes are by St. Alban's, Daventry, and Southam, as in Note [D]; or by Kineton, or by Gaydon Inn, from Banbury, as in the next page.

[F]

WARWICK	94½
Hatton	97½
Rowington	100½
Lapworth Street ..	103
HOCKLEY	104½
Monkspath Street -	107½
Shirley Street	109
Hall Green	112
Camphill	113½
Deritend Bridge ..	114½
BIRMINGHAM -	114½

L.D.	M. from Tyburn Turnpike.	
	56	BUCKINGHAM. [*Prospective Distances:* Banbury ...... 16 *m.* Warwick ...... 38½ Birmingham.... 59] On R. Stow, Duke of Buckingham (*a*).
	61	Westbury.
		Northamptonshire.
29	63½	BRACKLEY.
	67	Farthingho, on R. Cross the river Charwell and the Oxford Canal.
		Oxfordshire.
20	72	BANBURY.
18	74½	Little Bourton.
		Warwickshire.
16	76½	Mollington.
	80	Fenny Compton, on L.
7	84	Ladbroke.
	85½	SOUTHAM. Another R. is by St. Alban's and Daventry [D].
	88	Ufton.
2	90½	Radford.
*	92½	LEAMINGTON. L. *to Coventry by Stoneleigh 8m.*

L.D.	M. from Tyburn Turnpike.	
	94½	WARWICK [E]. [*Prospective Distances:* Birmingham .. 20½ *m.* Wolverhampton 34 Shrewsbury .... 64½ Holyhead ......171½] On L. Warwick Castle, E. of Warwick (*b*). On R. the Priory, H. C. Wise, Esq.
	96½	On L. Grove Park, Lord Dormer.
17	97½	Hatton. L. *to Birmingham by Hockley* [F].
	98½	Haseley.
	100½	Wroxhall.
10	105½	KNOWLE.
	107½	Malvern Hall, H. G. Lewis, Esq.
7	108	SOLIHULL.
6	109	World's End.
	110½	Acock's Green.
1	113½	Spark Brook.
	114½	Deritend Bridge.
*	115	BIRMINGHAM. *To Shrewsbury & Holyhead.* See R. 8.

(*a*) A very copious account of this princely mansion, accompanied with descriptive particulars of its pictures, &c. &c. will be found in Britton and Brayley's Topography of the county.

(*b*) See Brewer's Topography of Warwickshire, referred to in the next page, for an ample account of this imposing edifice.

LONDON TO BANBURY, BY BICESTER;

And thence to WARWICK, by Gaydon Inn. Continued to KENILWORTH and STONE BRIDGE.

Variations of Route, and Branch Routes.

	M.
[A]	
BICESTER......	54¾
Middleton Stoney,	58
On L. Middleton Park, Earl of Jersey.	
Heyford Purcell ..	60¼
Hopcroft's Holt ..	62¼
Steeple Barton....	63¼
Middle Barton....	63¾
Westcott Barton ..	64¼
Sandford	65½
Gaging Well......	67
Church Enstone ..	68¼
Junction of road from Oxford	68¾
CHAPEL HOUSE..	72¼
CHIPPING NORTON	73
[B]	
Another R. is by Kineton.	
BANBURY......	68¾
Drayton	71
Wroxton	71¼
[Warw.] Upton ..	76
EDGE HILL......	76¾
KINETON	81
Compton Verney ..	82¾
Wellesburne Hastings	85¼
Barford	89¼
Cross the river Avon.	
Longbridge	90¼
WARWICK	91¾
[C]	
Another Route:	
COVENTRY (R. 8)	91¼
Stivichall	92¼
Milbourne Grange	95¼
KENILWORTH,	96¼

L.D.	M. *from Tyburn Turnpike.*
	Buckinghamshire.
49	38¾ AYLESBURY (p. 15)
	43¾ Waddesden.
41	46¾ Ham Green.
	On L. Wotton, Duke of Buckingham.
	Oxfordshire.
	51½ Black Thorn Heath.
33	54¾ BICESTER.
	L. *to Chipping Norton* [A].
	56 Caversfield.
	61 Ploughley Hill.
	Souldern, on L.
	Buckinghamshire.
25	62½ Aynhoe on the Hill.
24	63¾ Nell Bridge.
	Cross the river Charwell.
	Oxfordshire.
	65 Adderbury.
	66¾ Weeping Cross.
19	68¾ BANBURY.
	Another Route is by Aylesbury and Buckingham, as in the preceding page.
	L. *to Edge Hill.*
	70 On L. Wroxton Abbey, Countess Guildford.

L.D.	M. *from Tyburn Turnpike.*
	Warwickshire (*a*).
14	73¾ Warmington.
9	79 Gaydon Inn.
	82 Harwood House.
*	87¼ WARWICK [B].
	L. *to Birmingham*, as in R. 5.
	89 Guy's Cliff.
3	90¾ Leek Wotton.
5	93 KENILWORTH [C].
	R. *to Coventry;* L. *to*
	97 George in the Tree.
	101 Moulding Bridge.
14	102 STONE BRIDGE.
	Forward to Coleshill 4 m.; thence to Lichfield 15 *m.*
	R. *to Coventry* 8½*m.*
	L. *to Birmingham* 9½*m.*

(*a*) The topography of this interesting county has been very ably delineated by Mr. Brewer, in his "Topographical and Historical Description of the County of Warwick," accompanied with views of the principal seats, and other objects of prominent interest. The village of Kenilworth, the borough of Warwick, and the fashionable watering-place of Leamington, being situate nearly in the centre of the county, the tourist will be amply gratified by reference to the above work, for a rich fund of information, relative to those places and the adjoining districts.

* WARWICK.

LONDON TO BIRMINGHAM, BY OXFORD [E].

Thence to SHREWSBURY and HOLYHEAD, page 20; to CHESTER, p. 26; and to LIVERPOOL and MANCHESTER, p. 27.

Variations of Route, and Branch Routes.

[A] Thence to Shrewsbury and Holyhead, p. 23.

[B] *Prospective and Cross R. Distances from Chapel House:*

	M.
Alcester, through Stratford	29
Aylesbury	34
Banbury	11
Bicester	17
Birmingham	44
Buckingham	25
Burford	12
Deddington	10
Morton in Marsh	12
Oxford	19
Warwick (turn off at Tredington)	27
Woodstock	11
Worcester	39

[C] On the R. a circle of stones, of supposed Druidical origin, called Rollrich Stones. Without the circle is a larger stone, called the King's Stone, and five others.

[D] Another R. to Stratford is by Aylesbury (p. 23), 89 miles.

In the church, Shakspeare's monument, respecting which, and other reminiscences, many interesting particulars will be found in Cooke's Topography of the county.

[E] Another Route to Birmingham, from Oxford, is through Banbury and Warwick; thus, to Banbury, p. 3, and thence pp. 15 and 16.

L.D.	M. from Tyburn Turnpike.	
		Oxfordshire.
*	54	OXFORD, as in R. 3.
		[*Prospective Distances:* Chapel House .. 19 m. Shipston on Stour 29; Stratford on Av. 39½; *Kidderminster* [A] .... 70; Birmingham .. 62½; Wolverhampton 76; *Chester* ......134½; Shrewsbury ....106½; Holyhead ......213½; *Manchester* ..140½; *Liverpool* ....161]
		From Oxford to
8	62	WOODSTOCK, and
15	69	ENSTONE, p. 10.
19	72¾	CHAPEL HOUSE [B].
21	75	Little Rolright [C].
22	75¾	Compton Hill.
		On R. Weston House, Earl of Clonmell.
		Warwickshire.
23	77	Long Compton.
27	81	Burmington.
		Cross the river Stour.
		Worcestershire.
	81¾	Tidmington.
29	83	SHIPSTON ON STOUR.
31	85	Tredington.
		R. *to Warwick* 14*m.*
	87	Newbold.
27	89	Alderminster.
		Warwickshire.
	93	Bridge Town.
		Cross the Avon.
23	93½	STRATFORD ON AVON [D].
		R. *to Warwick* 7¾*m.*
		L. *to Alcester* 8*m.; thence to Kidderminster and Shrewsbury*, p. 23.
	97	On R. Bearley....
	100	Wotton Wawen.
15	101¼	HENLEY IN ARDEN.
10	106¼	HOCKLEY HEATH.—Junction of the road from Warwick.
		Thence, as in p. 15, to
*	116½	BIRMINGHAM.

Other Routes are,

	M.
1. By Coventry, as in the Holyhead Mail Route (p. 20)	109½
2. By a diversion from the Holyhead Mail Route at Daventry, through Leamington and Warwick (p. 15)	112
3. By Aylesbury and Banbury to Leamington and Warwick (p. 15)	115
4. By Bicester to Banbury, and thence to Warwick by Gaydon Inn (p. 16)	108½

LONDON TO HOLYHEAD;

The Mail Route by COVENTRY, BIRMINGHAM, and SHREWSBURY (a).

Variations of Route, and Branch Routes.

M.

[A]

At Islington Green . 1
R. to Ball's Pond .. 2¼
On L. *Canonbury Lane.*
Forward to Newington Green & Enfield; R. *to*
Kingsland T. G..... 3
Forward to Hackney.
L. *to Ware;* R. *to*
Dalston 3¼
Lea Bridge 4¾
[Essex] Whip's Cross 6¾
Snaresbrook, Eagle - 7½
R. *to Chigwell.*
Woodford 8½
EPPING 17¼

[B]

To Highgate,
From St. Giles's Pound:
Camden Town 1¼
Mother Red Cap's.. 1¾
Kentish Town....... 2¼
Highgate.......... 4½
[*From Holborn Bars 5m.*]

[B 2]

To Mill Hill,
From Holborn Bars:
Mother Red Cap's .. 2¼
Haverstock Hill.... 3¼
Hampstead 4
Hampstead Heath .. 4½
½*m. farther* R. *to Highgate 2m.* L. *to*
North End 5
Goulder's Green.... 6
Hendon 7
R. *to Finchley 1½m.*
Mill Hill.......... 9

L.D.	M. *from Hicks's Hall.*
	Middlesex.
	½ Pentonville.
	1 Islington Green [A].
	2¼ Holloway T. G.
	3½ Foot of Highgate Hill.
	L. *to Highgate, up the Hill, ½m.* [B].
	4 Highgate Archway.
	4½ R. *to Muswell Hill 1¼m.*
	L. *to Hampstead Heath, thro' Highgate, 2m.*
	6 Finchley.
	9 Whetstone.
10	11 BARNET. (Herts.)
	11¾ The Obelisk, in commemoration of the Battle of Barnet.
	R. *to Hatfield;* L. *to*
9	12¼ Kitt's End.
	On R. G. Byng, Esq.
	On L. J. Trotter, Esq.
6	14¾ SOUTH MIMS.
	Hertfordshire.
5	16 Ridge Hill.
	On R. North Mims, H. Brown, Esq.
3	18 London Colney.
	On R. Tittenhanger, Earl of Hardwick.
*	21 ST. ALBANS [C].
	23 On L. Gorhambury, Earl Verulam.

L.D.	M. *from Hicks's Hall.*
	25¼ Redburn.
	29¼ Market Street.
	Bedfordshire.
76	33½ DUNSTABLE.
	R. *to Ampthill and Bedford* [D].
72	37¼ Hockliffe.
	R. *to Woburn 4½m.*
	L. *to Leighton 3½m.*
	Buckinghamshire.
66	43¼ LITTLE BRICKHILL.
	Great Brickhill, on L.
	On R. Bow Brickhill ....
	45 Fenny Stratford.
	48¼ Shenley.
57	52¼ STONEY STRATFORD (a).
	R. *to Northampton and Leicester, p. 30.*
	Northamptonshire.
	53 Old Stratford.

(a) A shorter route, by 3 miles, from the west end of the metropolis, and through a fine part of the country, is by Bushey Heath to Hemel Hempstead (p. 14), and thence to Stoney Stratford, through Leighton Buzzard.

* BIRMINGHAM.

Variations of Route, and Branch Routes.

[C] M.

Another Route:

EDGWARE (p. 14) 8
Brockley Hill 10
[Herts.] Elstree, or Idlestry 11
Radlet 14
Colney Street 16½
Frogmore 17½
St. Stephens...... 18½
(49) ST. ALBANS.... 20

Thence to Luton and Bedford:

Harpenden (Harden) 24
Gibraltar Inn 28
On R. Luton Park, Marquis of Bute.
[Beds.] LUTON .. 30
Over the Downs to Barton in the Clay - 36½
(46) Silsoe............ 39½
On R. Wrest Park, Countess de Grey.
Clophill 41
L. to *Ampthill* 3m.
(37) West End 43
Willshamstead 45¾
Elstow 48
BEDFORD 50

[D]

DUNSTABLE ... 33¼
Houghton Regis .. 34¼
Chalgrave 37
Toddington 38
Westoning 41
Dennel End 43½
AMPTHILL 45
Another Route is by Luton 44m. See note [C].
(29) On L. Ampthill Park, Lord Holland.
Houghton Conquest 46½
Hempston Hardwick 49
BEDFORD 53
Another Route is by Woburn:

M. *from Hicks's Hall.*

55 Potterspury. Whittlebury Forest on L. and Wakefield Lodge, Duke of Grafton.

59 Heavencote.
On R. Stoke Park, L. Vernon, Esq.

(49) 60 TOWCESTER.

R. *to Northampton*—
[60 TOWCESTER.
63½ Blisworth.
65½ Milton.
69 NORTHAMPTON.]

On R. Easton Neston, Earl of Pomfret.

(46) 63½ Foster's Booth.

68 Weedon Beck. Grand Military Depot.

(37) 72¼ DAVENTRY.
L. *to Southam, thence to Leamington & Warwick.* See p. 15.

75¾ Braunston. Junction of the Oxford and Grand Junction Canals.

Warwickshire.

76¾ Willoughby.

(29) 80 DUNCHURCH.

R. *to Lutterworth*—
[80 DUNCHURCH.
82¾ RUGBY.
84¾ Brownsover.
88¼ [Leic.] Cottesbatch.
90½ LUTTERWORTH.]

M. *from Hicks's Hall.*

(21) 85 Stretton upon Dunsmoor.

85¾ Knightlow Cross.

(22) 86¾ Ryton.

88½ Willenhall.

89½ Whitley.

(18) 91¼ COVENTRY.

[*Prospective Distances:*
Birmingham .. 18¼ m.
Wolverhampton 31½
Shrewsbury 62
Holyhead 169¼
Chester (p. 26). 96]

R. *to Atherstone and Tamworth* [E].

94 Allesley (Ausley).

(12) 97½ Meriden.
On L. W. Digby, Esq.

99 On R. Packington Hall, Earl of Aylesford.

(10) 99¾ STONE BRIDGE (a).
R. *to Coleshill and Lichfield.* See p. 27.

100 Bickenhill, on L.

(7) 102¼ Elmdon.

(a) It is in contemplation (see 4th Report of the Parliamentary Commissioners, 1822) to form a new line of road, diverging from the present line at Stonebridge, and rejoining it at Moxley Bridge, near Wolverhampton, leaving Birmingham out of the mail route. Another new line is proposed from the Cock Inn, or Watling Street, to Chirk, leaving Shrewsbury and Oswestry on the left; which will shorten the distance from Watling Street to Chirk seven miles.

* BIRMINGHAM.

Variations of Route, and Branch Routes.

	M.
WOBURN	41¾
On R. Woburn Abbey, Duke of Bedford.	
Through the Park to Ridgemont	43¾
Lidlington T. G. ..	46
AMPTHILL	49
Thence to Bedford 8m. as above.	

[E]

To Atherstone:	
COVENTRY	91¼
Foleshill	93¼
Longford	94
Bedworth	96¼
Griff	97½
Attleborough	99
NUNEATON	99½
R. *to Hinckley 5m.*	
L. to Manceter....	103
ATHERSTONE ..	105

[E 2]

To Tamworth:	
COVENTRY	91¼
R. to Radford	92
Karesley Green ..	93½
Corley Moor.......	96
Fillongley	97
Upper Whitacre ..	101
L. *to Coleshill 3½m.*	
Nether Whitacre ..	103
Kingsbury........	105¾
London Road	109¼
L. *to Fazeley ½m.*	
TAMWORTH....	111
Another Route:	
COVENTRY	91¼
Wishaw (p. 27) ..	108
TAMWORTH....	113¾

[F]

WOLVERHAMPTON	122¾
Gosbrook Mill	124
Ford Houses......	126
Standyford Lane ..	129
Spread Eagle	131
PENKRIDGE ..	133
Cross the riv. Penk.	
Dunston..........	135¾

L.D.	M. *from Hicks's Hall.*	
5	104¼	Wells Green.
		On R. Sheldon....
4	105½	Yardley.
	108¾	Small Heath T. G.
*	109½	BIRMINGHAM.
		For other Routes to Birmingham see page 17.

[*Prospective Distances:*

Wolverhampton	13¼m.
Shiffnal	26
Shrewsbury	44
Holyhead	151
Chester (p. 26)..	72
Parkgate	84
Manchester (p. 27)	78
Liverpool	98½

On Return Route:

Coventry	18¼
Daventry	37¼
Towcester......	49½
Stoney Stratford	57½
Dunstable......	76
St. Albans	88½

L. *to Halesowen 7¾m.; thence to Stourbridge 4½m.*

L.D.	M.	
	111	Hockley Brook.
		R. *to Walsall and Stafford.* See p. 27.

Staffordshire.

L.D.	M.	
	111¼	On L. M. R. Boulton, Esq.
2	111½	Soho.
		On R. Handsworth
	113	Sandwell Green.
		On R. Sandwell Park, Earl of Dartmouth.
	114	L. *to Dudley and Stourbridge.* See page 23 [B].

L.D.	M. *from Hicks's Hall.*	
	114½	Bromwich Heath.
	117½	WEDNESBURY.
		R. *to Walsall 3m.*
	118¾	Moxley Bridge.
	120	Bilston.
31	122¾	WOLVERHAMPTON.
		R. *to Stafford and Stone* [F].
	124½	New Bridge.
	124¾	Tettenhall.
		R. *to Ivetsey Bank* (p. 26).
27	126	The Wergs.

Shropshire.

L.D.	M.	
	129¾	Boningale.
	134½	Upton.
18	135¼	SHIFFNALL.
		L. *to Coalbrook Dale, and thence to Shrewsbury* [G].
	138¼	Prior's Leigh.
12	141	Ketley Iron Works.
	141¾	COCK INN, Watling St.
		[See Note [*a*] for projected new line of road from hence to Chirk.]
		R. *to Wellington ½m.; thence to Whitchurch*—

[142½ WELLINGTON.
146½ Crudington.
154 Hodnet.
159 Sandford.
164 WHITCHURCH.]

L.D.	M.	
10	143	Hay Gate.
		On L. the Wrekin Hill.

Variations of Route, and Branch Routes.

	M.
STAFFORD	139
Yarley	143
Walton	145¾
STONE..........	146¾

Thence to Manchester and Liverpool, as in R. 12, p. 27.

[G]

SHIFFNALL	135½
Hem	137½
MADELEY MARKET	139¼
COALBROOK DALE	141¼
Adney	143¼
Leighton	145¼
Tern Bridge	150½

Thence as in the opp. col.

Other R. to Coalbrook Dale:

BRIDGNORTH, (p. 23)	132½
Morvil	134¾
Willey	136¼
BROSELEY	138¾
Cross the Severn, at the iron bridge, to COALBROOK DALE	140¾

Or,
At Lower Town,

BRIDGNORTH..	132
R. to Stockton	136¾
Sutton Maddock ..	138¼
Brocton..........	139¼
MADELEY MARKET	140¾
COALBROOK DALE	142¾

[H]
To Whitchurch:

SHREWSBURY.	153¼
Albrighton	157
Harmer Hill......	159½
Broughton........	161
WEM	164¼
Edstaston	166¾
Tilstock	170¾
WHITCHURCH .	173

L.D.	M. from Hicks's Hall.	
7	146½	Uckington.
	148½	Tern Bridge.
4	149¼	Atcham.
		Cross the river Severn.
7	152	Lord Hill's Column.
	152¾	Abbey Foregate.
		Cross the Severn.
*	153¼	SHREWSBURY [H].

Other Routes are by Coalbrook Dale, as in [G]; or by Aylesbury and Kidderminster, p. 23; or by either of the variations of route to Birmingham, specified in p. 17.

[*Prospective Distances:*

Oswestry	18 m.
Llangollen	31
Corwen........	41
Capel Curig	68½
Bangor	83¼
Menai Bridge ..	86
Holyhead	107½

On Return Route:

Shiffnal........	18
Wolverhampton	30½
Birmingham ..	44]

R. *to Ellesmere* 16¼*m.; thence to Wrexham* 12½*m.* [I].

L.D.	M.	
		Welsh Bridge.
		Cross the Severn again.
		R. *to Llanfyllin* [K].
2	155½	Shelton.
	157¾	Montford Bridge.
		Cross the Severn.
6	159¼	Ensdon.
	161¾	Nesscliff.
		L. *to Bala;* R. *to*
13	166½	West Felton.

L.D.	M. from Hicks's Hall.	
	167½	Queen's Head T. G.
		R. *to Ellesmere* 9*m.*
89	171¼	OSWESTRY.
	174	Gobowen.

Denbighshire.

L.D.	M.	
83	177	Chirk (*b*).

[The projected alteration of the road to Chirk (see note *a*) will reduce the distance 7m.]

L.D.	M.	
	179	Whitehurst T. G.
76	184	LLANGOLLEN.
		R. *to Ruthen* 13½*m.*

Merionethshire.

L.D.	M.	
	191½	Llansaintfraid.
66	194	CORWEN.
		Cross the river Dee.

Denbighshire.

L.D.	M.	
56	204	Cerrig y Druidion.
	207	Cernioge Mawr.

(*b*) Near Chirk, see the Aqueducts of the Ellesmere Canal, one of which is over the river Dee.

The scenery here is remarkably beautiful. As the route proceeds, it becomes more mountainous and romantic; but the limits of this work not admitting of any particularization of the many interesting objects of attention worthy the traveller's particular notice throughout this district, distinguished by its grandeur and magnificence, the reader is referred to Thomas Evans's "Walks through Wales," for any desired topographical information.

* HOLYHEAD.

Variations of Route, and Branch Routes.

M.

[J]

To Holywell:
SHREWSBURY .. 153¾
Albrighton 157
Harmer Hill....... 159½
Middle 161
Burlton Grove.... 162¾
Cockshut 165
ELLESMERE .. 169¾
[Flint.] Overton .. 175
[Denbigh.] Eyton.. 177¾
WREXHAM 182
R. to *Chester* 12m.
CAERGWRLE .. 187½
MOLD 194
Northope 197
R. to *Flint* 3m.
Halkin 199¾
HOLYWELL..... 202¼

[K]

To Llanfyllin:
SHREWSBURY - 153¾
Frankwell......... 153¾
Cross Gates 158¾
Alderbury 162
[Mont.] Llandrinio 167
Cross the Severn.
Llan St. Fraid 172
Cross the river Virnwy.
LLANFYLLIN .. 178

[L]

Prospective Distances from Holyhead on Route to London:
Menai Bridge .. 21½m.
Bangor 24
Capel Curig 49
Corwen......... 66¼
Llangollen 76¾
Oswestry 89¼
Shrewsbury 107¾
Birmingham.... 151
Coventry 169¾
Daventry 186¾
St. Albans 239¾

L.D. M. *from Hicks's Hall.*

31 209½ Pentre Foelas.
R. to *Llanwrst* 9m.
— to *Conway* 21m.
216 Iron Bridge.
Cross the riv. Conway.

Caernarvonshire.

24 216½ Bettws y Coed.
39 221½ CAPEL CURIG.
L. to *Beddgelert* 13m.
On L. Snowdon Mountain.
35 225½ Ogwen Lake.
31 229¾ Tyn y Maes.
234¾ Llandygai.
34 236½ BANGOR.
L. to *Caernarvon* 9½m.
239 MENAI BRIDGE, across the Menai Strait.

This bridge is 560 feet between the points of suspension. The road-way is 30 feet broad, and 100 feet above the level of high water spring tides. The sum voted by Parliament for its erection, in the year 1819, was 20,000*l.*—For the improvement of the road between Bangor and Chirk, the sum of 47,594*l.* has been voted at different times since 1817; and for other parts of the road 20,000*l.*; exclusive of 42,200*l.* for the works at Holyhead, and improvement of the harbour.

The receipts of the toll-houses between Shrewsbury and Holyhead, from Feb. 1, 1822, to Feb. 1, 1823, amounted to 6731*l.* 13*s.* 6*d.* of which it is worthy of remark, that the proprietors of the Regent, and Prince of Wales coaches, paid each 982*l.* 16*s.*—*See Parliamentary Report.*

L.D. M. *from Hicks's Hall.*

Enter the Island of

Anglesea.

241 Llanfair.
15 245½ Pentre Berw.
246¾ Llangistiolus.
247½ Cefn Cernydd.
12 248½ CAER MON INN.
250½ Gwalchmai.
5 255¾ Caer Caliog.
257 Old road.
257¾ Stanley Sands.
* 260½ HOLYHEAD [L].

Great improvements have been made throughout this line of road, by direction of the Parliamentary Commissioners; the width of the road having been enlarged wherever requisite, its surface considerably improved, and the abrupt declivities of the hills diminished. An entirely new road has been made through the island of Anglesea. Previously to these improvements, the direct mail route was by Chester to Bangor, and thence to Holyhead, as follows:

M.
BANGOR (p. 25)......... 251¼
Bangor Ferry.............. 252¼
Across the Menai Strait.
[Anglesea.] Braint......... 255¼
Llangefni 260¾
Gwyndi 265¼
Bodedern 269¾
Llanygenedi 271
Four Mile Bridge 274
HOLYHEAD 276

The new road through Anglesea crosses the main ridge of the island at 160 feet below the level of the old road, the circuity of which is avoided by means of the embankment at Stanley Sands.

* HOLYHEAD.

LONDON TO SHREWSBURY;

By AYLESBURY and KIDDERMINSTER.

Variations of Route, and Branch Routes.

	M.
[A]	
ALCESTER	97
Ridgway	100
Feckenham	103
Bradley	104
Meer Green	106½
Hanbury	107½
DROITWICH ..	110
Ombersley	114
STOURPORT ..	119¼
Another Route:	
WORCESTER (p. 10)	111
Northwick	112½
Ombersley	116
STOURPORT....	121¼
[B]	
BROMSGROVE -	109¾
Cat's Hill	112
Holy Cross	115½
Hagley	116¾
On R. Lord Lyttelton.	
Pedmore	117¾
Old Swinford	118¾
STOURBRIDGE -	119
Another Route:	
BIRMINGHAM, (p. 20)	109½
Hockley Brook ..	111
[Staff.] Soho	111½
Sandwell	113
[Worc.] DUDLEY	118¾
STOURBRIDGE.	123¾
Or,	
BIRMINGHAM..	109½
[Salop.] Halesowen	117¼
[Worc.] STOURBRIDGE	121½

L.D.	M. from Tyburn Turnpike.	
		Oxfordshire.
*	68¾	BANBURY, by Bicester, as in p. 16.
	71	Drayton.
	71¾	Wroxton.
		Warwickshire.
	76	Upton.
8	76¾	EDGE HILL. [The distance to Edge Hill, as travelled by the Leamington mail to Banbury, R. 5, is 80 miles.]
	81	Pillerton.
14	83	Upper Eatington.
		Worcestershire.
	85	Goldicote.
		Warwickshire.
20	89	STRATFORD ON AVON.
	93	Red Hill. Temple Grafton, on L.
28	97	ALCESTER. L. to Evesham 10m. — to Droitwich and Stourport [A].
30	98¾	Coughton.
	102¼	Crab's Cross.
		Worcestershire.
	103¾	Headley's Cross. R. to Redditch 1½m.
38	106¾	Tardebig.
	109¾	BROMSGROVE. R. to Stourbridge [B].
	114½	Chaddesley Corbet.
	115¾	Winterfold.
	117	Stone.
35	119¼	KIDDERMINSTER. [By Buckingham 122½m.] [Prospective Distances: Bridgnorth .... 13 m. Much Wenlock . 22 Shrewsbury .... 35¼ Holyhead ...... 142¾ On Return Route: Alcester ...... 22¼ Stratford on Av. 30½ Banbury ...... 50¾] R. to Stourbridge 7m. L. to Bewdley 3m. — to Stourport 4m.
	123	Shatterford.
		Shropshire.
	128½	Quat.
	130½	Quatford.
22	132¼	BRIDGNORTH. R. to Coalbrook Dale. See page 21.
19	135½	Morvil.
17	137½	Muckley Cross.
13	141	MUCH WENLOCK.
	143	Harley.
	145	Cressage.
	147	Cound.
3	151½	Weeping Cross.
	154	Abbey Foregate.
*	154½	SHREWSBURY. Thence to Holyhead, p. 21.

LONDON TO CHESTER;

The Mail Route by NORTHAMPTON and STAFFORD: continued to HOLYHEAD.

Variations of Route, and Branch Routes.

[A] M.

NEWPORT PAGNELL 50
Cross the riv. Ouse.
Sherrington 52½
Emberton 54½
Cross the Ouse.
Olney 55½
Warrington 57
[Nthamp.] Bozeat, 60¼
Wollaston........ 63½
WELLINGBOROUGH 67¼
Great Harrowden, 68½
Isham 70½
KETTERING.... 74½

[B]

NORTHAMPTON 66
Harlestone 70
East Haddon 73½
West Haddon 77
Crick............ 79½
[Warw.] Hill Morton 82½
RUGBY 85

[C]

WELFORD 80½
[Leic.] Husband's Bosworth 83
Shearsby 87½
Vigston 93
LEICESTER 96½

[D]

By keeping forward along Watling street to the Harrow Inn, and leaving Hinckley on R. the line of Route will be shortened about a mile and a half.

[E]

HINCKLEY 99½
Stapleton 102½
Cadeby 105
L. to *Ashby-de-la-Zouch*, 11m.
MARKET BOSWORTH 106½

L.D.	M. *from Hicks's Hall.*
	Bedfordshire.
	37¼ Hockliffe, (p. 18.)
24	41¾ WOBURN.
	Buckinghamshire.
	45½ Wavenden.
	47¾ Broughton.
	Cross the river Ouse.
16	50 NEWPORT PAGNELL.
	R. *to Kettering* [A].
	54½ Stoke Golding.
	R. *to Olney 4m.*
	Northamptonshire.
	58½ Horton.
6	60 Hackleton.
	64 Queen's Cross.
*	66 NORTHAMPTON.
	Other Routes are by Stoney Stratford, (p. 30), or by Towcester, (p. 19).
	L. *to Rugby* [B].
	67½ Kingsthorpe.
4	70¼ Chapel Brampton.
	73¾ Upper Creaton.
	77¼ Thornby.
14	80½ WELFORD.
	R. *to Leicester* [C].
	Cross the river Avon.
	Leicestershire.
18	84 North Kilworth.
	87 Walcote.

L.D.	M. *from Hicks's Hall.*
	89 LUTTERWORTH.
	Another Route is by Daventry and Dunchurch, (p. 19.)
	90 Bitteswell.
	93 Upper Claybrook.
20	95 High Cross, on Watling Street.
	96 Smockington [D].
	98½ Burbage.
24	99½ HINCKLEY.
	R. *to Market Bosworth* [E].
	101¼ Harrow Inn.
	L. *to Nuneaton 3½m.* [F].
	106½ Witherley.
	Cross the river Anker.
	Warwickshire.
16	107½ ATHERSTONE.
	Another Route is by Coventry (p. 20).
	R. *to Burton on Trent* [G]
12	111½ Hall End.
	113 Wilnecote.
	Staffordshire.
	114½ Fazeley.
8	115¾ TAMWORTH [H].
	118 Hoppas.
*	123¾ LICHFIELD.
	127½ Longdon.
	130 Brereton.
8	131½ RUGELEY.
10	133½ Wolseley Bridge.

Variations of Route, and Branch Routes.

	M.
[F]	
Another R. to Nuneaton is by Coventry (p. 20.)	
[G]	
ATHERSTONE..	107¼
[Leic.] Sheepy	110¼
Twycross	112¾
Snareston	116
Cross the riv. Mease.	
MEASHAM	117¾
Crickett's Inn	119¾
Over Seal........	120¾
[Derby.] Castle Greasley	123
Stanton	125
Stapenhill........	126
Cross the riv. Trent.	
[Staff.] BURTON ON TRENT ..	127
[H]	
Another Route:	
At ATHERSTONE	107¼
L. to Grendon	110¼
Polesworth	112¼
TAMWORTH....	116½
Other R. are by Coventry (p. 20.)	
[I]	
NEWCASTLE, (p. 28)	149½
Keele............	152
Little Madeley....	153¾
Betley	157
[Chesh.] Gorsty Hill,	158½
The Hough	161¼
NAMPTWICH ..	164¼
Or, Little Madeley,	153¾
[Salop] WOORE ..	158¼
Thence as in the opp. column.	
Or, NEWCASTLE,	149½
Chesterton	151¾
Audley	154
[Chesh.] Gorsty Hill,	158¼
NAMPTWICH ..	164¼
[K]	
Tarvin	183¾
Alvanley	189¼
Netherton........	191
FRODSHAM....	192¼
Sutton	194
HALTON	195¼

L.D.	M. from Hicks's Hall.
	137¼ Milford.
	139 Weeping Cross.
48	141 STAFFORD.
	Other Routes are by Birmingham. See page 27.
	144¾ Bridgeford.
	146 Walton.
41	148 ECCLESHALL.
	153¼ Broughton.
	L. to *Drayton* 3½m.
	157 Muckleston.
	159 Knighton.
	Shropshire.
29	160¼ WOORE.
	Cheshire.
	162¼ Bridgemore.
	165 Walgherton.
	166¾ Stapeley.
20	169 NAMPTWICH.
	Other Routes are by Newcastle [I].
	170¼ Acton.
	171½ Hurleston.
	172¾ Barbridge.
	175¼ Highway Side.
11	178¼ TARPORLEY.
	180¾ Clotton.
	181½ Dutton.
6	183½ Tarvin.
	R. to *Frodsham* [K].
	185½ Stamford Bridge.
2	187¼ Vicar's Cross.
	188½ Little Boughton.
*	189¼ CHESTER.
	[By Coventry to Lichfield, (p. 27) 184¼ miles.] For Prospective Distances see next page [C].

L.D.	M. from Hicks's Hall.
	Cross the river Dee.
	Flintshire.
	193½ Broughton.
	L. to *Mold* 6½m.; *thence to Ruthen* 8m.
79	196 HAWARDEN.
	197¾ Ewloe.
	201 Northrop.
	204 Halkin.
68	207½ HOLYWELL.
	213¼ Brick Kiln.
58	217½ ST. ASAPH.
	220½ Cross Foxes.
	Denbighshire.
	222¼ Llan St. Sior, or St. George's.
51	224¼ ABERGELEY.
	227 Llandulas.
39	235¼ Conway Ferry House.
	Caernarvonshire.
39	236¼ ABERCONWAY.
	238¾ Pont Sychnant.
33	242¼ Penmaen Mawr T.G.
30	245½ Aber.
	R. *to Beaumaris, across the Lavan Sands and Ferry,* 4½m.
	248¾ Talybont.
	249¼ Llandygau.
24	251¼ BANGOR.
	Thence across the Menai Strait (see p. 22) to
*	275¼ HOLYHEAD.

LONDON TO CHESTER;

By COVENTRY and BIRMINGHAM: continued to PARKGATE.

[For Mail Route, see p. 24].

Variations of Route, and Branch Routes.

[A]

Another Route from Birmingham is through Walsall:

	M.
BIRMINGHAM..	109½
Hockley Brook ..	111
Forward to Wolverhampton, R. *to*	
Handsworth	112
Snail's Green	114½
Great Barr	115¾
WALSALL......	118¾
Bloxwich	121
Church Bridge....	125
Streetway........	126
Four Crosses Inn..	127
Spread Eagle	129½
IVETSEY BANK ..	134½

Thence, as in the opposite column.

[B]

CHESTER	181½
Backford	182¼
Great Sutton	187½
Eastham	190¼
Great Bebbington..	193
Tranmere Ferry ..	196
LIVERPOOL....	198

At Eastham a passage boat daily to and from Liverpool.

[C]

At Chester, *Prospective Distances to Holyhead:*

Holywell	18½m.
St. Asaph	28¾
Abergeley......	35¼
Aberconway....	47
Bangor	62
Holyhead	86

L.D.	M. *from Hicks's Hall.*	
		Warwickshire.
*	109½	BIRMINGHAM (p. 20)
	111	Hockley Brook.
		R. *to Walsall* [A].
		Staffordshire.
2	111½	Soho.
	112½	New Inn.
	113	Sandwell Green.
5	114½	Bromwich Heath.
8	117½	WEDNESBURY.
	118¾	Moxley.
	120	Bilston.
13	122¾	WOLVERHAMPTON.
	124¾	Tettenhall.
		L. *to Shiffnall*, p. 20.
	127½	Codsall.
23	132½	IVETSEY BANK [A].
	134½	Weston under Lizard.
27	136½	Parney Corner.
		Shropshire.
	138	Woodcot.
	139½	Chetwynd Aston.
31	140½	NEWPORT.
	144½	Stanford Bridge.
	146½	Hinstock.
		R. *to Drayton* 6m.
	150½	Sutton Heath.
43	152½	TERN HILL.
	153¾	Bletchley.
47	156½	Sandford.
	160	Great Ash.

L.D.	M. *from Hicks's Hall.*	
	161½	WHITCHURCH.
		[*By Shrewsbury* (p. 21) 173m.]
		Cheshire.
18	163¾	Grindley Bridge.
		L. *to Malpas* 3m.
17	164½	Bell on the Hill.
	166	No Man's Heath.
14	167½	Hampton Guide Post.
	170	Broxton.
10	171	Barnhill.
	173¾	Handley.
	174½	Golbourn Bridge.
	176½	High Halton.
	180	Little Boughton.
*	181½	CHESTER [C].

Other Routes are by Northampton and Stafford. See p. 24; or, by Coventry to Lichfield, as in the opposite page.

[*Prospective Distances on Return Route:*

Whitchurch	20 m.
Tern Hill	29
Newport	41
Ivetsey Bank ..	49
Wolverhampton	58½
Birmingham ..	72
Coventry	90

On Return Route by Stafford; see p. 25.]

L.D.	M.	
		R. *to Liverpool* [B]
	183¾	Mollington.
5	186½	The Yacht.
10	191	Enderton.
11	192	GREAT NESTON.
12	193¾	PARKGATE.

LONDON TO LIVERPOOL;

The Mail Route by COVENTRY and LICHFIELD: continued to PRESTON. Thence to CARLISLE, GLASGOW, and EDINBURGH.

Variations of Route, and Branch Routes.

[A]

To Stone by Birmingham and Stafford:

	M.
BIRMINGHAM, (p. 20).	109½
Hockley Brook	111
[Staff.] Handsworth	112
Barr	115½
WALSALL	118¼
Bloxwich	121
Great Wyrley	123
Cannock	125½
Huntingdon	127½
Over Cannock Chase.	
Weeping Cross	133
STAFFORD	135
Yarley	139
Little Aston	140¼
Walton	141¾
STONE	142½
Or, by Birmingham and Wolverhampton to Stafford, as in page 20 [F]	146½

[B]

TALK ON THE HILL	154¼
[Chesh.] Lawton Gate	155½
Oddrode	156¾
Smallwood	158½
Brown Edge	161
Brereton	162
Holmes Chapel	164
Cranage	165
Over the Heath to Lach Dennis	169
Lostock	171
Great Budworth	173
Higher Whitley	176
Stretton	177
Wilder's Pool	179½
[Lanc.] WARRINGTON	181
LIVERPOOL	199

L.D.	M. from Hicks's Hall.	
		Warwickshire.
*	91¼	COVENTRY (p. 19). [*Prospective Distances:* Coleshill 12¼m. Lichfield 27½ Wolseley Bridge 37 Stone 49½ Newcastle 58¼ *Manchester* 94¼ Liverpool 115]
	94	Allesley.
6	97½	MERIDEN. On L. W. Digby, Esq.
8	99	On R. Packington Hall, Earl of Aylesford.
19	99¾	STONE BRIDGE. L. *to Birmingham;* R. *to*
15	103¾	COLESHILL.
	106	Curdworth Bridge.
11	108	Wishaw.
		Staffordshire.
	112	Basset's Pole.
6	112¾	Canwell.
	115	Weeford.
	116½	Swinfen.
*	118¾	LICHFIELD. Another Route is by Northampton (p. 24), 123½ m. [*Prospective Distances:* Stone 22 m. Newcastle 31 Congleton 43½ *Manchester* 67 Warrington 69½ Liverpool 87½]
	122	Longdon. On L. Beaudesert, Marq. of Anglesea.
	125	Bruerton.
23	126¼	RUGELEY.
21	128¼	WOLSELEY BRIDGE. Cave. On L. Sir C. Wolseley, Bt. L. *to Stafford,* p. 25. Cross the Trent.
	129¼	Colwich.
19	130½	Great Haywood.
	133	Shirleywich.
	134	Weston on Trent.
13	136¼	SANDON. R. *to Leek* 18½*m.; thence to Buxton* 12*m.* (p. 31.)
10	139½	Stoke.
9	140½	STONE [A]. R. *to Lane End 7m.; thence through the Potteries, as in p. 33.*
	142	Cross the river Trent.
7	142½	Darlaston.
	143	Tittensor Heath.
4	145½	On L. Trentham Park, Marq. of Stafford. On R. a Mausoleum.
	146	Trentham Inn.
	147	Handford. R. *to Stoke upon Trent,* 1½*m. thence to Handley and Burslem, as in p. 33.*

* NEWCASTLE.

Variations of Route, and Branch Routes.

	M.
[B 2]	
Talk on the Hill ..	154½
[Chesh.] Lawton Gate	155½
Dean Hill........	159
SANDBACH	160½
Booth Lane	161½
MIDDLEWICH ..	165¼
Bostock	168½
Davenham	170
NORTHWICH ..	172½
Great Budworth ..	175½
LIVERPOOL, as in Note [B]	201½
[C]	
Monk's Heath	169
Alderley	170½
Street Lane Ends..	171½
WILMSLOW....	173½
Ulbart	175½
Cheadle	178½
Cross the Mersey.	
[Lanc.] Didsbury..	180
Withington	181½
Rusholme T. G. ..	183½
MANCHESTER ..	185¾
Or, by Birmingham and Stafford, to STONE, as in Note [A]............	142½
TALK ON THE HILL	156
Thence by Congleton & Wilmslow to MANCHESTER..	187½
[D]	
KNUTSFORD ..	176¼
Mere Heath	177
Buckley Hill	179
ALTRINCHAM..	183
[Lanc.] Stretford..	187
MANCHESTER..	191
[E]	
MACCLESFIELD (p. 31)	167½
Long Moss	168¾
Birtles	170
Monk's Heath	172
Thence, as in the annexed column, to Knutsford and LIVERPOOL.	

L. D. — M. *from Hicks's Hall.*

149½ NEWCASTLE-UNDER-LINE.

[*Prospective Distances:*

Congleton	12¼ m.
Knutsford	27
Warrington....	38½
Liverpool	56½
Manchester ..	36½]

R. *to Burslem* 2½*m.*

152 Chesterton.

52 154¼ TALK ON THE HILL.

L. *to Liverpool by Holmes Chapel* [B], *or by Middlewich* [B 2].

Cheshire.

155½ Lawton. Red Bull.

159 Morton Hall.

160½ Asbury.

44 162 CONGLETON.

R. *to Macclesfield* 8¼*m.*

165¼ Morton.

166¼ Siddington T. G.

37 169 Monk's Heath.

R. *to Wilmslow, and thence to Manchester* [C].

171 Chelford.

174 Ollerton Gates.

30 176¼ KNUTSFORD.

R. *to Manchester* [D].

179 Mere.

181 High Leigh.

20 186 Latchford.

Cross the river Mersey.

L. D. — M. *from Hicks's Hall.*

Lancashire.

18 188 WARRINGTON.

[*By Holmes Chapel* 181*m.*]

R. *to Wigan.* See p. 29.

189½ Sankey Bridge.

L. *to Liverpool by Penketh* 14¼*m.*

190½ Great Sankey.

11 195 Rainhill.

8 198 PRESCOT.

202 Knotty Ash.

* 206 LIVERPOOL.

Thence to Preston, as in the next page, col. 3.

Other Routes are by Birmingham and Stafford to Talk on the Hill, as in Note [A], and thence, either by the Mail Route above, or by Middlewich, or Holmes Chapel, as in Notes [B] & [B 2]. Other Routes are by Leicester and Derby, as in the Manchester Mail Route, [E]; or through the Potteries, from Leicester, as in page 33. Or, by Birmingham, and through the Potteries.

[*Prospective Distances:*

Ormskirk	13 m.
Preston........	31½
Lancaster	53½
Burton	65
Kendal	76
Penrith........	101½
Carlisle........	120
Glasgow	221
Edinburgh	211

On Return Route:

Warrington	18
Knutsford......	30
Congleton......	44
Newcastle	56½
Stone	65½
Stafford	72
Birmingham ..	98½
Coventry	115]

* LIVERPOOL.

LONDON TO PRESTON;

By WARRINGTON and WIGAN, and by LIVERPOOL. Thence to CARLISLE, GLASGOW, and EDINBURGH.

L.D.	M. from Hicks's Hall.	
		Lancashire.
29	181	WARRINGTON, by Holmes Chapel, page 28.
	183½	Hulme.
24	186	NEWTON.
		R. *to Leigh* 6¼m. [D].
	188½	Ashton.
	191	Goose Green.
17	193½	WIGAN.
	195¼	L. *to Chorley* 6m.; *and thence to Preston*, as in p. 32.
	196½	Standish.
	199½	Welsh Whittle.
	202½	Euxton.
5	205	Clayton.
	206¼	Bamber Bridge.
	208¼	Walton le Dale.
*	210	PRESTON.
		[*By Congleton to Warrington*, 217*m*. *By Manchester* (p. 32) 218*m*.]
	213	Ashton.
	216½	Clifton.
6	219	KIRKHAM.
	222	Weeton.
		R. *to Poulton* 5½*m*.
	225	Newton.
17	227	BLACKPOOL.

L.D.	M. from Hicks's Hall.	
		BY LIVERPOOL.
31	206	LIVERPOOL, as on the opposite page.
		L. *to Crosby Sea Bank* [A].
29	208	Kirkdale.
	209	Walton.
	211	Warbeck Moor.
23	214½	Maghull Brook.
		L. *to Southport* [B].
	217	Aughton.
	219	ORMSKIRK [C].
	222	BURSCOUGH BRIDGE.
13	224½	Rufford.
	228	Tarleton Bridge.
5	230	Great Hoole.
	232½	Longton.
	236¼	Penwortham Bridge.
		Cross the river Ribble.
*	237½	PRESTON.
		Continued to Carlisle and Glasgow, p. 32; *and to Edinburgh*, p. 46.

[*Prospective Distances:*

Lancaster	22 m.
Burton	33¾
Kendal	44¼
Penrith	70
Carlisle	88¼
Glasgow	189¼
Edinburgh	179¼]

Variations of Route, and Branch Routes.

[A]	M.
LIVERPOOL	206
Bootle	209
Linacre	210
CROSBY SEA BANK	212

[A 2]

To Parkgate:

LIVERPOOL	206
Cross the Mersey.	
Tranmere	208
Bebbington	209¾
Thornton Mayes	212¼
Neston	214¼
PARKGATE	215¼

[B]

Maghull Brook	214½
Lydiate	216
Heskayne	218
Barton	219
Shirley Hill	222
Southport	226

[C]

Another Route:

WARRINGTON	181
Sankey	183½
Bold Heath	186
ST. HELLEN	191
Rainford	196½
Bickerstaffe	200
ORMSKIRK	203

[D]

NEWTON	186
LEIGH	192¼
Chowbent	194
MIDDLE HULTON,	196¼
BOLTON	199¼
R. *to Bury* 6*m*.	
BLACKBURN	212
Whalley	218¼
CLITHEROE	222¼

LONDON TO MANCHESTER;

The Mail Route by NORTHAMPTON and DERBY. Continued to LANCASTER and CARLISLE. Thence to GLASGOW and EDINBURGH.

Variations of Route, and Branch Routes.

[A]

To Buxton, and thence to Manchester.

	M.
ASHBORNE	139¾
Sandy Brook	140½
Bentley	142
New Inn	145
Newhaven Inn ..	149
Hardlow House ..	153
Street House	154
BUXTON	160
White Hall	162¼
Shall Cross Mill ..	165¼
Whalley Bridge ..	166½
[Chesh.] Disley ..	170
BULLOCK SMITHY	173½
STOCKPORT	176
MANCHESTER .	182¼

Another Route to Buxton:

LICHFIELD (p.27)	118¾
Hansacre	123
Hill Ridware	124¼
Blythbury	126
ABBOT'S BROMLEY	129
On R. Bagot's Park, Lord Bagot.	
UTTOXETER ..	136
R. *to Ashborne 10m.; thence to Matlock*, p. 34.	
Stramshall	137¼
Beamhurst	139
Checkley	141½
Nether Tean	142¾
Upper Tean	143
CHEADLE	146
Holt	147¾
Ipstones	151
Bottom House	153
Onecote	154½
Broadham Oak ..	160
Longnor	162
[Derb.] BUXTON .	167

L.D.	M. *from Hicks's Hall.*	
	52¼	STONEY STRATFORD (p. 18).
		Cross the river Ouse.
		Northamptonshire.
11	55	Yardly Gobyon.
10	56½	King's Grafton.
	64½	Queen's Cross.
*	66¼	NORTHAMPTON.
		Another Route is by Newport Pagnell, p. 24.
		[*Prospective Distances:* Market Harbro' 17¼m. Leicester 32. Loughborough 43¼. Derby 60. Ashborn 73¼. Leek 88¼. Macclesfield 101¼. Stockport 113¼. Manchester 120]
	68	Kingsthorpe.
6	72¾	Brixworth.
9	75	Lamport.
	76¾	Maidwell.
	79	Kelmarsh ....
15	81	Oxenden.
		Cross the riv. Welland.
		Leicestershire.
17	83½	MARKET HARBOROUGH.
		Other Routes are by Kettering, p. 36.
		R. *to Hallaton 7m.*
		— *to Billesdon 10m.*
	89¼	Kibworth.
	92	Great Glen.
	94¾	Oadby.
28	98	LEICESTER.
		Other Routes are by Newport Pagnell and Welford, as in p. 24; or by Bedford and Kettering to Market Harborough.
		[*Prospective Distances:* Loughborough 11½m. Derby 28. Ashborn 42. Leek 57. Macclesfield 69¼. Stockport 81½. Manchester 88]
		L. *to Burton on Trent, and through the Potteries.* See p. 33.
26	100	Belgrave.
		Cross the river Soar.
21	105¼	MOUNTSORRELL.
	106½	Quarn (Quarndon).
17	109½	LOUGHBOROUGH.
		R. *to Nottingham and Mansfield*, p. 36.
	111¼	Dishley.
14	112	Hathern.
	115½	KEGWORTH.
7	119¼	Cavendish Bridge.
		On L. Donnington Park.
		Cross the river Trent.
		Derbyshire.
	119½	Shardlow.
2	123¾	Alvaston.

Variations of Route, and Branch Routes.

M.

[B]

Other R. to Leek are by Lichfield:

To Sandon (p. 27) 136¼
Hilderston 139¾
Weston Coyney .. 145¾
Cellar Head 148
Wetley Rocks 149
Cheadleton 151¼
LEEK 154¾

Or,

CHEADLE, as in Note [A] 146
Wetley Rocks 151½
LEEK 156¾

Thence to Buxton 12m.

[C]

To Rochdale:

MANCHESTER . 186
Cheetham 187½
MIDDLETON .. 193
Trub Smithy 196
ROCHDALE 199

Thence to Burnley 15m.

[C 2]

MANCHESTER . 186
Cheetham 187½
Great Heaton 190
Whitefield 191½
BURY 195
Shuttleworth 200
HASLINGDEN .. 204
Accrington 208
Cook Bridge 211½
Whalley 212¾
CLITHEROE 216½

Thence to Skipton 18¼m.

[C 3]

To Colne:

Shuttleworth, as above 200
Crawshaw Booth .. 205
BURNLEY 210½
Marsden 212¾
COLNE 216½

Thence to Skipton 26½m.

L.D.	M. from Hicks's Hall.	
		On R. Earl of Harrington.
	125¾	Osmaston T. G.
		On L. Sir R. Wilmot, Bart.
*	126	DERBY.
		[*Prospective Distances:* Ashborn ...... 14 m. Leek .... 29 Macclesfield .... 41½ Stockport ...... 53¾ Manchester .... 60]
	129½	Mackworth.
5	131¼	Langley.
		On R. Lord Scarsdale.
	133¾	Brailsford.
		Over Shirley Common.
	138¾	Hardy T. G.
14	139¾	ASHBORNE.
		R. *to Buxton* [A].
	141½	Hanging Bridge.
		Cross the river Dove.
		Staffordshire.
17	143	Swinescote.
	146½	Milk Hill Gate.
24	150¼	Bottom House.
27	153¾	Low Hill T. G.

L.D.	M. from Hicks's Hall.	
	154¾	LEEK [B].
11	156½	Poolend.
8	159½	Rushton Marsh.
		L. *to Congleton* 5½m.
7	160¾	Hog Bridge.
		Cross the river Dane.
		Cheshire.
	162	Bosley.
*	167½	MACCLESFIELD.
	169¾	Flash.
	171	Butley.
7	174½	Poynton.
	175½	Norbury.
	177	Bullock Smithy.
12	179½	STOCKPORT.
		Cross the riv. Mersey.
		Lancashire.
13	180¾	Heaton Norris.
	182	Levenshulme.
17	184½	Ardwick Green.
	186	MANCHESTER (*a*).
		[*Prospective Distances:* Chorley ...... 22½m. Preston .... 32 Garstang 43

(*a*) Other Routes to Manchester are, M.

1. By Buxton, as in Note [A] 182½
2. By Derby and Matlock (page 34) 186½
   Subject, in either of the above cases, to the variations of route to Leicester.
3. By Nottingham and Matlock (p. 36) 191¾
4. By Coventry, Lichfield, and Congleton (p. 27) 185¾
5. By Birmingham and Stafford (subject to the variations of route to Birmingham) p. 27 .... 186¾
6. Through the Potteries, as in p. 39 .... 194½

Variations of Route, and Branch Routes.

[D]	M.
IRLAM ON THE HEIGHT	189½
Pendlebury	190½
Clifton	192
Farnworth	194½
Great Lever	196
BOLTON	197½
Halliwell	200
Horwich	203
Smithy Bridge	203½
Nightingale House	206
CHORLEY	208½
[D 2]	
BOLTON (above)	197½
Astley's Bridge	199
Walmsley	201½
Over Darwen	206½
BLACKBURN	210½

[E]

The Passage across the sands saves 11½ miles; but should never be attempted without a guide, nor even with one during heavy gales.

LANCASTER	240
Slyne	243
Hest Bank	243¾
Cross the Sands.	
Carter, or Guide's House	251
CARTMEL	254
Thence to Whitehaven (p. 40).	
[E 2]	
CARTMEL, as above	254
Holker	256
Cross the Leven Sands.	
ULVERSTON	261
Kirkby	267
Broughton in Furness	270½
Duddon Bridge	272
[Cumb.] RAVENGLASS	280

[E 3] See next page.

L.D.	M.	*from Hicks's Hall.*
		Lancaster 54
		Burton 65¼
		Kendal 76¾
		Penrith 102
		Carlisle 120
		R. *to Rochdale* [C].
		— *to Bury* [C 2].
		Cross the river Irwell.
	188¼	Pendleton.
	189½	IRLAM ON THE HEIGHT.
		R. *to Bolton, and thence to Chorley* [D].
47	193	Walkden Moor.
	195	Little Hulton.
43	197	MIDDLE HULTON.
		R. *to Bolton 3m.*
42	198	Over Hulton.
		L. *to Wigan 6½m.*
40	200	Win Yate.
	203	Blackrode.
34	206	Nightingale House.
	207¼	Yarrow Bridge.
	208½	CHORLEY.
29	211	Whittle in the Woods.
	212¼	Clayton Green.
26	214	Bamber Green.
	216	Walton le Dale.
		Cross the river Ribble.
22	218	PRESTON.
	220½	Cadley Moor.
18	222	Broughton.
	223½	Barton.
14	226	Brock's Bridge.
	227	Claughton T. G.
11	229	GARSTANG.
	231	Fooler Hill.
	234¼	Hole of Ellel.
4	236	Golgate Bridge.

L.D.	M.	*from Hicks's Hall.*
	238½	Scotforth.
*	240	LANCASTER.
		R. *to Sedbergh* [F].
		Cross the river Loyne.
		R. *to Kirkby Lonsdale.*
3	243	Slyne.
		L. *to Cartmel, across the Sands* [E].
7	244½	Bolton le Sands.
	246¾	Carnforth.
	248¾	Dare Bridge.
	249½	Borwick.
		Westmorland.
11	251½	BURTON.
		L. *to Cartmel* [G].
	256½	End Moor.
19	259	Barrow's Green.
	261	Mill Beck.
22	262¼	KENDAL.
		R. *to Appleby* [H].
		L. *to Ambleside and Keswick*, p. 40.
	267¾	Gate Side.
	271	Hausse Foot.
28	278	SHAP.
25	281¼	Thrimby.
	283½	New Village.
		Lowther, on L. & Castle, Earl of Lonsdale.
	285¾	Clifton.
	287	Lowther Bridge [I].
18	288	PENRITH; thence to
*	306½	CARLISLE, GLASGOW, and EDINBURGH, p. 46.

* LANCASTER.

LONDON TO MANCHESTER, AND LIVERPOOL;

Through the POTTERIES (a).

Variations of Route, and Branch Routes.	M.
[E 3]	
ULVERSTON ..	261
Linnal	263½
DALTON	265
[F]	
LANCASTER ..	240
Caton	245
Claughton	247
HORNBY	249
Melling	250¾
Tunstall..........	252¼
Casterton	256¼
Middleton..........	260¼
New Bridge	263
[Yorkshire.] SEDBERGH	265½
Rother Bridge	270
[Westm.] KIRKBY STEPHEN	279
BROUGH (p. 46) .	283¾
[G]	
BURTON	251½
Holme	253
Millthorpe	256
Cross the Ken and Winster rivers.	
[Lanc.] Linsdale ..	262
CARTMEL	265½
[H]	
KENDAL	262¼
Grayrigg	269
Low Borrow Bridge	272
Cross the Loyne.	
Tebay	274
ORTON	276¼
Hough	284
Burrells..........	285
APPLEBY	286
[I]	
PENRITH	288
Eden Hall	291
Longwarthly	292¼
Melmerby.........	296¼
Hartside Cross	300½
ALDSTONE MOOR	307
[North.] Knaresdale	312¼
HALTWHISTLE.	318¾

L.D.	M. from Hicks's Hall.	
		Leicestershire.
*	98	LEICESTER.
	102	Grooby.
7	105	Markfield.
	109½	Hagglescote.
	112	Ravenscote.
17	115	ASHBY-DE-LA-ZOUCH.
		R. *to Derby* 19*m.*
		L. *to Measham* 3½*m.*
		Derbyshire.
23	121	Stag and Hounds. On R. Bretby Park, Earl of Chesterfield.
		Staffordshire.
26	124	BURTON on TRENT.
		R. *to Derby* 11¼*m.*
	125	Horninglow.
30	128¼	Tutbury.
		Derbyshire.
33	131¼	Foston.
35	133¼	Aston.
	133½	Sudbury. On R. Sudbury Park, Lord Vernon.
		R. *to Ashborne* 8*m.*
39	137	Dovebridge. On L. Lord Waterpark.

L.D.	M. from Hicks's Hall.	
		Staffordshire.
19	139¼	UTTOXETER.
	140½	Stramshall.
16	142¼	Beamhurst.
	144¼	Checkley.
13	145¼	Nether Tean.
	146¼	Upper Tean.
		R. *to Cheadle* 3*m.*
11	147¾	Draycott.
	150	Blithe Bridge.
	151½	Mere.
6	152¼	LANE END (*a*).
		L. *to Stone* 7*m.*
5	153¾	Lane Delph.
	155	Stoke upon Trent.
		L. *to Newcastle* 1¼*m.*
	156	Shelton.
		R. *to Handley* 1*m.*
	157½	Cowbridge T. G.
*	158½	BURSLEM.
		L. *to Longport* ½*m.*; *thence to Newcastle* 2*m.*
	159¼	Tunstall T. G.
3	161½	Golden Hill.
	163	Kidcrew.
5¼	164	Lawton. Red Bull. Thence (p. 28) to
36	194¼	MANCHESTER, *and to Liverpool.*

(*a*) Another Route to Lane End, and thence through the Potteries, is by Birmingham and Stafford to Stone, p. 27.

LONDON TO MANCHESTER, THROUGH MATLOCK;

The Route to Matlock, either by Derby, Lichfield, or Nottingham.

Variations of Route, and Branch Routes.

[A] M.

Another R. from Derby:

	M.
DERBY	126
Allestrey	128
Duffield	130
On L. Kedleston Pk.	
Cross the Derwent.	
Milford	131
On L. J. D. Strutt, Esq.	
BELPER	134
On L. G. B. Strutt, Esq.	
Cromford	141
On R. Willersley Castle, R. Arkwright, Esq.	
MATLOCK BATH	142
R. *to Matlock village* 2m.	

The tour through this district is extremely picturesque and beautiful. It is well observed in Cooke's Topography of the County of Derby, that "Matlock Dale is perhaps superior in natural beauty to any of the most finished places in the kingdom. It consists of a winding vale, through which the river Derwent flows in a very diversified manner: the boundaries of the vale being cultivated hills on one side, and very bold rocks with pendent woods on the other." The route is farther interesting by its local associations and the many natural curiosities of the neighbourhood, which will be found very agreeably detailed in the little compendium above quoted.

L. D.	M. *from Hicks's Hall.*	
		Derbyshire.
*	126	DERBY (p. 31).
3	129¼	Kedleston Inn.
		On L. Lord Scarsdale.
		Through the Park to
	132½	Weston under Wood.
9	135	Cross Hands.
	137	Black Swan.
	138½	Bateman Bridge.
14	140	Wall Brook.
	140¼	WIRKSWORTH.
16	142	Cromford.
		L. *to Matlock Bath* 1m. [A].
		Cross the riv. Derwent.
18	144	MATLOCK (Village).
	147¼	Darley.
		Cross the Derwent.
37	149½	Rowsley.
	151	On R. Haddon Hall.
34	152½	BAKEWELL.
		On R. Chatsworth, Duke of Devonshire.
32	154½	Ashford.
	155½	Little Longstone.
	158	Wardlow.
	160	L. *to Tideswell* ½m.
23	163½	New Dam.
	165½	Sparrow Pit T. G.
19	167½	CHAPEL EN LE FRITH.
	170¾	L. *to Buxton* 6m.
	171	Whaley Bridge.

L. D.	M. *from Hicks's Hall.*	
		Cheshire.
12	174¼	Disley.
	176	Hoo Lane.
		On R. Marple....
9	177½	BULLOCK SMITHY.
	180	STOCKPORT.
*	186½	MANCHESTER (p. 31).

ANOTHER ROUTE TO MATLOCK.

L. D.	M.	
		Staffordshire.
37	118¾	LICHFIELD (p. 27).
32	123¾	King's Bromley.
	126	Yoxall.
	128	Forest Church.
23	132½	Draycott.
		Derbyshire.
21	134¾	Sudbury.
	138	Cubley.
	141½	Clifton.
13	142¾	ASHBORNE.
		L. *to Buxton* (p. 30.)
11	145¾	Kniveton.
6	149½	Carsington.
4	151¾	WIRKSWORTH.
*	155½	MATLOCK.
		Another R. is by Nottingham, as on the opposite page [C].

* MANCHESTER.

LONDON TO NOTTINGHAM;

And thence to SHEFFIELD and LEEDS; the Mail Route. Continued to HARROWGATE, RIPON, and NORTHALLERTON. Thence to EDINBURGH.

Variations of Route, and Branch Routes.

[A]

	M.
BEDFORD	50
Wilden	54½
Bonhurst	55½
Keysoe	57½
Pertenhall	60
[Hunt.] Park Lane T. G.	60½
KIMBOLTON	62
Thence to Stamford:	
Great Catsworth	66
Brington	68
[Northam.] Clapton	71
OUNDLE	76
Cotterstock	78
Wood Newton	81
KING'S CLIFFE	83½
Easton	89
STAMFORD	91
Thence, p. 41.	

[B]

By leaving Higham Ferrers out of the route, and keeping the left-hand road to Kettering, the traveller will save two miles. The roads rejoin at Finedon.

[C]

NOTTINGHAM	124
Bobber's Mill	125½
Cinder Hill	127½
Nuthall	128½
Watnal	130
Griesley	131
Selstone	136
[Derb.] Somercotes	138
ALFRETON	140
Higham	142
Stretton	143½
Butterby	146½
Tansley	147½
MATLOCK	149½
MATLOCK BATH	151½

L. D.	M. from Hicks's Hall.
	Middlesex.
	½ Pentonville.
	1 Islington Green.
	2¼ Holloway T. G.
	4 Highgate Archway.
	6 Finchley.
	9 Whetstone.
	Hertfordshire.
39	11 BARNET.
	Middlesex.
	11¾ Obelisk.
	L. *to St. Alban's*, R. *to*
36	14 Potter's Bar.
	Hertfordshire.
	16 R. *to Hertford* 8m.
	16¾ Bell Bar.
31	19½ HATFIELD.
	On R. Hatfield House, Marq. of Salisbury.
	R. *to Hertford* 7½m.
	L. *to St. Alban's* 5m.
29	21¼ Stanborough.
	L. *to Wheathampstead* 3½m.
28	22 Lemsford Mills.
	Cross the river Lea.
	On L. Brocket Hall, Visc. Melbourne.

L. D.	M. from Hicks's Hall.
27	23 Brickwall T. G.
25	25 WELWYN.
	R. *to Stevenage and Biggleswade*. See R. 17.
	26½ Codicote.
	29½ Langley.
16	34 HITCHIN.
	R, *to Baldock* 5m.
	On R. Ickleford...
	Bedfordshire.
9	41 SHEFFORD.
4	46¼ Cotton End.
2	48¼ Fenlake.
*	50 BEDFORD.
	Other Routes are by Barnet and St. Alban's, 51m.; by Edgware and St. Alban's, 50m.; and by Dunstable and Ampthill 53m. See p. 19.
	[*Prospective Distances:* Higham Ferrers - 15 m. Kettering 24½ Rockingham 33 Uppingham 39 Oakham 45½ Melton Mowbray 55 Nottingham 74 Sheffield 113]
	R. *to St. Neots* 12m.
	— *to Kimbolton* [A].
	52 L. *to Olney* 9½m.
2	52¼ Clapham T. G.
	On L. Oakley House, Marquis of Tavistock.

* BEDFORD.

Variations of Route, and Branch Routes.

[D] M.
Irthlingborough .. 66½
Little Addington .. 68½
Great Addington .. 69½
Woodford 71
THRAPSTON .. 73½
Thence to Oundle 8m.

[E]
KETTERING.... 74½
Rothwell 78½
Desborough 80
Fox Inn 82
Little Bowden 85
[Leic.] MARKET HARBOROUGH 85½
Thence, p. 30, to
LEICESTER 100
From Market Harboro' to Billesdon 10m.

[F]
OAKHAM 95½
Burleigh on the Hill 97¾
Cottesmere 99¾
Greetham 101½
[Linc.] WITHAM. 105½
Thence along the North Road, p. 41.

[G]
Another Route:
STAMFORD (p.41) 89½
Empingham 94½
[Rutl.] Whitwell.. 96¾
OAKHAM 101½
Thence, as in the opposite col. to
MELTON MOWBRAY 110¾

[H]
LOUGHBOROUGH (p. 30) 109½
Cotes 111
Hoton 112¾
[Notts.] Rempston 114
Cortlingstock 115
Bunney 117½
Bradmore 118½
Ruddington 120
Trent Bridge 123¾
NOTTINGHAM . 124½

L.D.	M. from Hicks's Hall.
	55 Milton Ernest.
	56½ Bletsoe.
	60 Knotting: Fox Public House. Division of the Road [B].
	Northamptonshire.
	63½ Rushden.
	L. *to Wellingborough* 5*m.*
59	64½ HIGHAM FERRERS.
	66½ Irthlingborough.
	R. *to Thrapston* [D].
	68½ Finedon.
	71 Burton Latimer.
	72½ Barton Seagrave.
50	74½ KETTERING.
	Another Route is by Newport Pagnell, p. 24.
	L. *to Market Harborough* [E].
45	79½ Oakley Inn.
	[83¾ Weldon.
	92 Duddington.
	97½ STAMFORD.]
	80 Rockingham Forest.
41	83 ROCKINGHAM.
	Rutlandshire.
	84½ Caldecote.
35	89 UPPINGHAM.
	90½ Preston.
	92½ Manton.
29	95½ OAKHAM.
	R. *to Witham* [F].
	96½ Barleythorpe.
	97½ Langham T. G.

L.D.	M. from Hicks's Hall.
	Leicestershire.
	103½ Burton Lazars.
	R. *to Waltham* 3½*m.*
19	105 MELTON MOWBRAY [G].
	108½ Kettleby.
13	110¾ Nether Broughton.
	Nottinghamshire.
	111½ Over Broughton.
	Stanton, on L.
	117½ Normanton.
6	118 Plumtree.
	122¾ Trent Bridge.
*	124 NOTTINGHAM.
	Another Route is by Northampton and Leicester [H].
	[*Prospective Distances:* Mansfield ...... 14 m. Chesterfield .... 26½ Sheffield ...... 39 Barnsley ...... 52½ Wakefield .... 63 Leeds .... 72 Harrowgate .... 87 Newcastle ....166 Edinburgh ....285]
	L. *to Matlock* [C]; *thence to Manchester*, p. 34.
	126¾ Daybrook T. G.
4	128½ Red Hill.
	R. *to Southwell* 10*m.*
	Enter Sherwood Forest.
	133¾ Newstead T. G.
14	138 MANSFIELD.
	R. *to Worksop* [I].
	140½ Pleasley Hill.

* NOTTINGHAM.

Variations of Route, and Branch Routes.

[I] — M.

MANSFIELD .. 138
Mansfield Woodhouse 139¼
Market Warsop .. 142¾
Church Warsop .. 143
Norton 145
Worksop Manor .. 147¼
WORKSOP 149¾
Thence to Doncaster 17*m.* p. 41.

[K]

MANSFIELD .. 138
[Derb.] Pleasley .. 141
Stoney Houghton · 142
L. *to Bolsover* 3½*m.*
Scarcliff 143½
Clown 148
Knitacre 149½
[York.] Aughton.. 156
Whiston 158
ROTHERHAM .. 160
Thence to Barnsley:
Greasborough 161¾
Nether Hough 162¾
Wentworth 165½
Junction of Road from Sheffield .. 166½
Worsborough 170
BANK TOP INN .. 171¼
BARNSLEY 172¾

[L]

DERBY (p. 31) .. 126
Little Chester 127
Little Eaton 129½
Coxbench 131¼
Kilburn T. G. 133
Denby College 134½
Butterley 136¾
Swanwick 138
ALFRETON 139½
Higham 141½
Stretton 142¾
Clay Cross 144
Tupton 145¼
CHESTERFIELD 149¾
Another Route is through Allestrey and Duffield from Derby, 150½m.

L.D.	M. *from Hicks's Hall.*	
		Derbyshire.
22	141	Pleasley.
		R. *to Rotherham* [K].
19	143¾	Glapwell.
	145½	Heath.
16	147¼	Temple Normanton.
14	149¼	Hasland T. G.
	150½	CHESTERFIELD.
		[*By Derby* [L] 149¾*m.*]
10	153	Whittington Common.
	156½	DRONFIELD.
	158½	Greenhill Common.
2	161¼	Healey.
		Yorkshire.
*	163	SHEFFIELD.

Other Routes are by Derby [L], 162 miles; or, by Newark and Worksop [M], 164m.

[*Prospective Distances:*
Barnsley .... 13¼*m.*
Wakefield....... 24
Leeds 33
Harrowgate 48
Ripon 60
Northallerton .. 77¼
Durham 112¾
Newcastle 127
Edinburgh ....246]

R. *to Rotherham 6m.; thence to Doncaster* 11¼*m.*

L. *to Huddersfield*, p. 39.

L.D.	M. *from Hicks's Hall.*	
	164¼	Pitt's Moor.
5	168	Ecclesfield.
	169	Chapel Town.
7	170	Woodhill.
11	174	Worsborough.
	175¼	BANK TOP.
19	176½	BARNSLEY.

Another Route is by Rotherham from Mansfield [K].

L.D.	M.	
	177¼	Old Mill Inn.
16	180	Staincross.
14	181¼	Woolley Park.
	183½	New Miller Dam.
11	185	Sandall.
9	187	WAKEFIELD.

Another Route is by Newark and Doncaster [N].

L. *to Bradford* [N].

L.D.	M.	
7	188½	Newton.
5	190½	Lofthouse.
	194¾	Hunslet T. G.
*	195¾	LEEDS.

Other Routes are by Ferry Bridge [O]; or, by Newark to Worksop, and thence through Sheffield, as in Note [M].

[*Prospective Distances:*
Harrowgate .... 15¼*m.*
Ripley 19½
Boroughbridge 25½
Ripon 27½
Northallerton .. 45
Darlington 61½
Durham 80
Newcastle 94½
Edinburgh 213¾
Stockton (p. 48) 61]

R. *to Tadcaster* 14½*m.; thence to York* 9*m.; continued to Scarborough*, p. 50.

L. *to Otley; thence to Skipton and Kendal* [O 2].

L.D.	M.	
3	198½	Chapel Allerton.

Variations of Route, and Branch Routes.

	M.
[M]	
WORKSOP (p. 41 [C])	146½
Gateford	148½
[York.] South Anston	152¼
Todwick	154¼
Aston	156¼
Hansworth	160½
Darnal	162
Attercliffe	163
SHEFFIELD	164
[N]	
DONCASTER (p. 42)	162
Red House	167
North Elmsall	171
Over Ackworth Moor.	
Wragby	176
Foldby	177
Crofton	178
WAKEFIELD	182
Thence to Skipton:	
East Ardaley	185½
Tingley	187
Bruntcliff	189½
Adwalton	191
Wisket Hill	193
Dudley Hill	194½
BRADFORD	196
Cottingley	199½
BINGLEY	201¾
KEIGHLEY	206
Thence as in R. 16.	
SKIPTON	216
[O]	
FERRY BRIDGE, (p. 42)	177
Brotherton	178
Fairburn	179½
Peckfield	182
West Garforth	185½
Whitchurch	187¾
Halton	189
LEEDS	192
Thence to Skipton: See col. 3 [O 2].	

L.D.	M. *from Hicks's Hall.*	
	199¾	Moor Town.
10	201	Alwoodley Gate.
7	204	HAREWOOD. On L. Earl of Harewood.
5	205¼	Dun Keswick.
	208½	Spacey House.
*	211	HARROWGATE.

Another Route is by Ferry Bridge [P].

[*Prospective Distances:*

Ripon	12m.
CatterickBridge	32½
(Thence, pp. 45, 46) Northallerton	29½
Darlington	46
Durham	64½
Newcastle	79
Edinburgh	198]

R. *to Knaresborough 3m.; thence to Boroughbridge 7m.*

[At Boroughbridge, to Guisborough, Stockton, and Sunderland, p. 48.]

L.D.	M.	
	213¾	Killenhall.
4	215¼	RIPLEY [Q]. L. *to Pateley Bridge 9½m.*
7	217¾	South Stainley.
12	223	RIPON. [*By Boroughbridge, as in R. 17, 212m.*]
16	227½	Cross the Carlisle Rd. L. *to Catterick Bridge 16m.; thence to Edinburgh, by Jedburgh, p. 45; or,* L. *to Carlisle and Glasgow, p. 46.*

L.D.	M. *from Hicks's Hall.*	
	228¾	Baldersby.
10	230¼	Skipton Bridge.
9	231½	Busby Stoop. R. *to Thirsk 3½m.*
8	232½	Sand Hutton.
	236	South Otterington.
3	237½	North Otterington.
*	240½	NORTHALLERTON.

Thence, p. 43, to

Darlington	16½m.
Durham	35
Newcastle	49½
Edinburgh	168½

Variations of Route, and Branch Routes, continued from column 1.

	M.
[O 2]	
LEEDS	192
Headingley	194
Cookridge	197½
OTLEY	201¼
Burley	203¾
Ilkley	206
Addingham	210½
SKIPTON	216
Thence to Kendal and Whitehaven, p. 39.	
[P]	
FERRY BRIDGE (p. 42)	177
WETHERBY	193½
Spofforth	196¾
HARROWGATE	201
[Q]	
Another Route:	
WETHERBY (p. 43)	193½
Spofforth	196¾
KNARESBOROUGH	201½
RIPLEY	206

LONDON TO HALIFAX;

Continued to KENDAL, and thence to WHITEHAVEN.

Variations of Route, and Branch Routes.

	M.
[A]	
BARNSLEY, p. 38,	172¾
Darton	175½
Bretton	179
Midgley	180
Hill Top	181¾
Flockton	182½
Highgate Lane....	185
Almondbury.......	187
HUDDERSFIELD	189
[B]	
WORKSOP, p. 41,	146½
Gateford	148½
[York.] South Anston	152½
Todwick	154½
Aston..............	156½
ROTHERHAM ..	162
Greasborough	163¾
Nether Hough....	164¾
Wentworth	167¼
Worsborough	172
BANK TOP INN ..	173¾
BARNSLEY	174½
Thence as above [A].	
[C]	
HALIFAX	197
Beggarinton......	200
Great Horton	203¾
BRADFORD	205½

Other Routes are by Sheffield and Wakefield, p. 37, 201 miles; or by Doncaster and Wakefield, 196 miles.

[D]	
Another Route:	
LANCASTER, p. 32	240
Caton	245
Claughton........	247
HORNBY	249
Melling...........	250¼
Tunstall...........	252½
KIRKBY LONSDALE	255½

L.D.	M. from Hicks's Hall.	
		Yorkshire.
*	163	SHEFFIELD, as in page 37.
		[*Prospective Distances:* Huddersfield .. 26 m. Halifax........ 34 Skipton ...... 55½ Settle .... 71 Kirkby Lonsdale 88½ Kendal ....101 Ambleside ....115 Keswick ......131 Cockermouth ..142½ Whitehaven....156]
3	166	Wadsley Bridge.
		Cross the river Don.
5	168	Grina Side.
8	171	Wortley.
		On R. Wortley Hall, J. S. Wortley, Esq.
	172½	Thurgoland.
12	175½	PENISTONE.
	177½	Inchbirchworth.
		Cross Denby Moor.
18	181	Over Shepley.
	184	High Burton.
	185½	Highgate Lane.
24	187	Almondbury.
		Cross the river Coln.
26	189	HUDDERSFIELD.
		Other Routes are as in Note [A], or by Newark and Worksop [B].
	191½	Clough Cliff.
31	194	Ealand.
	195¼	Salter Hebble Bridge.
21	197	HALIFAX.
		R. to *Bradford* [C].
	198¼	Ovenden.
	199½	Illingworth.
16	202½	Denholm Gate.
		Through Denholm Park.
13	205	Cullingworth.
		L. *to Colne* 11*m*.
	207	Hainworth Common.
9	209	KEIGHLEY.
	211¼	Steeton.
	212¾	Eastburn.
5	213½	Cross Hills.
	214	Kildwick.
*	218¼	SKIPTON.
		Other Routes are by Wakefield, p. 38, [N], or by Ferry Bridge and Leeds, p. 38, [O], or by Manchester, p. 31.
		On R. the Castle, Earl of Thanet.
2	220¼	Sturton Thorlby.
	222	Holme Bridge.
5	223	Gargrave.
	225	Cold Coniston.
10	228	Hellifield Cochins.
	230	Long Preston.
16	234	SETTLE.
	234¾	Giggleswick.
22	240½	Clapham.

Variations of Route, and Branch Routes.

[E]	M.
KENDAL	264
Bonning Yate	267
Quaker's Meeting..	269½
Bowness	272½
Ferry across Winander Mere.	
[Lanc.] Claife	275
HAWKSHEAD..	278

Another Route; and thence to Whitehaven:

	M.
CARTMEL, (across the Sands, as in R. 13)	254
Broughton.........	256
Staveley	258½
Newby Bridge ..	259½
Cross the Leven Water.	
Finsthwaite	262
Highdale Park....	265
HAWKSHEAD..	267½
[Cumb.] Wastdale,	280
Enerdale	289
WHITEHAVEN..	294

[F]	M.
RAVENGLASS, as in R. 13.......	280
Carleton	282½
Ponsonby	288
EGREMONT	292½
WHITEHAVEN..	298
Thence to Workington:	
Moresby	300½
Distington	302½
WORKINGTON..	306½

[G]	M.
KESWICK	293¾
Little Crosthwaite,	297½
High Side.........	299½
Orthwaite	302
Uldale	304½
IREBY	306
WIGTON	311½

L.D.	M. from Hicks's Hall.	
		On R. Ingleborough Mountain.
20	244½	Ingleton.
	245½	Thornton.
		Lancashire.
15	249½	Cowan Bridge.
		Cross the river Loyne.
		Westmorland.
13	251½	KIRKBY LONSDALE [D].
	252¾	Kearswick.
9	255	Old Town.
	258¾	Old Hutton.
	259½	Chapel House.
*	264	KENDAL.
		[*By Manchester* 262½*m.*]
		R. *to Carlisle and Glasgow*, p. 32.
		L. *to Hawkshead* [E].
	265¾	L. *to Winander Mere* 7*m.*
	266½	Gate Side.
5	269	Staveley.
	270½	Garth Chapel.
10	274	Trout Beck Bridge.
		On L. Winander Mere.
	277½	Low Wood Inn.
14	278	AMBLESIDE.
	279½	Rydal.
20	284	Dunmail Raise.
		Cumberland.
21	285½	Wyntburn Chapel.

L.D.	M. from Hicks's Hall.	
	288	Thirlspot.
30	289	Smalthwaite Bridge.
	292½	Castlerigg.
26	293¾	KESWICK.
		R. *to Wigton* [G].
	294¾	Crossthwaite.
	295½	Portingscale.
23	296½	Braithwaite.
		On R. Bassenthwaite Water.
	301½	Lorton.
14	305½	COCKERMOUTH.
		R. *to Maryport* 7½*m.*
9	310	Little Clifton.
		R. *to Workington* 3*m.*
	314½	Distington.
	316½	Moresby.
*	319½	WHITEHAVEN.

Other Routes are as in [E], or by Ravenglass [F].

Branch Routes, referred to on the opposite page.

[A]	
BUCKDEN	60¼
Brampton Cross ..	63¼
Hinchinbrook	64¼
HUNTINGDON .	65
Another Route is by Ware (p. 49) 58¾m.	

[B]	
Great Ponton T. G.	107
Cold Harbour	111
Londonthorpe	112
Ancaster	115¼
Baynard's Leap ..	118¾
GREEN MAN	126
Dunston Pillar....	127¾
LINCOLN	134

LONDON TO EDINBURGH.

The Great North Road; and Route also of the Glasgow Mail to BOROUGHBRIDGE, subject to the Variation at [C].

Variations of Route, and Branch Routes.

[A] [B]. See page 48.

[C]

The route travelled by the Glasgow Mail, from Newark to Doncaster, is by Worksop and Tickhill, as below. Whence, the distances beyond Doncaster will each be 1½m. greater on the mail route to Glasgow, than on the annexed line by Scarthing Moor.

	M.
NEWARK	124¼
Kelham..........	126¾
Caunton	129½
Beesthorpe Common	130
Kneesall	134
Ompton..........	135
Wellow..........	136¼
OLLERTON (*a*)..	137¾
Budby	140½
On R. Thoresby Park.	
Carburton........	142¼
On R. Clumber Park.	
On L. Welbeck Abbey.	
Sparkenhill	145
WORKSOP	146½
On L. Worksop Manor.	
Carlton..........	149¾
Goldthorpe	154
[York.] TICKHILL	156
Wadworth	159
Loversall	160
Balby	161¾
DONCASTER ..	163½

(*a*) The tourist, on leaving Ollerton, may pass through Thoresby and Clumber Parks, and re-enter the turnpike road at Sparkenhill.

L.D. | M. *from Hicks's Hall.*

Hertfordshire.

By BARNET to

64 | 25 WELWYN, p. 35.

27 Woolmer Green.

29¼ Broadwater.

58 | 31½ STEVENAGE.

[*By Hertford* (p. 49) 33*m*.]

33¾ Graveley.

37¼ BALDOCK.

49 | 40¼ New Inn T. G.

On R. Caldecote

Bedfordshire.

44 | 45 BIGGLESWADE.

R. *to Potton* 3½*m*.

46½ Lower Caldecote.

48 Beeston Cross.

48¾ Girtford.

38 | 51 Tempsford.

53¾ Little Barford.

Huntingdonshire.

33 | 55¼ ST. NEOTS.

57¾ Little Paxton.

28 | 60¾ BUCKDEN.

R. *to Huntingdon* [A].

66 Alconbury.

67 Weston.

21 | 68 ALCONBURY HILL.

[*By Ware* (p. 49) 64*m*.]

71½ Sawtry St. Andrews.

L.D. | M. *from Hicks's Hall.*

14 | 75 STILTON.

13 | 76 Norman's Cross.

R. *to Peterborough* 5½*m*.

8 | 81 Water Newton.

Northamptonshire.

83¾ WANDSFORD.

84½ Thornhaugh, on L.

2 | 87 White Water T. G.

On R. Burleigh House, Marq. of Exeter.

Lincolnshire.

* 89¼ STAMFORD.

[*Prospective Distances:*

Grantham......	21¼*m*.
Newark	35½
Scarthing Moor.	46½
East Retford ..	55¼
Barnby Moor ..	59
Doncaster......	73
Ferry Bridge ..	88
York	110]

R. *to Bourn* 11½*m*.

Rutlandshire.

2 | 91½ Bridge Casterton.

6 | 95½ Horn Lane T. G.

8 | 97 GREETHAM.

Lincolnshire.

12 | 101 WITHAM. Black Bull.

13 | 102¼ Coltersworth.

18 | 107 Great Ponton T. G.

R. *to Ancaster* [B].

* STAMFORD.

Variations of Route, and Branch Routes.

[D] M.

NEWARK 124½
Winthorpe 126¼
Langford 128
Collingham 130
Besthorpe 132
Girton 133½
Linc.] Newton .. 138½
Torksey 142
GAINSBORO' .. 149
Another Route is by Lincoln (p. 56) 147m.

[E]

BAWTRY 153¼
Rossington Bridge - 157¾
Hatfield 163
THORNE 167
Thence to York:
New Bridge 171½
SNAITH 174
L. *to Pontefract* 13m.
Carleton 175½
Camblesforth 177
Over the Moor.
SELBY 181½
L. *to Cawood* 4½m.
Cross the Ouse.
Barlby T. G. 183¾
Riccall 186
Escrick Bridge 190
Fulford 194
Walmgate Bar.... 195½
YORK 196

[E 2].

To Market Weighton:
THORNE 167
New Bridge 171½
Cross the Dutch riv.
Roccliffe 173¾
Armyn 177
BOOTH FERRY .. 178½
Cross the Ouse.
HOWDEN 180½
Welham Bridge .. 185½
Holme 187½
L. *to Pocklington* 9½m.
MARKET WEIGHTON 192½

L. D. | M. *from Hicks's Hall.*

109½ Spittlegate.
14 110½ GRANTHAM.
112 Gunnerby.
114¼ Marston T. G.
116 Foston.
118 Long Bennington.
6 119¾ Shire Bridge.

Nottinghamshire.

122¼ Balderton T. G.
* 124½ NEWARK [C].
[132½ Halfway House.
138½ Brace Bridge.
140¾ LINCOLN.]
L. *to Southwell* 8½m.
R. *to Gainsborough*, [D].
Cross the river Trent.
127 South Muskham.
128 North Muskham.
130 Cromwell........
7 131½ Carlton.
133 Sutton.
10 134¾ Weston..........
135½ SCARTHING MOOR.
13 137½ TUXFORD.
139½ West Markham.
22 140 Markham Moor T. G.
141¼ Gamston.
142½ Eaton.
144½ EAST RETFORD.
R. *to Gainsborough* 9¼m.
14 148 BARNBY MOOR.
L. *to Blythe* 3m.
149½ Torworth.
150½ Rauskill.
10 152 Scrooby.

L. D. | M. *from Hicks's Hall.*

Yorkshire.

9 153¼ BAWTRY.
L. *to Tickhill* 4m.
4½ 157¾ Rossington Bridge.
R. *to Thorne, and thence to York* [E].
159½ Race Ground.
* 162 DONCASTER.
[*Prospective Distances:*
Ferry Bridge .. 15 m.
Abberford 24
York 37
Boroughbridge.. 44
Northallerton .. 62½
Darlington 79
Durham 97½
Newcastle 112
Edinburgh ....231]
R. *to Thorne* 10m.
164 York Bar.
5 167 Red House.
L. *to Wakefield* 15½m.
7 168¾ Robin Hood's Well.
172½ Went Bridge.
174 Darrington.
15 177 FERRY BRIDGE.
[*By Ware* (p. 40) 173m.]
16 178 Brotherton.
R. *to* YORK; *thence to Northallerton* [F].
Another Route is by Thorne and Snaith [E.]
179½ Fairburn.
22 182 Peckfield T. G.
183½ Micklefield.
24 186 ABBERFORD.
R. *to Tadcaster* 4m.; *thence to York as in* [F].

* DONCASTER.

Variations of Route, and Branch Routes.

	M.
[F]	
FERRY BRIDGE ..	177
Brotherton	178
South Milford	181½
Sherburn	183
Barkston	184½
Towton	186¾
TADCASTER....	190
Street Houses	193
Dring Houses	197½
YORK	199
Clifton	200½
Skelton	203
Skipton...........	204½
Tollerton Lanes ..	208
L. *to Tollerton* 1½*m.*	
R. *to Sutton* 4*m.*	
EASINGWOLD .	212
Thormanby	216½
Stockwell T. G. ..	220¼
THIRSK	222½
Thornton in the Street	225½
NORTHALLERTON	231½
[G]	
NEWCASTLE ..	274
Newbiggin	277½
Ponteland.........	281½
Nun Hill	285½
Corridge	292
CAMBOE	295
Harwood Head ..	300½
Elsdon	304
Otterburn	306
ELISHA BRIDGE .	309½
[H]	
NEWCASTLE ..	274
Useborn	275
Biker.............	276
Chirton	280½
NOR. SHIELDS -	281½
TYNEMOUTH	283
[I]	
MORPETH......	289
Leaning T. G.	291
L. *to Rothbury* 13*m.*	
Longhorsley T. G. -	296
Weldon Bridge ..	298½

L.D.	M. *from Hicks's Hall.*	
	189½	Bramham.
	193½	WETHERBY.
	196¾	Warkford Bridge.
	206	BOROUGHBRIDGE
		[*Prospective Distances:* Northallerton .. 18½m. Darlington .... 35 Durham ...... 53½ Newcastle .... 68 Morpeth ...... 83 Berwick ......131½ Edinburgh ....187]
		L. *to Leeming Lane* 12*m.; thence to Carlisle and Glasgow,* p. 46.
	210	Dishforth.
47	212½	Topcliffe.
		R. *to Thirsk* 4*m.*
	216½	Sand Hutton.
41	218½	Newsham.
	220	South Otterington.
	221½	North Otterington.
35	224½	NORTHALLERTON.
		[*By York* [F] 231½*m.* *By Leeds,* see p. 38.]
		L. *to Catterick Bridge* 13*m.*
31	228½	Lowsome Hill.
	230¼	Little Smeaton.
	232	Great Smeaton.
	233	Enter Common T. G.
		R. *to Yarm* 9½*m.*
	236	Dalton.
22	237½	Croft.
		Cross the river Tees.
		Durham.
	241	DARLINGTON.
	245	Coatham Mandeville.
	246	Aycliffe.
	247	Traveller's Rest.
11	248½	Woodham.
	250	RUSHYFORD.
7	252½	Ferry Hill.
5	254½	Butcher Race.
	256	Sunderland Bridge.
		Cross the river Wear.
*	259½	DURHAM.
		Other Routes are by Catterick Bridge, p. 45.
		L. *to Shotley Bridge* 15*m.*
	260½	Durham Moor House.
	263	Plausworth T. G.
	265½	Chester le Street.
9	268½	Birtley.
	270	Ayton Bank.
		R. *to Sunderland, over the Iron Bridge,* 10½*m.*
13	272½	Gateshead.
14	273½	Tyne Bridge.
		Northumberland.
	274	NEWCASTLE-ON-TYNE.
		[*Prospective Distances:* Morpeth ...... 15 m. Alnwick ...... 34 Belford........ 48½ Berwick ...... 63½ Dunbar ...... 90½ Edinburgh ....119]
		L. *to Elisha Bridge* 33½*m.* [G]*; thence to Jedburgh,* p. 45.
		R. *to Shields* [H].

* DURHAM.

Variations of Route, and Branch Routes.

	M.
Long Framlington	300
Rimside Moor Guide Post	304
R. *to Alnwick* 8m.	
L. *to Rothbury* 4m.	
WHITTINGHAM	308½
Glanton	310
Percy's Cross	313¼
WOOLER HAUGH HEAD	318½
WOOLER	320½
Millfield	326
CORNHILL	333
On R. *to Berwick* 12m.	
Across the Tweed into SCOTLAND.	
[Berwickshire] COLDSTREAM	334½
Coldstream T. G.	335½
L. *to Kelso* 7m.	
Orange Lane Inn	340
Ploughland T. G.	342
GREENLAW	344½
Tibby's Inn	347½
Dodd's Mill	353
Thirlestone	354
L. *to Lauder* 2½m. *and thence to Edinburgh*, p. 45, *or forward to*	
NORTON	356
Carfra Mill	359½
Channel Kirk	361½
Thence (p. 45) to EDINBURGH	381

[K]

	M.
WOOLER	320½
Akeld	322½
Kirk Newton	325½
Mindrum	331
Enter SCOTLAND	332½
[Roxb.] Pott's Close,	335
KELSO	340
Smailholm	346
[Berw.] Bridge End,	353¼
LAUDER	357
Thence (p. 45) to EDINBURGH	382½

L.D.	M. *from Hicks's Hall.*	
12	277	Gosforth T. G.
9	280	Six Mile House.
	282	Shotton Edge.
5	284	Stannington.
	286	Clifton.
*	289	MORPETH.
		[*Prospective Distances:* Alnwick ...... 19 m. Berwick ...... 40 Dunbar........ 75½ Edinburgh ....104]
		L. *to Elisha Bridge* 25m.
		— *to Edinburgh, by Wooler and Coldstream* [I].
5	294	Earsdon Moor.
10	299	Felton Bridge.
	302	Newton.
30	308	ALNWICK.
23	314½	Charlton.
	318½	Warrenford.
15	322½	BELFORD.
	324¾	Detchon.
10	327½	Fenwick.
7	330½	Haggerston.
	337	Tweed Mouth T. G.
*	337¾	BERWICK ON TWEED.
52	340½	Pass Berwick Bounds into SCOTLAND.
		Berwickshire.
	345	Ayton, or Eyeton.
44	349½	RENTON INN.
	354	Old Cambus.
36	357	Path Head.
		Haddingtonshire.
34	359	Thornton Brook.
28	364½	DUNBAR.
	366½	West Bourn.
26	367	Belton Ford.
		R. *to North Berwick* 7m.
	370	Linton.
17	376	HADDINGTON.
	379½	Gladesmuir.
10	383	Tranent.
		Edinburghshire.
6	387	MUSSELBURGH.
3	389½	Porto Bello.
		R. *to Leith* 2½m.
*	392½	EDINBURGH (*b*).
		For Prospective Distances on Return Route see next page [D].

(*b*) The Mail Route to Edinburgh is by Ware to Alconbury Hill (p. 49), and thence as above, along the Great North Road to York and Northallerton. The distance to Edinburgh, as travelled by the Mail, is 398m.

Another Route to Edinburgh is by Wooler and Coldstream, as in Note [I], diverging from the above line at Morpeth. It has been recommended, by a Committee of the House of Commons, to alter and improve this branch line, and to make it a mail route, thereby shortening the Post-office line of communication with Edinburgh about 19 miles; the Mail, in such case, running direct from London to Boroughbridge, and thence as above.

Another Route branches from the last-mentioned Route to Kelso, and thence to Lauder. See Note [K]. Other Routes are by Jedburgh, as on the opposite page, and by Carlisle, p. 47.

LONDON TO EDINBURGH;

By CATTERICK and JEDBURGH.

Variations of Route, and Branch Routes.

[A]	M.
PIERCE BRIDGE -	239½
West Auckland ..	246½
BISHOP'S AUCKLAND	249
Sunderland Bridge	255½
Cross the river Wear.	
DURHAM	259
Another Route:	
PIERCE BRIDGE -	239½
Heighington	245
Eldon	248¼
Merrington	251¾
Sunderland Bridge	256½
DURHAM	260

[B]	
WOLSINGHAM -	257½
Muggleswick	265½
[North.] Sleaton ..	274½
HEXHAM	280
Cross the river Tyne.	
Picts' Wall	284
Chollerton	285½
Barrysford	286½
Wark	291
BELLINGHAM .	295

Another Route to Wolsingham is by Bernard Castle, p. 46.

[D]

EDINBURGH.

Prospective Distances on Route to London:

Dunbar	28¼ m.
Berwick	55
Alnwick	85
Morpeth	104
Newcastle	119
Durham	133¼
Darlington	152
Northallerton ..	168
Boroughbridge ..	187
Ferrybridge	216
Doncaster	231
Newark	266½
Stamford	303½

L.D.	M. from Hicks's Hall.	
		Yorkshire.
*	206	BOROUGHBRIDGE (p. 42).
	207	Kirby Hill.
		L. *to Ripon* 5m.
7	213	York Gate Inn.
12	218	LEEMING LANE.
14	220	Londonderry.
	221½	Leeming T. G.
22	228	Catterick.
23	229	CATTERICK BRIDGE.
27	233	Scotch Corner.
33	239¼	Cross the river Tees.
		Durham.
	239½	PIERCE BRIDGE.
	246½	West Auckland.
		R. *to Bishop's Auckland.*
43	249	Low Toft Hill [A].
	251	Witton le Wear.
48	254	HARPERLEY LANE HEAD.
		L. *to Wolsingham* 3½m.; *thence to Hexham* [B].
58	264	Cold Rowley.
		Cross the riv. Derwent.
		Northumberland.
	265½	Allan's Ford.
62	267¾	Green Head.
	270½	Unthank.
	275½	Riding.
93	277½	CORBRIDGE.
90	280¼	Wheat Sheaf Inn.
		Cross the Military Rd.
86	284½	Collell.
		L. *to Chollerton* 3m.
	289	Tone Pit Inn.
	298	Troughend.
70	300	ELISHA BRIDGE.
		Junction of Road from Newcastle, p. 43.
63	307½	Buryness.
		Across the Cheviot Hills into SCOTLAND.
		Roxburghshire.
56	314½	Carter Fell T. G.
	319	Doveford Bridge.
45	325	JEDBURGH.
	328	Ancrum T. G.
	334	Newton.
34	336	FLY BRIDGE.
		Berwickshire.
25	345	LAUDER.
	351	Channel Kirk.
		Edinburghshire.
14	356	FALLA.
12	358	CASTERTOWN.
11	359	Path Head.
6	364	DALKEITH.
*	370½	EDINBURGH.

LONDON TO CARLISLE AND GLASGOW;

The Mail Route by NEWARK and DONCASTER [A].

Variations of Route, and Branch Routes.

	M.
[A]	
Another Route is by Manchester & Preston, p. 32.	
[B]	
York Gate	213
Nosterfield	220
MASHAM	223½
Low Ellington	226
Jervaux Abbey	228½
East Witton	230½
Cover Bridge	231
L. to *Middleham* 1m.	
Spennythorne	233
LEYBURN	235
Wensley	236
Redmire	239½
Carperby	242
ASKRIGG	246½
L. to *Hawes*, 5½m.	
[C]	
PENRITH	283
Hutton	288½
Seberham Bridge,	296
Rosley	299
WIGTON	304
Thence to Abbey Holme 6*m*.	
[D]	
MOFFAT	346½
Tweed Shaws	353
Bield Inn	361
Broughton	368½
Blyth Bridge	375
LINTON	379½
EDINBURGH	395½
[E]	
CARLISLE	301¼
LONGTOWN	310½
Kirk Andrews	313
Enter SCOTLAND,	314
[Dumfriesshire.]	
Cannobie Bridge	316
Cross the river Esk.	
LANGHOLM	322

L.D.	M. from Hicks's Hall.	
		Yorkshire.
*	206	BOROUGHBRIDGE
	207	Kirkby Hill. [p. 42.
7	213	York Gate Inn.
		L. to *Masham* [B].
12	218	LEEMING LANE.
14	220	Londonderry.
	221½	Leeming T. G.
22	228	Catterick.
23	229	CATTERICK BRIDGE.
27	233	Scotch Corner.
		R. to *Pierce Bridge*, p. 45.
	240¼	Smallways.
59	242¼	GRETA BRIDGE.
		[245¼ BERNARD CASTLE.
		252½ West Pits.
		261½ WOLSINGHAM.]
53	248½	Bowes.
	254	Spittle House.
		Westmorland.
40	261¾	BROUGH.
		[263 Brough Sowerby.
		266½ KIRKBY STEPH.]
31	270	APPLEBY.
		[*By Manchester*, 286m.]
30	271½	CRACKENTHORPE.
	274½	Kirkbythore.
25	276	Temple Sowerby.
	282	Lowther Bridge.
19	282½	Emont Bridge.
		Cumberland.
17	283	PENRITH.
		L. to *Wigton* [C].

L.D.	M. from Hicks's Hall.	
14	287½	Salkeld Gate.
9	292½	High Hesket.
7	294	Low Hesket.
	295	Inglewood Forest.
3	298¾	Carlton.
*	301¼	CARLISLE.
		[*By Manchester* 306½m.]
		[*Prospective Distances:*
		Moffat .... 45m.
		Glasgow 101
		Edinburgh [E] 91
		On Return Route:
		Penrith 18¼
		Appleby 31½
		Greta Bridge .. 57
		Boroughbridge.. 95½
		Doncaster......129½]
		Cross the river Eden.
		[301¼ CARLISLE.
		305½ High Crosby.
		311 Brampton.
		318½ GILSLAND SPA.]
1	302½	Stanwix.
4	305½	Blackford.
6	307½	Westlington.
		Cross the river Line.
9	310½	LONGTOWN.
		Cross the river Esk.
		R. to *Edinburgh* [E].
13	314½	Cross the river Sark, and enter SCOTLAND.
		Dumfriesshire.
14	315	GRETNA GREEN.
		L. to *Dumfries*. See next page, col. 3.

* CARLISLE.

Variations of Route, and Branch Routes.

	M.
Ewes Kirk	326½
Fiddleton Toll Bar	330
[Roxburghshire.]	
MOSPAUL INN ..	332½
HAWICK	345
R. *to Jedburgh 10½m.; thence to Edinburgh by Lauder* (p. 45).	
Wilton	345½
Ashkirk	351
Selkirk Toll Bar ..	353
[Selk.] SELKIRK,	356
R. *to Melrose* 10*m.*	
Cross the river Etterick.	
Cross the Tweed ..	359½
Fairnielie Haugh ..	360
Crosslee Toll Bar ..	365
[Edinb.] TORSANCE	368
MIDDLETON	380
Leswade	386½
On L. Dalhousie Castle.	
Libberton	389½
EDINBURGH ..	392½
Another Route is by Moffat and Linton [D].	

[F]

DUMFRIES	340½
Dalswinton	347½
Gateside	353½
THORNHILL	357
Carron Bridge	359
SANQUHAR	369
Thence to Glasgow:	
[Ayr.] MUIRKIRK,	385
[Lanarkshire.]	
STRATHAVEN	398
Kilbride	406
RUTHERGLEN,	412
Gorbals	414½
GLASGOW	415

Thence to Edinburgh:
By Bathgate .. 44*m.*
— Midcalder, 45
— Falkirk .. 48

L.D.	M. *from Hicks's Hall.*	
16	317	Graham's Hill.
	320½	Langshaw.
23	324	ECCLESFECHAN.
25	326½	Brackenhill.
29	330	LOCKERBY.
	331	On R. Lockerby House.
	335	Dinwoodie Green.
	339	Wamphray.
		On R. Dumerief, Mar. of Queensberry.
56	346½	MOFFATT.
		L. *to Dumfries 25m.*
	351	Brickston Brae Head.
		R. *to Edinburgh* [D].

Lanarkshire.

L.D.	M.	
43	359	ELVAN FOOT BRIDGE.
41	361½	Crawford.
		Cross the river Clyde.
38	364½	Abingdon T. G.
36	366½	Duneton Bridge.
	373	DOUGLAS MILL INN.
		On R. Douglas Castle.
	379	Lesmehagow T. G.
15	387½	Lark Hall.
		R. *to Lanark* 10*m.*
11	391½	Hamilton.
		On L. the Palace, Duke of Hamilton.
9	393½	Bothwell Bridge.
		Cross the river Clyde.
		On L. Bothwell Castle.
6	396½	Clyde Side.
*	402½	GLASGOW.
		[*By Manchester* 407½*m.*]

L.D.	M. *from Hicks's Hall.*	

ADDENDA.

TO PORTPATRICK.

L.D.	M.	
25	315	GRETNA GREEN (p. 46.)
	317	Rigg.
19	321	Dornock.
17	323½	ANNAN.
	334	Mousewald.
*	340½	DUMFRIES.
		R. *to Sanquhar* [F].

Kirkcudbrightshire.

L.D.	M.	
	344½	Lochrutton.
8	348½	Milltown of Urr.
	353	Haugh of Urr.
16	356½	CASTLE DOUGLAS.
17	357¼	CARLINGWARK.
	359	Kelton Hill.
19	359½	Dee Bridge.
25	365½	Twynholm.
30	370½	GATE HOUSE OF FLEET
	372½	Anworth.
40	380	CREETOWN.
45	385½	Lead Mines.

Wigtownshire.

L.D.	M.	
32	388	NEWTON STEWART.
27	392½	Shanatown.
16	403½	GLENLUCE.
12	407½	Drumflower.
6	413½	STRANRAER.
*	419½	PORTPATRICK.
		Thence, across the Channel to Donaghadee about 16*m.*

LONDON TO STOCKTON-ON-TEES;

And thence to SHIELDS and TYNEMOUTH.

Variations of Route, and Branch Routes.

[A]

	M.
TONTINE INN....	230
Arncliffe	232
STOKESLEY....	239
Ayton	241½
Newton	243¾
Pinchingthorp ..	244¾
GUISBOROUGH,	247¼
Another Route:	
YORK (p. 43)....	199
Kettlestring	201½
Sutton on the Forest,	207
Stillington........	210
Gilling	217
Oswaldkirk	218
Sproxton	220½
HELMSLEY	222
Bilsdale	231½
STOKESLEY ..	238½
Thence, as above, to GUISBOROUGH,	247

[A 2]

To Kirby Moorside:

HELMSLEY (above)	222
Newton..........	224
KIRBY MOORSIDE	227½

[B]

Another Route:

YORK (p. 43)....	199
THIRSK	222½

Thence, as in the opposite column.

[C]

STOCKTON	241½
NORTON INN	243
Thorpe	247½
Layton	249½
SEDGFIELD....	251½
Black Gate	257
Four Mile Bridge,	258½
Shencliffe	260½
DURHAM	262½

[D]

Wolviston........	246½
Greatham	249½
Stranton	252½
R. *to Seaton* 1*m.*	
HARTLEPOOL..	254

L.D.	M. *from Hicks's Hall.*	
		Yorkshire.
*	206	BOROUGHBRIDGE (p. 44).
4	210	Dishforth.
	212½	Topcliffe.
	215½	Thornfield Houses.
12	218	THIRSK.
13	219	South Kilvington.
	220	North Kilvington.
16	222	Knayton.
17	223	Barrowby.
	224	Leake.
15	226½	Chaytor Houses.
	230	TONTINE INN.
		R. *to Guisborough* [A].
7	234½	Crathorne.
	236	Kirklavington.
	238	YARM.
		Cross the river Tees.
		Durham.
*	241½	STOCKTON ON TEES [B].
	243	NORTON INN.
		L. *to Durham* [C].
3	244½	Billingham T. G.
5	246½	Wolviston.
		R. *to Hartlepool* [D].
	253	Sheraton.
14	255½	CASTLE EDEN INN.
		On R. Castle Eden, R. Burton, Esq.

L.D.	M. *from Hicks's Hall.*	
	256½	Shotton.
	259	Easington.
15	262	Dalton le Dale.
	265	Rhyhope.
9	268	BISHOP WEARMOUTH.
		On L. Hilton Castle.
8	268¾	SUNDERLAND.
	269½	Over the Iron Bridge.
7	269¾	Monk Wearmouth.
	271¼	Fulwell T. G.
		L. *to Newcastle* 10*m.*
	273	Cleadon.
2	274¾	Harton.
	275½	Westoe.
	276½	SOUTH SHIELDS.
		Northumberland.
*	277	NORTH SHIELDS.
	278½	TYNEMOUTH.

ANOTHER ROUTE.

L.D.	M.	
13	259½	DURHAM (p. 43.)
	262	Blue Houses.
8	264½	East Raynton.
	266¼	Houghton-le-Spring.
4	268½	East Harrington.
	271½	BISHOP WEARMOUTH.
*	272¼	SUNDERLAND.

Thence, as above.

ANOTHER ROUTE is by Newcastle, p. 43.

LONDON TO LINCOLN;

Continued to HULL, and thence to SCARBOROUGH [A].

Variations of Route, and Branch Routes.

M.

[A]

Another Route to Alconbury Hill, on the following line of Route, is by Barnet and Hatfield. See p. 41.

[B]

HODDESDON .. 17
Hertford Heath .. 19¼
HERTFORD 21
Waterford........ 23¼
Stapleford........ 24½
Watton 26¼
Bragbury End 28¼
Broadwater 30¾
STEVENAGE .. 33

[C]

PETERBOROUGH 77½
Newark.......... 79
Eye 81
[Camb.] THORNEY 84
Guyhorn Chapel .. 90
St. Mary's........ 94
WISBEACH 97

[D]

PETERBOROUGH 77½
Long Thorpe 79½
Castor 82
Ailesworth 82¾
Wandsford 85½
STAMFORD 91

[E]

SLEAFORD 111½
Anwick.......... 116
Billinghay 120
TATTERSHALL, 125
Haltham 129
HORNCASTLE.. 133½
L. *to Wragby* 10m.
West Ashby...... 135½
Cawkwell 139½
Maltby 144½
LOUTH 147½

L.D. — M. *from Shoreditch Church.*

Middlesex.

1¼ Kingsland T. G.
2½ Stoke Newington.
3¼ Stamford Hill.
4¼ Tottenham.
7 Edmonton.
L. *to Enfield* 2¾*m.*
8¼ Ponder's End.
9¼ Enfield Highway.
10 Enfield Wash.

Hertfordshire.

(26) 11¼ Waltham Cross.
R. *to Waltham Abbey,* 1¼*m.*
12 Turner's Hill.
13 Cheshunt Street.
14 Cheshunt Wash.
14¾ Wormley.
(22) 15¼ Broxbourn.
17 HODDESDON.
L. *to Stevenage* [B].
(18) 19¼ Amwell.
21 WARE.
(15) 22¾ Wade's Mill.
24¾ Collier's End.
R. *to Standon* 2*m.*
(11) 26¼ PUCKERIDGE.
R. *to Cambridge* (p. 52).
31 BUNTINGFORD.
(5) 32¼ Chipping.
33¾ Buckland.
* 37½ ROYSTON.
R. *to Cambridge* 13½*m.*

L.D. — M. *from Shoreditch Church.*

Cambridgeshire.

40 Kneesworth.
44 ARRINGTON.
On R. Wimpole Hall, Earl of Hardwicke.
(28) 49¼ CAXTON.
(25) 52¼ Papworth St. Everard.

Huntingdonshire.

(20) 57¾ Godmanchester.
(19) 58¾ HUNTINGDON.
[*By Barnet and Welwyn, p. 41, 65 miles.*]
61 Great Stukeley.
(16) 61¾ Little Stukeley.
64 ALCONBURY HILL.
Junction of the road by Barnet and Hatfield. See p. 41.
(6½) 71 STILTON.
(5½) 72 Norman's Cross.
On R. Whittlesea Mere.

Northamptonshire.

* 77½ PETERBOROUGH.
R. *to Wisbeach* [C].
L. *to Stamford* [D].
80 Walton.
81 Werrington.
83 Glinton.
R. *to Crowland* 6*m.*; *thence to Spalding* 8*m.*
(7) 84¼ Norborough.
84¾ R. *to Spalding*, p. 51.

Variations of Route, and Branch Routes.

	M.
[F]	
LINCOLN	129
Saxilby	135
Fenton	138½
Torksey	140
Manton	142
Knaith	144
Lea	145
GAINSBORO' ..	147
[G]	
HULL	170½
Kirk Ella	176
Riplingham	180
SOUTH CAVE ..	183
Another Route:	
HOWDEN (p. 42)	180½
North Cave	190½
SOUTH CAVE ..	193½
HULL	206
[H]	
YORK (page 42)..	195
Lobster Inn	202¼
Spittle Beck	206
Whitwell	207½
NEW MALTON,	213
L. *to Whitby* [H 2]	
Norton	213½
Scagglethorp T. G.	216
Rillington	217½
YEDDINGHAM BRIDGE	222
SNAINTON	225
Brompton	227
Wykeham	228½
East Ayton	230½
Falsgrave	234
SCARBOROUGH	235
[H 2]	
NEW MALTON .	213
Old Malton	214
How Bridge	216½
PICKERING	221½
Sleights	237½
Ruswarp	240
WHITBY	242

L. D.	M. *from Shoreditch Church.*	
		Lincolnshire.
43	86	MARKET DEEPING.
	88½	Langtoft.
	89½	Baston.
	91½	Thurlby.
36	93½	BOURN.
	94	L. *to Corby* 8*m.*; *thence to Colterworth* 4½*m.*
32	96½	Morton.
		R. *to Donnington* 13*m.*; *thence to Boston* [K].
	100	Aslackby.
27	102	FOLKINGHAM.
		R. *to Boston* 17*m.*
	105	Osbornby.
	106	Aswarby.
	109	Silk Willoughby.
18	111½	SLEAFORD.
		R. *to Horncastle* [E].
	113	Holdingham.
	113½	Leasingham.
		L. *to Newark* 18*m.*
8	121	GREEN MAN.
	122½	Dunston Pillar.
*	129	LINCOLN.
		L. *to Gainsborough* [F].
		R. *to Market Raisin and Wragby*, p. 51.
	134½	Midge Inn.
11	140½	SPITTAL INN.
16	147	Redbourn.
	148½	Hibalston.
		L. *to Burton on Strather* 11½*m.*

L. D.	M. *from Shoreditch Church.*	
18	152½	BRIGG, or GLANDFORD BRIDGE.
7	163½	BARTON WATERSIDE INN.
		Cross the Humber.
		A mail packet sails across: the computed distance 7 miles.
		Yorkshire.
*	170½	HULL.
		R. *to Hornsea* 16*m.*
		— *to Hedon* 8*m.*; *thence to Patrington* 10*m.*
		L. *to South Cave* [G].
2	172½	Newlands.
	175	Duncehill.
	177½	Woodmansea.
9	179½	BEVERLEY.
		[188 BRANDSBURTON. L. *to Frodingham* 4*m.* 203 BRIDLINGTON [I].]
		L. *to Hessle* 9*m.*
		R. *to Hornsea* 13*m.*
10	180½	Molescroft.
	182½	Leckonfield.
	186	Beswick.
	188	Watton.
	190	Hutton Cranswick.
23	193½	GT. DRIFFIELD.
	195	Kendall House.
29	199½	Langtoft.
33	203½	Foxholes.
	208	Staxton.
41	211	Seamer.
	214	Falsgrave.
45	215	SCARBOROUGH.
		Another R. is by York [H].

LONDON TO BOSTON AND LOUTH;

Continued to GRIMSBY.

Variations of Route, and Branch Routes.

M.

[I]

Another Route:

	M.
YORK (p. 42)....	195
Grimston	198
Gate Helmsley	201
Stamford Bridge ..	202¼
GARRABY STREET	207¾
Fridaythorpe	213¾
Fimber	215
SLEDMERE	219
Rudstone	231
Boynton	233
BRIDLINGTON .	236
Flamborough	239½
Flamborough Head	241½
Or,	
Fridaythorpe	213¾
KELHAM	216¾
BRIDLINGTON .	234¾

[K]

Another Route:

	M.
BOURN (p. 50) ..	93¼
Morton	96½
Dunsby	98
Dowsby	99¾
Pointon	101¼
Sempringham	102¼
Billingborough....	102¾
Horbling	104
Bridgend Causeway	105¼
DONNINGTON..	109¾
SWINESHEAD..	112¾
Kirton Holme	114
BOSTON	118

[L]

	M.
BOSTON........	112¾
Benington........	117¾
Leverton	118¾
Leake	120
Wrangle	121
Friskney	124
WAINFLEET ..	128
Croft	129¾
R. *to Skegness* 4m.	
Burgh	133

L.D.	M. *from Shoreditch Church.*
	77½ PETERBOROUGH.
28	84¼ Norborough (p. 49).
	Lincolnshire.
	86 St. James Deeping.
	[The Route of the Boston and Louth Mail is through Market Deeping, from Norborough, to St. James Deeping, 87½m.]
	92 Littleworth.
15	97 SPALDING.
	R. *to Holbeach* 8m.
	99 Pinchbeck.
	101 Surfleet.
9	103¼ Gosberton T. G.
	L. *to Swineshead* 6m.; *thence to Boston* 5½m.
6	106½ Sotherton.
	109 Kirton.
*	112¾ BOSTON [K].
	R. *to Frieston Shore* 4m.
	— *to Wainfleet* [L].
5	117½ Sibsey.
10	122½ Stickney.
	125 Stickford.
	127 L. *to Bolingbroke* 2m.
	128 East Keal.
18	130 Spilsby.
	L. *to Horncastle* 10m.
	131½ Partney.
20	132½ Dalby.
	134½ R. *to Alford* 2m.
	136 Calseby Beck.
	139 Barwell.

L.D.	M. *from Shoreditch Church.*
*	144 LOUTH.
	Another Route is by Sleaford and Horncastle, p. 49 [E].
	R. *to Saltfleet* 10m.
2	146 South Elkington.
	154 Wold Newton.
	156½ Ravendale.
14	158 Brigsley.
	159½ Waltham.
17	161½ Scartho.
19	163½ GRIMSBY.

ANOTHER ROUTE.

L.D.	M.
*	129 LINCOLN (p. 49).
6	135 Langworth Bridge.
	R. *to Wragby* 5m.
	136½ Stainton.
9	138½ Snelland.
	140¾ Baslingthorpe.
15	144 MARKET RAISIN.
	146 Wailsby.
26	155½ Ravendale.
34	162¾ GRIMSBY, as above.
	Or,
20	144 MARKET RAISIN.
	151½ Nettleton.
12	152¾ CAISTOR.
	154½ Caborn.
	155½ Swallow.
8	158 Irby.
	160½ Laceby.
*	164 GRIMSBY.

LONDON TO CAMBRIDGE AND LYNN;

Continued to BURNHAM MARKET and WELLS.

Variations of Route, and Branch Routes.

[A]	M.
Another Route:	
ROYSTON (p. 49)	37½
[Camb.] Melbourn	41
Harleston	45¼
Trumpington	48¾
CAMBRIDGE ..	51
Quy	56
Bottisham........	57¾
Devil's Ditch	62¼
NEWMARKET..	64
[B]	
Another Route:	
CAXTON (p. 49) ..	49¼
Papworth St. Everard	52¼
[Hunt.] Hilton ..	56
ST. IVES	59½
Somersham	65¼
Chatteris Ferry ..	70
Cross the river Nen.	
[Camb.] Isle of Ely.	
CHATTERIS	72
Doddington	76
Wimblington	77½
MARCH	80½
Cross the river Nen.	
Guyhorn Ferry....	85
WISBEACH	90
R. *to Downham* 13*m.*	
L. *to Holbeach* 13½*m.*	
Cross the river Nen.	
[Norf.] Walsoken .	91¼
West Walton	93¼
Walpole St. Peter.	95
Terrington St. John	96¼
Islington	99
St. Germains	101
LYNN	105½
[C]	
South Wootton ..	99
Castle Rising	101
Darsingham	105
Ingoldsthorpe	106½
Snettisham	108
Hunstanton	113½
Holme	115½
BURNHAM M...	124

L.D.	M. *from Shoreditch Church.*	
		Hertfordshire.
	26½	PUCKERIDGE (p. 49).
24	27¼	Braughing.
	30½	Hare Street.
	34½	Barkway.
14	36¾	Barley.
		Cambridgeshire.
9	41¾	Fulmere.
	44½	Newton.
4	47	Hauxton.
	48¾	Trumpington.
*	51	CAMBRIDGE.
		R. *to Newmarket* [A].
		Cross the river Cam.
	52	Chesterton.
3	54¼	Milton.
10	61¼	Stretham Bridge.
	62¾	Stretham.
16	67¼	ELY.
18	69	Chittisham T. G.
	72	Littleport.
		Norfolk.
25	76	Brandon Creek Bridge.
	78	Southery.
	79¾	Modney Bridge.
30	81	Hilgay.
	82	Fordham.
	83¼	Denver.
33	84½	DOWNHAM MARKET.
		L. *to Wisbeach* 13*m.*
		R. *to Swaffham* 14½*m.*

L.D.	M. *from Shoreditch Church.*	
9	87	Stow Bardolph.
	88½	Runcton.
4	92	Setchy.
	93½	West Winch.
	95	Hardwick.
*	96	LYNN [B].
	97½	Gaywood.
3	99	South Wootton.
		[*To Burnham Market by Docking* 19½*m.* *By Holme* [C] 25*m.*]
	104½	Hillington Guide Post.
9	105	Flitcham.
	109½	Great Bircham.
	110½	Bircham Newton.
17	113	Stanhoe.
21	117	BURNHAM MARKET [C].
23	119½	Holkham New Inn.
25	121½	Holkham Staith.
27	122¾	WELLS.
		OR,
	104½	Hillington Guide Post.
15	110	Houghton.
		On L. Houghton Hall, Marquis of Cholmondeley.
	111¾	West Rudham.
12	113	East Rudham.
		R. *to Fakenham* 6½*m.*
	118½	South Creak.
3	122	Holkham Park, T. W. Coke, Esq.
*	125	WELLS.
		Another Route is by Brandon and Swaffham, as on the opposite page.

LONDON TO NEWMARKET;

Continued to SWAFFHAM and WELLS.

Variations of Route, and Branch Routes.

	M.
[A]	
Mile End	1
Bow	2½
[Essex] STRATFORD	3¾
Laytonstone	5¾
Snaresbrook, Eagle	6¾
Woodford Bridge	9
CHIGWELL	10½
ABRIDGE	13¾
Passingford Bridge	16
Hare Street	18½
CHIPPING ONGAR	21
Moreton End	24½
Hatfield Heath	30
DUNMOW	40½
[B]	
HARLOW	23½
Sheering Street	26¼
Hatfield Heath	27¾
Broad Oak	29¾
DUNMOW	37¾
THAXTEAD	44
[C]	
Newport	38½
SAFFRON WALDEN	42
Little Walden	44
Hadstock	46½
[Camb.] LINTON	48
Or,	
Great Chesterford	44¼
LINTON	49
[D]	
GREAT CHESTERFORD	44¼
[Camb.] Sawston	48¾
Trumpington	53¾
CAMBRIDGE	56
[E]	
NEWMARKET	60¾
[Suff.] Kentford	65¾
Saxham	70¾
BURY ST. EDMUNDS	74½

L.D.	M. from Shoreditch Church.	
		Middlesex.
	1	Cambridge Heath T. G.
	2	Hackney.
	3½	Lea Bridge T. G.
		Essex.
	6	Whip's Cross.
10	6¾	Snaresbrook, Eagle. Same distance from Whitechapel Church [A].
	8	Woodford.
	9¼	Woodford Wells.
7	10	Bald Stag.
	11½	Loughton.
*	16¾	EPPING.
	21½	Potter's Street.
7	23½	HARLOW. L. to Dunmow [B].
		Hertfordshire.
9	25½	Sawbridgeworth.
	27½	Spel Brook.
13	29½	L. to Bishop's Stortford [¼m.
	30	HOCKERILL. R. to Dunmow 8½m.
		Essex.
16	32¾	STANSTEAD.
	36	Quendon.
22	38½	Newport. R. to Linton [C].
	42¼	Littlebury.
27	43½	Little Chesterford.
16	44¼	GREAT CHESTERFORD.
	45¾	L. to Cambridge [D].
		Cambridgeshire.
11	49½	BOURN BRIDGE.
	55¼	Green Man.
	59	Devil's Ditch.
*	60¾	NEWMARKET. R. to Bury St. Edm. [E]. L. to Soham 8m.; thence to Ely 4m.
		Suffolk.
5	66¼	Red House T. G. L. to Mildenhall 3¾m.
8	69¼	BARTON MILLS. R. to Thetford, p. 55.
11	72¼	Hobb's Cross.
	75¼	Wangford, on L.
17	78¼	BRANDON.
		Norfolk.
22	83	Mundford.
	87¼	Hillborough.
32	93	SWAFFHAM.
	95¾	Castle Acre Guide P. L. to Castle Acre 1¼m.
	97¼	Newton.
41	102	Weasenham St. Peter.
	105	RAINHAM.
47	108	FAKENHAM. [By East Dereham, p. 58. By Lynn, p. 52.]
52	113	WALSINGHAM.
57	118	WELLS.

LONDON TO BURY ST. EDMUNDS;

And thence to NORWICH.

Variations of Route, and Branch Routes.

[A]	M.
STRATFORD	3½
West Ham	4
East Ham	6
Barking	7
Another Route:	
Limehouse Church	1¾
[Essex] Plaistow	4¼
Barking	7
Thence to South End:	
Beam River Gate	11
Rainham	12½
Wennington	14
Purfleet	16
West Thurrock	18
GRAY'S THURROCK	20½
Chadwell	23½
West Tilbury T. G.	24
R. *to Tilbury Fort, 2½m.*	
Muckingford	25½
Stanford	27¾
Vange	31¾
Pitsey	33½
Hadleigh	38
Adam's Elm	40
SOUTH END	43¼

[B]	
ROMFORD	11¾
Hornchurch	14
Upminster	15½
Corbet's Tye	16¾
South Ockendon	20
Stifford	22¼
GRAY'S THURROCK	24½
Thence, as above, to SOUTH END	47¼

[C]	
Margretting Street	25
Gallywood Common	27
Great Baddow	29½
Danbury	33
MALDON	37½

L.D.	M. from Whitechapel Church.	
		Middlesex.
	1	Mile End.
	2½	Bow
		Cross the river Lea.
		Essex.
	3½	STRATFORD.
		R. *to Barking* [A].
	6¾	ILFORD.
20	9	Chadwell.
17	11¾	ROMFORD.
		R. *to South End* [B].
16	13	Hare Street.
	16½	Brook Street.
11	17¾	BRENTWOOD.
10	19	Shenfield.
		R. *to Rochford* [D].
	21	Mountnessing Street.
6	23	INGATESTONE.
4	25	Margretting Street.
		R. *to Maldon* [C].
	26½	Stisted.
	27½	Widford.
	28¾	Moulsham,
*	29	CHELMSFORD.
	31½	Broomfield.
4	33¼	Little Waltham T. G.
		L. *to Dunmow 8½m.*
7	36	Blackwater St. Anne's.
	37½	Young's End.
11	40	BRAINTREE.
12	40¾	BOCKING STREET.
	42½	High Garret.
		L. *to Haverhill* [E].

L.D.	M. from Whitechapel Church.	
25	46½	HALSTEAD.
22	49	Maplestead.
19	52	Bulmer Tye.
		L. *to Castle Hedingham 5½m.*
		Suffolk.
17	54½	SUDBURY.
		R. *to Stowmarket*, p. 55.
	56½	Rodbridge Street.
13	58	LONG MELFORD.
9	62	Alpheton.
5	66	Bradfield.
	68½	Welnetham T. G.
*	71	BURY ST. EDM.
		[*By Newmarket* (p. 53) 74½m.]
		L. *to Thetford* [F].
		— *to Brandon* [F 2].
3	74	Barton.
	77½	Ixworth.
9½	80½	Stanton.
	81½	Hepworth.
15	86½	BOTESDALE.
21	92	Sturston.
		L. *to Diss 2m.*
	92½	Junction of road from Ipswich.
	93½	Cross the riv. Waveney.
		Norfolk.
22	93¾	SCOLE INN.
		Thence, p. 56, to
44	115½	NORWICH.

LONDON TO NORWICH;

By NEWMARKET and THETFORD (col. 2), and by SUDBURY and STOWMARKET (col. 3). Continued to YARMOUTH.

Variations of Route, and Branch Routes.

	M.
[D]	
BRENTWOOD ..	17¾
Shenfield	19
BILLERICAY....	23
South Green	24½
Cray Hill	26¾
Wickford	29
Raleigh	33¾
Hockley	36
ROCHFORD	39½
Sutton............	40¾
R. *to South End* 3m.	
South Church......	44
North Shoebury ..	46
Great Wakering ..	47½
[E]	
BOCKING STREET,	40¾
High Garret	42½
Gosfield	44½
Swan Street	47
SIBLE HEDINGHAM	47½
R. *to Castle Hedingham* ½m.	
Great Yeldham	50½
R. *to Clare* 5m.	
Ridgewell	53
Baythorn End	55
Sturmer	57
[Suffolk.] HAVERHILL	58½
[F]	
BURY ST. EDMUNDS	71
Fornham St. Martin,	73
Ingham	75½
Rymer House	79
Barnham	81
Cross the Little Ouse.	
[Norf.] THETFORD	83½
[F 2]	
Rymer House, above,	79
BRANDON	87

L.D.	M. *from Shoreditch Church.*	
	60¾	NEWMARKET.
		Suffolk.
40	69½	BARTON MILLS, p. 53.
33	76	Elvedon.
		Cross the Little Ouse.
		Norfolk.
29	80	THETFORD.
		[*By Bury* [E] 83½m.]
21	88	Larlingford.
		R. *to East Harlinge* 5½m.
15	94	ATTLEBOROUGH.
		L. *to Hingham* 5¼m.; *thence to Norwich* 14½m. p. 58.
9	100	WYNDHAM (Wymondham).
	103¼	Hetherset.
3	106	Cringleford.
	106¾	Easton.
*	109	NORWICH.
	111½	Thorpe.
	113½	On L. F. Gostling, Esq.
7	116	Blofield.
9	118	Burlingham.
	120½	Acle.
	121½	Wey Bridge.
15	124½	Burgh.
17	126	Filby.
	129¼	Caistor.
23	132¼	YARMOUTH.

L.D.	M. *from Whitechapel Church.*	
		Suffolk.
*	54½	SUDBURY, p. 54.
	56½	Chilton Park.
	57¾	L. *to Lavenham* 3m.
	59	Little Waddingfield.
6	60½	R. *to Bildestone* 3m.
	61	Brent Illeigh.
	63	Kettlebastone.
	64	Hitcham.
	65	Cross Green.
12	66½	Hoistead Green.
	67¼	Great Finborough.
15	67½	STOW MARKET.
		L. *to Botesdale* 13½m.
	71	Thorney Green.
21	75½	Mendlesham.
22	76½	Brockford Street.
		Junction of the road from Ipswich, p. 56.
30	77½	THWAITE.
26	80¾	Yaxley.
		R. *to Eye* 2m.
		L. *to Buckenham* [G].
		Norfolk.
22	84¾	SCOLE INN.
*	107	NORWICH, p. 56.

[G]	
Yaxley..............	80¾
Sturston	84
[Norf.] DISS	86
Shelfanger	88½
Windmill............	93¼
R. *to Attleborough* 5m.	
NEW BUCKENHAM	93½
Thence, 15½m. to NORWICH	109

LONDON TO NORWICH;

By IPSWICH.

Variations of Route, and Branch Routes.

	M.
[A]	
COLCHESTER ..	51
Ardleigh	56
Wignell Street....	58½
MANNINGTREE	60½
[*Or, leave Manningtree on* L. *distance nearly the same.*]	
Mistley Thorn	61
Bradfield	63
Ramsey Street....	67½
Ramsey..........	68½
Dover Court......	69½
HARWICH	71½
[A 2]	
COLCHESTER ..	51
Greenstead	52
Turn of the road ..	53
R. *to Wivenhoe* 2m.	
Elmstead Market,	55
Frating	57
St. Osyth	62
[B]	
COPDOCK	65½
Bramford	68
Great Blackenham,	71
NEEDHAM	74½
STOW MARKET,	78
[C]	
To Aylsham & Holt:	
NORWICH	114½
Horsham St. Faith,	118½
Newton St. Faith..	120
Heavingham.......	123½
Marsham	124½
AYLSHAM........	126½
R. *to Cromer* 10½m.	
Blickling	127½
Saxthorpe........	132
HOLT	138
CLEY	142½
[C 2]	
To Cromer:	
See next page, col. 3.	

L.D.	M. *from Whitechapel Church.*
	Essex.
*	29 CHELMSFORD, p.54.
	[*Prospective Distances:* Colchester .... 22m. *Harwich* ...... 42½ Ipswich........ 40 *Yarmouth* .... 95 Scole Inn ...... 63 Norwich ...... 85½]
	30 Springfield.
4	33 Boreham Street.
6	34½ Hatfield Peverill.
8½	37½ WITHAM.
	39½ Riven Hall End.
12	41 KELVEDON.
	L. *to Coggeshall* 3m.
	42 Gore Pits.
18	47 Stanway.
	49 Lexden.
22	51 COLCHESTER.
	R. *to Harwich* [A].
	— *to St. Osyth* [A 2].
	L. *to Reyland* 6m.
	52½ Killridge.
	55½ Arleigh.
29	57½ Stratford Bridge.
	R. *to Dedham* 1m.
	Suffolk.
	58½ Stratford.
	L. *to Hadleigh* 5½m.
	61½ Bentley.
36	65½ COPDOCK.
	L. *to Stow Market* [B].

L.D.	M. *from Whitechapel Church.*
*	69 IPSWICH.
	R. *to Woodbridge*, p. 57.
6	72½ Claydon.
	75 Coddenham Bridge.
11	79½ STONHAM PYE.
	80 R. *to Debenham* 3m.
	83½ Brockford Street.
	R. *to Eye* 5½m.
18	84½ THWAITE.
19	87 R. *to Eye* 2m.
	88 Yaxley.
	89½ L. *to Diss*, p. 55.
	Norfolk.
22	92 SCOLE INN.
	R. *to Harleston* [F].
	L. *to Diss* 2½m.
20	94½ Dickleburgh.
	96½ Tivet's Hall Green.
14	100½ Stratton St. Mary.
13	101½ Stratton St. Michael.
10	104½ Newton Flotman.
5	109 Hartford Bridge.
	Cross the river Yare.
*	114½ NORWICH.
	Other Routes are, By Sudbury and Stow Market (p. 55) 107m. By Newmarket and Thetford (p. 55) 109m. By Bury St. Edmunds (p. 54) 115½m. By Hingham (p. 58) 114m.

To Aylsham and Holt [C].
To Walsham and Cromer [C 2].

LONDON TO YARMOUTH.

Variations of Route, and Branch Routes.

	M.
[D]	
Yoxford	94
Bramfield	98½
HALESWORTH,	101
Stone Street	104
St. Laurence Ilketshall	107
BUNGAY	110
Another R. is by Scole Inn, below.	
[E]	
Blythburgh	99½
Bulchamp	100½
Brampton	104
Shaddingfield	105
Weston	107
BECCLES	109¼
Thence to Yarmouth as below, 15*m*.	
[F]	
Scole Inn (p. 56)	92
Billingford	93½
Thorpe Abbots	95
Brockdish Street	96¾
Needham	98¼
HARLESTON	100
Reddenhall	101½
Wortwell	102½
Dove Alehouse	103½
Earrham	105½
Cross the river Waveney.	
[Suff.] BUNGAY	107
L. *to Loddon* 6¼*m*.	
Mettingham	108½
Ship Meadow	110
Barsham	111
BECCLES	112½
Cross the river Waveney.	
[Norf.] Gillingham,	114
Hadiscoe	118½
St. Olave's Bridge	120½
Cross the Waveney.	
[Suff.] Fritton	121
Gorleston	125¼
[Norfolk.]	
YARMOUTH	127½

M. *from Whitechapel Church.*

L.D.	M.	
		Suffolk.
*	69	IPSWICH (p. 57).
		[*Prospective Distances:* Wickham Mark. 13*m*. Saxmundham .. 21; Yoxford .. 25; *Bungay* .. 41; *Beccles* .. 40½; Lowestoft .. 45; Yarmouth .. 55]
	72½	Kesgrave.
	75½	Martlesham.
8	77	WOODBRIDGE.
	78½	Melton T. G.
		R. *to Orford* 11*m*.
	79¾	Ufford Street.
12	81	Petistree.
13	81¾	Wickham Market.
		L. *to Framlingham* 5¾*m*.
	84½	Glenham.
17	86	Stratford St. Andrew.
18	86¾	Farnham.
		R. *to Aldborough* 7½*m*.
34	89¾	SAXMUNDHAM.
	91	Kelsale.
30	94	Yoxford.
		R. *to Dunwich* 6*m*.
		L. *to Bungay* [D] 16*m*.; *thence to Norwich* 14*m*.
24	99½	Blythburgh.
		L. *to Beccles* [E].
		R. *to Southwold* 4½*m*.
21	102½	Wangford.
18	105¾	Wrentham.
	107¼	Benacre T. G.
		On R. Benacre Park, Sir T. Gooch, Bart.
15	109	Kessingland.
	112	Pakefield.
	112½	Kirkley.
10	113¾	LOWESTOFT.
	118¼	Hopton T. G.
2	121½	Gorleston.
	122¼	South Town.
	123½	Yarmouth Bridge.
		Cross the river Yare.
		Norfolk.
*	123¾	YARMOUTH.
		Other Routes are by Beccles [E]; or by Scole Inn [F]; and by Norwich, p. 55.

* Yarmouth.

[C 2]	
NORWICH	114¼*m*.
Crostwick	119
Cross Stone Beck.	
Horstead Mill	121
Scottow	124
R. *to Worstead* 2¼*m*.	
Westwick Park	125½
NORTH WALSHAM	128½
Antingham	131
Thorpe Market	133½
CROMER	137½
Or, by Aylsham, p. 56.	
At North Walsham, forward to Happisburgh 5*m*.; thence, along the Coast to Cromer 15*m*.	

LONDON TO CROMER AND CLEY.

Variations of Route, and Branch Routes.

M.

[A]

WATTON 92¼
Carbrook Common 94¼
Upgate 95¾
Scoulton T. G..... 98
HINGHAM 99½
Kimberley Green . 103
Colney 111
Earlham 113
NORWICH 114

[B]

REPEHAM 114
Caurton.......... 116½
AYLSHAM...... 121
Banningham Bridge 124½
NORTH WALSHAM.......... 128
Another R. is by Norwich, p. 57.

[C]

BRANDON 78¼
[Norfolk.] Weeting All Saints...... 79¼
METHWOLD .. 84
STOKE FERRY .. 88¼
R. *to Swaffham* 14m.
Wereham 90
DOWNHAM MARKET 95

[C 2]

Wereham, above.. 90
Stradset.......... 93
Foston 95
Setchy 98½
LYNN 102¼

[D]

Another Route is by Brandon & Swaffham (p. 53) to
FAKENHAM.... 108
Snoring Common . 111
Stock Heath...... 113¼
SharingtonCommon 116¼
HOLT 119¼
L. *to Cley* 4½*m.*
R. *to Cromer* 10*m.*

L.D.	M. *from Shoreditch Church.*
	60¼ NEWMARKET.
	Suffolk.
11	69¼ BARTON MILLS (p. 53).
4	76 Elvedon.
	Cross the Little Ouse.
	Norfolk.
*	80 THETFORD.
	R. *to Wyndham*, p. 55.
	82½ Croxton.
8	88 Tottington.
	90½ Merton.
12	92½ WATTON.
	R. *to Hingham; thence to Norwich* [A].
	97½ Shipdam.
18	98¼ Market Street.
	99¾ Westfield Common.
23	103 EAST DEREHAM.
	L. *to Fakenham* 12½*m.*
	—*to Holt.* See next col.
28	108 Swanton.
	Cross the riv. Wensom.
	110 Bawdeswell.
	L. *to Foulsham* 3*m.*
34	114 REPEHAM.
	R. *to N. Walsham* [B].
41	121 Itteringham.
	125 Thurgarton.
46	126 Sustead.
	128¼ Felbrigg.
51	131½ CROMER.
	Other Routes are by Norwich, p. 57, [C 2].

L.D.	M. *from Shoreditch Church.*
	ANOTHER ROUTE TO EAST DEREHAM.
*	78¼ BRANDON (p. 53).
	L. *to Stoke Ferry* [C].
	Norfolk.
4	82¼ Lindford Lodge.
	83½ West Tofts Hall.
	85 Stanford.
10	88 Clermont Lodge.
	91 WATTON.
23	101½ EAST DEREHAM, as in opposite col.
	R. *to Repeham;* L. *to*
	107 Elmham.
31	109½ Guist Bridge.
	L. *to Foulsham* 2½*m.*
	114½ Melton Park.
	117½ Thornage.
42	120 HOLT [D].
46	124¼ CLEY.
	[*By Norwich*, p. 56.]

[C]

Another Route to Gosport:

ALTON (p. 60).... 47½
Filmer Hill 56
West Meon 58¾
WARNFORD 60¼
Exton 62
Droxford 63¾
Wickham 69¼
FAREHAM 73
Brookhurst........ 76½
GOSPORT 78¼

LONDON TO PORTSMOUTH.

Variations of Route, and Branch Routes.

[A] M.

Another Route:
From Hyde Park Corner,
Brompton 1
Little Chelsea...... 2
Parsons Green 3
Fulham Bridge 4
Cross the Thames.
[Surrey] Putney .. 4½
Putney Heath 5¾
Bald Face Stag 6¾
KINGSTON 10
Thence to Chertsey:
Cross the Thames.
[Middlesex.]
HAMPTON COURT, 11½
Cross the Thames.
[Sur.] East Mousley 12¼
West Mousley 13½
Walton 16
Weybridge 18¼
CHERTSEY 21
Or, HAMPTON CT. 11½
HAMPTON 12¼
Sunbury 15
Lower Hawford .. 17½
Shepperton 18
Chertsey Bridge .. 20¼
Cross the Thames.
[Surrey.] CHERTSEY 21

[A 2]
Fulham Bridge, above 4
[Surrey.] Barnes Common......... 5
R. *to Kew* 2*m*.
East Sheen......... 7
RICHMOND 8¾

[B]
Another Route is by Leatherhead, p. 57.

[C]
See opposite page.

L.D.	M. *from London Bridge.*
	Surrey.
	1 Newington T. G.
	2¼ Vauxhall T. G.
	[*From Hyde Park Corner over Vauxhall Bridge* 1¼*m*.]
	4½ Battersea Rise.
	6 WANDSWORTH.
22	7½ Putney Heath.
	On L. Wimbledon Park, Earl Spencer.
	9½ On R. Earl Besborough
	10 Robin Hood T. G.
	On R. Richmond Park, New Lodge, Lord Sidmouth.
	11 On L. Combe House, Earl of Liverpool.
	12 KINGSTON [A].
17	12½ On R. Hampton Court.
16	13¾ Thames Ditton.
	16 ESHER.
	R. *to Weybridge* 4½*m*.
	On L. Claremont, Pr. of Saxe Cobourg.
10	19½ COBHAM STREET.
	20 On L. Pain's Hill, Earl of Carhampton.
	23 On L. Ockham Park, Lord King.
6	23½ RIPLEY.
	R. *to Woking* 2¼*m*.
	26 On L. Clandon Park, Earl of Onslow.

L.D.	M. *from London Bridge.*
*	29½ GUILDFORD [B].
	R. *to Farnham* 10*m*.
	30½ Catherine Hill.
2	31½ On R. Loseley, J. M. Molyneux, Esq.
4	33¾ GODALMING.
6	35¼ Milford.
	36 Mousall.
	41 Hind Head Hill.
	44 Seven Thorns.
	Hampshire.
	46 LIPHOOK.
23	49½ Rake (Sussex).
	53 Sheet Bridge.
18	54¼ PETERSFIELD.
14	58½ Horndean Down.
10	62 HORNDEAN.
	L. *to Havant* 4¼*m*.
	Through Bere Forest.
6	66 Purbrook.
	On L. Lord Keith.
	Over Portsdown Hill: on the summit a monument to the memory of Ld. Nelson.
	68 Cosham.
4	68½ Enter Portsea Island.
	69 Hilsea.
*	72½ PORTSMOUTH.
	Across the Ferry to Gosport ½*m*. [C].
	To Ryde, Isle of Wight, about 6*m*.

* GUILDFORD.

LONDON TO SOUTHAMPTON AND POOLE.

[From Southampton to Cowes, Isle of Wight, about 14 miles. Vessels sail every Morning and return in the Afternoon.]

Variations of Route, and Branch Routes.

[A]	M.
WINCHESTER..	65
Hursley...........	69½
Amphiel	72¾
Abbott's Wood ..	73
ROMSEY	76
Oure Bridge......	79¼
Cadnam..........	82
Stoney Cross	84½
Picked Post	90½
RINGWOOD....	93½
[B]	
ALTON	47¼
Chawton	48½
Farringdon	50
East Tisted	52
Filmer Hill	56
BISHOP'S WALTHAM	65¼
BOTLEY	68¾
Northam Bridge ..	74
SOUTHAMPTON	75
[C]	
RINGWOOD....	97
Lower Kingston ..	99
Avon	101
Sopley	102½
Staples Cross	105
CHRISTCHURCH	106
Mudeford	107
[D]	
WIMBORN MINSTER	106½
Bushels	111
Lychett Minster ..	114½
WAREHAM [E],	120
Stowborough	120¾
CORFE CASTLE,	125
Langton	130
SWANAGE	132
[E]	
To Weymouth:	
WAREHAM	120
Stoke Green.......	123
Wool Bridge	126
Winfrith	129
Osmington	135½
WEYMOUTH ...	140

L.D.	M. from Hyde Park Corner.
	Surrey.
38	27¼ Golden Farmer, as on the opposite page.
35	30 Frimley.
33	32 Farnborough (Hants).
27	38 FARNHAM.
	[*By Guildford* 39½*m.*]
	On R. B. of Winchester.
	On L. R. Lang, Esq.
	Hampshire.
23	42 Bentley Green.
21	44¼ Froyle.
	46¼ Holybourn.
18	47¼ ALTON.
	[Same distance by Hartford Bridge, p. 61.]
	48½ Chawton.
	L. *to Filmer Hill* [B].
12	52¾ Ropley Stoke.
	54½ Ropley Dean.
	55¾ Bishop's Sutton.
8	57 ALRESFORD.
	58¼ Seward's Bridge.
	Winchester Downs.
*	65 WINCHESTER.
	[*By Basingstoke* 62½*m.*]
	R. *to Romsey* [A].
	66 St. Croix.
	67½ Compton.
4	69½ Otterborne.
	71½ Chandler's Ford.
12	77 SOUTHAMPTON [B]
	79 Milbrook.
	80½ Redbridge.

L.D.	M. from Hyde Park Corner.
	81 Totton.
	85½ Cadnam.
25	88 Stoney Cross.
	94 Picked Post.
16	97 RINGWOOD [A].
	L. *to Christchurch* [C].
	100½ St. Leonard's Bridge.
12	101¼ New Bridge.
	Dorsetshire.
	106½ WIMBORN MINSTER.
	R. *to Corfe Castle* [D].
*	113 POOLE.

ADDENDA.

L.D.	M.
*	77 SOUTHAMPTON.
	79 Milbrook.
4	81 Totton.
	86½ LYNDHURST.
13	90 Brockenhurst.
	92½ Boldre.
18	95½ LYMINGTON.

ANOTHER ROUTE.

77 SOUTHAMPTON.
Cross Southampton Water.
84 Beaulieu.
90½ LYMINGTON.
Thence to Christchurch 11*m.*

LONDON TO FALMOUTH;

The Great Western Road, and Route of the Falmouth Mail.

Variations of Route, and Branch Routes.

[A] M.
HOUNSLOW 9¾
Feltham 13¾
Littleton 17
Chertsey Bridge .. 19¼
Cross the Thames.
[Sur.] CHERTSEY 20
Another Route:
BRENTFORD .. 7
Isleworth 8½
Twickenham...... 10¼
Teddington 12
Through Bushy Park.
HAMPTON COURT- 13½
Thence, p. 50, to
CHERTSEY 23
Other Routes are by Kingston, p. 59.

[B]
EGHAM.......... 17¾
Englefield Green .. 18¾
[Berks.] Through Windsor Gt. Park.
Hatchet Lane 24¼
Winkfield 25½
Thence, p. 1, to
READING 38½

[C]
EGHAM 17¾
Virginia Water.... 20½
[Berk.] Sunning Hill 23½
Sunning Hill Wells 24
Ascot Heath 24½
Bracknell 28
WOKINGHAM .. 32
King Street 34¼
Loddon Bridge .. 35½
READING 39

[D]
BASINGSTOKE. 45
POPHAM LANE .. 50¾
Popham 52
East Stratton Park 53¾
Lunways Inn 57¼
King's Worthy.... 60¾
WINCHESTER.. 62½

L.D. | M. from Hyde Park Corner.

Middlesex.

½ Knightsbridge.
1½ Kensington.
4 Hammersmith.
5 Turnham Green.
7 BRENTFORD.
7½ On L. Sion House, D. of Northumberland.
9 Smallberry Green T. G.
9¾ HOUNSLOW.
R. *to Maidenhead*, p. 1.
L. *to Chertsey* [A].
32 13¾ BEDFONT (or Belfont).
16½ STAINES.
Cross the Thames.

Surrey.

27 17¾ EGHAM.
R. *to Reading through Binfield* [B].
Over Englefield Heath.
On R. Windsor Gt. Park.
20½ Virginia Water.
R. *to Ascot Heath; thence to Wokingham and Reading* [C].
23 21¾ Shrubs Hill.
23 Bagshot Heath.
25 On R. Bagshot Park, Duke of Gloucester.
19 26 BAGSHOT.
18 27½ Golden Farmer.
L. *to Farnham* p. 60.

L.D. | M. from Hyde Park Corner.

Hampshire.

15 30¼ BLACKWATER.
10 35¼ HARTFORD BRIDGE.
9 36 Hartley Row.
36½ L. *to Odiham* 3½m.
[40¼ ODIHAM.
42¾ South Warnborough.
48¼ ALTON.]
7 38 MURRELL GREEN.
39 Hook.
42¼ Maplederwell Hatch.
* 45 BASINGSTOKE.
L. *to Winchester* [D].
— *to Salisbury by Stockbridge* [E].
R. *to Kingsclere* [F].
2 47¼ WORTING.
49 Clerken Greeu.
8 52¾ OVERTON.
56½ WHITCHURCH.
14 58½ Hurstborne.
61½ Down House.
19 63½ ANDOVER.
R. *to Amesbury*—
[63½ ANDOVER.
66¾ Weyhill.
72¼ Park House.
77½ AMESBURY.]
Thence to Exeter by Ilchester and Ilminster (p. 65); *to Warminster & Frome* (p. 71).
65½ Little Ann.
23 68 Down Farm.
71 Middle Wallop.

* BASINGSTOKE.

Variations of Route, and Branch Routes.

[E]

	M.
BASINGSTOKE.	45
POPHAM LANE ..	50½
SUTTON	58½
Leckford Hut	62¼
STOCKBRIDGE .	66
[Wilts.] Lobcombe Corner	72¾
Winterslow Hut ..	74
SALISBURY	80½

[F]

BASINGSTOKE..	45
Ramsdale	49
Woolverton	52
KINGSCLERE ..	54½
Another Route:	
READING (p. 72)	39
THEAL	43½
ALDERMASTON ..	48½
[Hants.] Fair Oak,	54
KINGSCLERE ..	56½

[G]

SALISBURY	81
Fisherton	81½
Fuggiestone	84
Wilton	84½
Burcombe........	85¾
Barford..........	87¼
Dinton	89¾
Teffont	91¼
Chilmark	93
Fonthill	95¼
HINDON	96¾

[G]

SALISBURY	81
Combe Bisset	84
Tipput	89
[Dorset.]	
CRANBOURN ..	92
Horton Inn	96½
Stanbridge	100
WIMBORN MINSTER	102½
POOLE	109

[H]

BLANDFORD ..	103½
Milton Abbey	111¼
CERNE ABBAS.	120¼
SYDLING	122¾
Evershot	127
BEAMINSTER ..	133

L.D.	M. from Hyde Park Corner.
	Wiltshire.
8	73½ Lobcombe Corner.
7	74¼ Winterslow Hut.
*	81 SALISBURY.
	[*Prospective Distances:* Blandford........ 22½m. Dorchester .... 38½ *Weymouth* .... 47 Bridport .... 53½ Axminster .... 66 Exeter .... 92 Oakhampton ..114 Launceston ....132¼ Truro...........175¾ Falmouth ....187½]
	R. to *Hindon* [G].
	Cross the river Avon.
1	82½ R. to *Shaftesbury*, p. 67.
3	84¼ Combe Bisset.
	L. to *Poole* [G].
	Dorsetshire.
28	91¼ Woodyates Inn.
23	96¼ Cashmoor Inn.
	99 Tarrant Hinton.
18	101½ Pimperne.
16	103½ BLANDFORD.
	R. to *Cerne Abbas* [H].
11	108½ Winterbourne Whitchurch.
8	111½ MILBOURNE.
5	114¾ Piddle Town.
*	119½ DORCHESTER.
	L. to *Weymouth*— [119½ DORCHESTER. 122 Monckton. 127¼ Melcomb Regis. 127½ WEYMOUTH.]
	R. to *Beaminster* 17½m.
	122½ Junction of road from Weymouth 8m.
	L. to *Abbotsbury* 5m.
	124½ Winterbourne Abbas.
	127½ Longbredy.
	Over Askerwell Down.
42	131 Traveller's Rest.
	134¼ R. *Beaminster* 6¼m.
39	134½ BRIDPORT.
	137¼ Chidiock.
32	141¼ Charmouth.
	L. to *Lyme Regis*, p. 68.
	Devonshire.
	145 Hunter's Lodge Inn.
26	147 AXMINSTER.
	148½ Kilmington.
	152¾ Wilmington.
	156 Mount Pleasant.
16	157 HONITON.
	160¼ Fenny Bridges.
11	162¼ Fair Mile Inn.
4	169 Honiton's Clyst.
	171¼ Heavitree.
*	173 EXETER.
	[*Prospective Distances:* Oakhampton .. 22m. Launceston .... 40½ Bodmin ...... 61½ Truro .... 83¼ Falmouth ...... 95½ Penzance ......113 *On Return Route:* Axminster ..... 26 Bridport ...... 38½ *Weymouth* .... 55½ Dorchester .... 53½ Blandford...... 69½ Salisbury ...... 92 Andover ....109½]

Variations of Route, and Branch Routes.

	M.
[I]	
OAKHAMPTON	195
Sourton	199½
Pig's Lea	200½
Downton	203
Lidford	204
Cross the river Lid.	
Brent Tor T. G.	207¼
TAVISTOCK	211½
[K]	
LAUNCESTON	213½
St. Stephen's Down	215
Egloskerry	216¼
Haleworthy	222¾
Davidstow	224
R. *to Bossiney* 10*m.*	
CAMELFORD	228
Tramagennow	229
Helson	230
Knert's Mill	231¼
St. Teath	231½
R. *to Padstow* 12*m.*	
Trelill	235
Wadebridge	239
High Ranridge	244
ST. COLUMB	251
INDIAN QUEEN	254
TRURO, as in the opposite column	266½
[L]	
ST. MICHAEL	249½
Zealla	253
Perran Alms House	255
3*m* farther, R. *to St. Agnes* 3½*m.* L. *to Truro* 6*m.*	
Black Water	259½
REDRUTH	263½
Pool	265¼
Terswithian	266¾
Angarrack	271½
R. *to St. Ives* 6*m.*	
Trelowith	275
Crowless	277
PENZANCE	281
[M]	
Stricken Bridge	262¾
PENRYN	265½
Buttress	269¼

L.D.	M. *from Hyde Park Corner.*	
*	173	EXETER.
		R. *to Crediton and Bow*, p. 65.
		L. *to Plymouth*, p. 69.
		— *to Liskeard*, p. 66.
2	175¼	Adderwater.
6	179¼	Lilly Bridge.
7	180	Tap House.
	182¼	Cheriton Cross.
11	184	CROCKERNWELL.
	187¾	Merrymeet.
	191	South Zeal.
		Cross the river Taw.
	191½	Stickle Path.
22	195	OAKHAMPTON.
		Cross the river Oakment.
		R. *to Hatherleigh* 7*m.*
		L. *to Tavistock* [I].
28	201	Bridestow.
37	210	LYFTON.
	212	Poulston Bridge.
		Cross the Tamar.
		Cornwall.
21	213½	LAUNCESTON.
		R. *to Camelford* [K].
	218	Hickshaw Mill.
15	219½	Trerethick Bridge.
	221	Five Lanes Inn.
13	221½	Trewint.
	224	Palmer's Bridge.
		Over Temple Moor.
	228	Temple.
*	234½	BODMIN.
	236½	Lanevet Ford.
15	241½	East Lane End.
	244	INDIAN QUEEN.
	245	Fradden.
9	247½	Summer Court.
7	249½	ST. MICHAEL.
		R. *to Penzance* [L].
4	252¼	Trespen.
	255¼	Buckshead.
*	256½	TRURO [H].
	260½	Carnan.
5	261½	Perranwell.
6	262¾	Stricken Bridge.
		R. *to Helstone; thence to Penzance, below.*
9	265¼	PENRYN.
12	268½	FALMOUTH QUAY.

ADDENDA.

L.D.	M.	
24	262¾	Stricken Bridge, above.
18	268¼	Buttress.
		Or, *thro' Penryn* [M].
	269	Pollen Green.
	271	Menehy.
	272	Trevenen.
13	273¼	HELSTONE.
10	276½	Breage.
	279	St. Hilary Down.
	282¼	MARAZION.
*	286½	PENZANCE.
		Thence to Land's End, through Sennen, 10 miles (p. 66); or, through Newlyn & Trevelloe 11 miles.

LONDON TO EXETER, BY BATH AND WELLS.

The Route of the Bath, Exeter, and Plymouth Mail.

Variations of Route, and Branch Routes.

[A]	M.
BATH	106½
Radstoke	114
Stratton	117½
Oakhill	120½
SHEPTON MALLET	122½
CANNARD'S GRAVE INN	123½
Pylle Street	125¼
Wraxell	127¾
Four Foot Inn	129½
Lydford	131
ILCHESTER	137¼
Thence, p. 65, to	
HONITON	164½
EXETER	180½

[A 2]	
HONITON	164½
Sidbury	170½
Sidford	172
SIDMOUTH	173½
Thence, p. 68, to	
EXMOUTH	183¼

[B]	
FROME (p. 71)	103½
Whatley	106
Little Elm	107½
Over Mendip Hills.	
Long Cross	111
To Shepton Mallet 2m.	
East Horrington	117
WELLS	119
Thence to Axbridge:	
Wokey	120½
Westbury	123
Draycot	125
Cheddar	127
AXBRIDGE	129

[C]

Another Route from Bath to Bridgewater:

BATH	106½
AXBRIDGE	132
BRIDGEWATER	149½

L.D.	M.	*from Hyde Park Corner.*
		Somersetshire.
18	106½	BATH, by Devizes (p. 79).
		[*Prospective Distances:* Wells 18*m.*; Glastonbury 23½; Bridgewater 38¾; Taunton 49½; Wellington 56½; Collumpton 69¼; Exeter 81; Ilchester [A] 31; Honiton 58; Sidmouth [A 2] 67; Exmouth 76¼]
14	110½	Dunkerton.
	114	Radstoke.
8	116½	L. *to Shepton Mallet* [A].
	117	Chilcompton Inn.
6	118½	OLD DOWN INN.
		Cross the Mendip Hills.
*	124½	WELLS.
		Other Routes are by Andover and Frome [B].
	130	GLASTONBURY.
7	131¾	Street.
		L. *to Somerton 6m.*
9	133¼	Walton.
10	134¾	PIPER'S INN [D].
	135¾	Ashcot.
	141	Bawdrip.
11	145	BRIDGEWATER [C]
	148½	North Petherton.
5	151	Thurloxton.
	152½	Walford Bridge.
*	156	TAUNTON [D].
	157½	Bishop's Hull.
	159	Runwell.
	160½	Heatherton Park.
	162	Chilson.
25	163	WELLINGTON.
		Devonshire.
	166½	Bluet's Cross.
20	167½	MAIDEN DOWN, White Ball.
18	169¾	South Appleford.
	170	R. *to Tiverton 6½m.*
	173¼	Welland.
12	175¾	COLLUMPTON.
		R. *to Bradninch 2½m.*
	177¾	Wedcote.
7	180½	Beer.
	183	Broad Clyst.
		On R. Killerton House, Sir T. D. Ackland, Bart.
2	185½	Whipton.
*	187½	EXETER.
		To Plymouth, p. 69.
		To Falmouth, p. 62.

[D]

From Piper's Inn to Taunton, direct, leaving Bridgewater out of the line of route, 17¼ miles, thus:

	M.
At PIPER'S INN	134¾
L. to Pedwell	136
Sedgmoor T. G.	138
Burrowbridge	142
Alfred's Pillar	143
Durston	147
TAUNTON	152

LONDON TO EXETER, BY ILMINSTER [A];

Continued to LISKEARD and TRURO, and thence to the LAND'S END.

Variations of Route, and Branch Routes.

[A]

Other Routes to Exeter are,

1. By Bath and Wells, as in the opposite page.
2. By Salisbury and Bridport, as in the Route of the Exeter and Falmouth Mail, p. 62.
3. By Salisbury and Sherborne, p. 67.

[B]	M.
DEPTFORD INN ..	87
Codford St. Mary .	90
Upton Lovel	91½
Heytesbury	93¼
Boreham	95¼
WARMINSTER ..	97½

[C]	
WINCAUNTON ..	108
North Cheriton ..	110½
Charlton	112¾
SHERBORNE ..	117¼

[D]	
EXETER........	164½
Newton St. Cyres..	169
CREDITON	172
Morchard Bishops..	179
New Inn	181½
Chawleigh	184
CHUMLEIGH ..	186

[E]	
CREDITON, above	172
Coleford	176
BOW	179½
North Tawton	182½
L. *to Oakhampton* 7m.	
Sampford Courtenay	186
Exborn	187½
Jacobstow........	188½
HATHERLEIGH	192
Golden Inn	196
R. *to Sheepwash* 1½m.	
Houlsworthy	205½
Cross the riv. Tamar	209½
[Cornw.] STRATTON	213

L.D.	M. *from Hyde Park Corner.*	
		Hampshire.
*	63½	ANDOVER, p. 61.
		[*Prospective Distances:* Amesbury...... 14m. Deptford Inn .. 23½ Hindon........ 31 Mere.......... 37½ Wincaunton.... 44½ Ilchester ...... 58 Ilminster ...... 70 Honiton ...... 85 Exeter ....101]
3	66¾	Weyhill.
		R. *to Ludgershall*, p. 71.
9	72½	Park House.
		Wiltshire.
14	77½	AMESBURY.
16	79½	Stonehenge.
		R. *to Warminster*, p. 71.
19	82½	Winterton Stoke.
	87	DEPTFORD INN.
		R. *to Warminster* [B].
	87½	Wiley.
29	92½	New Inn.
		On L. Fonthill Abbey.
31	94½	HINDON.
		[*By Salisbury* (p. 62) 96½m.
		L. *to Shaftesbury* 7½m.
	97	Willoughby Hedge T. G.
		R. *to Bruton*, p. 70.
	101	MERE.
		Dorsetshire.
41	104½	Bourton.
		Somersetshire.
	107½	Bayford.
56	108	WINCAUNTON.
		R. *to Bruton* 4½m.
		— *to Castle Cary* 6½m.; *thence to Bridgewater*, p. 67.
		L. *to Sherborne* [C].
	110	Holton.
49	115½	Sparkford.
		L. *to Yeovil* 8m.
43	121½	ILCHESTER.
		L. *to Crewkerne* 12m.
37	127	Petherton Bridge.
		Junction of Road from Yeovil, p. 67.
	130	Sevington.
		On L. Hinton St. George, Earl Poulett.
	132	White Lackington.
31	133½	ILMINSTER.
		R. *to Taunton* [L].
		L. *to Chard* 5m.
25	139½	Buckland St. Mary.
		Cross the river Haven.
		Devonshire.
23	141½	Yarcomb.
16	148½	HONITON.
		R. *to Collumpton* 10½m.; *thence to Tiverton*, p. 70 [C].

* EXETER.

Variations of Route, and Branch Routes.

[F]	M.
TAVISTOCK	196½
Redford	198¾
Milton Abbott	201½
Greston Bridge	204
Cross the Tamar.	
[Cornw.] LAUNCESTON	206

[G]	M.
TAVISTOCK	196½
Whitechurch	198
Harra Bridge	202
Jumps	205
Nacker's Hole T. G.	207½
PLYMOUTH	210½

[H] To St. Mawes:	M.
Sticker	237¼
TREGONY	243
Treworlas	248
ST. MAWES	253

[I]	M.
REDRUTH	257
CAMBORNE	260½
HeyleCopperHouse	265½
Cross the riv. Heyle.	
Lelant	267½
ST. IVES	270½

[K]	M.
PLYMOUTH	207
Weston	209¾
Cross the Tamar.	
[Cornwall.] SALTASH	211½
Nottar Bridge	214½
Landrake	215½
LISKEARD	223½

The passage across the Tamar, at Saltash, is by a ferry. It has been proposed to erect a suspension bridge, of sufficient altitude to admit of frigates passing under it; the practicability of such an improvement having been ascertained, but requiring £60,000 to carry it into effect.

L.D.	M. from Hyde Park Corner.	
13	151½	Fenny Bridge.
11	153¾	Fair Mile Inn.
4	160½	Honiton Clyst.
*	164½	EXETER.
		[*Prospective Distances:* Moreton Hampstead 11*m.*; Tavistock 32; Liskeard 50; Lostwithiel 61½; Grampound 76; Truro 83¾; Redruth 92¾; Penzance 110]
		R. *to Oakhampton*, p. 63.
		— *to Chumleigh* [D].
		— *to Hatherleigh* [E].
		L. *to Chudleigh*, p. 69.
4	168½	Longdown End.
	171½	Green.
11	175½	MORETON HAMPSTEAD.
	178½	Wormhill.
15	179½	Dartmoor Forest.
18	182½	New House.
·	189½	Two Bridges.
28	192½	Merriville Bridge.
32	196½	TAVISTOCK.
		Another Route is by Oakhampton, p. 63.
		R. *to Launceston* [F].
		L. *to Beeralston* 5½*m.*
		— *to Plymouth* [G].
	200	New Bridge.
		Cross the Tamar.
		Cornwall.
41	205½	CALLINGTON.
48	212½	Pangover.

L.D.	M. from Hyde Park Corner.	
34	214½	LISKEARD.
		Junction of Road from Plymouth [K].
27	221	Tap House.
		R. *to Bodmin* 7*m.*
22	226	LOSTWITHIEL.
		L. *to Fowey* 5½*m.*
18	230	St. Blaizey.
	234½	St. Austle.
11	237¼	Sticker.
	238¾	L. *to Tregony* [H] 4½*m.*
	240½	GRAMPOUND.
5	243	Probus.
	245½	Tresilian.
*	248	TRURO.
		L. *to Penryn*, p. 63.
	253½	Chasewater.
9	257	REDRUTH.
		R. *to St. Ives* [I].
11	259	Pool.
·	260½	Terswithian.
17	265	Angarrack.
	266	R. *to St. Ives* 5*m.*
20	268½	Trelowith.
	270½	Crowless.
26	274½	PENZANCE.
	275¾	Trereife.
		R. *to St. Just* 6*m.*
	282½	Sennen.
36	284½	Land's End.

[L]	
ILMINSTER	133½*m.*
Horton	135½
Ashill	137½
Hatch	140
TAUNTON	148

LONDON TO EXETER, BY SHERBORNE.

Variations of Route, and Branch Routes.

M.

[A]

SHAFTESBURY 101
Litton Bridge 104½
Gillingham 105½
[Som.] Cucklington 109
Bayford 111
WINCAUNTON - 112
Thence to Bridgewater:
CASTLE CARY.. 118½
Cross Keys 124
PIPER'S INN 132¼
BRIDGEWATER 142¾

[B]

SHAFTESBURY 101
Todbere 104¼
Marnhall 107½
STURMINSTER - 109

[C]

YEOVIL 122
ILCHESTER 126¾
SOMERTON 131

[D]

YEOVIL 122
Preston 123
Odcomb 125
Montacute........ 126
Stoke............ 128
Petherton Bridge.. 129½
Sevington 132¾
White Lackington - 134½
ILMINSTER 136
CHARD 141

[E]

At Crewkerne, R. to Ilminster 8*m*., thence to Taunton, as on the opposite page [L].

L.B. | M. *from Hyde Park Corner.*

Wiltshire.

* 81 SALISBURY, p. 62.
[*Prospective Distances:*
Shaftesbury .... 20*m*.
Sherborne 36
Yeovil 41
Crewkerne 51
Chard 59
Honiton 71
Exeter .... 87]

84½ Wilton.
On L. Wilton House, Earl of Pembroke.

5 86 Burcombe.
87¼ Barford.
89½ Compton Chamberlain.
10 91 FOVANT.
14 95 Wardour Park.
On R. Wardour Castle, Lord Arundel.
15 96 White Sheet T. G.
17 98 Ludwell.

Dorsetshire.

20 101 SHAFTESBURY.
R. to *Wincaunton* [A].
L. to *Sturminster* [B].
24 105¼ East Stoure.
106½ West Stoure.

Somersetshire.

30 110¾ Henstridge.
L. to *Stalbridge* 1½*m*.
33 114 Milborne Port.

L.B. | M. *from Hyde Park Corner.*

Dorsetshire.

115½ Osborne.
51 116¾ SHERBORNE.
Another Route is by Hindon and Wincaunton (p. 65) 117¾*m*.
[*Prospective Distances:*
Crewkerne .... 15*m*.
Chard 23¼
Honiton 35¼
Exeter .... 51¼]
On L. Sherborne Castle, Earl of Digby.
49 119 Nether Compton.

Somersetshire.

46 122 YEOVIL.
R. to *Ilchester* [C].
→ to *Chard, by Ilminster* [D].
41 127 East Chinnock.
129¼ Haselbury.
36 131¼ CREWKERNE [E].
On R. Hinton St. George, Earl Poulett.
33 135 White Down.
28 140 CHARD.
R. to *Taunton* 13*m*.

Devonshire.

22 146 Stockland.
16 152 HONITON.
Thence, p. 65, to
* 168 EXETER.

LONDON TO SIDMOUTH, AND EXMOUTH;

Thence, along the Coast, to BRIXHAM QUAY (a).

Variations of Route, and Branch Routes.

[A]	M.
LYME REGIS ..	143
[Devon.] Colyford	149½
Division of the Rd.	156
Sidford............	159
Newton Poppleford	162
R. *to Exeter, by Bp.'s Clyst* 11m.	
Woodbury	167
TOPSHAM	170
EXETER.........	173½
[B] *Another Route:*	
EXETER (p. 66)..	164½
TOPSHAM	168
Lympstone	173
EXMOUTH	175½
[C]	
EXETER (p. 66) ..	164½
Alphington	166
Exminster	169
Kenton	171½
On L. Powderham Castle.	
Star Cross	173½
DAWLISH	177
TEIGNMOUTH ..	180½
Or, from Exminster to Dawlish, along the Banks of the Exe, with Powderham Pk. on R.	
Another Route:	
EXETER.........	164½
Alphington	166
Kenford	168
Haldon Hill......	170
TEIGNMOUTH	180
[D]	
Haldon Hill(above)	176
Sandy Gate	176½
NEWTON BUSHEL	179
King's Kerswell ..	181
Compton	184
Marldon	185
Galmpton	190
BRIXHAM	192

L.D.	M. from Hyde Park Corner.	
		Dorsetshire.
24	134½	BRIDPORT (p. 63).
		[Or, to Bridport by Southampton and Weymouth. See next column.]
	137½	Chidiock.
17	141	Charmouth.
15	143	LYME REGIS.
		Cross the river Axe.
		Devonshire.
9	149½	Colyford.
		R. *to Colyton* 1m. *thence to Honiton* 10m.
	156	Division of the Road.
		R. *to Exeter* [A].
*	158½	SIDMOUTH.
		Other Routes are by Honiton, p. 64.
	162	Otterton.
	163	Budleigh Salterton.
8	164½	Knole.
10	168½	EXMOUTH [B].
		Ferry across the Exe.
13	171½	DAWLISH.
17	175½	TEIGNMOUTH.
		Other Routes are by Exeter [C].
18	176½	Shaldon.
	178½	Comb Puffords.
22	180½	St. Mary Church.
	183½	Hope's, or Bob's Nose.
	185	TORQUAY.
29	187½	Tor Mohun.

L.D.	M. from Hyde Park Corner.	
	188½	Cockington.
	191	Paington.
		R. *to Totness* 4m.; *thence to Plymouth*, p. 69.
	195	Churston Ferrers.
	196½	BRIXHAM.
		Another R. is by Exeter [D].
	197	Brixham Quay.

ADDENDA.

L.D.	M.	
63	77	SOUTHAMPTON (p. 60).
		Thence, by Wimborn Minster and Wareham, to
*	140	WEYMOUTH.
5	145	Brodeway.
11	151	Winterborne St. Martin's.
23	163	BRIDPORT.

(a) The tour of the Devonshire coast is extremely beautiful, the different watering-places possessing each a distinctness of feature equally pleasing and diversified from the others. The mildness and salubrity of this part of the kingdom are evinced by the luxuriance which the myrtle trees attain in the open air; this beautiful shrub extending itself over the entire breadth of the cottages to which it is attached. This is particularly observable in the sheltered villages about Exmouth.—See "Cooke's Topography of Devon," for many interesting particulars of this county.

LONDON TO PLYMOUTH;

Thence to FOWEY.

Variations of Route, and Branch Routes.

[A]	M.
Another Route:	
TOTNESS	186¾
Wonton	191
MODBURY	198
Yealmpton	201½
PLYMPTON EARL	205½
Plympton St. Mary	206
PLYMOUTH	210½
[B]	
NEWTON BUSHEL.............	179
Abbots Kerswell ..	181
Compton	184
Marldon	185
1½m. *farther*, L. *to Paington* ½m.	
Galmpton	190
L. *to Brixham* 2m.	
Kingsweare	194½
Cross the Ferry.	
DARTMOUTH ..	195
Another Route:	
TOTNESS	186¾
Harburton Ford ..	189¾
New Inn	192
R. *to Kingsbridge* 6½m.	
DARTMOUTH ...	200
[C]	
Another Route:	
PLYMOUTH	207
Weston	209¾
Cross the Tamar.	
[Cornwall.]	
SALTASH	211½
See p. 66 [K].	
Nottar Bridge	214¼
Landrake	215¾
ST. GERMANS..	219
[D]	
Another Route:	
LOSTWITHIEL, (p. 66)	226
FOWEY	231½

L. D.	M. *from Hyde Park Corner.*	
		Devonshire.
*	164½	EXETER (p. 66).
	166	Alphington.
3	167½	Shillingford.
4	168½	Clopton Bridge.
		Over Haldon Hill.
9	173¾	CHUDLEIGH.
11	175¾	Knighton.
	176	Jew's Bridge.
	179½	Bickington.
24	183	ASHBURTON.
		Cross the river Dart.
	186	Buckfastleigh.
	187½	Dean Prior.
18	189	Harburton Ford.
	191	Brent.
	194	Bideford Bridge.
11	196	IVY BRIDGE.
	196¾	Woodland.
10	197¼	Cadleigh.
	198½	Lee Mill.
5	202¼	RIDGEWAY.
	203½	River Plym.
*	207	PLYMOUTH.
	208	Stonehouse.
		R. *to Saltash, across the Ferry*, 4½m.
2	209	PLYMOUTH DOCK.
		Ferry across the Tamar; on left, across the Crimble Passage to Maker; R. to Torpoint.

L. D.	M. *from Hyde Park Corner.*	
		Cornwall.
22	209¾	Torpoint.
	212¾	St. Anthony.
16	215¼	Croft Hole T. G.
		R. *to St. Germans 3m.* [C].
		— *to Liskeard* 10m.
	218½	Downderry.
	221¼	Bodigga.
8	223	EAST LOOE.
	223¼	West Looe.
	226½	Treweers.
*	231	FOWEY [D].

ANOTHER ROUTE.

L. D.	M.	
*	164½	EXETER.
	166	Alphington.
	168	Kenford.
	170	Haldon Hill.
12	176½	Sandy Gate.
		Cross the river Teign.
	179	NEWTON BUSHEL.
		L. *to Dartmouth* [B].
	181	Two Mile Oak.
19	183½	Bow.
		Cross the river Dart.
22	186¾	TOTNESS [A].
	191	Wonton.
	195	Bideford Bridge.
23	197	IVY BRIDGE.
45	209	PLYMOUTH, as in the opposite col.

LONDON TO BARNSTAPLE;

And thence to ILFRACOMBE.

Variations of Route, and Branch Routes.

	M.
[A]	
Another Route:	
SALISBURY, p. 62	81
Fisherton Ainger ..	81¼
Wilton T. G.	84¾
Burcombe........	86
Burford..........	87¼
Dinton	89¾
Teffont	91½
Chilmark	93
Fonthill..........	95¼
HINDON	96¾
Willoughby Hedge T. G.	99¼
[Som.] BRUTON.	112¾
Or,	
Heytesbury (p. 71)	92
Newnham........	94
Deverill	96
Maiden Bradley ..	100¼
[Som.] Yarnfield..	101¾
Brewham	105¾
BRUTON	108½
[B]	
BARNSTAPLE..	189
Hamacot	193¼
East Leigh	195
BIDEFORD	197¼
Ford	200¾
Holwell	203¾
HARTLAND	210¾
[C]	
WELLINGTON..	148¼
Rockwell Green ..	149¾
[Dev.] Biuet's Cross	152
MAIDEN DOWN..	153
South Appledore..	155
Sampford Peverll.	158
Halberton........	160
TIVERTON	163
Another Route:	
HONITON, p. 65.	148¼
Awliscombe......	150¾
Blue Ball	152¾
COLLUMPTON..	159
TIVERTON	164½

L. D.	M. *from Hyde Park Corner.*
	Wiltshire.
	87 DEPTFORD INN (p. 65).
49	92½ New Inn.
	L. *to Hindon 2m.*
	93¾ Chicklade.
45	96½ Willoughby Hedge T.G.
	97½ L. *to Mere 3m.*
	Somersetshire.
	102 Kilmington.
	106 Hardway.
34	107½ *Forward to Ainsford Inn, leaving Bruton on* R. *4½m.*
	109 BRUTON [A].
	110½ Pitcombe.
28	113¾ AINSFORD INN. On L. CASTLE CARY.
	L. *to Ilchester 11m.*
	115 Alford.
	120 King's Weston.
16	123½ SOMERTON.
	128 LANGPORT.
11	130½ Curry Rivell.
7	134¼ Rock House.
6	135½ Wrantage.
*	141½ TAUNTON.
	Other Routes are by Ilminster, p. 66; by Bath and Wells, p. 64; or by Warminster & Frome, as on the opposite page.
	L. *to Wellington and Tiverton.* See next column.

L. D.	M. *from Hyde Park Corner.*
	143 Staple Grove.
	144 Norton Fitzwarren.
40	149 MILVERTON.
36	153 WIVELISCOMBE.
	L. *to Bampton 9½m.*
	155½ Chipstable.
29	160 Skilgate.
	162 Bury.
24	164¾ DULVERTON.
	Devonshire.
	170½ Durleyford.
	176 Bush Bridge.
11	177½ SOUTH MOLTON.
	179½ South Hill.
8	181 Filleigh.
	184½ Swimbridge.
2	186¾ Landkey.
	188 Newport.
*	189 BARNSTAPLE [B].
	R. *to Comb Martin 9½m.*
	190 Pilton.
3	192 Prexford.
10	199 ILFRACOMBE.

ADDENDA.

L. D.	M.
*	141½ TAUNTON.
	143 Bishop's Hull.
3	144½ Ramwell.
	147½ Chilson.
7	148½ WELLINGTON.
	Thence [C] 14½m. to
	163 TIVERTON.

LONDON TO BRIDGEWATER:

Thence to MINEHEAD; and to SOUTH MOLTON.

L.D.	M. from Hyde Park Corner.	
		Hampshire.
*	63½	ANDOVER (p. 61).
3	66¾	Weyhill.
		R. *to Ludgershall* [A].
9	72½	Park House.
		Wiltshire.
14	77½	AMESBURY.
16	79¾	Stonehenge.
	83	Shrewton.
	88	Chiltern.
	92	Heytesbury.
31	94½	Boreham.
	96	WARMINSTER.
		Another Route is by Deptford Inn (p. 65) 97½m.
	97	Bugley.
36	99½	Whitbourn.
37	100½	Corsley Heath.
		Somersetshire.
40	103½	FROME [B].
	107	Holiwell.
	109	Layton.
49	112½	Doulting.
51	114½	SHEPTON MALLET.
		R. *to Wells 5m.*
	117	Pilton.
18	120	West Pennard.
	122	Edgarly.
15	123	GLASTONBURY.
		[*By Bath and Wells* (p. 64) 130*m.*]
13	124¾	Street.
	126½	Walton.
10	127¾	PIPER'S INN.
		L. *to* TAUNTON 17½*m.* See p. 64 [D].
9	128¾	Ashcot.
4	134	Bawdrip.
*	138	BRIDGEWATER.
		Other Routes are by Bruton [C], and by Bath and Wells, p. 64.
	142½	Cannington.
9	147	NETHER STOWEY.
10	148	Doddington.
	149½	Holford.
	155	Donniford.
18	156	WATCHET.
	159½	Carhampton.
23	161	DUNSTER.
	163½	MINEHEAD.
		To Porlock 6m.; thence to Ilfracombe 28m.

TO SOUTH MOLTON.

L.D.	M.	
*	138	BRIDGEWATER.
	139½	Durleigh.
4	142	Enmore.
9	147	West Bagborough.
	150½	Willet.
	154½	Raleigh's Cross.
18	156	Holwelslade.
	159½	Woolcot.
	163½	Heal Bridge.
27	165	DULVERTON.
		Thence, p. 70, to
40	177¾	SOUTH MOLTON.
		L. *to Torrington* [D].

Variations of Route, and Branch Routes.

[A]	M.
ANDOVER	63½
Weyhill	66¾
[Wilts.]	
LUDGERSHALL	70¾
East Everley	75¾
West Everley	76¾
Uphaven	80¾
Rushall	81½
Charlton	82¾
Connock	86
R. *to Devizes 5m.*	
Urchfont	87½
Easterton	89
EAST LAVINGTON	90
Littleton Pannel	91½
Little Cheverel	92
Earl Stoke	94
Eddington	96¼
Bratton	97
WESTBURY	99½
[B] Another Route:	
DEVIZES (p. 72),	88¼
Summerham Bridge,	91½
Seend	92¾
Littleton	94¾
Hilperton	97¾
R. *to Bradford 3m.*	
TROWBRIDGE	98¼
Studley	99¾
Southwick	101
[Som.] Road	103¼
Beckington	104¾
FROME	107¾
[C] Another Route:	
BRUTON (p. 70)	109
King's Weston	120
PIPER'S INN	126¾
BRIDGEWATER	137
[D]	
SOUTH MOLTON	176¾
Kingsland	178
Blackmantle	182
Atherington	185¼
TORRINGTON	192¼

* BRIDGEWATER.

LONDON TO BATH, BY DEVIZES.

Route of the BATH, EXETER, and PLYMOUTH Mail.

Variations of Route, and Branch Routes.

[A]	M.
READING	39
Purley	44
PANGBOURN	45
Streatley	48
Compton	52
EAST ILSLEY	54
West Ilsley	55½
Farnborough	58
Fawley	60
LAMBOURN	65
Another Route:	
Speen	56¾
Welford	62¼
Great Shefford	64¼
LAMBOURN	68¼
[B]	
To Wotton Basset:	
HUNGERFORD,	64
[Wilts.] Chilton	65½
Ramsbury	68
Albourne	71
Liddington	76
SWINDON	80
WOTTON BASSET	86½
Another Route:	
FARRINGDON, p. 8	69¼
HIGHWORTH	76
SWINDON	82½
WOTTON BASSET	89
[C]	
BECKHAMPTON INN	81
Shepherd's Shore	84
Sandy Lane	89
On R. Bowood, Mar. of Lansdown.	
On L. Spy Park.	
Bowden Hill	91
Laycock	92½
On R. Laycock Abbey.	
Corsham	95¾
Pickwick	96¾
Box	99¼
[Som.] Bath Easton	102¼
BATH	105¼

L.D.	M. from Hyde Park Corner.
	Berkshire.
13	26 Maidenhead (p. 1).
	26¾ Golden Fleece.
11	28 Maidenhead Thicket.
	Shottesbrook, on L.
7	32 Hare Hatch.
5	34 Twyford (Wilts).
	36 On R. Sunning.
*	39 READING.
	Other Routes are by Windsor (p. 1), or by Egham and Wokingham, p. 61.
	R. to *East Ilsley* [A].
	41½ Calcot Green.
	43¾ THEAL.
8	47 L. to *Kingsclere*, p. 62.
10	49 WOOLHAMPTON.
	52¾ Thatcham.
	55 On R. Shaw.
17	55¾ SPEENHAMLAND.
	On L. NEWBURY.
	56 SPEEN HILL.
18	56¾ Speen.
	R. to *Lambourn* [A].
	59½ Halfway House.
25	64 HUNGERFORD.
	R. to *Swindon* [B].
	Wiltshire.
28	67 Froxfield.
	L. to *Great Bedwin* 2¼m.
	69 On R. Ramsbury Park, Sir F. Burdett, Bt.
32	71 Savernake Forest.

L.D.	M. from Hyde Park Corner.
	74 MARLBOROUGH.
30	76½ Fifield.
	77¾ Overton.
	79 West Kennet.
	80 Silbury Hill.
25	81 BECKHAMPTON INN.
	R. to *Bath by Sandy Lane* [C].
	84 Wand's Dyke.
18	88¼ DEVIZES.
	Another Route is by Andover and Ludgershall (p. 71), 91 miles.
15	91¼ Selves Green.
	92¼ L. to *Trowbridge* 6¼m.
	Seend, on L.
11	95¼ MELKSHAM.
	L. to *Bradford* 6m. [E].
	97 Shaw.
	97½ Shaw Hill.
8	98½ Atford.
	101 Blue Vein T. G.
	Wraxhall, on L.
	102 Kingsdown Hill.
	Somersetshire.
3	103½ Bathford.
	104 Bath Easton.
	105¼ Walcot T. G.
*	106½ BATH.
	Other Routes are by Calne, see next page, or by Sandy Lane [C].

LONDON TO BRISTOL;

Continued to SWANSEA and CAERMARTHEN, and thence to MILFORD HAVEN.

Variations of Route, and Branch Routes.

M.

[D]

CHIPPENHAM .. 92¾
Corsham House .. 96
Pickwick 97
Box T. G. 99¾
[Som.] Bath Easton 103¼
BATH 105¾
Thence to Bristol:
Twyverton 108¼
L. *to Pensford* 8m.
Keynsham 114¼
Brislington 117
Redcliffe 119¼
Cross the riv. Avon.
[Glouc.] BRISTOL 119¾

[E]

Another Route:
EAST LAVINGTON (p. 71).... 90
Worton 93¼
Bulkington 95¾
Hilperton 100
TROWBRIDGE . 101
Cross the riv. Avon.
BRADFORD 103
Thence to Bath 8¼m.

[F]

NEWPORT 141
Bassalig 144
[Glamorganshire.]
CAERPHILLY .. 153¼
Bridgewater Arms. 156¾
Quaker's Yard 161¾
MERTHYR TYDVIL 169¼
Or, CARDIFF .. 153¼
Whitchurch 156¾
Bridgewater Arms - 164¾
MERTHYR TYDVIL 176½

[G]

SWANSEA 199¼
Olchfa 202½
Penmaen 209
PENRICE 212

L.D. | M. *from Hyde Park Corner.*

Wiltshire.

32 | 81 BECKHAMPTON INN, as on the oppos. page.
84¼ Cherhill.
26 | 87 CALNE.
88 On R. Bremhill ..
On L. Bowood, Marq. of Lansdown.
90¼ Derry Hill.
26 | 92¾ CHIPPENHAM.
L. *to Bath* [D].
98½ Ford T. G.
13 | 100 Wraxhall.

Gloucestershire.

11 | 102 MARSHFIELD.
8 | 105 Tog Hill.
107 Wick.
4 | 109 Warmley.
111 St. George's.
* | 113 BRISTOL.

[*Prospective Distances:*
Black Rock Inn. 13¼m.
Newport 28
Cardiff 40¼
Cowbridge 58
Neath 78
Swansea 86½
Caermarthen ..113
Tenby 141½
Haverfordwest..146
Milford Haven -153½]

L. *to Weston on the Sea* [K].

L.D. | M. *from Hyde Park Corner.*

120 Compton Greenfield.
122 R. *to Aust, or Old Passage House,* 3m.; *thence to Monmouth,* p. 76.
3 | 123½ NEW PASSAGE.
Cross the Severn at High Water.

Monmouthshire.

* | 126½ BLACK ROCK INN.
R. *to Chepstow* 5m.
1 | 127½ Portskewit.
129 Crick.
4 | 130½ CAERWENT.
R. *to Uske* 8m.; *thence to Pontypool* 7m.
6 | 132¼ Rock and Fountain.
8 | 134½ On R. Wentworth Lodge.
136 Catt's Ash.
137½ R. *to Caerleon* 1½m.
12 | 138¼ Christchurch.
141 NEWPORT.
[*By Gloucester* 146½m.]
R. *to Pontypool* 8m.
144 Bassalig.
R. *to Caerphilly* [F].
20 | 146¼ Halfway House.
22 | 148¼ St. Melons.
150 Rumney Bridge.

Variations of Route, and Branch Routes.

	M.
[H]	
PONTARDILLIS ..	208½
Caerm.] Llanelly .	215
KIDWELLY	224
[I]	
HAVERFORD-WEST	259¼
Pelcombe	261½
Trecoyd	263
Newgal Sands	268
Solvach	272
ST. DAVIDS	275
By Gloucester and Brecon to Haverfordwest 265m. By Llandovery and Cardigan (p. 75) *265m., thus,*	
CARDIGAN	232
Pemb.]	
St. Dogmael's	233½
Velindre	240
NEWPORT	243
FISHGUARD ...	250
Marthree	256
Penlan	258
ST. DAVIDS	265
[K]	
BRISTOL	113
Som.] Bedminster	114½
Long Ashton......	116
Bourton	118¾
Blackwall........	121
Congresbury	125
Paxton	127
Worll	129½
Weston on the Sea	132½
[L]	
Horsley, p. 76	101½
DURSLEY	108
Berkeley Heath ..	111½
BERKELEY	113
L. *to Thornbury* 8m.	
Or,	
CIRENCESTER, p. 8	88¼
TETBURY	96¼
DURSLEY	108½

L.D.	M. *from Hyde Park Corner.*
	Glamorganshire.
	151¾ Roath.
46	153¼ CARDIFF.
	Cross the river Tafe.
	R. *to Llandaff* 2½m.; *thence to Llantrissent* 8½m.
44	155¾ Ely Bridge.
	159¼ St. Nicholas.
	161¼ Bonvilston.
34	165¾ COWBRIDGE.
	171 Corntown.
	172 EWENNY BRIDGE.
	R. *to Bridgend* 2m.
21	178¾ PYLE INN.
19	180¼ Margram.
	184 Taybach.
	185 Aberavon.
	188 Briton Ferry.
8½	191 NEATH.
3	196½ Morriston.
	On R. Clasemont, Sir J. Morris, Bart.
	Forward to Cross Inon, 4m., leaving Swansea on the left, which saves 4m. of distance.
*	199½ SWANSEA.
	L. *to Penrice* [G].
	— *to Llanelly, by Llwghor Ferry,* 11m.
	203 Cadley.
5	204½ Cross Inon.
9	208½ PONTARDILLIS.
	L. *to Llanelly* [H].

L.D.	M. *from Hyde Park Corner.*
	Caermarthenshire.
	210 Gibrantwyd.
56	210¾ Brymind.
53	213¼ LLANNON.
50	216½ Pontyberem.
46	220½ Llangyndeyrn.
	226 CAERMARTHEN.
39	227½ Stony Bridge.
	233 Pool-y-Gravel.
31	235½ ST. CLARES.
29	237½ Llandowror.
	Pembrokeshire.
24	242¼ TAVERNSPITE.
20	246½ Cold Blow.
	L. *to Tenby* 8m.
18	248¼ NARBETH.
	250 Robbeston.
	251 Caniston Bridge.
13	253¾ Mid County House.
7	259¼ HAVERFORD-WEST.
	R. *to St. Davids* [I].
6	260 Merlin's Bridge.
3	263 Johnston.
	265 Stainton.
*	266½ MILFORD HAVEN.
	[*By Gloucester and Brecon, as on the opposite page,* 256½m.]

LONDON TO CAERMARTHEN;

By GLOUCESTER and BRECON. Thence to TENBY.

Variations of Route, and Branch Routes.

[A]

Another Route from Gloucester to Monmouth is through Mitchel Dean, as follows:

	M.
GLOUCESTER ..	103¼
Highnam	105¾
Churcham........	107½
Huntley T. G.	111
MITCHEL DEAN	116
R. *to Ross* 6m.	
Through the Forest of Dean.	
COLFORD	124
Red Brook	126½
MONMOUTH....	129
Wonastow	131½
RAGLAND	137
Clytha	140
ABERGAVENNY	146

[A 2]

To Pontypool:

RAGLAND (above)	137
USKE	142
PONTYPOOL ..	149

Another R. is by Bristol and New Passage (p. 73), 145½m.

[B]

TRECASTLE	177½
[Carm.] Talsarn ..	184½
LLANGADOCK -	188

Thence to Llandilo Vaur 8½m.

[C]

LLANDOVERY -	186¾
Pymsaint	194½
[Card.] LLANBEDER	203
R. *to Tregarron* 11m.	
Rhydowen	212½
[Caerm.] NEWCASTLE IN EMLYN	222
L. *to Kilgarron* 8m.	
[Card.] CARDIGAN	232

L.D.	M. *from Tyburn Turnpike.*	
		Herefordshire.
10	120	ROSS, p. 5 [A].
	120¾	Wilton T. G.
7	123¼	Pencraig.
6	124½	Goodrich.
4	126¼	Whitchurch.
		Monmouthshire.
*	130¼	MONMOUTH.
		Other Routes are by Aust Passage and Chepstow, p. 76.
2	132¼	Wonastow.
		R. *to Ragland, thence to Abergavenny* [A].
4	134	Dinastow.
7	137	Tregare.
8	138½	Bryngwyn.
13	143	Llangattock.
17	147	ABERGAVENNY.
	148½	Pentre.
	149¼	Llanwenarth.
		Brecknockshire.
	151¼	Llangranach.
	153¼	CRICKHOWEL.
12	155	Pontybrynert.
9	158	Bwlch.
6	160½	Llansaintfraid.
	162	Skethrog.
	163¼	Llanhamlach.
*	166¼	BRECON.

L.D.	M. *from Tyburn Turnpike.*	
	169	Llanspyddyd.
	172	Penpont.
	175	Rhyd-y-Brue.
67	177½	TRECASTLE.
		L. *to Llangadock* [B].
66	178½	Llwyel.
		Caermarthenshire.
	186	Velindre.
58	186¾	LLANDOVERY.
		R. *to Cardigan* [C].
	194	Llanwrda.
50	194½	Maesgoed Inn.
	198¼	Cledvulch.
	200	Rosmana.
43	201¼	LLANDILO VAUR.
41	203¼	Golden Grove.
	208	Llanarthy.
	215	Llangwnnor.
	216	CAERMARTHEN.
27	217½	Stony Bridge.
	223	Pool-y-Gravel.
19	225½	ST. CLARE'S.
		L. *to Laugharn* 3m.
17	227½	Llandowror.
		Pembrokeshire.
12	232½	TAVERNSPITE.
	236¼	Cold Blow.
		R. *to Milford Haven.* See opposite page.
7	237½	Templeton.
		R. *to Pembroke* 11m.
	240	Begelly.
*	244½	TENBY.

LONDON TO CHEPSTOW, BY AUST PASSAGE;

And thence to MONMOUTH.

Variations of Route, and Branch Routes.

	M.
[A]	
GLOUCESTER by High Wycombe (p. 4)	103½
Highnam	105½
Minsterworth	107½
Westbury	112
NEWNHAM	115
Blakeney	118
Lydney	121½
Alveston	124
Woolaston	125
Tiddenham	128½
Cross the Wye.	
[Monm.] CHEPSTOW	130
St. Pierre's	133½
Crick	134½
Thence, p. 73, to NEWPORT	146½
[B]	
FARRINGDON, p. 8	69¾
Coleshill	72¾
[Wilts.] HIGHWORTH	76
Cold Harbour Inn.	79¾
Water Eaton	82¼
CRICKLADE	84
Another Route:	
SWINDON, p. 72	80
Cold Harbour Inn.	84½
CRICKLADE	88¾
R. *to Cirencester* 6¾m.	
[C]	
Another Route:	
SWINDON, p. 72	80
Purton	86
Garsden	94
MALMESBURY	96½

L.D.	M. *from Hyde Park Corner.*	
		Wiltshire.
*	92¾	CHIPPENHAM, p. 73.
	96½	Yatton Keynell.
5	98	Castlecombe.
8	101	Nettleton.
		Gloucestershire.
	102	Acton Turville.
12	105	CROSS HANDS INN.
	106½	Old Sodbury.
15	108	CHIPPING SODBURY.
	109	Yate T. G.
	111½	Iron Acton.
22	115½	Alveston.
		R. *to Thornbury* 2½m.
	116	Rudgway.
	118	Olveston.
28	121	AUST PASSAGE INN.
		Cross the Severn to
19	122½	BEACHLEY PASSAGE HOUSE.
		Cross the river Wye.
		Monmouthshire.
15	126	CHEPSTOW.
		Other Routes are by Gloucester [A]; and by Bristol, p. 73.
12	129½	St. Arvans.
5	136½	Trelleck.
*	141½	MONMOUTH.
		[*By Bristol* 145½m.]

L.D.	M. *from Hyde Park Corner.*	
		ANOTHER ROUTE.
	84	CRICKLADE [B].
8	87½	Cove House.
2	93½	Charlton.
*	95½	MALMESBURY [C].
	99	Easton Grey.
5	100	Pinkney.
	101	Sherston.
8	103	Luckington.
		Gloucestershire.
11	106½	Acton Turville.
14	109½	CROSS HANDS INN.
		Thence, as in the annexed column.

ADDENDA.

L.D.	M.	
*	88½	CIRENCESTER, p. 8. Keep Oakley Park on R.
10	98½	MINCHING HAMPTON.
	[101½	RODBOROUGH.
	103	Cain's Cross.
		L. *to Frocester* 4m.
	103¾	Ebley.
	104¼	Stonehouse.]
12	100½	Nailsworth.
13	101½	Horsley.
	108	WOTTON UNDER EDGE.

LONDON TO CHICHESTER:

Thence to BOGNOR. With Branches to ARUNDEL.

Variations of Route, and Branch Routes.

[A]

	M.
Another R. is by	
EWELL (p. 79)..	12¾
EPSOM	14¼
LEATHERHEAD	18¼
Great Bookham ..	20¾
Effingham........	22
East Hornby	23¾
Merrow..........	28¾
GUILDFORD ..	30¼

These distances are from Westminster Bridge.

[B]

DORKING (p. 79)	23¼
Bear Green	27¼
OCKLEY GREEN..	30
[Sussex] Park Street,	37
Billinghurst	41
Adversane........	43
PULBOROUGH ..	46
Bury	51
Houghton Hill....	52¼
ARUNDEL [D] ..	55
Walberton	58
Yapton	60½
Felpham	64
BOGNOR	65½

[C]

PETWORTH	49
Fittleworth	52¼
Cross the riv. Rother.	
Bury	56
Houghton Hill....	57½
ARUNDEL......	60
LITTLE HAMPTON	64½

Another Route is by Horsham and Steyning:

STEYNING, p. 79,	50¼
Sompting	55¼
Broadwater Green,	56½
ARUNDEL......	65

[D]

At Arundel,
L. *to Worthing* 10*m.*
— *to New Shoreham* 16*m.*
— *to Brighton* 22*m.*

L. D.	M. *from London Bridge.*
	Surrey.
33	29½ GUILDFORD, by Kingston, p. 59, [A].
29	33¾ GODALMING.
	35¼ Milford.
	L. *to Petworth.* See next column.
24	38½ Brook Green.
	40¾ Gray's Wood.
20	42½ HASLEMERE.
	L. *to Petworth* 9½*m.*
	Sussex.
19	43½ Blue Bells.
	45½ Fernhurst.
	46½ Furley Hill.
12	50¼ MIDHURST.
	L. *to Petworth* 6*m.*
10	52¾ Cocking T. G.
	55¼ Singleton.
6	56½ West Dean.
	60 Mid Lavant.
	On L. Goodwood, D. of Richmond.
*	62½ CHICHESTER.
4	66½ Elbridge.
6	68½ South Berstead.
	70 BOGNOR.

Other Routes are by Petworth, as in the next column, or by Dorking and Arundel [B].

L. D.	M. *from London Bridge.*
	Surrey.
29	33¾ GODALMING, as in the preceding col.
	35¼ Milford.
	37 Witley.
23	40 Chidingfold.
21	42 Cripple Crouch Hill.
	On L. Shillingley, Earl Winterton.
	Sussex.
20	43 Fisher Street.
	R. *to Midhurst* 8½*m.*
	44 North Chapel.
	48½ On R. E. of Egremont.
14	49 PETWORTH.
	L. *to Arundel and Little Hampton* [C].
	Another Route to Arundel is by Dorking [B].
12	51½ Coultershall Mill T.G.
10	53 Duncton.
	55½ Waltham.
6	57 Benge's.
	L. *to Bognor* 10*m.*
	59½ Halnaker.
	On R. Duke of Richmond.
*	63 CHICHESTER.

LONDON TO BRIGHTON (a).

Variations of Route, and Branch Routes.

M.

[A]

From Westminster Bridge to

	M.
Kennington T. G.	1¼
Stockwell	2¼
Clapham Common	3¾
Upper Tooting	5¼
Lower Tooting	6
Upper Mitcham	7¼
Lower Mitcham	8¼
SUTTON	11¼
Obelisk on Banstead Downs	13
Canhatch Farm	15
Tadworth T. G.	16
R. *to Dorking* 9m.	
Over Walton Heath.	
Gatton Inn	19¼
REIGATE	21
Kinnersley Bridge	23
[Sussex] County Oak	28½
CRAWLEY	30¼

[B]

	M.
CROYDON	9½
GODSTONE GREEN,	19
New Chapel Green,	25
[Sussex.] Turner's Hill	30
Hapstead Green	34½
LINDFIELD	37
Wivelsfield	41
Ditchling T. G.	45
Clayton	47½
Piecombe	48½
Patcham	51
BRIGHTON	54½

[C]

	M.
GRINSTEAD	28½
Wych Cross T. G.	33½
Dane Hill	36½
Sheffield Bridge	38¼
CHAILEY COMMON,	41
Chailey	42½
Offham Street	47
LEWES	49
BRIGHTON	57½

L. D.	M. *from Westminster Bridge.*	
		Surrey.
	1¼	Kennington T. G.
	3¼	Brixton Causeway.
4	5¼	Streatham.
		R. *to Mitcham* 2m.
	6	Streatham Common.
*	9½	CROYDON.
	11½	Purley.
		L. *to Godstone Green; R. to*
	12	Foxley Hatch T. G.
4	13½	Leaden Cross.
	17½	Merstham.
	19	Division of the road.
		R. *to Reigate* 2¼m.
11	20¼	RED HILL.
13	22½	Salfords T. G.
15	24	HORLEY COMMON.
		L. *to Brighton through Balcombe.* See next column.
	26	Kimberham Bridge.
		Sussex.
20	29	CRAWLEY. Junction of the road through Reigate [A].
	33½	Hand Cross.
17	35	Staplefield Common.
12	40	HICKSTED.
10	42	Albourn Green.
7	45¼	Dale T. G.
6	46	Piecombe.
	48½	Patcham.
	50½	Preston T. G.
*	52	BRIGHTON.

By BALCOMBE *and* CUCKFIELD.

[This road is hilly, but affords very extensive prospects.]

L. D.	M.	
	24	HORLEY COMMON.
		Sussex.
22	29½	Worth.
	33	Balcombe.
14	37¼	CUCKFIELD.
	41	St. John's Common.
	43	Friar's Oak Inn.
6	45½	Piecombe.
	48	Patcham.
*	51½	BRIGHTON.

(a) The Route to Brighton admits of the following variations;

1.	By Croydon, Crawley, and Hicksted, as above	52 m.
2.	By a diversion from the above route at Horley, through Balcombe and Cuckfield	51½
3.	By Sutton, Reigate, and Crawley [A], the King's Route	53¼
4.	By Godstone Green and Lindfield [B]	54½
5.	By Grinstead and Lewes through Uckfield, p. 79	58
6.	By Ditto, through Chailey [C]	57½
7.	By Dorking and Horsham [G]	57¾

LONDON TO BRIGHTON, BY LEWES.

L.D.	M. from Westminster Bridge.
	Surrey.
*	9½ CROYDON, p. 78. [*From Cornhill* 10½*m.*]
2	11½ Purley.
	14 Rose and Crown.
6	15½ Marden Park.
	19 GODSTONE GREEN. R. *to Bletchingley* 1½*m.*
	23 Blindley Heath T. G.
	25 New Chapel Green. *To Brighton by Lindfield* [B].
	Sussex.
17	26¾ Fellbridge.
21	28½ EAST GRINSTEAD.
	31 Forest Row.
16	33½ Wych Cross T. G. R. *to Chailey* [C].
13	36½ Nutley.
10	39½ MARESFIELD.
8	41½ UCKFIELD. L. *to Horsbridge* [D].
6	43½ Horstead.
*	49½ LEWES. L. *to Seaford* [E].
2	51½ Ashcomb.
4	53¾ Falmer.
8½	58 BRIGHTON.

ROUTE XLVII.]

LONDON TO WORTHING.

L.D.	M. from Westminster Bridge.
	Surrey.
	1¼ Kennington T. G. [H].
	2¼ Stockwell.
	3¾ Clapham Common.
9	5¼ Upper Tooting.
	6 Lower Tooting.
	7 Merton.
5	9¼ Morden.
4	10¼ North Cheam.
	12¾ EWELL.
*	14¼ EPSOM.
	16¼ ASHTEAD.
4	18¼ LEATHERHEAD. R. *to Guildford* 12½*m.*
6	20¼ Mickleham.
	23¼ DORKING.
10	26½ Holmwood T. G.
	27¼ Bear Green. R. *to Arundel*, p. 77.
7	29¼ Capel.
	Sussex.
	32 Kingsfold T. G.
*	36¼ HORSHAM. L. *to Brighton* [G].
6	42¾ West Grinstead. L. *to Steyning* [F].
11	47 Ashington T. G.
15	51½ Finden.
18	54¾ Broadwater.
20	56 WORTHING.

Variations of Route, and Branch Routes.

	M.
[D]	
UCKFIELD	41½
Little Horstead	44
East Hoathley	46½
Whitesmith Green	48½
HORSBRIDGE	52½
R. *to Hailsham* 1½*m.*	
Swine's Hill T. G.	56½
Willingdon	57¾
EAST BOURNE	59¾
SOUTH BOURNE	60½
Another Route, p. 80.	
[E]	
LEWES	49½
Iford	51½
Piddinghoe	55½
NEWHAVEN	56½
Bishopstone	58½
SEAFORD	60
[F]	
HORSHAM	36¼
West Grinstead	42¾
Partridge Green	44¾
STEYNING	50½
R. *to Worthing* 10*m.* —*to Arundel* 14½*m.* See page 77.	
Bramber	51½
L. *to Brighton* 9½*m.*	
Beeding	52
NEW SHOREHAM	55¾
[G]	
HORSHAM	36¼
Cowfold	43¼
Corner House T. G.	45¼
HENFIELD	47¼
Saddlescombe	52¼
BRIGHTON	57¼

[H]

From London Bridge to Kennington T. G. 2*m.*
From Vauxhall Bridge 1*m.*
From Hyde Park Corner over ditto 2½*m.*

LONDON to HASTINGS.

Variations of Route, and Branch Routes.

[A]	M.
Another Route:	
London Bridge to Elephant and Castle	1
Walworth........	2
Camberwell Green	3
[*From Hyde Park Corner* 3½*m.*]	
Denmark Hill	3½
Dulwich Hill	4½
Dulwich	5
L. *to Sydenham* 2¼*m.*	
Penge T. G.......	6
[Kent.] Beckenham	9
BROMLEY......	10½
Thence to Westerham:	
Keston	15¼
Leaver Green	16¾
South Street.......	19½
WESTERHAM ..	22¼

[B]	
Hurst Green T. G.	47½
Silver Hill	48¾
Springate's Hill ..	49½
Knowl Hill T. G...	51
Staple Cross.......	53½
Horn's Cross	56½
Beckley	57¾
Peasmarsh	59½
RYE............	63¼
WINCHELSEA..	66½
Another Route:	
Flimwell	44½
Seacock Heath.....	45¾
[Kent.] HIGHGATE	47½
Sandhurst.........	50¼
Newenden	52½
[Sus.] Northiam ..	54½
Beckley	56
Four Oaks.......	57½
Peasmarsh	59
RYE............	63

Another Route is by Maidstone (p. 81) 68*m.*

L.D.	M. *from London Bridge.*
	Kent.
	3½ New Cross T. G.
	[*From Hyde Park Corner, over Vauxhall Bridge, 6m.*]
	5½ Lewisham.
	7½ South End.
	9 Bromley Hill.
20	9¾ BROMLEY [A].
	R. *to Westerham 7m.*
	10½ Mason's Hill.
	13 Lock's Bottom.
16	14 FARNBOROUGH.
15	15 Green Street Green.
	16½ Pratt's Bottom.
	17½ Rushmore Hill.
10	20 Morant's Court Hill.
9	21 Dunton.
8	22 RIVER HEAD.
	L. *to Maidstone* 17½*m.*
	23½ SEVEN OAKS.
	24½ SEVEN OAKS COMMON.
5	25 River Hill.
	27 Watt's Cross.
*	30 TUNBRIDGE.
	L. *to Tunbridge Wells.*
5	35 Wood's Gate T. G.
	36½ Kipping's Cross.
	Sussex.
18	40 LAMBERHURST.
	Kent.
13	42¾ STONE CROUCH.

L.D.	M. *from London Bridge.*
	Sussex.
	44½ Flimwell.
	47½ Hurst Green T. G.
	L. *to Rye* [B].
14	50 ROBERTSBRIDGE.
	52½ Vine Hall.
	L. *to Rye* 11¾*m.*
10	54 Wartlington.
8	56 BATTLE.
	R. *to Bexhill 9m.*
	58 Crowhurst Park.
5	59 Beauport.
	61½ Ore.
*	64 HASTINGS.

ANOTHER ROUTE.

L.D.	M.
36	30 TUNBRIDGE.
33	33 Southborough.
	35½ TUNBRIDGE WELLS.
	Sussex.
28	37¾ Frant.
	[43½ Mayfield.
	48 Cross in Hand.
	51 Horeham.
	55 HORSEBRIDGE.
	62¼ EAST BOURNE.
	63 SOUTH BOURNE.]
24	42 Wadhurst.
	48½ Flimwell.
14	52 ROBERTSBRIDGE.
	Thence, as above, to
*	66 HASTINGS.

LONDON TO MAIDSTONE;

Continued to HYTHE and FOLKSTONE; and to TENTERDEN and NEW ROMNEY.

Variations of Route, and Branch Routes.

[A]	M.
ELTHAM	8
Southend	9
Chislehurst	11½
ST. MARY CRAY	13½
Or, LEE	6
Mottingham	8¼
Chislehurst	11
ST. MARY CARY	13¼
[B]	
WROTHAM HEATH	26
Teston	31
Linton	35½
Staplehurst	41
CRANBROOK ..	45½
Hartley Street	47½
HIGHGATE	50
Newenden	55¼
[Sussex.] Northiam -	57¼
Four Oaks	60
Peasmarsh	61¾
RYE	65½
Another Route:	
MAIDSTONE	34¼
Loose	36¾
Linton	38
Stile Bridge	40
Staplehurst	43½
CRANBROOK ..	48
HIGHGATE	52½
Thence as above.	
[C]	
Charing	48
Westwell	50¾
Eastwell	52¼
Boughton Lees	53¼
WYE	55¼
[D]	
TUNBRIDGE, p. 80	30
Kipping's Cross	36¾
Matfield Green	38¼
Brenchley	39¾
Horsemonden Heath	41½
Goudhurst Gore....	43
Idon Green	45½
Thence, col. 3. to NEW ROMNEY..	70

L.D.	M. *from London Bridge.*
	Kent.
	3½ New Cross T. G.
	[*From Hyde Park Corner* 6*m.*]
29	5¼ Lewisham.
	R. *to Bromley* 5*m.*
	6 LEE.
26	8 ELTHAM.
	9 Southend.
	To St. Mary Cray [A].
23	11½ Sidcup.
22	12 FOOT'S CRAY.
	14 Birchwood Corner.
17	17½ FARNINGHAM.
13	21¼ Kingsdown.
10	24 WROTHAM.
8	26 WROTHAM HEATH.
	R. *to Cranbrook* [B].
6	28½ — *to West Malling* ½*m.*
	30 Larkfield.
4	30½ Ditton.
	L. *to Aylesford* 2*m.*
	Cross the Medway.
*	34¼ MAIDSTONE.
	To Tenterden. See next col.
1	35½ On R. the Mote, Earl of Romney.
5	39¼ On R. Leeds Castle.
	43 Harrietsham Street.
10	44½ LENHAM.
14	48 Charing.
	L. *to Wye* 7½*m.* [C].
18	52 Hothfield Heath.

L.D.	M. *from London Bridge.*
20	54¼ ASHFORD.
22	56½ Willesborough.
24	58¼ Mersham Heath.
27	61½ Sellinge.
	65 Pedling Street.
33	67 HYTHE.
	69¾ SANDGATE.
37	71½ FOLKESTONE.
	Other Routes are by Canterbury, p. 82.

To NEW ROMNEY.

L.D.	M.
*	34¼ MAIDSTONE.
	36¾ Loose.
4	38 Linton.
6	40 Stile Bridge.
	43½ Staplehurst.
	To Cranbrook [B].
10	44 Idon Green.
	47¼ Milkhouse Street.
	L. *to Smarden* 7½*m.*
14	48 Gofford Green.
	51 Forston Green.
20	54 TENTERDEN.
	55¼ Leigh Green.
	57½ Reding Street.
26	60 Appledore.
28	62¼ Snargate.
	63¾ Brenzett Corner.
32	66¼ Old Romney.
	R. *to Lydd* 3*m.*
34	68½ NEW ROMNEY.
	Another Route is by Tunbridge [D].

LONDON TO CANTERBURY;

Thence to DOVER, DEAL, MARGATE, and RAMSGATE.

Variations of Route, and Branch Routes.

	M.
[A]	
Another Route:	
New Cross T. G. ..	3½
Lewisham	5¼
Lee..............	6
ELTHAM	8
Blendon	11½
Bexley Heath ..	13
DARTFORD	16¾
[B]	
ROCHESTER	29¼
The Bull..........	33
Boxley Hill	33½
MAIDSTONE	37¾
[C]	
Key Street........	38
King's Ferry	42
QUEENBORO' ..	45
SHEERNESS	47
[D]	
CANTERBURY ..	55¼
Bridge............	58¼
Halfway House	63
Lydden	66
Ewell T. G.	67¾
Buckland	69¼
DOVER..........	71
[E]	
CANTERBURY ..	55¼
Littlebourn........	59¼
Brandling	60½
Wingham	62
Ash	64½
SANDWICH	68
How Bridge	72
Cottington	72¾
Upper Deal........	74
LOWER DEAL ..	75
Another Route:	
Brandling, as above,	60½
Knowlton	64½
How Bridge	69
DEAL............	72

L.D.	M. from London Bridge.	
		Kent.
	3½	New Cross T. G.
		[*From Hyde Park Corner 6m.*
	4	Deptford Bridge.
		L. *to Greenwich* 1m.; *thence to Woolwich* 3.
	5	BLACKHEATH.
		L. *to Woolwich through Charlton 4m.*
21	8	SHOOTER'S HILL.
		R. *to Eltham* 1½m.
		L. *to Woolwich* 1½m.
19	10¼	Welling.
18	11¼	BEXLEY HEATH.
	13	Crayford.
		R. *to Foot's Cray 5m.*
14	15	DARTFORD [A].
	17	Horn's Cross.
9	20½	Northfleet.
7	22	GRAVESEND.
	23	Milton.
6	26¼	Chalk Street T. G.
	26½	Gad's Hill.
	28½	Strood.
		Cross the riv. Medway.
*	29¼	ROCHESTER.
		R. *to Maidstone* [B].
1	30¼	CHATHAM.
5	34	Rainham.
	34¾	Mool Street.
	36¾	Newington Street.
9	38	Key Street.
		L. *to Sheerness* [C].
10	39	Chalk Well.
		L. *to Milton* 1m.

L.D.	M. from London Bridge.	
	39¾	SITTINGBOURNE.
	41	Bapchild.
	42½	Green Street.
26	46	Ospringe.
		L. *to Faversham* 1m.
	49	Boughton Street.
22	50	Boughton Hill.
	52¾	Harbledown T. G.
17	55¼	CANTERBURY.
		R. *to Dover* [D].
		— *to Deal* [E].
		— *to Folkestone* 17m. *or through Elham* 18m.
	57¾	Sturry.
	61½	Upstreet.
		Enter Isle of Thanet.
8	64	Sarr.
7	65¼	On L. St. Nicholas at Wade.
	68½	Birchington.
	70¼	Street.
*	72	MARGATE.
2	74¼	St. Peters.
	75½	BROADSTAIRS.

To RAMSGATE.

L.D.	M.	
9	64	Sarr, as above.
	66½	Monkton.
		To Margate 3½m.
	68½	Mount Pleasant.
	69½	Minster Mills.
1	72	Nether Court.
*	73	RAMSGATE.

LONDON TO SOUTH END. [A]

L.D.	M. from Whitechapel Church.
	Middlesex,
	1¾ Limehouse Church.
	3¼ Iron Bridge across the Lea.
	Essex.
	4¼ Plaistow.
	6 East Ham.
*	7 BARKING.
	10¼ L. *to Dagenham* 1*m.*
4	11 Beam River Gate.
	12½ Rainham.
7	14 Winnington.
	15 L. *to Aveley* [B].
9	16 Purfleet.
11	18 West Thurrock.
	20½ GRAY'S THURROCK.
	23½ Chadwell.
19	24 West Tilbury T. G.
	R. *to Tilbury Fort* 2½*m.*
	25½ Muckingford.
16	27 Junction of the road through Aveley and Stifford.
	27¾ Stanford le Hope.
12	31½ Vange.
	33½ Pitsea.
6	37½ Junction of road from Billericay.
	38 Hadleigh,
3	40 Adam's Elm.
	R. *to Leigh* ½*m.*
	41¾ L. *to Prittlewell* ½*m.*
*	43¼ SOUTH END.

ROUTE LII.]

LONDON TO HARROW:

Continued to AMERSHAM and AYLESBURY. Thence to Buckingham, Banbury, and Warwick, pp. 14, 15.

L.D.	M. from Tyburn Turnpike.
	Middlesex.
	¾ Paddington.
	Cross Grand Junction Canal.
	1½ Westborn Green.
	3 Kensell Green.
	4¼ Holsden Green.
	5¾ Stone Bridge.
	7 Wembley Green.
	10 HARROW ON THE HILL.
	R. *to Watford.*
	13 Pinner.
	15½ Northwood.
	Hertfordshire.
24	16½ Bacher Heath.
	18 RICKMANSWORTH [C].
21	19¾ Chorley Wood.
	Buckinghamshire.
19	21¼ Cheynies.
	26¼ AMERSHAM [D.]
12	28½ Little Missenden.
	31 GREAT MISSENDEN.
5	35½ WENDOVER.
	40 Walton T. G.
*	40½ AYLESBURY.

Variations of Route, and Branch Routes.

[A]

Other Routes are by Romford and Gray's Thurrock, p. 54, and by Billericay and Rochford, p. 55; or by Billericay, avoiding Rochford, as follows:

	M.
BILLERICAY....	23
South Green	24½
Cray Hill	27
Wickford	29
Raleigh	34
Hadleigh Common	36½
SOUTH END	42

[B]

By turning on the left through Aveley and Stifford, leaving Gray's Thurrock out of the route, the distance will be reduced about 3½ miles.

[C]

Another Route:

EDGEWARE(p.84)	8
Stanmore	10
Hatch End	12
Pinner Green......	14½
North Wood	16
Bacher Heath	17
RICKMANSWORTH	18½

Or, by Watford (See next page) leaving Cashiobury Park on the right, 17½ miles.

[D]

Another Route:

UXBRIDGE (p. 9)	15
Tatling End	18
Chalfont, St. Pe.er's	20½
Chalfont, St. Giles..	22½
AMERSHAM	26

LONDON TO COVENTRY, CHESTER, &c.

From the West-end of the Metropolis,

Through HEMEL HEMPSTEAD and LEIGHTON BUSSARD: with Branches to WOBURN, AMPTHILL, and NORTHAMPTON. [A]

Variations of Route, and Branch Routes.

[A]

This forms the shortest line of communication between the west end of the metropolis, and the great roads leading to Liverpool, Chester, Holyhead, and Manchester.

[B]

From St. Giles's Pound to

Camden Town 1¼
Mother Red Caps .. 1½
R. *to Highgate* 2½*m.*
Haverstock Hill.... 2¾
Hampstead.......... 3½
Over the Heath to North End......... 4¼
Goulder's Green.... 5½
Hendon 8¼
R. *to Mill Hill* 2*m.*
EDGEWARE 9½

[C]

Another road from Leighton, saving half a mile of distance, is thro' Stoke Hammond and Water Eaton, which here enters the Holyhead road at the 45th mile stone from Hicks's Hall.

[D]

LEIGHTON....... 37
Cross the Holyhead Road 40½
WOBURN 42¾
Through the Park.
Ridgemont......... 44¾
Lidlington T. G. .. 47
AMPTHILL........ 50
Thence to Bedford 8*m.*
Other Routes to Ampthill are by St. Albans and Luton, and by Dunstable. See p. 19.

L.D.	M. *from Tyburn Turnpike.*
	Middlesex.
	½ Paddington T. G.
	2¼ Kilburn.
	4 Cricklewood.
	6¼ Hyde.
	6½ Junction of Road from Hampstead and Hendon [B].
15	8 EDGEWARE.
	9¾ R. *to St. Alban's* 12*m.*; *thence to Luton and Bedford.* See p. 19.
	Turn on L. to
13	10 Stanmore.
	11½ Bushey Heath.
	On L. Bentley Priory, Marq. of Abercorn.
	Hertfordshire.
10	13¼ BUSHEY.
	14½ WATFORD.
	On L. Cashiobury Park, Earl of Essex.
	L. *to Rickmansworth.*
6	16¾ On L. Grove Park, Earl of Clarendon.
	17¾ Upper Highway.
2	21 Belswains.
	21¾ Corner Hall.
*	23 HEMEL HEMPSTEAD.
	23¾ Picket's End.
2	25¼ Water End.

L.D.	M. *from Tyburn Turnpike.*
	28 Mile Barn.
	L. *to Ivingho* 5*m.*
	Buckinghamshire.
	29¾ Dagnal.
	R. *to Dunstable by the New Road.*
	31¼ Cross Icknield Way.
20	32 Eddlesbrough, Rev. W. B. Wroth.
	33¼ Northall.
	Bedfordshire.
	35 Billington.
15	37 LEIGHTON BUSSARD.
	[*From Hicks's Hall, by Barnet and Hockliffe,* (p. 18) 40¾ *m.*]
13	39 Heath and Reach.
	40½ Enter the Holyhead Road, near the 41st mile stone from Hicks's Hall.
	Forward to Woburn and Ampthill [D].
	Turn on the L. to
11	41¼ Shire Ash.
	Buckinghamshire.
	42¼ LITTLE BRICKHILL.
7	44¾ Fenny Stratford [C].
	R. *to Newport Pagnell* 6*m.*; *thence to Olney* 5½*m.* See page 24.

* STONEY STRATFORD.

Variations of Route, and Branch Routes.

[E]

These distances from Tyburn Turnpike differ only a quarter of a mile from those measured from Hicks's Hall.

[F]

	M.
Erdington	107½
WALSALL	115¾
Bloxwich	118¾
Streetway	123¾
Four Crosses	124¾
Spread Eagle	127
IVETSEY BANK	132

[G]

	M.
WHITCHURCH	160
[Flintsh.] Bangor Is-coed	171
Cross the Dee	
[Denb.] Marchwiail	173½
WREXHAM	175¾
[Flint.] Caergwrle	181
Hope	181¾
MOLD	189
R. *to Flint* 6¼*m.*	
DENBIGH	205

[H]

Dawpool is about a mile and a half north of Parkgate, on the eastern bank of the Dee. Its site offering great facilities of communication between London & Dublin, as a packet station, an experimental trip was made by the Mountaineer steam packet, August 3, 1823. The passage was effected within 19 hours, though with a heavy gale of wind right in the teeth of the vessel on getting under weigh. The return voyage was effected in about 14 hours.

L.D.	M. *from Tyburn Turnpike.*
	48½ Sheuley.
39	52 STONEY STRATFORD.
	R. *to Northampton* (see p 30); *thence to Leicester, Derby, and Manchester.*
	Forward, (see p 19) to
	Warwickshire.
*	91 COVENTRY, and
	98½ STONE BRIDGE [E].
	L. *to Birmingham*, p. 19.
	Turn on R. (the old road to Chester) to
9	100 Little Packington.
	R. *to Lichfield*, p. 27.
	102½ Bacon's Inn.
14	105 Castle Bromwich.
	L. *to Birmingham* 5½*m.*
	107½ Erdington.
	R. *to Sutton Colefield* 3*m.*; *thence to Lichfield* 8½.
19	110 L. *to Walsall* [F].
	Staffordshire.
	113½ Mill Green.
24	115 Stonall.
	119½ Norton.
30	121 R. *to Cannock* 1*m.* *thence to Stafford* 9¾*m.*; *and through Namptwich to Chester*, p. 25.
	122½ Street Way. Junction of Road from Walsall [F].
	123½ Four Crosses Inn.
	L. *to Brewood* 5*m.*
	126 Spread Eagle.
	R. *to Penkridge* 2½*m.*

L.D.	M. *from Tyburn Turnpike.*
49	131 IVETSEY BANK.
	L. *to Shrewsbury* 23*m.*
	133 Weston under Lizard.
45	135 Parney Corner.
	Shropshire.
	136½ Woodcot.
	138 Chetwynd Aston.
41	139 NEWPORT.
	143 Stanford Bridge.
35	145 Hinstock.
	149 Sutton Heath.
29	151 TERN HILL.
	152½ Bletchley.
	155 Sandford.
	158½ Great Ash.
20	160 WHITCHURCH.
	R. *to Wrexham* [G].
	Cheshire.
18	162 Grindley Bridge.
	163 Bell on the Hill.
	164½ No Man's Heath.
14	166 Hampton Guide Post.
	R. *to Tarporley* 9½*m.*
	168½ Broxton.
	169½ Barnhill.
8	172 Handley.
	173 Golbourn Bridge.
5	175 High Halton.
	178½ Little Boughton.
*	179½ CHESTER.
	To Parkgate 12*m.* p. 26.
	To Dawpool 13½*m.* [H].

The mail route to Chester is by Northampton and Stafford, p. 24. Other routes are, through Birmingham from Coventry, p. 26.; or through Lichfield to Stafford, p. 27.

FROM THE WEST END OF THE METROPOLIS,

To the EAGLE at SNARESBROOK, on EPPING FOREST; thence to EPPING, CHIPPING ONGAR, &c. communicating with the North-east and Norfolk Roads.

L. D.	M. fr. Regent's Park Entrance.
	Middlesex.
	Along the New Road to
1	Battle Bridge T. G.
	L. to Highgate 3¼m.
1½	Pentonville, Angel.
	On L. into Islington.
	L. to Highgate; R. to
2¾	Ball's Pond T. G.
	To Enfield 8m. [A].
3¼	Kingsland T. G.
	L. to Tottenham and Edmonton, and onwards to WARE, *&c.* p. 49.
3¾	Dalston.
4¼	Hackney.
	R. to Homerton ½m.
5¼	Clapton T. G.
6	Lea Bridge.

L. D.	M. fr. Regent's Park Entrance.
	Essex.
6¾	*L. to Walthamstow ¾m.*
7¾	Low Layton.
8½	Whip's Cross.
9¾	Snaresbrook, the Eagle.
	L. to Woodford Wells; thence to EPPING, *and onwards to Cambridge, Newmarket, &c.* p. 53.
11½	Woodford Bridge.
13	CHIGWELL.
15½	ABRIDGE.
18½	Passingford Bridge.
21	Hare Street.
23½	CHIPPING ONGAR.
	To Dunmow 19½m. p. 53.
	To Chelmsford [B]; *thence to Colchester,* p. 56.

FROM HYDE PARK CORNER,

Over Vauxhall Bridge, to LEWISHAM and FOOT'S CRAY: with Branches communicating with the Sussex and Kent Roads.

L. D.	M. from Hyde Park Corner.
1½	Vauxhall Bridge.
	Surrey.
1¾	Vauxhall T. G.
	R. to Wandsworth 3½m.
2¼	Kennington Oval.
2½	Kennington T. G.
	To Streatham & Croydon. p. 78.
3½	Camberwell Green.
	R. to Dulwich 2m.
	— to Sydenham 4m.
4½	Peckham.

L. D.	M. from Hyde Park Corner.
	Kent.
6	New Cross T. G.
	L. to Greenwich 1¾m.; thence to Woolwich 2½m. [C].
	To Shooter's Hill, and thence along the Dover Road, p. 82.
8	Lewisham.
	L. to Bromley, thence to Seven Oaks and Tunbridge, p. 80.
10¾	ELTHAM.
	L. to Dartford, 8¾m.
	R. to Foot's Cray; thence to Wrotham and Maidstone, p. 81.

Variations of Route, and Branch Routes.

[A]

From Hicks's Hall:

Islington T. G.	1
Ball's Pond T. G.	2
Newington Green	2½
Paradise Row T. G.	3
Green Lane T. G.	5½
Wood Green	6
Bow's Farm	7¼
Palmer's Green	7¾
Ford Green	8¾
Bush Hill	9¼
ENFIELD	10

From St. Giles's Pound:

New Road	¾
Southampton Arms, Camden Town	1¼
Mother Red Caps	1½
Kentish Town	2¼
Holloway	3¼
Cross the North Road.	
Crouch End	4¾
Hornsey	5½
Wood Green	6
Thence, as above.	

[B]

CHIPPING ONGAR	23½
Norton Heath	26½
Cook's Mill Green	29
Oxney Green	30¼
The Lordship	31½
Clip Elm	32
CHELMSFORD	34

At the Entrance of Chelmsford, to Braintree and Bury St. Edmunds, p. 54.

[C]

New Cross	6
GREENWICH	7¾
WOOLWICH	10¼
Plumstead	11½
Belvidere	14½
Erith	15½

CROSS ROADS.

The Cross Roads in the Environs of London, as well as the direct Roads, are many of them connected by the auxiliary lines of communication contained in the three preceding pages; the New Road from Hyde Park Corner (for instance), over Vauxhall Bridge, connecting the Sussex and Kent with the Western and North-west Roads; and the Road to Snaresbrook, on Epping Forest, the South-west with the North-east and Norfolk Roads. The western Environs of the Metropolis communicate with the Holyhead, Chester, Manchester, and North Roads, through Edgeware, p. 84.

THE novel and improved Plan of the Cross Roads here adopted, differing entirely from that of every other Road Book, will be easily comprehended from the following brief explanation:—

1. In the arrangement of the roads, every continuous line of route is concentred, as far as practicable, within one opening of the book. See five leaves forward, for exemplification sake, Be § 19 to 23, containing the entire line of route from Weymouth to Chester and Liverpool, through Bristol, Hereford, and Shrewsbury, a length of 224 miles; and again, Br § 35 to 40, containing the line of route from Exeter to Sheffield, through Bristol, Gloucester, Worcester, Birmingham, and Derby, a length of 238 miles, with branches from Torquay, Teignmouth, and the various watering places on the Devonshire coast.

2. Every continuous line of route, from one extreme point to another, is distinguished by the alphabetical letters prefixed, as by Be, Br, in the routes above re-

ferred to. See also A § 1, on the opposite page, &c. &c. The first and third columns of each page contain the continuous line, and the middle column shews the branch distances to the points of junction on that line where the roads converge. The utility of this column will be best appreciated by considering the map of England as a mathematical figure, and every continuous line as a right line; in which case the branch lines become either converging lines to, or diverging lines from, the continuous line.

3. The continuous lines of route are subdivided into sections of distance from one principal place to another, thus,—

§ 1. Aberystwith to Shrewsbury;
§ 2. Shrewsbury to Derby;
§ 3. Derby to Lincoln;

as exemplified on the opposite and two following pages; these sections not comprising any particular periods of distance, but terminating at such points d'appui as best comport with facility of reference, and convenience of arrangement.

4. The arched figures shew the distances to and from the points d'appui. Thus, Montgomery, on the opposite page, is seen to be 54 miles from Aberystwith, and 22 from Shrewsbury. By means of these figures, the computation of distances, generally, is much facilitated: the distance from Newtown to Nottingham, for instance, on the annexed line of route, is seen with very little exertion of mind, to be 111½ miles; thus, Newtown to Shrewsbury 31; thence to Derby 65½; and Derby to Nottingham 15.

5. The general index is so arranged, that reference may at once be had to any required line of route, from any considerable town or watering place. For exemplification, suppose the route from Shrewsbury to Barmouth be required; or Barmouth to Shrewsbury. See index, under Shrewsbury, which directs to [§ 1 *c*], where, as seen on the opposite page, the road diverges at Mallwyd to Barmouth, through Dolgelly. On reversing the order of route, and travelling from Barmouth to Shrewsbury, Mallwyd becomes, *vice versa*, the converging point, where the branch joins the main line.

6. When there are two lines of route from one place to another, they are placed, as far as practicable, in juxta-position, as on the opposite page, where § 1[a] shews the route from Aberystwith to Shrewsbury, through Montgomery, and § 1[b] that through Welshpool.

☞ On travelling by cross roads, it should always be borne in mind that the best roads generally are those which lead to large towns; and though such lines of route may be, occasionally, somewhat circuitous, their circuity is well compensated by the better state of the road, the facilities afforded by the more frequent intercourse of stage coaches, the additional recommendation of good inns, &c. &c.

Cardiganshire.

	* ABERYSTWITH..	76
2	Piccadilly	74
9	Eskynald	67
12	Devil's Bridge ..	64
13½	Yspytty..........	62½
18½	Eisteddfagerrig ...	57½

Montgomeryshire.

26½	Llangerrig........	49½
31½	LLANYDLOES ..	44½
38	Llandinam	38
42	Penstrywad.......	34
45	NEWTOWN [a]..	31
52	Llandyssil	24
54	MONTGOMERY .	22

Shropshire.

57	Chirbury	19
60½	Marton...........	15½
62½	Brocton	13½
63½	Worthin..........	12½
67	Westbury	9
68¾	Stretton	7¼
70	Yockleton	6
71	Nox..............	5
72	Cruckleton........	4
76	SHREWSBURY [e] *	

L. *to Whitchurch, p.* 21.
— *to Drayton* 19*m.*
R. *to Wellington and Wolverhampton p.* 21.

Points of Junction.

[a] *To Bishop's Castle* (p. 12.) 17m.
L. *to Welshpool* 16*m.*

[b] TOWYN
To Machynlleth, 12m.

[c] BARMOUTH
To Dolgelly, 11m.

DOLGELLY
To Mallwyd 14½m.

HARLECH
To Dolgelly 18½m.

[d] NEWTOWN
To Welshpool 16m.

[e] OSWESTRY
To Shrewsbury 18m.
Page 21.

CAERNARVON
To Bala 42 miles, and thence to Shrewsbury 14½m.
Page 13.

LLANFYLLIN
To Shrewsbury 25m.
Page 22.

BISHOP'S CASTLE
To Shrewsbury, 23m.

ANOTHER ROUTE.

Cardiganshire.

	* ABERYSTWITH.	73½
4¼	Rhydd-y-penne ...	69¼
7½	Tal-y-bont........	66
11½	Eglwy's Fach	62

Montgomeryshire.

18½	MACHYNLLETH [b]...........	55
25½	Cemmes..........	48

Merionethshire.

30½	Mallwyd [c]....	43
	L. *to Dynasmouthy 2m.*	
33½	Nantyrhedyd.....	40

Montgomeryshire.

36	Dollymain	47½
41	Cann's Office Inn	32½
47½	LLANFAIR.....	26
55½	WELSHPOOL [d]	18
	Cross the Severn.	
56½	Buttington	17
58½	Uppington	15

Shropshire.

62	Trevenant........	11½
66½	Rowton	7
68¼	Cross Gates.......	5¼
73	Frankwell	½
73½	SHREWSBURY[e]*	

A § 2	CROSS ROADS.	A § 2 *cont.*

Shropshire.

*	SHREWSBURY	65½
4	Atcham	61½
4¾	Tern Bridge	60¾
6¾	Uckington	58¾
10¼	Hay Gate	55¼
11½	Cock, Watling St.	54
12¾	Hadley	52¾
14	French Lane	51½
15½	Dunnington	50
16½	Lilleshull Hill	49
19¼	NEWPORT [*a*]	46¼

Staffordshire.

20½	Forton	45
21½	Sutton	44
27	Wooton	38½
28¼	ECCLESHALL	36¼
33¼	Walton	31¾
34¼	STONE [*b*]	31¼
35¼	Stoke	30¼
37	Hardwick Hill	28½
39	Cotton	26½
44¼	Bramshall	21¼
46¾	UTTOXETER [*c*]	18¾

Derbyshire.

48½	Dovebridge	17
52	Sudbury	13½
52½	Aston	13
54	Foston	11½
57½	Hilton	8
59½	Etwall	6
62	Mickle Over	3½
65½	DERBY	*

Points of Junction.

[*a*] WELLINGTON
To Newport 8m.

[*b*] WOORE
To Stone 14m.

DRAYTON
To Stone 16m.

[*c*] NAMPTWICH
To Newcastle 15m.
Page 25.

DRAYTON
To Newcastle 14½m.

NEWCASTLE
To Uttoxeter 17m.
Page 33.

[*d*] ASHBY DE LA ZOUCH
To Nottingham 21m.

WARWICK
To Coventry 10m.

COVENTRY
To Leicester 26m.
§ 55.

LEICESTER
To Loughborough 11½m.

LOUGHBOROUGH
To Nottingham 15m.

A § 3

*	DERBY	51¼
2	Chaddesden	49¼
4½	Borrows Ash	46¾
7½	Risley	43¾
9	Sandyacre	42¼

Nottinghamshire.

10¼	Stapleford	41
13½	Lenton	37¾
15	NOTTINGHAM [*d*]	36¼
16	Trent Bridge	35¼
19	Holme Lane	32¼
20¾	Ratcliffe	30½
23½	Saxondale	27¾
27½	Red Lodge	23¾
31¼	East Stoke	20
35	NEWARK	16¼

Lincolnshire.

43	Halfway House	8¼
49	Brace Bridge	2¼
51¼	LINCOLN	*

To Wragby 10*m.*; *thence to Horncastle* 10½*m.*

To Market Raisin and Grimsby, p. 51.

Ae § 4

Cardiganshire.

*	ABERYSTWITH	33
7½	Tal-y-bont........	25½
11½	Eglwy's Fach.....	21½
	Montgomeryshire.	
18½	MACHYNLLETH	24½
23½	Pontabercous	9½
	Merionethshire.	
33	DOLGELLY	*

Ae § 5

*	DOLGELLY [e]..	63¼
8½	Drws-y-nant......	54¾
12½	Llanwchllyn......	50¾
17½	BALA [f].......	45¾
	Cross the river Dee.	
25½	Llandrillo	37¾
28	Cynwyd..........	35¼
30½	CORWEN	32¾
33	Llan St. Fraid T.G.	30¼
	Denbighshire.	
40½	LLANGOLLEN ..	22¾
46½	Ruabon	16¾
52	WREXHAM [g] .	11¼
56	Gresford..........	7¼
58¼	Pulford	5
63¼	CHESTER	*

Another Route from Aberystwith to Chester is by Llanydloes to Newtown and Welshpool, § 1; thence to Oswestry 15m. [g].

Points of Junction.

[e] BARMOUTH
To Dolgelly 11m.

[f]
MACHYNLLETH
To Dinasmouthy 13½m.

DINASMOUTHY
To Bala 18m.

[g] WELSHPOOL
To Oswestry 15m.

OSWESTRY
To Wrexham 15m.

[h] RUTHIN
To Chester 21m.

FLINT
To Chester 14½m.

PARKGATE
To Chester 12m.
Page 24.

[i] WHITCHURCH
To Tarporley 20½m.

TARPORLEY
To Northwich 10m.

Ae § 6[a]

Cheshire.

*	CHESTER[h]....	38½
1	Boughton.........	37½
4	Stanford Bridge...	34½
6	Tarvin	32½
8	Kelsall...........	30½
13	Crab Tree Green..	25½
14½	Sandway Lane	24
16¼	Hartford..........	22¼
17¼	Holloway Head ...	21¼
18	NORTHWICH [i]	20½
19½	Lostock	19
24	High Tabley......	14½
26½	Buckley Hill	12
28½	New Bridge	10
30½	ALTRINGHAM..	8
33½	Cross Street	5
	Lancashire.	
34½	Stretford	4
36	Old Trafford......	2½
38½	MANCHESTER..	*

Ae § 6[b]

ANOTHER ROUTE.

CHESTER
To Warrington 20½m.

WARRINGTON
To Manchester 18½m.

See *Liverpool to Manchester.*

Ai § 7

Cardiganshire.

*	ABERYSTWITH	72½
2	Piccadilly T. G. ..	70½
9	Eskynald	63½
12	Devil's Bridge ..	60½
15	Pentrebrunant	57½
18	Cwm Ystwith	54½
	Cross the river Wye.	

Radnorshire.

29	RHAYADER-GWY [b]......	43½
33¾	Nantmell	38¾
39½	Penybont	33
41¼	Llandegley	31½
45¾	Llanvihangel Nant Mellan	26¾
48	N. RADNOR [a].	24½
51	Kinnerton	21½
54	Beggar's Bush	18½
56	PRESTEIGN	16½

Herefordshire.

58	Comb Bridge	14½
60	Kinsham	12½
61	Darvold Bridge ...	11½
64¾	Wigmore	7¾
66¼	Lenthall Starkes ..	6¼
68	Elton	4½
69	Aston	3½

Shropshire.

72½	LUDLOW	*

Points of Junction.

[a] TREGARRON
To Llangammarch 23¼m.; thence to Builth 8¼m.

BUILTH
To New Radnor 12m.
Page 6.

[b] *To Knighton* 11½*m.*

[b 2] KNIGHTON
To Ludlow 17m.

[c] LEOMINSTER
To Tenbury 11m.

TENBURY
To Bewdley 13m.

[d] BROMYARD
To Kidderminster 22m.
§ 130.

[e] BRIDGNORTH
To Stourbridge 11½m.

STOURBRIDGE
To Birmingham through Halesowen 12¼m.; thro' Dudley 13¾m.

DUDLEY
To Birmingham 9m.
Pp. 20, 23.

Ai § 8

*	LUDLOW [b 2] ..	42
3½	Caynham	38½
5¾	Hope Baggot	36¼
10½	Hopton Wafers ...	31½
13	CLEOBURY MORTIMER ..	29

Worcestershire.

18½	Mopson's Cross....	23½
21	BEWDLEY [c] ..	21
24	KIDDERMINSTER [d]	18
30	Hagley	12

Shropshire.

34	Halesowen [e]....	8

Warwickshire.

42	BIRMINGHAM..	*

To Coventry and Cambridge. See Index.

Ai § 9

*	BIRMINGHAM ..	20½
2	Saltley	18½
6	Castle Bromwich ..	14½
8½	Bacon's Inn	12
10½	COLESHILL	10
13½	Shustock..........	7
14	Upper Whitacre...	6½
16½	Bentley Chapel....	4
20½	ATHERSTONE ..	*

To Hinckley 8*m.; thence to Leicester* 13*m.*

Ao § 10

*	ABERYSTWITH	39½
	As in § 12 to	
9½	Llanrhystid	30
12	Llanon	27½
17	Aberayron	22½
21	Llanarth	18½
24	Tynewydd	15½
28½	New Inn	11
33½	Blaneporth	6
35½	Tremayn	4
37½	Warren	2
39½	CARDIGAN	*

To St. David's 33m. (p. 74.)

Ao § 11

*	CARDIGAN	33½
	Pembrokeshire.	
3½	Llantwood	30
6	Eglwyswrw	27½
7½	Pontydnon	26
8	Hendra Gate	25½
9½	Pontbrynbairn	24
14	New Inn	19½
16½	Brook's End	17
23	Beggar's Bush	10½
25½	Prendergast	8
26¼	HAVERFORD-WEST	7¼
30	Johnston	3
32	Stainton	1½
33½	MILFORD HAV.	*

Points of Junction.

[*f*]

LLANDILOVAUR

To Llanbeder 17m.

LLANDOVERY

To Llanbeder 16¼m.

[*g*] *Tour of the Welsh Coast.*

SWANSEA

To Tenby 55m. Page 74.

TENBY

To Pembroke 10m.; thence across the Ferry to Haverfordwest 9m.

HAVERFORD-WEST

To New Inn 12m.; thence to Cardigan 14m.

CARDIGAN

To Aberystwith 43m. § 10.

ABERYSTWITH

To Dolgelly (§ 4) 33m.; thence to Caernarvon 39m. Page 13.

At Dolgelly, L. to Barmouth 11m.

CAERNARVON

To Bangor 9½m.

BANGOR

To Chester 62m.—Page 25.

Au § 12

	Pembrokeshire.	
*	TENBY	76½
4½	Begelly	72
7	Templeton	69½
8	Cold Blow	68½
12	TAVERNSPITE	64½
	Caermarthenshire.	
17	Llandowror	59½
19	St. Clare's	57½
21½	Pool-y-Gravel	55
27	Stony Bridge	49½
28½	CAERMARTHEN	48
32¾	Rhydyrgay	43¾
36½	Llangwilli	40
39½	Gwirgrig	37
40½	New Inn	36
41¼	Troedyrhw	35¼
46¼	Llanbyther	30¼
	Cardiganshire.	
51½	LLANBEDER [*f*]	25
58½	Talsarn	18
64	New Inn	12½
65½	Pontyperris	11
67	Llanrhystid	9½
69	Tavernspite	7½
73	Pontllanychaiarn	3½
74	Ridalvin	2½
76½	ABERYSTWITH [*g*]	*

B § 13

*	BRIGHTON	29½
7½	SHOREHAM BRIDGE	22
8½	Upper Lancing ...	21
10	Sompting..........	19½
12	Offington	17½
15	Patching Pond....	14½
19½	ARUNDEL [a]...	10
22½	Avisford Hill	7
23¾	Ball's Hut.........	6
25¼	Crocker Hill	4
27¼	Maudlin...........	2
28	West Hampnet....	1½
29½	CHICHESTER [b]	*

B § 14

*	CHICHESTER ..	53¼
	See opp. p. § 18, to	
13½	Cosham [c].......	39¾
16¾	Southwick.........	36½
20¼	WICKHAM	32½
25	BOTLEY	28¼
28¾	West End	24½
29¾	Mansbridge.......	23½
33½	Chilworth	19¾
37½	ROMSEY [d]....	15¾
	Wilts.	
44¼	Cowsfield	9
45¼	White Parish	8
49¼	Whaddon.........	4
50¼	Alderbury........	3
53¼	SALISBURY [e].	*

Points of Junction.

[a] WORTHING
To Arundel 10m.

LITTLE HAMPTON
To Arundel 4½m.

[b] BOGNOR
To Chichester 7½m.

[c] Junction of Roads from Portsmouth and Southampton.

[d] PORTSMOUTH
To Romsey 28½m.

SOUTHAMPTON
To Romsey 12m.

[e] WINCHESTER
To Salisbury 22½m.—§ 29.

[f] SHAFTESBURY
To Warminster 14½m.

HINDON
To Warminster 10½m.

[g] MAIDEN BRADLEY
To Frome 7m.

FROME
To Bath 13m.

BRADFORD
To Bath 8½m.

MELKSHAM
To Bath 11½m.—Page 72.

B § 15

Wiltshire.

*	SALISBURY	38¾
½	Fisherton..........	38¼
2¾	Fugglestone	36
4	Chilhampton	34¾
5	South Newton.....	33¾
5½	Stoford	33¼
7	Stapleford	31¾
9	Steeple Langford..	29¾
10¾	DEPTFORD INN....	28
13¼	Codford St. Mary..	25½
13¾	Codford St. Peter .	25
15½	Upton Lovel......	23¼
17	Heytesbury	21¾
20½	Boreham	18¼
21¾	WARMINSTER [f]............	17
25	Broomfield	13¾

Somersetshire.

27¼	Standerwick	11½
28½	Beckington	10¼
30	Woolverton.......	8¾
31¾	Norton St. Philips.	7
33½	Hinton	5¼
35½	Midford	3¼
36¾	South Stoke.......	2
38¾	BATH [g].......	*

Thence to Bristol, (p. 73) 13½m.

*	BRISTOL [h]	56¼
5	Compton Greenfield	51¼
10½	NEW PASSAGE HOUSE [m]	45¾
	Cross the Severn.	

Monmouthshire.

13½	BLACK ROCK INN ..	42¾
14½	Portskewit	41¾
16	Crick	40¼
17½	CAERWENT	38¾
25½	USKE	30¾
30½	Clytha	25¾
31½	Llanvihangel......	24¾
32½	Llangattock	23¾
36½	ABERGAVENNY [i]	19¾
38	Pentre	18¼
38½	Llanewenarth	17¾

Brecknockshire.

40½	Llangranach	15¾
42½	CRICKHOWEL .	13¾
44½	Pontybrynaert	11¾
47½	Bwlch	8¾
50	Llansaintfraid.....	6¼
51½	Skethrog	4¾
53	Llanhamlach......	3¼
56¼	BRECON [k]....	*

To Llandovery 20m. [l]. Page 75.

Points of Junction.

[h] CHIPPENHAM
To Bristol 20½m.
Page 73.

WELLS
To Bristol 17m.
§ 46.

[i] MONMOUTH
To Abergavenny 17m.
Page 75.

[k] CAERPHILLY
To Merthyr Tydvil 16m.
Page 73.

CARDIFF
To Merthyr Tydvil 24m.

MERTHYR TYDVIL
To Brecon 18½m.

[l] LLANDOVERY
To Llanbeder 16½m.

LLANBEDER
To Aberystwith 24½m.
§ 12.

[m] Another Route from Bristol to Aberystwith is through Hereford. See next page, § 20, Bristol to Hereford; thence to Rhayadergwy and Aberystwith, p. 5.

*	BRECON	58
2¾	Llandivilog	55¼
5	Lower Chapel	53
8¾	Upper Chapel	49¼
15	BUILTH	43
20	Ithon Bridge......	38
29	RHAYADERGWY [m]......	29
58	ABERYSTWITH	*

Ba § 18

Sussex.

*	BRIGHTON	59
	See opp. p. § 13, to	
29½	CHICHESTER ..	29½
31¼	Old Fishbourne ...	27¾
35	Nutbourne........	24

Hampshire.

36¾	EMSWORTH	22¼
38¾	HAVANT	20¼
39½	Bedhampton	19½
43	Cosham...........	16
	L. *to Portsmouth* 4½*m.*	
45½	Porchester........	13½
47¾	FAREHAM......	11¼
48½	Blackbrook	10½
50	Titchfield	9
53½	Bursledon Bridge .	5½
58	Northam Bridge...	1
59	SOUTHAMPTON	*

To Sherborne and Taunton, § 25, 26.

Dorsetshire.

*	WEYMOUTH....	64
½	Melcomb Regis ...	63½
6½	Monckton	57½
8¼	DORCHESTER ..	55¾
18	Revel's Inn	46
22½	Long Burton	41½
25½	SHERBORNE [a]	38½

Somersetshire.

31½	Thackston	32½
34½	Cattle Hill	29½
38	Ainsford Inn [b]..	26
42½	Presley	21½
43½	Cannard's Grave Inn	20½
44½	SHEPTON MALLET [c]........	19½
	R. to *Bath* 16*m.* § 41.	
48	Gurney Slade	16
49¾	Old Down Inn....	14¼
50¾	Stone Easton......	13¼
52	Farringdon Gurney	12
53¾	Temple Cloud	10¼
54¼	Clutton	9¾
57½	PENSFORD	6½
60	Whitchurch........	4
64	BRISTOL........	*

To Gloucester, and Cheltenham § 37.

Points of Junction.

[a] CHRISTCHURCH
To Blandford, 24m.
BLANDFORD
To Sherborne, 23m.

[b] SHAFTESBURY
To Wincaunton, 11m.
WINCAUNTON
To Ainsford Inn, 6½m.

[c] BRUTON
To Shepton Mallet, 7m.

[d] WELLS
To Bristol, 17m.
§ 46.
BRIDGEWATER
To Bristol, 37m.
§ 36.

[e] DEVIZES
To Chippenham, 10m.
CHIPPENHAM
To Aust Passage, 28½m.
Page 76.

[f] NEWPORT
To Abergavenny, 16½m.
ABERGAVENNY
To Hereford, 24m.

Gloucestershire.

*	BRISTOL [d]....	50¼
3¾	Westbury.........	46½
7	ComptonGreenfield	43¼
12	Aust Passage House [e]......	38¼
	Cross the Severn.	
13½	Beachley Passage House	36¾

Monmouthshire.

17	CHEPSTOW	33¼
19¼	St. Arvans.........	31
23	Llanvihangel Tor y Mynd	27¼
27	Trelleck	23¼
32¼	MONMOUTH....	18
	To Ross 10½*m.*	

Herefordshire.

35¾	Welch Newton....	14½
39¾	St. Weonards	10½
43¾	Wormelow Stump Inn............	6½
45½	Cross in hand T. G.	4¾
46¼	Callow	4
48½	Red Hill	1¾
50¼	HEREFORD [f]	*

L. *To Kington and Radnor*, p. 5.

Be § 21

*	HEREFORD [g]	53
1¾	Holmer	51¼
4¼	Morton	48¾
5½	Wellington	47½
8¾	Hope	46¼
10½	Wharton	42½
13	LEOMINSTER [h]	40
	R. *to Tenbury 11m.; thence to Bewdley and Kidderminster, and onward to Birmingham,* § 8 c.	
15¼	Lucton	37¾
18½	Portway	34½
19½	Bilberry	33½
	Shropshire.	
21½	Overton	31½
23¼	LUDLOW [i]	29¾
	R. *To Bridgnorth and Wolverhampton.*	
26	Bromfield	27
28½	Onibury	24½
31	Newton Green	22
36	Fell Hampton	17
38½	Little Stretton	14½
40	CHURCH STRETTON	13
41	All Stretton	12
43¾	Lebotwood	9¼
46¼	Dorington	6¾
50¾	Pulley Common	2¼
53	SHREWSBURY	*

To Chester by Whitchurch 40*m.* [*l*]

Points of Junction.

[g] GLOUCESTER
To Ross 16½m.

ROSS
To Hereford 14¼m.
Page 5.

[h] HAY
To Leominster 23m.

[i] BROMYARD
To Tenbury 12m.

TENBURY
To Ludlow 9m.

WORCESTER
To Ludlow 30½m.
Page 12.

[k] BISHOP'S CASTLE
To Shrewsbury 23m.

BRIDGNORTH
To Wenlock 9m.

WENLOCK
To Shrewsbury 13½m.
Page 23.

[l] SHREWSBURY
To Whitchurch 20m.

WHITCHURCH
To Chester 20m.

Be § 22

*	SHREWSBURY [k]	40
3¾	Abrighton	36¼
6	Harmer Hill	34
7¾	Middle	32¼
9¼	Burlton	30¾
12	Cockshut	28
16½	ELLESMERE	23½
	Flintshire.	
21¾	Overton	18¼
	Denbighshire.	
24½	Eyton	15½
26½	Marchwiail	13½
28¾	WREXHAM	11¼
32¾	Gresford	7¼
	Cheshire.	
35	Pulford	5
40	CHESTER [l]	*

To Parkgate 12*m.* page 24.

Be § 23

*	CHESTER	17
1	Backford	16
6½	Great Sutton	10¾
9	Eastham	8
11½	Great Bebbington	5½
15	Tranmere Ferry	2
17	LIVERPOOL	*

Bh § 24

Hampshire.

*	PORTSMOUTH..	20½
3¼	Hilsea............	17¼
4½	Cosham	16
	To Romsey and Salisbury, § 19.	
7	Porchester........	13½
9¼	FAREHAM [*a*]..	11¼
10	Blackbrook	10½
11¼	Cattisfield	9¼
12	Titchfield House ..	8½
15½	Bursledon Bridge..	5
19½	Northam Bridge...	1
20½	SOUTHAMPTON	*

Bh § 25

*	SOUTHAMPTON	62½
2	Millbrook	60½
3½	Redbridge........	59
4	Totton	58½
8½	Cadnam	54
11	Stoney Cross......	51½
17	Picked Post	45½
20	RINGWOOD	42½
24¼	New Bridge	38¼
	Dorsetshire.	
29½	WIMBORN MINSTER [*b*]......	33
32¼	Barford	30¼
34¾	Shapwick	27¾
37¾	Langton	24¾
39¼	BLANDFORD [*c*]	23¼
	To Dorchester, Honiton, and Exeter, p. 62.	
42½	Durwestone	20
45½	Shillingstone......	17
49¼	Newton	13¼
52¾	Lidlinch..........	9¾
57¼	Bishop's Caundell..	5¼
58¾	Caundell Meuse...	3¾
61	North Wootton....	1½
62½	SHERBORNE...	*

Bh § 26

*	SHERBORNE [*d*]	33¾
2¼	Nether Compton ..	31½
	Somersetshire.	
5¼	YEOVIL	28½
	To Honiton and Exeter, p. 67.	
6¼	Preston	27½
8¼	Odcomb..........	25½
9¼	Montacute........	24½
11¼	Stoke	22½
12¾	Petherton Bridge .	21
19¼	ILMINSTER [*e*]..	14½
21¼	Horton	12½
23¼	Ashill	10½
25¾	Hatch	8
33¾	TAUNTON [*f*] ..	*

Points of Junction.

[*a*] Or, from Portsmouth, across the Ferry, to Gosport ½m.; thence to Fareham 5½m.

[*b*] LYMINGTON
To Christchurch 13m.

CHRISTCHURCH
To Wimborn Minster 12m.

[*c*] POOLE
To Blandford 15m.

[*d*] SHAFTESBURY
To Sherborne 15½m.
Page 67.

[*e*] ILCHESTER
To Ilminster 12½m.
Page 65.

[*f*] CHARD
To Taunton 13m.; thence to Barnstaple and Ilfracomb, p. 70.

TAUNTON
To Minehead 23m.
To Wellington 7m.
To Bampton 21m.
Page 70.

Sussex.

*	BRIGHTON	65½
9¼	Bramber..........	56¼
10¼	STEYNING......	55¼
16	Storrington	49½
20¾	PULBOROUGH [g] ..	44¾
21¾	Stopham..........	43¾
23½	Fittleworth	42
26½	PETWORTH.....	39
28	Tillington	37½
30	Halfway Bridge ...	35½
32½	Easebourn	33
33½	MIDHURST	32
37½	Trotton	28
39½	Rogate	26

Hampshire.

42¼	Sheet Bridge......	23¼
43½	PETERSFIELD [i]	22
	Over Stonar Hill.	
47	Week Green......	18½
50	Rumsden Bottom ..	15½
53	Ropley	12½
55	Ropley Dean......	10½
56¼	Bishop's Sutton....	9¼
57½	ALRESFORD....	8
58½	Seward's Bridge ..	7
60	Staple Green T. G..	5½
65½	WINCHESTER [k]	*

To Romsey 11m. (p. 69).
To Salisbury. See opp. col. § 29.

Points of Junction.

[g] WORTHING
To Pulborough 14½m.

[h] BASINGSTOKE
To Andover 18½m.
Page 61.

[i] CHICHESTER
To Petersfield 15m.

[k] PORTSMOUTH
To Bishop's Waltham 16½m.

BISHOP'S WALTHAM
To Winchester 10½m.

ALTON
To Winchester 18m.
Page 60.

[l] SOUTHAMPTON
To Romsey 12m.

ROMSEY
To Salisbury 16m.
§ 14.

*	WINCHESTER ..	40½
9¾	Wherwell	30¾
13	ANDOVER [h] ..	27½
16¼	Weyhill	24¼

Wiltshire.

20¼	LUDGERSHALL.	20¼
24¾	East Everley......	15¾
26	West Everley	14½
30	Uphaven..........	10½
31	Rushall	9½
31¾	Charlton	8¾
35½	Connock	5
40½	DEVIZES........	*

To Bath (p. 72) 18¼*m.*

Bk § 29

*	WINCHESTER ..	22½
1	Week	21½
8½	STOCKBRIDGE .	14

Wiltshire.

14¾	Lobcomb Corner...	7¾
	R. *to Amesbury* 8*m.*; *thence to Warminster and Frome,* p. 71.	
16	Winterslow Hut ...	6½
22½	SALISBURY [l].	*

To Bath § 15; *thence to Bristol and Aberystwith.*

Bo § 30

Sussex.

	* BRIGHTON	81
4	Rottingdean	77
9	NEWHAVEN	72
12½	SEAFORD	68½
14¾	Exet Bridge	66¼
17½	Friston	63½
18	East Dean	63
19½	East Bourne [a]	61½
20½	SOUTH BOURNE	60½
23¼	Langley T. G.	57¾
25¾	Westham	55¼
26	Pevensey Castle	55
29	Sluice Haven	52
33¼	Bexhill	47¾
35¼	Glynd	45¾
39¼	HASTINGS [b]	41¾
43	Guestling	38
45	Icklesham	36
46½	WINCHELSEA	34½
49½	RYE [c]	31½
50½	Playdon T. G.	30½

Kent.

59	Old Romney	22
61	NEW ROMNEY	20
65	Dymchurch	16
70	HYTHE	11
72¾	Sandgate Castle	8¼
74	FOLKSTONE	7
81	DOVER	*

CROSS ROADS.

Points of Junction.

[a] LEWES
To East Bourne 17½m.

[b] LEWES
To Horsbridge 10½m.

HORSBRIDGE
To Battle 14m.

BATTLE
To Hastings 8m.

[c] BATTLE
To Rye 14m.

[d] Another Route from Brighton to Canterbury:

BRIGHTON
To Lewes 8½m.

LEWES
To Cross in Hand T. G. (leaving Uckfield on L.) 12m.; thence to Cranbrook 17½m.

CRANBROOK
To Charing 15m.; thence to Canterbury 17½m.

[e] At Tunbridge,
L. *to Seven Oaks 6½m.; thence to Dartford 13½m.*

Bo § 31

	* DOVER	28
6	Ringswould	22
7¼	Walmer	20¾
9	DEAL	19
11½	Halfway House	16½
14½	SANDWICH	13½
18	Cliff's End	10
20½	St. Lawrence	7½
21½	RAMSGATE	6½
23½	BROADSTAIRS	4½
25½	Kingsgate	2½
26¾	North Down	1¼
28	MARGATE	*

Bp § 32

Sussex.

	* BRIGHTON	35½
4¼	Falmer	31¼
6½	Ashcomb	29
8½	LEWES [d]	27
14½	Horstead	21
16½	UCKFIELD	19
20	Handell Gate	15½
25	Boar's Head Street	10½
27¾	Eridge Green	7¾

Kent.

30	TUNBRIDGE WELLS	5½
32¼	Nonsuch Green	3¼
32¾	Southborough	2¾
35½	TUNBRIDGE [e]	*

Kent.

*	TUNBRIDGE ...	40¼
3¾	Hadlow	36½
4¾	Goose Green	35½
6¾	Mereworth Cross ..	33½
8½	Wateringbury	31¾
9½	Teston............	30¾
11	Barming Cross	29¼
13	The Bower........	27¼
13½	MAIDSTONE [*f*]	26¾
	L. *to Rochester* 8½*m.*	
14¾	Pennenden T. G. ..	25½
16¼	Detling	24
20	StocktonburyValley	20¼
21½	Danaway	18¾
23	Key Street........	17¼
	L. *to Queenborough* 8*m.*	
	— *to Sheerness* 10½*m.*	
24	Chalk Well	16¼
24¾	SITTINGBOURNE ...	15½
26	Bapchild	14¼
27½	Green Street......	12¾
31	Ospringe	9¼
34	Boughton Street ...	6¼
37¾	Harbledown T. G...	2½
40¼	CANTERBURY [*g*]	*

To Margate, (p. 82.) 17*m.*
To Ramsgate, 18*m.*
To Broadstairs, 20¼*m.*

Points of Junction.

[*f*] GUILDFORD
To Dorking 11½m.
DORKING
To Reigate 5½m.
REIGATE
To Westerham 13½m.
WESTERHAM
To Maidstone 21m.
Or, at Westerham, R. *To Seven Oaks* 6*m.*; *thence to Maidstone* 15½*m.*

[*g*] TENTERDEN
To Ashford 11m.
ASHFORD
To Canterbury 14½m.
NEW ROMNEY
To Canterbury 22m.
FOLKSTONE
To Canterbury 17m.

[*h*] WORTHING
To Horsham 20m.
STEYNING
To Horsham 14½m.
HORSHAM
To Ewell 23½m.—P. 79.
ARUNDEL
To Dorking 32m.—P. 77.
DORKING
To Ewell 10½m.—P. 79.

Sussex.

*	BRIGHTON	51½
1¼	Preston T. G......	50
3½	Patcham	48
6	Piecombe.........	45½
6¾	Dale T. G.........	44¾
10	Albourne Green ...	41½
12	HICKSTED	39½
17	StaplefieldCommon	34½
18½	Hand Cross.......	33
23	CRAWLEY	28½
24¾	County Oak......	26¾

Surrey.

30¼	Kinnerley Bridge .	21¼
32¼	REIGATE.......	19¼
34	Gatton Inn	17½
35	Walton Heath	16½
37¼	Tadworth.........	14¼
38	Borough Street....	13½
40¾	EWELL [*h*]	10¾
43½	Talworth	8
46¼	KINGSTON	5¼

Middlesex.

46½	Hampton Wick ...	5
48	Teddington	3½
49	Twickenham......	2½
50	Worton	1½
51½	HOUNSLOW	*

Br § 35

Devonshire.

*	EXETER [a]	42½
2	Whipton	40½
4½	Broad Clyst	38
7	Beer	35½
10¼	Wedcote	32¼
12¼	COLLUMPTON	30¼
14½	Welland	28
17¾	South Appleford	24¾
20	MAIDEN DOWN [b]	22½
21	Bluet's Cross	21½

Somersetshire.

24½	WELLINGTON	18
25½	Chilson	17
27	Heatherton Park	15
28½	Runwell	14
30	Bishop's Hull	12½
31½	TAUNTON [c]	11
35	Walford Bridge	7½
36½	Thurloxton	6
39	North Petherton	3½
42½	BRIDGEWATER	*

To Bath (p. 64.) 38½*m.*

Br § 36

*	BRIDGEWATER [d]	36¾
5½	Pawlet	29¼
8	Huntspill	26¾
9	High Bridge Inn	25¾
13¾	Rook's Bridge	21

Points of Junction.

[a] TORQUAY
To Teignmouth 9½m.

TEIGNMOUTH
To Exeter 16m.
page 68.

[b] TIVERTON
To Maiden Down 10m.
page 70.

[c] EXMOUTH
To Sidmouth 10m.

SIDMOUTH
To Honiton 9m.

HONITON
To Taunton 18m.

LYME REGIS
To Chard 10½m.

CHARD
To Taunton 11½m.

[d] MINEHEAD
To Bridgewater 25½m.
Page 71.

[e] WELLS
To Bristol 17m.

SHEPTON MALLET
To Bristol 19½m.
§ 19.

Br § 36 *cont.*

16¼	Weare	18½
17¼	CROSS	17½
19¼	Sydcot	15½
21¼	Churchill	13½
22¾	LANGFORD	12
26¼	Red Hill	8½
33¾	Bedminster	1

Gloucestershire.

34¾	BRISTOL	*

Br § 37

*	BRISTOL [e]	33¾
2½	Horfield	31¼
4¼	Filton	29½
7¼	Almondsbury	26½
9	Rudgway	24¾
9¾	Alvaston	24
10¾	L. *to Thornbury* 2½*m.*	
14½	Falfield	19¼
16	Stone	17¾
17¾	NEWPORT	16
19	Berkeley Heath	14¾
23	CAMBRIDGE INN	10¾
25¼	Church End T. G.	8½
26¼	Whitminster Inn	7½
27¼	Putloe	6½
28	Parkin Green	5¾
29¾	Hardwick Elm	4
30½	Quedgley	3¼
33¾	GLOUCESTER	*

To Cheltenham 9¼*m.*

Br § 38

*	GLOUCESTER [*f*]	27
1½	Longford	25½
2¼	Twigworth	24¾
7	Swan Inn	20
11	TEWKESBURY [*g*]	16
13½	Twining	13½

Worcestershire.

15½	Stratford Bridge	11½
17	Naunton	10
19½	Severn Stoke	7½
21	Clifton	6
23	Kempsey	4
27	WORCESTER	*

To Kidderminster (§ 51) 14*m.*; *thence to Wolverhampton and Stafford; and to Bridgnorth and Shrewsbury.*

Br § 39

*	WORCESTER [*h*]	26
3	Fernhill Heath	23
6¾	DROITWICH	19¼
9½	Upton Warren	16½
12¾	BROMSGROVE	13¼
17¼	Lickey Hill	8¾
20	Northfield	6
22	Selly Oak	4
22¾	Bourn Brook	3¼

Warwickshire.

26	BIRMINGHAM	*

Points of Junction.

[*f*] SWANSEA
To Cardiff 46½m.

CARDIFF
To Chepstow 32m.
Page 73.

CHEPSTOW
To Gloucester 26½m.
Page 76.

STROUD
To Gloucester 10m.

[*g*] CHELTENHAM
To Tewkesbury 9m.
Page 7.

[*h*] HEREFORD
To Malvern 23½m.

MALVERN
To Worcester 8½m.
Page 7.

PERSHORE
To Worcester 9m.

[*i*] ALCESTER
To Birmingham 20m.

KIDDERMINSTER
To Birmingham 18m.

WARWICK
To Birmingham 20½m.
Page 15.

[*k*] WARWICK
To Lichfield 33½m.

Br § 40

*	BIRMINGHAM [*i*]	39¾
1½	Aston Park	38¼
4	Erdington	35¾
6½	Maney	33¼
7¼	SUTTON COLEFIELD	32½
9½	Barley Mow	30¼

Staffordshire.

11¼	Woodend T. G.	28½
12¾	Shenstone	27
15¾	LICHFIELD [*k*].	24

L. *to Wolseley Bridge; thence to Stone and Newcastle*, p. 27.

17¾	Streethay T. G.	22
22	Whichnor Bridge	17¾
	Cross the riv. Trent.	
25¾	Branston T. G.	14
28¼	BURTON ON TRENT	11½
31¼	Monk's Bridge	8½

Derbyshire.

37¾	Little Over	2
39¾	DERBY	*

To Matlock Bath 16*m.* *See* p. 34.

To Sheffield (p. 37) 32*m.*

Another Route from Birmingham to Sheffield is through Uttoxeter and Ashborne, from Lichfield. See *Lichfield to Uttoxeter* 17¼*m.* § 44; *thence to Sheffield* 45½*m.*

C § 41

Devonshire.

*	SIDMOUTH [a]..	67
1½	Sidford	65½
3	Sidbury...........	64
9	HONITON	58
16	Yarcomb	51

Somersetshire.

18	Buckland St. Mary	49
24	ILMINSTER [b] .	43
25½	White Lackington .	41½
27½	Sevington	39½
30½	Petberton Bridge ..	36½
36¼	ILCHESTER	30¾
42½	Lydford	24½
44	Fourfoot Inn	23
45¾	Wraxell	21¼
48	Pylle Street	19
50	CANNARD'S GRAVE INN	17
51	SHEPTON MALLET [d].......	16
53	Oakhill	14
56	Stratton...........	11
59½	Radstoke	7½
63	Dunkerton	4
67	BATH [c]	*

To Bristol (p. 73) *13¾m.; thence to Aberystwith,* § 16.

Points of Junction.

[a] EXMOUTH
To Sidmouth 10m.

[b] LYME REGIS
To Chard, 10½m.

Or, LYME REGIS
To Axminster, 4½m.

AXMINSTER
To Chard, 7½m.;
Thence to Ilminster, 4m.

[c] Another Route from Ilminster to Bath:

ILMINSTER
To Somerton 14m.—§ 46.

SOMERTON
To Wells 13½m.

WELLS
To Bath, 18m.
Page 64.

[d] WEYMOUTH
To Shepton Mallet, 44½m. § 19.

BRIDPORT
To Crewkerne, 13½m.

CREWKERNE
To Somerton, 14m.

SOMERTON
To Shepton Mallet, 14½m.

C § 42

*	BATH	40½
3	Swanswick........	37½

Gloucestershire.

5	Tog Hill..........	35½
6¾	Dyrham Park	33¾
8½	Toll Down House..	32
11½	CROSS HANDS INN..	29
14½	BEAUFORT ARMS, Petty France ...	26
15¼	Dunkirk..........	25¼
19	Lasborough	21½
20	Kingscote.........	20½
21½	Tipput's Inn	19
22¼	Horsley	18¼
23¼	Nailsworth........	17¼
25¼	RODBOROUGH	15¼
27¼	STROUD	13¼
30½	Painswick	10
	R. to Cheltenham, along the old road ¶.	
34¾	Cooper's Hill	5¾
37½	Shurdington	3
40½	CHELTENHAM..	*

¶ The new road, by Shurdington, avoids the Leckhampton and Birdlip Hills, and affords a fine expanse of picturesque scenery, extending over the fertile vale of Gloucester, and comprehending the cities of Gloucester and Worcester, and the towns of Cheltenham and Tewkesbury.

At 5 miles from Cheltenham, on R. Whitcomb House, Sir W. Hicks, Bart. on whose premises is the lately discovered Roman tessellated pavement.

Gloucestershire.

* CHELTENHAM [e] 46

3 Bishop's Cleeve .. 43

Worcestershire.

7½ Cross Hands 38½

Gloucestershire.

9 Beckford Inn 37

Worcestershire.

13 Sedgberrow 33

16 EVESHAM [f] .. 30

19 Norton 27

Warwickshire.

23 Dunnington 23

25 Arrow............ 21

26 ALCESTER...... 20

27¾ Coughton 18¼

30 Studley 16

31½ Mapleboro' Green . 14½

Worcestershire.

38¾ Drake's Cross 7¼

41½ Millpole Hill...... 4½

44 Moseley 2

Warwickshire.

46 BIRMINGHAM.. *

Another Route from Cheltenham to Birmingham is through Tewkesbury and Worcester, 51 miles, § 38, 39.

Points of Junction.

[e] GLOUCESTER
To Cheltenham 9¼m.

[f] TEWKESBURY
To Evesham 13m.

FARRINGDON
To Burford 10½m.

BURFORD
To Stow on the Wold 10m.

STOW ON WOLD
To Broadway 9m.

BROADWAY
To Evesham 6m.

[g] STRATFORD ON AVON
To Birmingham 23m.
Page 17.

WARWICK
To Birmingham 20½m.
Pp. 15, 16.

[h] WARWICK
To Lichfield 33¼m.

[i] *To Matlock Bath:*

UTTOXETER
To Ashborne 11m.

ASHBORNE
To Wirksworth 9¾m.

WIRKSWORTH
To Matlock Bath 2¾m.

Another Route from Lichfield to Matlock is through Derby, § 40.

BIRMINGHAM [g].. 64

As in § 40, to

Staffordshire.

* LICHFIELD [h] 48¼

4¼ Hansacre 44

5¾ Hill Ridware 42½

7¼ Blythbury........ 41

10¼ ABBOT'S BROMLEY 38

17¼ UTTOXETER ... 31

To Ashborne (§ 114) *11m.; thence to Buxton* (p. 30) *20½m.*

To Matlock Bath [i].

18¾ Stramshall........ 29½

20¼ Beamhurst 28

22¾ Checkley 25½

23¾ Nether Tean 24½

24¼ Upper Tean 24

27¼ CHEADLE 21

29 Holt 19¼

32¼ Ipstones.......... 16

34¼ Bottom House 14

35¾ Onecote 12½

41¼ Broadham Oak.... 7

43¼ Longnor 5

Derbyshire.

48¼ BUXTON........ *

To Huddersfield 33m.; thence to Leeds 15½m. (§ 116)

Ca § 45

Devonshire.

*	EXMOUTH	34
4	Knole	30
5¼	Budleigh Salterton,	28¾
6¼	Otterton	27¾
10	SIDMOUTH	24
11½	Sidford	22½
13	Sidbury	21
19	HONITON	15
26	Yarcomb	8

Somersetshire.

28	Buckland St. Mary	6
34	ILMINSTER.....	*

Ca § 46

*	ILMINSTER [a]..	44
2	Puckington	42
4¾	Hambridge........	39¼
6¾	Curry Rivell......	37¼
9¾	LANGPORT	34¼
13¾	SOMERTON [b]..	30¼
19¾	Street	24¼
21½	GLASTONBURY,	22½
27	WELLS [c]	17
34½	Blue Bowl........	9½
37	Chew Stoke	7
41½	Buishport	2½
43	Bedminster	1
44	BRISTOL........	*

To Gloucester, Worcester, and Birmingham, § 37.
To Cheltenham & Warwick, § 64.

CROSS ROADS.

Points of Junction.

[a] LYME REGIS
To Chard 10½m.

Or, LYME REGIS
To Axminster 4½m.

AXMINSTER
To Chard 7¼m.

CHARD
To Ilminster 4m.

[b] YEOVIL
To Ilchester 4½m.

ILCHESTER
To Somerton 4¼m.

BRIDPORT
To Crewkerne 13½m.

CREWKERNE
To Somerton 14m.

[c] SHAFTESBURY
To Wincaunton 11m.

WINCAUNTON
To Castle Cary 6½m.

CASTLE CARY
To Shepton Mallet 17m.

SHEPTON MALLET
To Wells 5m.

[d] WICKWAR
To Tetbury 13½m.

[e] WOTTON UNDER EDGE
To Minching Hampton 10m.

Cb § 47

Dorsetshire.

*	WEYMOUTH....	63½
½	Melcomb Regis....	63
5¾	Monckton	57¾
8¼	DORCHESTER ..	55¼
13	Piddle Town......	50½
16¼	MILBOURNE....	47¼
19¼	Winterbourne Whitchurch	44½
25¼	BLANDFORD ...	38¼
34¼	Melbury Abbas ...	29¼
37	SHAFTESBURY .	26½

Wiltshire.

42	East Knoyle	21½
48¾	Longbridge Deverill	14¾
49¾	Crockerton	13¼
51	Sambourne........	12½
51½	WARMINSTER..	12
55½	WESTBURY.....	8
58½	West Ashton	5
61½	Sevington	2
63½	MELKSHAM.....	*

Cb § 48.

*	MELKSHAM	45
1½	Benacre	43½
3	Laycock	42
4	Notton............	41
7	CHIPPENHAM..	38
12	Lower Stanton St. Quintin	33

Cb § 48 *cont.*

CROSS ROADS.

14 Corston Bridge.... 31
16½ MALMESBURY . 28½
19½ Long Newton 25½

Gloucestershire.

21 TETBURY [*d*]... 24
23 Upton Grove...... 22
27¼ MINCHING HAMPTON [*e*]. 17¾
29¾ Rodborough...... 15¼
31¾ STROUD [*f*] 13¼
35 Painswick 10
39¼ Cooper's Hill 5¾
42 Shurdington 3
45 CHELTENHAM.. *

To Birmingham § 43.

Cb § 49

* CHELTENHAM.. 25
1¾ Bedlam 23¼
2¾ Uckington 22¼
5 Swan Inn [*g*]..... 20
9 TEWKESBURY[*h*] 16
11½ Twining 13½

Worcestershire.

13½ Stratford Bridge .. 11½
15 Naunton.......... 10
17½ Severn Stoke...... 7½
19 Clifton 6
21 Kempsey 4
25 WORCESTER [*h*] *

To Birmingham § 39.
To Shrewsbury § 51.

Points of Junction.

[*f*] BRISTOL
To Wotton under Edge 20m.

WOTTON UNDER EDGE
To Stroud 12m.

[*g*] Junction of the Road from Gloucester.

GLOUCESTER
To Tewkesbury 11m.

[*h*] TEWKESBURY
To Pershore 9½m.

PERSHORE
To Worcester 9m.

[*i*] RODBOROUGH
To Stroud 2m.; thence to Gloucester 11m.

Another Route thence to Worcester:

GLOUCESTER
To Upton on Severn 15m.; thence to Worcester 10m.

[*k*] EVESHAM
To Alcester 10m.

ALCESTER
To Kidderminster 22½m. Page 23.

ALCESTER
To Droitwich 13m.; thence to Kidderminster 13m.

[*l*] BROMSGROVE
To Stourbridge 9½m.

STOURBRIDGE
To Bridgnorth 12½m.

Cc § 50

* BATH 42
See § 42, to
25¼ Rodborough [*i*].. 16¾
26¾ Cain Cross........ 15¼
28¾ King's Stanley 13¼
30½ Frocester 11½
42 GLOUCESTER [*i*] *

To Worcester § 38.

Cc § 51

Worcestershire.

* WORCESTER [*i*] 49¼
1½ Northwick........ 47¾
3 Hawford.......... 46¼
5¾ Ombersley........ 43½

To Bewdley 8½m.

10¼ Hartlebury 39
12¾ Ford Brook 36½
15 KIDDERMINSTER [*k*]...... 34¼
18 Shatterford........ 31¼

Shropshire.

23¼ Quat 26
25¼ Quatford 24
27 BRIDGNORTH[*l*] 22¼
30¼ Morvil 19
35¾ MUCH WENLOCK 13½
37¾ Harley 11½
39¾ Cressage.......... 9½
41¾ Cound............ 7½
46¼ Weeping Cross.... 3
49¼ SHREWSBURY.. *

Cd § 52

Hampshire.

*	SOUTHAMPTON	65
5½	Chandler's Ford Bridge	59½
7½	Otterborne	57½
9½	Compton	55½
11	St. Croix	54
12	WINCHESTER [a]	53
18½	Sutton	46½
20	Bullington	45
24	WHITCHURCH	41
29	Litchfield	36
33	Whitway	32
36¼	Newtown	29

Berkshire.

38	NEWBURY [b]	27
38¼	SPEENHAMLAND	26¾
39	Donnington	26
42¾	Chieveley	22¼
47¼	EAST ILSLEY	17¾
49¼	Kate's Gore	15¾
50½	Chilton	14½
54½	Steventon Green	10½
56½	Drayton	8½
58¾	ABINGDON	6¼
62	Bagley Wood	3

Oxfordshire.

65	OXFORD	*

To Northampton § 59.

[a] PORTSMOUTH
To Bishop's Waltham 16½m.

BISHOP'S WALTHAM
To Winchester 10½m.

[b] SALISBURY
To Andover 17¼m.

ANDOVER
To Newbury 16m. § 58.

[c] HUNGERFORD
To Wantage 14m.

WANTAGE
To Oxford 14m.

READING
To Henley on Thames 8m.

HENLEY
To Oxford 23m. Page 2.

[d] BUCKINGHAM
To Banbury 16m. Page 15.

[e] GLOUCESTER
Through Cheltenham to Evesham 25¼m.

EVESHAM
To Stratford on Avon 17½m.

STRATFORD
To Warwick 8m. § 65.

Cd § 53

Oxfordshire.

*	OXFORD [c]	49½
5	Kidlington Green	44½
12½	Hopcroft's Holt	37
16½	DEDDINGTON	33
19½	Adderbury	30
21	Weeping Cross	28½
23	BANBURY [d]	26½

To Leicester § 57.

Warwickshire.

27½	Mollington	22
35	Ladbroke	14½
37	SOUTHAM	12½

To Leamington 7m.
To Warwick 9*m.* See p. 7.

39¼	Long Itchington	10¼
41½	Marton	8
42¾	Princethorpe	6¾
46¼	Finford Bridge	3¼
47¼	Willenhall	2¼
48	Whitley Bridge	1½
49½	COVENTRY	*

To Leicester § 56.
To Derby § 55.

Cd² § 54

*	LEAMINGTON	12
2	WARWICK [e]	10
3	Guy's Cliffe	9
7	KENILWORTH	5
11	Stivichall	1
12	COVENTRY	*

Cd § 55

Warwickshire.

*	COVENTRY [*f*]	45
2	Foleshill	43
3	Longford	42
5	Bedworth	40
6¼	Griff	38¾
8¼	NUNEATON	36¾

To Leicester § 56.

11¾	Manceter	33¼
13¾	ATHERSTONE [*g*]	31¼

Leicestershire.

16¾	Sheepy	28¼
19	Twycross	26
22¼	Snareston	22¾
24	MEASHAM	21
27	Over Seal	18

Derbyshire.

29½	Castle Greasley	15½
31½	Stanton	13½
32½	Stapenhill	12½

Staffordshire.

33½	BURTON ON TRENT [*h*]	11½
36½	Monk's Bridge	8½

Derbyshire.

43	Little Over	2
45	DERBY	*

To Sheffield (p. 37.) 32*m.*

Points of Junction.

[*f*] RUGBY
To Coventry 13¼m.

[*g*] COLESHILL
To Atherstone 10m.

[*h*] SHIPSTON ON STOUR
To Warwick 17m.

WARWICK
To Coleshill 18½m.
Page 16.

COLESHILL
To Tamworth 10m.

TAMWORTH
To Burton on Trent 15m.

[*i*] OXFORD
To Banbury 23m. See opp. page, § 53.

[*k*] BRACKLEY
To Towcester 11m. § 59.

TOWCESTER
To Daventry 12½m.
Page 19.

Another and more direct route from Daventry to Lutterworth, is through Ashby Ledgers and Kilsby, 14m. but some parts of it are impassable in winter and wet seasons.

Ce § 56

Warwickshire.

*	COVENTRY	26

See opposite col. § 55. to

8¼	NUNEATON	17¾

Leicestershire.

11¼	Harrow Inn	14¾
13¼	HINCKLEY	12¾
17	Earl Shelton	9
26	LEICESTER	*

Ce § 57.

Oxfordshire.

*	BANBURY [*i*]	47¼
4½	Wardington	42¾

Northamptonshire.

9½	Byfield	37¾
11½	Charwelton	35¾
14¼	Badby	33
16¾	DAVENTRY [*k*]	30½
19¾	Braunston	27½

Warwickshire.

21¼	Willoughby	26
24½	DUNCHURCH	22¾
27¼	RUGBY	20
29¼	Brownsover	18

Leicestershire.

33	Cottesbatch	14¼
34¾	LUTTERWORTH	12½
43	Blaby	4¼
44¾	Ayleston	2½
47¼	LEICESTER	*

To Nottingham (p. 30) 26½*m.*

CROSS ROADS.

Cf § 58

*	SALISBURY [a]	33½
6¾	Winterton Hut	26¾
7½	Lobcombe Corner	26
	Hampshire.	
10	Middle Wallop	23½
13	Down Farm	20½
15½	Little Ann	18
17½	ANDOVER	16
20	Knights Enhane	13½
23	Hurstborne Tarrant	10½
29	Highclere Street	4½
	Berkshire.	
33½	NEWBURY	*

To Oxford § 52.

Cf § 59

Oxfordshire.

*	OXFORD	42
5	Gofford Bridge	37
9	Weston on the Green	33
12	MIDDLETON STONEY	30
14¼	Ardley	27¾
	Northamptonshire.	
18¾	Barley Mow Inn	23¼
22	BRACKLEY. [b]	20
26	Syersham	16
29	Silverston	13
33	TOWCESTER	9
36¾	Blisworth	5¼
38½	Milton	3½
42	NORTHAMPTON	*

To Leicester (p. 30.) 32m.
To Peterborough § 61.

Points of Junction.

[a] WEYMOUTH
To Salisbury 47m.
Page 62.

CHRISTCHURCH
To Ringwood 9m.

RINGWOOD
To Fordingbridge 6m.; thence to Salisbury 11m.

[b] WITNEY
To Woodstock 8m.

WOODSTOCK
To Deddington 11m.

CHAPEL HOUSE
To Deddington 10m.

DEDDINGTON
To Brackley 10½m.

[c] KETTERING
To Weldon 8½m.; thence to Stamford 13m.

STAMFORD
To Market Deeping 8½m.
Thence to Spalding 12m.

SPALDING
To Boston 15½m.

Or, STAMFORD
To Bourn 12¼m.
Thence to Boston, p. 51.

BOSTON
To Frieston Shore 4m.

Cf § 60

*	NORTHAMPTON	78
4	Overston	74
11	Broughton	67
14	KETTERING	64

To Weldon 8½*m.*
To Peterborough [c]

19	Oakley Inn	59
22½	ROCKINGHAM	55½
	Rutlandshire.	
24	Caldecote	54
28½	UPPINGHAM	49½
30	Preston	48
32	Manton	46
35	OAKHAM	43
37¼	Burleigh on the Hill	40¾
39	Cottesmere	39
41	Greetham	37
45	WITHAM	33
46½	Coltersworth	31½

To Grantham 8m.; thence to Newark (p. 42.)

54½	Cold Harbour	23½
59	Ancaster	19
62	Baynard's Leap	16
70	GREEN MAN	8
71¾	Dunston Pillar	6¼
78	LINCOLN	*

To Hull and Scarborough p. 50.
To Grimsby p. 51.
To Gainsborough p. 50.

Cf² § 61

	* NORTHAMPTON	42½
1¾	Abington	40¾
2¾	Weston Favel	39¾
4½	Great Billing	38
5½	Ecton	37
8½	Wilby	34
11½	WELLINGBOROUGH [d]	31
	To Kettering 7m.	
14½	Finedon	28
21½	THRAPSTON	21
24	Thorp Waterville	18½
27	Barnwell St. Andrews	15½
29	OUNDLE [e]	13½
32	Warmington	10½
	Huntingdonshire.	
34	Elton	8½
37	Chesterton	5½
37¼	Kate's Cabin	5¼
	Cross the North Road.	
37½	Alwalton	5
39	Overton Waterville	3½
40	Long Orton	2½
41½	Woodstone	1
	Northamptonshire.	
42½	PETERBORO'	*

To Lynn § 63; thence to Norwich [g].

Points of Junction.

[d] NEWPORT PAGNELL
To Wellingborough 17½m. Page 24.

[e] KETTERING
To Oundle 15m.

[f] MELTON MOWBRAY
To Oakham 9½m.

OAKHAM
To Stamford 12m.

STAMFORD
To Peterborough 14m.

UPPINGHAM
To Stamford 12m.

[g] *To Norwich:*

WISBEACH
To Downham Market 13m.

DOWNHAM
To Swaffham 13½m.

SWAFFHAM
To East Dereham 11½m.

EAST DEREHAM
To Norwich 17m.

[h] LYNN
To Swaffham 16m.; thence to Norwich 28½m. as above [g].

Cg § 62

	* LEICESTER	42
4¼	Bushby	37¾
6	Houghton	36
9	Billesdon	33
12	Tugby	30
	Rutlandshire.	
20	UPPINGHAM	22
22	Glayston	20
	Northamptonshire.	
28	Duddington	14
34	Wandsford	8
37	Ailesworth	5
40	Thorpe	2
42	PETERBORO'	*

Cg § 63

	* PETERBORO' [f]	35
1½	Newark	33½
3½	Eye	31½
	Cambridgeshire.	
6½	Thorney	28½
12½	Guyhorn Chapel	22½
16½	St. Mary's	18½
19½	WISBEACH [g]	15½
	Norfolk.	
20¾	Walsoken	14
22½	West Walton	12
24½	Walpole St. Peter	10
25½	Terrington St. John	9
28½	Islington	6
30½	St. Germains	4
35	LYNN [h]	*

Ch § 64

*	BRISTOL	44¾
2	Stapleton	42¾
5	Hambrook	39¾
9	Iron Acton	35¾
10½	Rangeworthy	34
14	Long Cross	30¾
15	Woodend	29¾
20	WOTTON UNDER EDGE	14¾
26½	Horsley	18¼
27½	Nailsworth	17¼
	Thence, § 42, to	
44¾	CHELTENHAM	*

Ch § 65

*	CHELTENHAM	39½
3½	Bishop's Cleeve	36
	Worcestershire.	
9½	Sedgberrow	30
16	EVESHAM	25½
19	Norton	22½
	Warwickshire.	
23	Dunnington	18½
25	Arrow	16½
26	ALCESTER	15½
30¼	Red Hill	11¼
33½	STRATFORD ON AVON	8
35½	Packsaddle Bridge	6
39½	Shirburn	2
41½	WARWICK	*

To Leamington 2m.

Points of Junction.

[*a*] HEREFORD
To Cheltenham 46m.—P. 4.

MONMOUTH
To Gloucester 25½m.—P. 75.

GLOUCESTER
To Cheltenham 9½m.

MALVERN
To Cheltenham 26m.—P. 7.

[*b*] MALVERN
To Upton on Severn 9m.

UPTON on SEVERN
To Tewkesbury 7½m.

TEWKESBURY
To Stow on the Wold 22m. Page 7.

CHELTENHAM
To Winchcomb 5m.

WINCHCOMB
To Stow on the Wold 13m.

[*c*] WORCESTER
To Pershore 9m.

PERSHORE
To Bengworth 7m.; thence to Broadway 6m.

BROADWAY
To Morton in Marsh 8½m.; thence to Chipping Norton 8½m.
Total, Worcester to Chapel House 39½m. See p. 10.

Ch^s § 66

	Gloucestershire.	
*	CHELTENHAM [*a*]	49½
2	Charlton Kings	47½
4	Dowdeswell	45½
14¼	Lower Swell	35¼
15¼	STOW ON THE WOLD [*b*]	34¼
17¼	Oddington	32¼
	Oxfordshire.	
20	Salford Hill	29½
22	Salford	27½
23¼	CHIPPING NORTON	26¼
24¼	CHAPEL HOUSE [*c*]	25¼
	To Banbury 11*m.*	
27½	Pomfrect Castle	22
33	Hempton	16
34¼	DEDDINGTON	15½
35½	Clifton	14
	Northamptonshire.	
37¾	Aynhoe on the Hill	11¾
39¾	Croughton	9¾
41¼	Barley Mow	8¼
	Oxfordshire.	
42½	Monk's House	7
45	Finmore	4½
	Buckinghamshire.	
46¼	Tingewick	3¼
49½	BUCKINGHAM	*

To Bedford and Cambridge, § 78.

* CHELTENHAM .. 58

As in § 66, to

Oxfordshire.

24¼ CHAPEL HOUSE [c]. 33¾
28 Church Enstone .. 30
29½ Gaging Well 28½
31 Sandford 27
32 Westcott Barton .. 26
33 Middle Barton 25
33½ Steeple Barton 24½
34¼ Hopcroft's Holt .. 23¾
36 Heyford Purcell .. 22
39 MIDDLETON STONEY 19
42 BICESTER 16
45½ Black Thorn Heath 12½

Buckinghamshire.

50 Ham Green 8
53 Waddesden 5
58 AYLESBURY .... *

To Leighton [d 2].

Ch³ § 68

* AYLESBURY [d] 39½
4 Aston Clinton 35½

Hertfordshire.

7 TRING 32½
10¾ North Church 28¾
12 BERKHAMPSTEAD 27½
17¼ HEMEL HEMPSTEAD 22¼
22¾ Redburn 16¾
27 ST. ALBANS [e]. 12½
29¾ Four Wants 9¾
32 HATFIELD 7½
33 Hatfield Mills 6½
35¾ Cole Green 3¾
38 Hartingfordbury .. 1½
39½ HERTFORD .... *

To Chelmsford [h].

Points of Junction.

[d] OXFORD
To Thame 13m.; thence to Aylesbury 9½m.—§ 74.

FARRINGDON
To Abingdon 14m.

ABINGDON
To Shillingford 8½m.; thence to Thame 11½m.

THAME
To Aylesbury 9½m.

[d 2] AYLESBURY
To Leighton 11m.

LEIGHTON
To Woburn 7½m.; thence to Bedford 15½m.—P. 20.

[e] WINDSOR
To Uxbridge 9m.

UXBRIDGE
To Rickmansworth 8m.; thence to St. Albans 11½m.

[f] WELWYN
To Hertford 7½m.

[g] HODDESDON
To Harlowe 6m.; thence to Dunmow 14¼m.

[h] HERTFORD
To Hoddesdon 4m.

HODDESDON
To Epping 5½m.; thence to Chelmsford 18m.

Ch³ § 69

* HERTFORD [f]. 49
3 WARE 46
5 Wade's Mill 44
7 Collier's End...... 42
9½ STANDON 39½
13 Hadhamon Ash 36
16 Bishop's Stortford.. 33
16½ HOCKERILL 32½

Essex.

20 Takeley Street.... 29
21 Bonington Green .. 28
22¾ Little Canfield 26¼
25 DUNMOW [g]... 24
28 Stebbing Ford 21
32 Raine 17
33½ BRAINTREE.... 15½
36¾ Blackwater 12¼
39½ COGGESHALL .. 9½
43½ Marks Tey 5½
45 Stanway 4
47 Lexden 2
49 COLCHESTER .. *

Ci § 70

Gloucestershire.

*	BRISTOL	35½
2½	Lower Easton	33
9¼	Nibley	26¼
10¼	Yate	25¼
11¼	CHIPPING SODBURY	24¼
14	Old Sodbury	21½
15	CROSS HANDS INN [a]	20½
18	BEAUFORT ARMS, Petty France	17½
18¾	Dunkirk	16¾
20¾	Didmarton	14¾
23½	Hare and Hounds	12
25½	TETBURY	10
32¼	Thames and Severn Canal	3¼
35½	CIRENCESTER [a 2]	*

Ci § 71

*	CIRENCESTER [b]	40½
4	Barnsley	36½
7	BIBURY	33½
10½	Aldsworth	30
	Oxfordshire.	
17	BURFORD	23½
28	CHIP. NORTON	12½
28¾	CHAPEL HOUSE	11¾
40½	BANBURY	*

To Coventry, § 53.
To Daventry and Leicester, § 57.

Points of Junction.

[a] Junction of Road from Bath, § 42.

[a 2] BATH
To Cirencester 32m.

CIRENCESTER
To Stow on the Wold 19m.

STOW on the WOLD
To Warwick 25½m.
To Stratford on Avon 21m.; thence to Birmingham 23m. Page 17.

[b] CHIPPENHAM
To Malmesbury 9½m.

MALMESBURY
To Cirencester 11½m.

[c] *Another Route:*

BRISTOL
To Chippenham 20½m. Page 73.

CHIPPENHAM
To Wotton Basset 15m. (or through Calne 16½m.); thence as in § 73.

[d] SWINDON
To Farringdon 12½m.

D § 72

Gloucestershire.

*	BRISTOL [c]	66½
2¼	Lower Easton	62¼
5½	Mangotsfield	61
7¾	Pucklechurch	58¾
11¾	Toll Down House	54¾
	Wiltshire.	
15½	Luckington	51
17¼	Sherston	49¼
18¼	Pinkney	48¼
19¼	Easton Grey	47¼
22¾	MALMESBURY	43¾
	To Cirencester 11½m.; thence § 71.	
24¾	Charlton	41¾
30¾	Cove House	35¾
34¼	CRICKLADE	32¼
35¾	Water Eaton	30¾
38½	Cold Harbour	28
42¼	HIGHWORTH [c]	24¼
	Berkshire.	
44½	Coleshill	22
48½	FARRINGDON [d]	18
53¼	Pusey Furze	13¼
56¼	KINGSTON INN	10¼
57½	Fifield	9
58¼	Tubney	8¼
60¾	Besselsleigh	5¾
64¾	Botley	1¾
	Oxfordshire.	
66½	OXFORD	*

To Aylesbury § 74.
To Buckingham § 77.

CROSS ROADS.

Da § 73

*	BATH	66½
2½	Bath Easton	64
	Wiltshire.	
6	Box T. G.	60
8¾	Pickwick	57¾
13	CHIPPENHAM [*e*]	53½
15½	Derry Hill	51
18¾	CALNE	47¾
22¼	Hillmarton	44¼
25	Lyneham	41½
29¼	WOTTON BASSET [*e*]	37¼
	To Cricklade 7½m.	
35¾	SWINDON [*f*]	30¾
37¾	Stratton St. Margt.	28¾
42¼	HIGHWORTH	24¼
	Thence, as in the opp. col. to	
	Oxfordshire.	
66½	OXFORD [*e* 2]	*
	To Buckingham § 77.	

Da § 74

*	OXFORD	22¼
7	Wheatley Bridge	15¼
9¼	Albury	13
11½	North Weston	10¾
13	THAME [*g*]	9¼
	Buckinghamshire.	
16	Haddenham (on R.)	6¼
18¼	Denton	4
19½	Stone	2¾
20½	Hartwell	1¾
22¼	AYLESBURY	*

Points of Junction.

[*e*] *Another Route:*

CHIPPENHAM

To Sutton Benger 4m.; thence to Lyneham 7m.; and thence to Wotton Basset 4m.

Another Route from Bath to Oxford is through Cirencester.

[*f*] **FROME**

To Trowbridge 9m.

TROWBRIDGE

To Devizes 10½m. Page 71.

DEVIZES

To Beckhampton Inn 7½m.; thence to Swindon 11½m.

WARMINSTER

To Devizes 16m.

[*g*] **WANTAGE**

To Wallingford 14m.

WALLINGFORD

To Thame 14½m.

[*h*] **BICESTER**

To Aylesbury 16m.

[*i*] **BEDFORD**

To Shefford 9m.

SHEFFORD

To Baldock 8m.

Da § 75

*	AYLESBURY	58
4	Aston Clinton	54
5½	Wendover Canal	52½
8½	Grand Junct. Canal	49½
11	Beacon Hill	47
	Bedfordshire.	
16	DUNSTABLE	42
18½	Lewsey	39½
21	Little Bramingham	37
	Hertfordshire.	
27½	Highdown Hill	30½
31	HITCHIN	27
32	Walsworth	26
33½	Letchworth	24½
36	BALDOCK [*i*]	22
40	Odsey Grange	18
44½	ROYSTON	13½
	Cambridgeshire.	
48	Melbourn	10
52½	Harleston	5½
58	CAMBRIDGE	*

Da § 76

*	CAMBRIDGE	13
5	Quy	8
6¾	Bottisham	6¼
11¼	Devil's Ditch	1¾
13	NEWMARKET	*

Thence (p. 55) *to Thetford, Norwich, and Yarmouth.*

Oxfordshire.

*	OXFORD	26
5	Gofford Bridge	21
10	Wendlesbury	16
13	BICESTER	13
17	Fringford	9
22	Finmere	4
	Buckinghamshire.	
23¼	Tingewick	2¾
26	BUCKINGHAM	*

De § 78

*	BUCKINGHAM	30¾
4	Thornton	26¾
5¼	Beachampton	25½
7	Calverton	23¾
8¼	STONEY STRATFORD	22½
9¾	Woolverton	21
12¼	Stanton Bridge	18½
14¼	NEWPORT PAGNELL	16½
19	OLNEY	11¾
	Bedfordshire.	
23	Turvey	7¾
27¾	Bromhead Bridge	3
30¾	BEDFORD	*

To Cambridge (§ 88) 30m.

Points of Junction.

[a] OXFORD
To Leicester, § 53, 57.

WARWICK
To Coventry 10m.

COVENTRY
To Leicester 26m.—§ 56.

BIRMINGHAM
To Atherstone 20½m.—§ 9.

ATHERSTONE
To Hinckley 8m.; thence to Leicester 13m.

[b] OAKHAM
To Witham 10m.; thence to Grantham 9½m.—P. 36.

[c] GRANTHAM
To Sleaford 11½m.

SLEAFORD
To Horncastle 22m.—P. 49.

HORNCASTLE
To Louth 14m.

LOUTH
To Saltfleet 10m.

[d] LINCOLN
To Market Raisin 15m. Page 51.

MARKET RAISIN
To Caistor 8½m.

CAISTOR
To Great Grimsby 11½m.

Leicestershire.

*	LEICESTER [a]	54½
3	Thurmaston	51½
5	Syston	49½
7	Rearsby	47½
9	Brocksby	45½
11	Frisby	43½
12½	Kirkby Bellers	42
15	MELTON MOWBRAY	39½
17	Thorpe Arnold	37½
20	Waltham on the W.	34½
24	Croxton Kyriell	30½
	Lincolnshire.	
28½	Harlaxton	26
31	GRANTHAM [b]	23½
33½	Belton [c]	21
34½	Syston	20
35¼	Barkston	19¼
36	Hunnington	18½
37½	Carlton Scrope	17
38½	Normanton	16
39¾	Claythorpe	14¾
40½	Fulbeck	14
41½	Leadenham	13
43¾	Welbourn	10¾
44¼	Wellingore	10¼
45	Navenby	9½
46	Boothby	8½
48	Coleby	6½
54½	LINCOLN [d]	*

Dg § 80

*	OXFORD	28
2½	Littlemore	25½
3½	Sandford	24½
5½	Nuneham Courtenay	22½
9	Dorchester	19
10½	Shillingford	17½
	Cross the Thames.	
	Berkshire.	
12½	WALLINGFORD	15½
16	Moulsford	12
18	Streatley	10
19½	Basildon	8½
22	PANGBOURN	6
	To Basingstoke, § 83.	
24	Purley	4
28	READING	*

Dg § 81

*	READING [e]	22¼
	Wiltshire.	
3	Three Mile Cross	19¼
5½	Swallowfield	16¾
6¼	Riseley	16
	Hampshire.	
7¾	Heckfield	14½
9½	Mattingley	12¾
11½	Hook	10¾
	Cross the Lond. Rd.	
13¼	North Warnborough	9
14¼	ODIHAM	8
16¾	South Warnborough	5½
22¼	ALTON [f]	*

Points of Junction.

[e] H. WYCOMBE

To Great Marlow 5m.

GREAT MARLOW

To Henley on Thames 7m.

HENLEY ON TH.

To Reading 8m.

[e 2] READING

To Basingstoke 16m.

BASINGSTOKE

To Winchester 17½m. Page 61.

WINCHESTER

To Southampton 12m. Thence to Lymington, Christchurch, &c.—Page 60.

[f] ALTON

To Warnford 13m.

WARNFORD

To Fareham 13m.

FAREHAM

To Gosport 5½m.; thence, across the Ferry, to Portsmouth ½m.—Page 58.

Or, ALTON

To Petersfield 13m. as in the opposite column.

PETERSFIELD

To Horndean 7½m.; thence to Portsmouth 10½m. Page 59.

Dh § 82

*	ALTON	34¾
1¼	Chawton	33½
2¾	Farringdon	32
4¾	East Tisted	30
10	Week Green	24¾
13	PETERSFIELD	21¾
17¼	Gravel Hill	17½
20½	HORNDEAN	14¼
25½	HAVANT	9¼
	Thence, § 18, to	
34¾	CHICHESTER	*

Dh § 83

*	OXFORD	51
	See opp. col. § 80, to **Berkshire.**	
22	PANGBOURN	29
23	Tidmarsh	28
25	Englefield	26
28½	Halfway House	22½
30	Aldermaston	21
	Hampshire.	
34	Pamber	17
36	East Sherborne	15
39	BASINGSTOKE [e 2]	12
	Thro' Hackwood Pk.	
42	Winslade	9
43¾	Herriard	7¼
46	Lasham	5
51	ALTON [f]	*

Di § 84

Warwickshire.

*	BIRMINGHAM [a]	57
4	Yardley	53
5¼	Wells Green	51¾
7¼	Elmdon	49¾
9¼	Stone Bridge	47¾
12	Meriden	45
15½	Allesley	41½
18¾	COVENTRY	38¼
19¾	Stoke	37¼
22	Binley	35
26	Brinklow	31
27	Stretton	30
28¾	Pailton	28¼

Leicestershire.

31	Cross in Hand T. G.	26
33	LUTTERWORTH	24
35	Walcote [b]	22
38¾	North Kilworth ...	18¼
40	Husband's Bosworth	17
41½	Theddingworth....	15½
44	Lubenham	13
46	MARKET HARBOROUGH....	11

Northamptonshire.

46½	Little Bowden	10½
49½	Fox Inn..........	7½
51½	Desborough.......	5½
53	Rothwell	4
57	KETTERING [c]	*

To Kimbolton [e]

CROSS ROADS.

Points of Junction.

[a] SHREWSBURY
To Shiffnal 18m.
SHIFFNAL
To Wolverhampton 12½m.
WOLVERHAMPTON
To Birmingham 13½m.
Page 20.

[b] LICHFIELD
To Atherstone 16½m.
ATHERSTONE
To Hinckley 8m.
HINCKLEY
To Lutterworth 10½m.
Page 24.

[c] DERBY
To Loughborough 16½m.
Thence to Leicester 11½m.
LEICESTER
To Market Harborough 14½m.
Page 30.
HARBOROUGH
To Kettering 11m.

[d] STAMFORD
To Stilton 14½m.
STILTON
To Huntingdon 12½m.

Di § 85

Northamptonshire.

*	KETTERING. [c]	41½
1¾	Barton Seagrave ..	39¾
4¼	Cranford St. John's	37¼
9¼	THRAPSTON ...	32¼

Huntingdonshire.

13½	Bythorne	28
18	Spaldwick	23½
20¼	Ellington	21¼
22¼	Creamer's Hut....	19¼
24	Brampton	17½
26	HUNTINGDON [d]	15½

To St. Ives 6½m.; thence to Cambridge 12½m.

26¾	Godmanchester....	14¾
31¼	Fenny Stanton	10¼

Cambridgeshire.

35	Lolworth	6½
38½	Girton............	3
41½	CAMBRIDGE ...	*

To Bury St. Edmunds § 89.

Another Route from Birmingham and Coventry to Cambridge is through Northampton [f].

Di § 86

*	CAMBRIDGE . .	47½
5	Babraham	42½
7	Abington	40½
9½	LINTON	38

Suffolk.

19	HAVERHILL ...	28½

Essex.

20½	Sturmer	27
22½	Baythorn End	25
24¼	Ridgewell	23
27	Great Yeldham....	20½
30¼	SIBLE HEDINGHAM.	17¼

To Sudbury 8¾m.; thence to Ipswich 21¼m.

30¾	Swan Street	16¾
32¼	Brook Street......	15¼
34¼	HALSTEAD	13¼
35¼	Blue Bridge	12¼
37¾	Earle's Colne	9¾
40	Colne Wake	7½
42½	Ford Street	5
45½	Lexden	2
47½	COLCHESTER ..	*

Di § 87

*	COLCHESTER ..	20½
5	Ardleigh	15½
7½	Wignell Street	13
9¼	MANNINGTREE	11¼
10	Mistley Thorn	10½
12	Bradfield	8½
16¾	Ramsey Street	3¾
17¼	Ramsey	3¼
18½	Dover Court......	2
20½	HARWICH......	*

Points of Junction.

[e] KETTERING
To Higham Ferrers 10m.

HIGH. FERRERS
To Kimbolton 8m.; thence to Eaton Socon 8½m.

[f] COVENTRY
To Daventry 19m.—P. 19.

DAVENTRY
To Northampton 13m.

NORTHAMPTON
To Olney 15½m.

OLNEY
To Bedford 11¾m.

BUCKINGHAM
To Bedford 31m.—§ 78.

[g] AYLESBURY
To Tring 7¼m.

TRING
To Dunstable 10½m.

DUNSTABLE
To Hitchin 15m.

HITCHIN
To Baldock 5m.; thence to Royston 8½m.

ROYSTON
To Cambridge 13¼m.

Dk § 88

*	BEDFORD [f]...	30
6	Great Barford	24
10½	Eaton Socon [e]...	19½

Huntingdonshire.

12	ST. NEOTS	18

Cambridgeshire.

18	Eltisley	12
23	Bourn Leyes Com..	7
30	CAMBRIDGE....	*

Dk § 89

*	CAMBRIDGE [g]	49½
5	Quy	44½
6¾	Bottisham.........	42¾
11¼	Devil's Ditch	38¼
13	NEWMARKET ..	36½

To Thetford and Norwich, p. 55.

Suffolk.

17½	Kentford..........	32
23	Saxham	26½
27	BURY ST. EDM.	22½
30	Barton...........	19½
33½	Ixworth	16
36½	Stanton	13
37½	Hepworth	12
42½	BOTESDALE	7
48	Sturston	1½

Norfolk.

49½	SCOLE INN	*

Thence to Yarmouth. (p. 57) 35½m.

Dm § 90

Lancashire.

	* MANCHESTER ..	52¼
2½	Rusholme T. G. ...	49¾
4¼	Withington........	48
5¾	Didsbury	46½

Cheshire.

7¼	Cheadle	45
10¼	Ulbart............	42
12¼	WILMSLOW.....	40
14¼	Street Lane Ends..	38
15¾	Alderley..........	36½
16¾	Monk's Heath	35½
19½	Siddington T. G. ..	32¾
20	Morton	32¼
23¾	CONGLETON [a]	28½
25¼	Asbury	27
30¼	Lawton, Red Bull .	22

Staffordshire.

31½	TALK ON THE HILL [b]	20¾
33¾	Chesterton	18½
36¼	NEWCASTLE UNDER LINE [c]	16
38¼	Handford	14
39¾	Trentham Inn	12½
42¾	Tittensor Heath ...	9½
43¾	Darlaston	8½
45¼	STONE [d]	7
48¼	Yarley	4
52¼	STAFFORD	*

To Birmingham, § 94.

CROSS ROADS.

Points of Junction.

[a] LIVERPOOL
To Congleton 44m.—P. 28.

[b] Junction of Road from Liverpool, through Middlewich, p. 28.

[c] BURSLEM
To Newcastle 2¼m.

[d] BUXTON
To Leek 12m.
LEEK
To Stone 16½m.

[e] WALSALL
To Dudley 9¼m.
DUDLEY
To Stourbridge 4¾m.
STOURBRIDGE
To Kidderminster 6¾m.

[f] WOLVERHAMPTON
To Dudley 6m.
DUDLEY
To Halesowen 4¾m.; thence to Bromsgrove 7¾m.
BROMSGROVE
To Worcester 13m.

Dm § 91

	* STAFFORD	45¼
3¼	Dunston	42
6¼	PENKRIDGE....	39
8¼	Spread Eagle	37
10¼	Standyford Lane...	35
13	Ford Houses	32¼
15	Gosbrook Mill.....	30¼
16¼	WOLVERHAMPTON	29

To Birmingham 13½m. See Page 20.

18¼	Upper Pen	27
21¾	Himley	23½
22¼	Seven Stars	23
26¼	Stew Poney.......	19
27¾	Whittington	17½

Worcestershire.

30¼	Broadwaters	15
31¼	KIDDERMINSTER [e]	14

To Bewdley 3m.
To Bromyard and Hereford, § 109.

32¾	Ford Brook	12½
35	Hartlebury........	10¼
39¾	Ombersley........	5½
42¼	Hawford..........	3
43¾	Northwick	1½
45¼	WORCESTER [f]	*

To Cheltenham, § 49.

To Malvern, Ross, and Monmouth, § 146.

Gloucestershire.

*	CHELTENHAM ..	46
2½	Leckhampton Court	43½
6½	Birdlip	39½
20	CIRENCESTER [g]	26
23¾	Cross Way	22¼

Wiltshire.

25¾	Latton	20¼
26¾	CRICKLADE	19¼
	To Wotton Basset, 7½m.; thence to Calne 10½m.	
27½	Corkett	18½
28¼	Water Eaton	17¾
30¾	Cold Harbour Inn .	15¼
35	SWINDON	11
	To Hungerford 16m.; thence to Newbury 8m.	
37½	Wroughton	8½
38½	Burdrope T. G.....	7½
	Over Ogbourn Downs.	
46	MARLBOROUGH	*

Dm § 93

*	MARLBOROUGH	48
4	Savernake Forest..	44
6	Burbage	42
11	East Everley [h]	37
15½	LUDGERSHALL.	32½

Points of Junction.

[g] HEREFORD
To Gloucester 31m.—P. 5.

GLOUCESTER
To Painswick 7m.; thence to Cirencester 11m.—P. 8.

[h] DEVIZES
To East Everley 15¾m. Thence to Andover 11¾m. as in the annexed col.

[i] WINCHESTER
To Bishop's Waltham 10½m. thence to Portsmouth, by Cosham, 16m.;—to Gosport 13¾m.

[k] WOLVER-HAMPTON
To Walsall 6m.

[l] *Another Route from Stafford to Birmingham:*

STAFFORD
To Penkridge 6m.; thence to Wolverhampton 10½m.

WOLVERHAMPTON
To Birmingham 13½m. Page 20.

BIRMINGHAM
To Coventry, § 84.
To Warwick and Leamington, p. 15.
To Alcester and Evesham, § 43.
To Oxford, p. 17.

Hampshire.

19½	Weyhill	28½
22¾	ANDOVER	25¼
26	Wherwell	22
	Over Barton Stacey Down.	
36	WINCHESTER ..	12
	To Bishop's Waltham; thence to Portsmouth and Gosport [i].	
37	St. Croix	11
38½	Compton	9½
40¼	Otterborne	7¾
42½	Chandler's Ford ...	5½
48	SOUTHAMPTON	*

Dn § 94

Staffordshire.

*	STAFFORD [l] ..	25½
2	Weeping Cross	23½
	Over Cannock Chase.	
7½	Huntingdon	18
9¾	Cannock	15¾
12	Great Wyrley	13½
14	Bloxwich	11½
16¾	WALSALL [k] ...	8¾
19½	Barr	6
23	Handsworth	2½
24	Hockley Brook....	1½

Warwickshire.

25½	BIRMINGHAM [l]	*

Do § 95

Lancashire.

*	LIVERPOOL [a]	36½
4	Knotty Ash	32½
8	PRESCOT	28½
11	Rainhill	25½
15½	Great Sankey	21
17½	Sankey Bridge ...	20
18	WARRINGTON[b]	18½
20¾	Woolston	15¾
23½	Rixton	13
25½	Cadishead Green ..	11
27½	Irlam	9
30¾	Part-a-croft Bridge	5¾
32	Eccles.............	4½
34¼	Pendleton	2¼
36½	MANCHESTER..	*

To Halifax & Leeds, § 99.

Do § 96

*	MANCHESTER[c]	25
3	Newton Heath	22
4¼	Failsworth	20¾
5½	Hollinwood	19½
7½	OLDHAM	17½

To Rochdale 8m.
To Halifax 19½m.

Yorkshire.

10	Austerland	15
13	Delph	12
17¾	Marsden	7¼
20	Bradley Brook....	5
21½	Black Moor Foot .	3½
25	HUDDERSFIELD	*

Points of Junction.

[a] PARKGATE
To Liverpool 9½m.
Page 29.
Or, Parkgate to Chester, (p. 26,) thence to Warrington as below.

[b] LLANGOLLEN
To Wrexham 11½m.

WREXHAM
To Chester 11½m.—§ 5.

CHESTER
To Warrington 20½m.

[c] CHESTER
To Northwich 18m.
Thence to Knutsford [c 2].

NORTHWICH
To Altringham 12½m.; thence to Manchester 8m.

[c 2] KNUTSFORD
To Altringham 7m.; thence to Stockport 9½m.

STOCKPORT
To Mottram 7¼m.; thence to Huddersfield 16m.

[d] BURNLEY
To Halifax 22m.

HALIFAX
To Wakefield 16½m.

COLNE
To Bradford 18m.

BRADFORD
To Wakefield 14m.
Page 38.

[e] LEEDS
To Ferry Bridge 15m. P. 38.

Do § 97

*	HUDDERSFIELD [c 2]...	45
2	Aldmondbury	43
4	Highgate Lane	41
8	Over Shitlington...	37
10½	Horbury	34½
13	WAKEFIELD [d]	32
17½	Aybridge	27½
20	Purston Jackling ..	25
22	PONTEFRACT ..	23

To Ferry Bridge 1½m. [e]*; thence to Snaith 12¾m.*

25	Knottingley	20
31¼	Great Heck	13¾
35½	SNAITH	9½
37¼	Turnbridge	7¾
38½	Roccliffe	6½
43	Booth Ferry	2
45	HOWDEN	*

Do § 98

*	HOWDEN	25
1½	Belby	23½
3½	East Linton	21½
5½	Gilberdike.........	19½
7½	New Village......	17½
10	North Cave......	15
12½	South Cave	12½
15¾	Riplingham T. G...	9¼
19¾	Kirk Ella	5¼
20¾	Anlaby	4¼
25	HULL...........	*

CROSS ROADS.

Dp § 99

*	MANCHESTER [f]	47
1½	Cheetham	45½
6½	Middleton	40½
9½	Trub Smithy	37½
12½	ROCHDALE [g]	34½
14½	Stubley	32½
15½	Littleborough	31½
	Yorkshire.	
20½	Baitings	26½
23	Ripponden	24
26	Sowerby Bridge	21
27½	King's Cross	19½
29	HALIFAX [f]	18
31½	Beggarinton	15½
35	Great Horton	12
37	BRADFORD [h]	10
41¼	Staningley	5¾
44	Kirkstall Bridge	3
45¼	Burley	1¾
47	LEEDS	*

Dp § 100

*	LEEDS [i]	23¾
2¼	Halton T. G.	21½
4¼	Seacroft	19½
8	Kidhall Inn	15¾
14¼	TADCASTER [k]	9½
17½	Street Houses	6¼
22	Dring Houses	1¾
23¾	YORK	*

To Hull, § 102.
To Bridlington, p. 51.

Points of Junction.

[f] MANCHESTER
To Halifax, through Oldham, 27m.
See opp. page, § 96.

[g] BOLTON
To Bury 4½m.

BURY
To Rochdale 7m.

[h] COLNE
To Bradford 16m.

[i] HUDDERSFIELD
To Leeds 15½m.

[k] SKIPTON
To Otley 15m.

OTLEY
To Harewood 8m.; thence to Tadcaster 11m.

[l] HARROWGATE
To Wetherby 7½m.; thence to York 14m.

PAITLEY BRIDGE
To Ripley 9½m.; thence to Knaresborough 4½m.

KNARESBORO'
To York 18m.

[m] RIPON
To Boroughbridge 7m.

BOROUGHBRIDGE
To York 17½m.

Dp § 101

*	YORK [l]	40
[illegible]	Lobster Inn	32¼
11	Spittle Beck	29
12½	Whitwell	27½
18	NEW MALTON	22
18½	Norton	21½
21	Scagglethorp T. G.	19
22¼	Rillington	17¾
27	YEDDINGHAM BRIDGE	13
30	SNAINTON	10
32	Brompton	8
33½	Wykeham	6½
35½	East Ayton	4½
39	Falsgrave	1
40	SCARBOROUGH.	*

Dr § 102

*	YORK [m]	38¾
2¾	Grimston	36
6½	Kexley Bridge	32¼
8¼	Wilberfoss	30½
11½	BARNBY MOOR INN	27¼
13¾	POCKLINGTON, New Inn	25
14½	Hayton	24¼
17	Shipton	21¾
19	MARKET WEIGHTON	19¾
26½	Bishop's Burton	12¼
29½	BEVERLEY	9¼
31½	Woodmansea	7¼
38¾	HULL	*

E § 103

Glamorganshire.

*	SWANSEA	52
3	Morriston Bridge	49
8½	NEATH	43½
14½	Newbridge	37½
17	Aberpegwin	35
20½	Pontneath Vaughan	31½
	Brecknockshire.	
24½	Ystradvellty	27½
37	BRECON [*b*]	15
41¼	Vellinvach	10¾
44¼	Bryntllys	7¾
48	Glasbury	4
52	HAY	*

To Leominster, § 112.

E § 104

*	HAY	61
	See § 112, to	
	Herefordshire.	
7½	Willersley	53½
9	Eardesley	52
11	Bullingham Chapel	50
12	Sponn Moor	49
15½	KINGTON	45½
	Radnorshire.	
21½	PRESTEIGN [*a*]	39½
24½	Norton	36½
28½	KNIGHTON	32½
	Shropshire.	
35	CLUN	26
39	Colebach	22

Points of Junction.

[*a*] TENBY

To Caermarthen 28½m.

CAERMARTHEN

To Llandovery 29½m. Page 75.

LLANDOVERY

To Llangammarch 14m.; thence to Builth 8½m.

BUILTH

To New Radnor 11½m.; thence to Presteign 8m.

Total—Tenby to Presteign 100m.

[*b*] CARDIFF

To Merthyr Tydvil 24m.

MERTHYR TYDVIL

To Brecon 18½m.

[*b* 2] BRECON

To Llandrindod Wells 7m.; thence to Newtown 22m.

NEWTOWN

To Welshpool 16m.

WELSHPOOL

To Oswestry 15m.

OSWESTRY

To Wrexham 15m.; thence to Chester 11½m.

Total—Brecon to Chester 86½m.

E § 104 *cont.*

40	BISHOP'S CASTLE	21
43¾	Norbury	17¼
48½	Stitt	12½
51¾	Castle Pulverbach	9¼
58	Nobold	3
61	SHREWSBURY	*

E § 105

*	SHREWSBURY [*c*]	57
7¼	Shawbury	49¾
8	Edgeboulton	49
13	Hodnet	44
16	TERN HILL	41
19	DRAYTON [*d*]	38
	Staffordshire.	
27½	Baldwin Gate	29½
29	Whitmore	28
31	Millstone Green	26
33½	NEWCASTLE UNDER LYNE	23½
34¾	Wolstanton	22¼
35½	BURSLEM	21½
37½	Norton	19½
40½	Endon	16½
42½	Bank End	14½
45½	LEEK	11½
49	Upper Holme	8
	Derbyshire.	
53¾	Flashgate	3¼
57	BUXTON [*c*]	*

Eb § 106 — CROSS ROADS. — Eb² § 108

Eb § 106

Shropshire.

*	SHREWSBURY [c]	30½
3¾	Albrighton	26¾
6	Harmer Hill	24½
7½	Broughton	23
11	WEM	19½
13½	Edstaston	17
17½	Tilstock	13
20	WHITCHURCH	10½
	Cheshire.	
25½	Newhall	5
29½	Shrew Bridge	1
30½	NAMPTWICH	*

Eb § 107

*	NAMPTWICH [d]	38¼
2¼	Wistaston	36
6	Crewe Green	32¼
7	Haslington	31¼
9	Wheelock	29
10½	SANDBACH	27¾
13	Brereton Green	25¼
15	Holmes Chapel	23¼
16½	Twemlow	21¾
21	Chelford	17¼

To Macclesfield 6m.
To Knutsford 5m.

22½	Warford	15¾
24	Street Lane Ends	14¼
26	WILMSLOW	12¼

Thence, § 90, to

38¼	MANCHESTER	*

Points of Junction.

[c] ABERYSTWITH

To Shrewsbury, by Montgomery (§ 1) 76m.; by Welshpool 73½m.

SHREWSBURY

To Stone (§ 2) 34½m.; thence to Newcastle 9m.

STONE

To Leek 16m.; thence to Buxton 12m.

[d] NEWTON

To Drayton 12m.; thence to Namptwich 13m.

NAMPTWICH

To Middlewich 13m.; thence to Northwich 7m.

NORTHWICH

To Warrington 11m.

WARRINGTON

To Wigan 12½m.

WIGAN

To Preston 16½m.; thence to Lancaster, page 29.

Eb² § 108

20	SHREWSBURY	

See § 106, to

*	WHITCHURCH	46½
	Cheshire.	
2	Grindley Bridge	44½
3	Bell on the Hill	43½
4½	No Man's Heath	42½
6	Hampton Guide Post	40½

To Chester (p. 26) 14*m.*; *thence to Parkgate.*

11	Peckforton	35½
15½	TARPORLEY	31
22½	Sandyway Head	24
24	Hartford	22½
26	NORTHWICH [d]	20½

To Knutsford 7m.

27½	Lostock	19
31¾	High Tabley	14¾
33	Mere Town	13½
34½	Buckley Hill	12
38½	ALTRINGHAM	8

To Stockport 9½m.; thence to Huddersfield 23¼m.

41½	Cross Street	5
	Lancashire.	
42½	Stretford	4
44	Old Trafford	2½
46½	MANCHESTER	*

To Halifax, § 99.

*	HEREFORD [a].	36
¼	Aylston Hill	35¾
2	Lugg Mills........	34
3½	Ewe Withington...	32½
7¾	Burley T. G.......	28¼
10	Stoke Lacy	26
14	BROMYARD	22
	To Worcester (p. 11) 14*m.*	
19½	Three Gates	16½
	Worcestershire.	
23½	Stanford Bridge ...	12½
26	HUNDRED HOUSE INN	10
29½	Dunley	6½
32	STOURPORT....	4
36	KIDDERMINSTER	*

Ed § 110

*	KIDDERMINSTER [b].......	31½
1	Broadwaters......	30½
6¾	STOURBRIDGE.	24¾
8	Brettel Lane......	23½
11½	DUDLEY........	20
	Staffordshire.	
14	Horsley Heath	17½
18	WEDNESBURY.	13½
21	WALSALL	10½
	See opp. col. to	
31½	LICHFIELD	*

Points of Junction.

[a] NEWPORT
To Abergavenny 16½m.

ABERGAVENNY
To Hereford 24m.

NEWPORT
To Uske 11½m.; thence to Monmouth 13m.

MONMOUTH
To Hereford 18m.
§ 20.

[b] MONMOUTH
To Ross 10½m.

ROSS
To Ledbury 13m.; thence to Malvern 8m.
§ 146.

MALVERN
To Worcester 8½m.

WORCESTER
To Kidderminster 14m.
§ 91.

[c] TENBY
To Llandovery 58m.

LLANDOVERY
To Presteign 42m.

PRESTEIGN
To Ludlow 16½m.

[d] LEOMINSTER
To Tenbury (§ 112), 11m.

TENBURY
To Cleobury 7m.; thence to Bridgnorth 14m.

72½	ABERYSTWITH.	
	See § 7, to	
	Shropshire.	
*	LUDLOW [c]....	51
2	Rocks Green......	49
5	The Moor	46
8	Clee Hills	43
10½	Botterell Aston....	40½
12	Wrickton	39
16½	Down	34½
20	BRIDGNORTH [d]	31
	To Shiffnall 11*m.*	
	Cross the Severn.	
22¾	Roughton	28¼
23¾	Wyken	27¼
26½	Shipley...........	24½
	Staffordshire.	
29½	Trescot	21½
31	Wightwick	20
32	Compton..........	19
33½	WOLVERHAMPTON	17½
37	Willenhall........	14
40½	WALSALL.......	10½
42	Rushall	9
44	Walsall Wood.....	7
47½	Muckley Corner ..	3½
49	Pipe Hill	2
51	LICHFIELD	*
	To Derby (§ 18) 24*m.*	

52 SWANSEA ....
See § 103, to
* HAY 49½

Herefordshire.

2½ Clifford 47
Cross the River Wye.
4¾ Whitney 44¾
6¾ Winforton 42¾
7½ Willersley 42
10½ Kinnersley 39
13 Sarnsfield 36½
16½ Great Delwyn 33
20 Monkland 29½
22½ LEOMINSTER .. 27
To Ludlow (§ 21) 10¼*m.*
24½ Stocktonbury Cross 25
26½ Ashton 23
29½ Brimfield Cross.... 20
30¾ Little Hereford.... 18¾
Cross the River Teme.

Worcestershire.

33½ TENBURY 16
To Cleobury 7m.; thence to Bridgnorth 14m.
37 Newnham 12½
40 Mamble 9½
44 Mopson's Cross.... 5½
46½ BEWDLEY 3
49½ KIDDERMINSTER .... *
To Birmingham (§ 8) 18*m.*

Points of Junction.

[e] HEREFORD
To Worcester 26m.

WORCESTER
To Birmingham 26m.
§ 39.

CHELTENHAM
To Eversham 16m.; thence to Alcester 10m.

ALCESTER
To Birmingham 20m.
§ 43.

[f] COLESHILL
To Atherstone 10m.

ATHERSTONE
To Measham 10½m.
Page 25.

[g] NOTTINGHAM
To Newark 20m.

NEWARK
To Lincoln 16½m.

LINCOLN
To Louth 28m.

LOUTH
To Saltfleet 12m.

LINCOLN
To Wragby 11m.; thence to Horncastle 9½m.

Warwickshire.

* BIRMINGHAM [e] 48
1½ Aston Park 46½
4 Erdington 44
6½ Maney 41½
7½ SUTTON COLEFIELD 40½

Staffordshire.

9½ Basset's Pole 38½
14½ TAMWORTH 33½
18½ Four County Gate . 29½

Leicestershire.

24½ MEASHAM [f] .. 23½
28 ASHBY-DE-LA-ZOUCH 20
33¾ Bredon 14¼
35¼ Isley Walton 12¾
37½ Castle Donington .. 10½
40 Harrington Bridge. 8
Cross the River Trent.

Derbyshire.

40½ Sawley 7½
41¼ Long Eaton 6¾

Nottinghamshire.

42¼ Toton 5¾
43¼ Chilwell 4¾
45¼ Beeston 3¾
46½ Lenton 1½
48 NOTTINGHAM .. *
To Lincoln, &c. [g]

Eg § 114

Staffordshire.

*	LICHFIELD [a]	63
4¼	Hansacre	58¾
5¼	Hill Ridware	57¾
7¼	Blythbury	55¾
10¼	ABBOT'S BROMLEY	52¾
17¼	UTTOXETER	45¾
21	Rocester	42
24	Ellaston	39
27	Church Mayfield	36
	Derbyshire.	
28¼	ASHBORNE [d]	34¾
30	Fenny Bentley	33
32½	Bradborn Mill	30½
39½	WINSTER	23½
46	BAKEWELL [b]	17
49	Hasop	14
53	Grindleford Bridge	10
	See opp. p. § 118, to	
63	SHEFFIELD	*

Eh § 115

*	LICHFIELD [a]	26½
5	King's Bromley	21½
7½	Yoxall	19
15	Draycott	11½
	Derbyshire.	
16¼	SUDBURY	10¼
26½	ASHBORNE	*

To Buxton (p. 30) 20¼m.

Points of Junction.

[a] BIRMINGHAM
To Lichfield 16m.—§ 40.

COVENTRY
To Lichfield 27¼m.—P. 27.

[b] MATLOCK
To Bakewell 8½m.—P. 34.

[c] Another Route from Lichfield to Ashborne is by Sudbury 26½m. as in § 115.—Thence, by Buxton to Sheffield, as on the opposite page, § 118, 120.

[d] SHREWSBURY
To Newcastle under Lyne 33½m

NEWCASTLE
To Buxton 23½m.—§ 108.

WORCESTER
To Wolverhampton 29m. § 91.

WOLVERHAMPTON
To Stone 23¼m.

STONE
To Leek 16½m.; thence to Buxton, § 108.

Eh § 116

Derbyshire.

*	BUXTON [c]	33
4¼	CHAPEL-EN-LE-FRITH	28¾
5½	Milton	27½
7¾	Chinley Head	25¼
12½	Chunall	20½
14	Whitefield	19
15	Glossop	18
19	Woodhead	14
	Yorkshire.	
24	Holme	9
27	Holmfirth	6
29½	Honley	3½
31½	Lockwood	1½
33	HUDDERSFIELD	*

To Halifax 8m.
To Wakefield, § 97.

Eh § 117

*	HUDDERSFIELD	15¼
3	Bradley	12¼
4¼	Nunbrook	11
6½	Mill Bridge	8¾
8½	Birstall	6¾
9¼	Holden Cliff	6
10	Bruntcliff	5¼
11	Morley	4¼
12	Chirwell	3¼
13	Beeston	2¼
15¼	LEEDS	*

To Harrowgate (p. 37) 15¼m.

Derbyshire.

*	BUXTON [e]	24
1	Fairfield	23
5	Hargate Wall Hill	19
7	TIDESWELL [h]	17
14	Grindleford Bridge	10
19	Ringinglow T. G.	5
	Yorkshire.	
20½	Hill Top	3½
24	SHEFFIELD	*

To Gainsborough, § 121.

Ei § 119

*	SHEFFIELD	17½
1½	Attercliff	16
3½	Tinsley	14½
6	ROTHERHAM	11½
9	Thrybergh	8½
10½	Hooton Roberts	7
12½	Conisbrough	5
15	Warmsworth	2½
16½	Bulby	1
17½	DONCASTER [i]	*

Ek § 120

*	BUXTON	26
4¾	CHAPEL-EN-LE-FRITH	21¼
7	Sparrow Pit	19
11	Castleton	15
17	Hathersage	9
26	SHEFFIELD	*

Points of Junction.

[e] MACCLESFIELD
To Buxton 11m.

CONGLETON
To Buxton 16m.

[f] MANCHESTER
To Sheffield 38m.—§ 125.

[g] HUDDERSFIELD
To Barnsley 16½m.

BARNSLEY
To Rotherham 12½m.
Page 39.

ROTHERHAM
To Bawtry 15m.

[h] BUXTON
To Tideswell 7m.; thence to Chesterfield 16m.

CHESTERFIELD
To Worksop 15m.

WORKSOP
To Retford 7¾m.; thence to Gainsborough 9½m.
§ 139.

[i] DONCASTER
To Thorne 10½m.; thence to Howden 12½m.

HOWDEN
To North Cave 10m.; thence to Hull 15m.—§ 99.

Yorkshire.

*	SHEFFIELD [f]	31½
1½	Attercliffe	30
2¼	Car Brook	29¼
3½	Tinsley	28
5	Crankley Mill	26½
9	Wickersley	22½
12	Maltby	19½
16	TICKHILL	15½
17½	Tickhill Spital	14
20	BAWTRY [g]	11½
	Nottinghamshire.	
21¼	Scafforth T. G.	10¼
23	Everton	8½
26	Gringley on the Hill	5½
28¾	Beckingham	2¾
30½	Flood Arches	1
	Lincolnshire.	
31½	GAINSBORO'	*

Ek § 122

*	GAINSBORO' [h]	36½
3½	Little Corringham	33
7¾	Harpswell	28¾
9¾	SPITAL INN	26¾
21	MARK. RAISIN.	15½
25	North Willingham	11½
32	Kelstorn	4½
36½	LOUTH	*

	Lancashire.	
*	MANCHESTER [a]	51
5	Audenshaw	46
7	ASHTON UNDER LINE	44
	Cheshire.	
8	Stayley Bridge	43
10¼	Mottram in Longden Dale [b]	40¾
12¾	Tintwistle	38¼
16	Woodhead	35
18	Further Woodhead	33
	Yorkshire.	
20½	Salter's Brook House	30½
27¼	Thurlston	23¾
31½	Silkstone	19½
33½	Dodworth	17½
35¼	BARNSLEY	15¾
38	Ardsley	13
41	Darfield	10
45	Hickleton	6
47	Marr	4
49½	York Bar	1½
51	DONCASTER	*

Em § 124

*	MANCHESTER	40
20½	Salter's Brook House	19½
23½	Board Hill T. G.	16½
32½	Bythorn Bridge	7½
40	SHEFFIELD	*

Points of Junction.

[a] LIVERPOOL
To Warrington 18m.

WARRINGTON
To Manchester 18½m. § 95.

Or, WARRINGTON
To Altringham 11½m.; thence as in [b].

[b] CHESTER
To Altringham 30½m.; thence to Stockport 9m.

STOCKPORT
To Mottram 7½m.

[c] MANCHESTER
To Whaley Bridge 15½m.; (§ 131); thence to Chapel-en-le-Frith 4m.

CHAPEL-EN-LE-FRITH
To Chesterfield 23½m.

CHESTERFIELD
To Mansfield 12½m.

MANSFIELD
To Newark 20m.

[d] The tourist may pass through Clumber and Thoresby Parks, instead of keeping the turnpike road from Sparkenhill to Ollerton.

Em § 125

*	MANCHESTER	38
	See § 123, to	
10¼	Mottram in Longden Dale	27¾
11¾	Woolley Bridge	26¼
	Derbyshire.	
15	Glossop	23
20	Lady Clough House	18
27	Cocks Bridge	11
	Yorkshire.	
32	Surry Arms	6
34	Rivelin Mill	4
36	Lidgate	2
38	SHEFFIELD	*

Em § 126

*	SHEFFIELD	39½
2	Darnal	37½
3½	Hansworth	36
7½	Aston	32
9½	Todwick	30
11½	South Anston	28
	Nottinghamshire.	
15¼	Gateford	24
17½	WORKSOP	22
19	Sparkenhill [d]	20½
21½	Carburton	18
23½	Budley	16
26¼	OLLERTON [d]	13¼
29	Ompton	10½
39½	NEWARK [c]	*

*	NEWARK	36¼
2½	Coddington	33¾
	Lincolnshire.	
4¾	Beckingham	31½
9¾	Leadenham	26½
14	Bayard's Leap	22¼
17	Leasingham	19¼
17½	Holdingham	18¾
18½	SLEAFORD	17¾
21	Kirkby Laythorpe.	15¼
24	Heckington	12¼
26	Garrick	10¼
30	North End	6¼
32	Kirton Holme	4¼
36¼	BOSTON.........	*

Em § 128

*	BOSTON [*e*]	33½

To Lynn by Spalding and Wisbeach, avoiding the Washes, 58m. [*e* 2]. *—Across the Washes* 33½*m. as follows:*

3¾	Kirton............	29¾
6	Sutterton	27½
9¼	Foss Dyke Wash ..	24¼
	Cross the Wash at the New Bridge.	
14	Saracen's Head....	19½
17	HOLBEACH	16½
19	Fleet............	14½
20	Gedney	13½
22	Long Sutton	11½

See the Tide Table, for Time of crossing Cross Keys Wash.

28½	Terrington	5
33½	LYNN	*

Em § 129

*	BOSTON	37½
22	Long Sutton	15½
26	Tid Gote..........	11½
28	Foul Anchor Ferry	9½
33½	Terrington	5
37½	LYNN	*

Em § 130

*	LYNN [*f*]	43½
1	Hardwick T. G. ...	42½
3¼	Middleton.........	40¼
5¼	East Winch	38¼
7	West Bilney	36½
9¾	Narborough	33¾
15½	SWAFFHAM [*g*].	28
19	Necton	24½
21	Little Framsham ..	22½
23	Wendling	20½
25	Scarning	18½
27	EAST DEREHAM	16½
32½	Hockering	11
35½	Honingham	8
37½	Easton............	6
43½	NORWICH	*

To Yarmouth (p. 55) 23¼*m.*

Points of Junction.

[*e*] DERBY
To Nottingham 16m.

NOTTINGHAM
To Bingham 10m.; thence to Grantham 14m.

GRANTHAM
To Donnington 19½m.

DONNINGTON
To Boston 8½.

[*e* 2] BOSTON
To Spalding 15½m.

SPALDING
To Holbeach 8m.; thence to Wisbeach 14m.

WISBEACH
To Lynn 15½m.

[*f*] GRANTHAM
To Coltersworth 8m.; thence to Bourn 12½m.

BOURN
To Spalding 9½m.

SPALDING
To Holbeach 8m.

HOLBEACH
To Lynn 16¾m.

[*g*] WISBEACH
To Downham 13m.

DOWNHAM
To Swaffham 14½m.

En § 131

*	MANCHESTER ..	22
1½	Ardwick Green....	20½
4	Levenshulme......	18
5¼	Heaton Norris,....	16¾
	Cheshire.	
6½	STOCKPORT....	15½
9	Bullock Smithy ..	13
12½	Disley............	9½
	Derbyshire.	
15½	Whaley Bridge ..	6½
	To Chapel-en-le-Frith 4m. [*a*].	
16¼	Shall Cross Mill ...	5¾
19½	White Hall	2½
22	BUXTON	*

To Bakewell, § 133.

En § 132

21	BUXTON	44¾
	As in the opp. col. to	
*	Matlock Bath ...	23¾
1	Cromford	22¾
6¼	Amber Gate [*d*]...	17½
	To Derby 9½m.	
7¼	Bull Bridge	16½
9¾	Ripley	14
12¼	Codnor	11½
15¾	Eastwood	8
19¼	Nuthall [*c*]	4½
20¼	Cinder Hill	3½
22¼	Bobber's Mill	1½
23¾	NOTTINGHAM [*d*]	*

Points of Junction.

[*a*] MANCHESTER
To Chapel-en-le-Frith 19½m. thence, through the Peak, to Wardlow T. G. 9½m.; thence to Chesterfield 14¼m.

CHESTERFIELD
To Mansfield 12½m.

MANSFIELD
To Southwell 12½m.; thence to Newark 7m.

[*b*] CHAPEL-EN-LE-FRITH
To Wardlow T. G. 9½m.; thence to Bakewell 5½m.

[*c*] Junction of the Road from Alfreton:

BAKEWELL
To Alfreton 18m.

ALFRETON
To Nottingham 16m.

[*d*] This, though the shortest line of route, is not the route usually travelled from Matlock Bath to Nottingham; for, a great part of it being through some very extensive collieries, the road is generally in a very rough state. The usual carriage route is through Derby, as in the opposite column; the circuity of which is amply compensated for, by the better state of the road and the beauty of the scenery.

[*e*] Another Route from Matlock to Derby is thro' Kedleston Park, page 34.

En § 133

*	BUXTON	52
6	Taddington	46
10½	Ashford in the Water	41½
12	BAKEWELL [*b*].	40
15	Rousley	37
17	Darley	35
20	Matlock Bridge [*e*]	32
21	Matlock Bath ...	31
22	Cromford	30
29	BELPER	23
32	Milford	20
33	Duffield...........	19
35	Allestrey	17
37	DERBY [*e*]......	15
39	Chaddesden	13
41½	Borrows Ash......	10½
44½	Risley............	7½
46	Sandyacre	6
	Nottinghamshire.	
47¼	Stapleford	4¾
50½	Lenton	1½
52	NOTTINGHAM ..	*

En § 134

*	NOTTINGHAM ..	24
1½	West Bridgeford...	22½
3¾	Holme Lane	20¼
5½	Ratcliffe..........	18½
8¼	Saxondale	15¾
9½	BINGHAM.......	14½
24	GRANTHAM [*f*].	*

Eo § 135

*	NOTTINGHAM	40½
6½	Normanton	34
12½	Over Broughton	28
	Leicestershire.	
13¼	Nether Broughton	27¼
15¾	Kettleby	24¾
19	MELTON MOWBRAY	21½
20¾	Burton Lazars	19¾
	Rutlandshire.	
26½	Langham	14
27½	Barleythorpe	13
28½	OAKHAM [g]	12
33	Whitwell	7½
	Lincolnshire.	
35	Empingham	5½
40½	STAMFORD	*

To Alconbury Hill, p. 41.

Eo § 136

*	STAMFORD	49
	Northamptonshire.	
5½	Wandsworth	43½
8¼	Ailesworth	41¼
11½	Long Thorpe	37½
13½	PETERBORO' [h]	35½
	Cambridgeshire.	
19½	Whittlesea [k]	29½
31½	MARCH	17½
37½	Chatteris	11½
49	ELY [k]	*

Points of Junction.

[f] GRANTHAM
To Donnington 20½m.

DONNINGTON
To Boston 9½m.

[g] LEICESTER
To Oakham 19m.; thence to Stamford 12m.

STAMFORD
To Market Deeping 8½m.

[h] LEICESTER
To Billesdon 9m.; thence to Uppingham 11m.

UPPINGHAM
To Wandsford 14m.; thence to Peterborough 8m.

PETERBOROUGH
To Huntingdon 19m.

[i] LEICESTER
To Market Harboro' 14½m.; thence to Kettering 11m.

KETTERING
To Thrapston 9½m.; thence to Huntingdon 16½m.

[k] This Route is not always passable in wet seasons; in such case, Peterborough to Ely, through Huntingdon [h] and Cambridge, § 85.

Eo § 137

*	ELY	25
5½	Soham	19½
9	Fordham	16
	Suffolk.	
13	Red House	12
15½	Kenford	9½
21	Saxham	4
25	BURY ST. EDMUNDS	*

Ep § 138

*	OAKHAM [g]	39
2½	Manton	36½
5½	Glayston	33½
	Northamptonshire.	
8	Harringworth	31
12	Deane	27
13½	Deane Thorpe	25½
17	Bensfield	22
21	Lilford	18
24	Clapton	15
	Huntingdonshire.	
26½	Molesworth	12½
28	Division of the Road	11
	To Kimbolton 5½m.; thence to Eaton Socon 8½m.	
31½	Spaldwick	7½
34	Ellington	5
39	HUNTINGDON [i]	*

To Cambridge (§ 85) 15½m.

F § 139

	* GAINSBORO' ...	32¼
	Nottinghamshire.	
2¾	Beckingham T. G. ..	29½
4¾	Wheatley	27½
7	Clareborough	25¼
8	Welham	24¼
9½	EAST RETFORD	22¾
10¾	Babworth	21½
15½	Manton	16¾
17¼	WORKSOP	15
	To Derby, § 143, 144.	
	Derbyshire.	
21	Whitwell	11½
24	Barlborough	8¼
27½	Staveley	4¾
29¾	Brimington	2½
32¼	CHESTERFIELD	*

To Matlock 9½m.

F § 140

	* CHESTERFIELD [*a*]	34
11	Stony Middleton.	23
14	Wardlow Myers T.G.	20
16	TIDESWELL	18
18	Hargate Wall Hill.	16
22	Fairfield	12
23	Buxton	11
	Cheshire.	
26	Moss House	8
29	Forest Chapel....	5
34	MACCLESFIELD	*

To Liverpool, p. 28.

Points of Junction.

[*a*] NEWARK
To Mansfield 19½m.

MANSFIELD
To Chesterfield 12½m.

MANSFIELD
To Matlock 16m.

[*b*]
GAINSBOROUGH
To Chesterfield 32¼m.

CHESTERFIELD
To Matlock 9½m.

MATLOCK
To Wirksworth 4m.; thence to Ashborne 9m.

ASHBORNE
To Cheadle 12½m.

CHEADLE
To Lane End 6½m.; thence to Newcastle 3½m.

CHEADLE
To Stone 10m.

[*c*] ELLESMERE
To Chirk 8m.; thence to Llangollen 7m.

LLANGOLLEN
To Corwen 10m.; thence to Bangor and Holyhead, page 21.

CORWEN
To Bala 12m.; thence to Dolgelly 18m.

F § 141

	* CHESTERFIELD [*b*]	43½
8½	Baslow	35
11	Hasop	32½
13½	Ashford	30
17	Moneyash	26½
19¼	Crankston Grange .	24¼
20½	Crowdy Cote	23
	Staffordshire.	
21½	Longnor	22
23	Harding's Booth ...	20½
28½	Upper Hulme	15
31½	LEEK	12
	Thence, § 108, to	
43½	NEWCASTLE UNDER LYNE [*b*]	*

F § 142

	* NEWCASTLE ...	32½
2½	Keele	30
4½	Little Madeley	26
5½	Great Madeley	27
	Shropshire.	
8½	Woore	24
10	Sandyford	22½
	Cheshire.	
11	Buerton	21½
13	Audlem	19½
14½	Cheley Bridge	18
	Shropshire.	
21½	WHITCHURCH..	11
32½	ELLESMERE [*c*].	*

Fa § 143

Yorkshire.

*	DONCASTER [d]	43
3½	Loversall	39½
4½	Wadworth	38½
7½	TICKHILL	35½

Nottinghamshire.

9½	Goldthorpe	33½
13¾	Carlton	29¼
17	WORKSOP	26
19¾	Worksop Manor	23¼
20¾	Norton	22¼
23	Church Warsop	20
24½	Market Warsop	18½
27½	Mansfield Woodhouse	15½
29	MANSFIELD [e].	14

To Derby, § 144, below.

33½	Newstead T. G.	9½

Thro' Sherwood Forest.

38½	Red Hill	4½
43	NOTTINGHAM	*

To Leicester, § 145.

Fa § 144

*	MANSFIELD	21½
6½	Annesley	15
10½	Eastwood	10½

Derbyshire.

12¾	Heanor	8¾
15½	Smalley	6
17½	Morley	4
21½	DERBY	*

To Lichfield (§ 40) 24m.

Points of Junction.

[d] YORK
To Ferry Bridge (p. 43) 22m.; thence to Doncaster 15m.

[e] HARROWGATE
To Leeds 15½m.

LEEDS
To Wakefield 8¾m.

WAKEFIELD
To Sheffield 24m.

SHEFFIELD
To Chesterfield 12½m.

CHESTERFIELD
To Mansfield 12¼m.
Pp. 36, 37.

[f] BUXTON
To Ashborne 20½m.; thence to Derby 13¾m.

DERBY
To Loughborough 16½m.; thence to Leicester 11¼m.
Pp. 30, 31.

LEICESTER
To Market Harboro' 14½m.; thence to Kettering 11m.

KETTERING
To Huntingdon (§ 85) 26m.; thence to Cambridge 15½m.

Fa § 145

*	NOTTINGHAM	57
1	Trent Bridge	56
4½	Ruddington	52½
6	Bradmore	51
7	Bunney	50
9½	Cortlingstock	47½
10½	Rempston	46½

Leicestershire.

11¾	Hoton	45¼
13½	Cotes	43½
15	LOUGHBORO'	42
18	Quarndon	39
19½	MOUNTSORRELL	37½
24½	Belgrave	32½
26½	LEICESTER	30½

To Market Harborough and Kettering [f].

30	Wigston	27
35½	Shearsby	21½
40	Husband's Bosworth	17

Northamptonshire.

42½	WELFORD	14½
45¾	Thornby	11¼
49¼	Upper Creaton	7¾
52¾	Chapel Brampton	4¼
55½	Kingsthorpe	1½
57	NORTHAMPTON	*

To Newport Pagnell (p. 24) 16m.; thence to Woburn 8½m.

*	WORCESTER [a]	39½
	Cross the Severn.	
1	St. John's	38½
3	Powick	36½
6½	Newland's Green	33
8½	GREAT MALVERN	31
10½	MALVERN WELLS	29
12	Little Malvern	27½
	Herefordshire.	
15	Lower Mitchel	24½
16½	LEDBURY	23
19½	Preston (*Glo'stersh.*)	20
21¼	Much Marcle	18¼
25½	Old Gore	14
29¼	ROSS	10¼
30	Wilton T. G.	9½
32¾	Pencraig	6¾
33¾	Goodrich	5¾
35½	Whitchurch	4
	Monmouthshire.	
39½	MONMOUTH	*

Fb § 147

*	MONMOUTH [d]	24½
2¼	Wonastow	22¼
8	Ragland	16½
13	USKE	11½
20½	Caerleon	4
22	Christchurch	2½
24½	NEWPORT	*

To Swansea (p. 73) 58½*m.*

Points of Junction.

[a] DERBY
To Lichfield 24m.

LICHFIELD
To Birmingham 16m.

BIRMINGHAM
To Worcester 26m.
§ 39, 40.

[b]
KIDDERMINSTER
To the Hundred House 10m.; thence to Bromyard 12m.

BROMYARD
To Hereford 14m.—§ 109.

HEREFORD
To Abergavenny 24m.

[c]
KIDDERMINSTER
To Tenbury 16m.

TENBURY
To Leominster 11m.

LEOMINSTER
To Hay 22½m.

[d] CHELTENHAM
To Gloucester 9½m.

GLOUCESTER
To Monmouth 25½m.
Page 75.

[e] BRECON
To Llandovery 20m.; thence to Tenby, p. 75.

*	WORCESTER	32
	As in the opp. col. to	
16½	LEDBURY	15½
	Thence, page 7, to	
32	HEREFORD	*

Another Route from Worcester to Hereford is through Bromyard, page 11; a very picturesque and beautiful ride.—A shorter Route is by Stifford's Bridge, page 7 B, but some parts of it are very indifferent as a carriage road.

Fb § 149

*	HEREFORD [b]	36
1¼	White Cross	34¾
2½	King's Acre	33½
4	Sugwas Pool	32
5	Ware	31
6½	Bridge Sollers	29½
8	Garnons	28
8¾	Portway	27¼
9¾	Stanton	26¼
10½	Hanmer's Cross	25½
11¾	Letton	24¼
13½	Willersley	22½
14¼	Winforton	21¾
16¼	Whitney	19¾
18½	Clifford	17½
	Brecknockshire.	
21	HAY [c]	15
25	Glasbury	11
28¼	Brynllys	7¾
31¾	Velinvach	4¼
36	BRECON [e]	*

WORCESTER [a,f] 62

See § 38, to

Gloucestershire.

TEWKESBURY . 46

Junction of Road from Malvern [g]

* GLOUCESTER .. 35

3¼ Quedgley 31¾

4 Hardwick Elm 31

To Frocester 7m.; thence to Lasborough, on this road, 6½m.

8½ Stonehouse 26½

11 Rodborough 24

Junction of Road from Stroud [h]

12½ Inchborough 22½

13¼ Nailsworth 21¾

To Horsley 1m. § 42.

14½ Tipput's Inn 20½

16 Lasborough 19

Junction of Road from Frocester.

19¾ Dunkirk 15¼

20½ Beaufort Arms, Petty France ... 14½

23½ Cross Hands Inn . 11½

26½ Toll Down House.. 8½

28¼ Dyrham Park 6¾

30 Tog Hill 5

Somersetshire.

32 Swanswick 3

35 BATH .... *

Points of Junction.

[f] CHESTER

To Shrewsbury 40m.—§ 22.

SHREWSBURY

To Bridgnorth 22½m.

BRIDGNORTH

To Worcester 27m.—§ 51. *Thence to Cheltenham,* § 49.

MANCHESTER

To Stafford 52½m.

STAFFORD

To Wolverhampton 16½m.; thence to Worcester 29m. § 91.

LIVERPOOL

To Stafford (pp. 27, 28) 73m.; thence to Worcester, as above, § 91.

Or, Liverpool to Birmingham; thence, through Cheltenham, § 42, 43, to Bath.

[g] MALVERN

To Tewkesbury 17m. Page 7.

[h] GLOUCESTER

To Painswick 7m.

PAINSWICK

To Stroud 4m.; thence to Rodborough ½m.

Somersetshire.

* BATH 39

3½ Midford 35½

5¾ Charterhouse Hinton 33¼

6½ Norton St. Philip.. 32½

8½ Woolverton 30½

10 Beckington 29

11¼ Oakford 27¾

13 FROME 26

15 Marston Inn 24

18½ Wanstrow 20½

24 BRUTON 15

25½ Pitcomb 13½

29 WINCAUNTON .. 10

31 Lotterford 8

Dorsetshire.

39 SHERBORNE .... *

To Weymouth, § 19.

Another Route is through Shepton Mallet:—

* BATH 60½

4 Dunkerton 56½

7½ Radstoke 53

11 Stratton 49½

14 Oakhill 46½

16 SHEPTON MALLET 44½

Thence (§ 19) to

60½ WEYMOUTH .... *

Fm § 152	CROSS ROADS.	Fm § 153

Lincolnshire.

	LOUTH [a]......	102
	See page 51, to	
*	BOSTON	71
4	Kirton Holme	67
5½	SWINESHEAD ..	65½
8¼	DONNINGTON ..	62¾
12½	Bridgend Causeway	58½
14	Horbling..........	57
15½	Sempringham......	55½
18½	Dowsby	52½
21¾	Morton	49¼
24½	BOURN	46½
26½	Toft...............	44½
32	Ryall (Rutlandsh.)	39
34½	STAMFORD	36½

To Uppingham 12 m; thence to Northampton (§ 60) 28½ m.

Northamptonshire.

35½	Worthop..........	35½
36½	Easton on the Hill .	34½
38	Collyweston.......	33
40	Duddington	31
42	Fineshade	29
44	Bulwick..........	27
48½	Weldon...........	22½
57	KETTERING	14
60	Broughton	11
67	Overston	4
71	NORTHAMPTON	*

Another Route from Louth to Northampton thro' Horncastle [a].

Points of Junction.

[a] SALTFLEET
To Louth 10m.

LOUTH
To Horncastle 14m.

HORNCASTLE
To Sleaford 22m.

SLEAFORD
To Coltersworth 22½m.; thence to Oakham 11½m.

OAKHAM
To Uppingham 6½m.; thence to Northampton 28½.—§ 60.

[b] LYNN
To Peterboro' 35m.—§ 63.

PETERBOROUGH
To Northampton 42½m. § 61.

NORTHAMPTON
To Oxford 42m.—§ 59. Thence to Bath, § 73.

LINCOLN
To Northampton 78m.—§60.

[c] *Another Route:*

NORTHAMPTON
To Daventry 13m.

DAVENTRY
To Banbury 17m.—§ 57.

BANBURY
To Chapel House 11¾m.; thence to Burford 12m.

BURFORD
To Bibury 10m.; thence to Cirencester 7m.—§ 71.

Northamptonshire.

*	NORTHAMPTON [b]	76
5¼	Blisworth.........	70¾
10	TOWCESTER....	66
13	Silverston	63
16	Syersham	60

To Banbury 11½m.; thence to Cirencester. [c]

20	BRACKLEY	56
23¼	Barley Mow Inn ..	52¾

Oxfordshire.

30¼	DEDDINGTON ..	45¾
36½	Pomfreet Castle ...	39½
40	CHAPEL HOUSE	36
41	CHIP. NORTON.	35
44¾	Salford Hill.......	31¼

Gloucestershire.

47	Oddington	29
49	STOW ON THE WOLD	27

To Tewkesbury (p. 7, A) 22*m.*

50	Lower Swell	26
53	R. *to Winchcombe* 9*m*.	23
60	Dowdeswell House.	16

To Cheltenham 4¼m.

63	Seven Wells.......	13
65	*To Gloucester 7¾m.* .	11
66	Birdlip	10
72	Painswick	4
76	STROUD	*

To Bath § 42.

DONCASTER [*d*] 105½
See § 143, to

Nottinghamshire.

WORKSOP 88½
Thence, 26m. to

* NOTTINGHAM .. 62½
Thence, § 145, to

Leicestershire.

26½ LEICESTER 36

To Lutterworth and Rugby, § 57. —*At Lutterworth, to Coventry* § 84.

35½ Earl Shilton 27
39¼ HINCKLEY 23¼
41¼ Harrow Inn 21¼

Warwickshire.

44¼ NUNEATON 18¼
46¼ Griff............. 16¼
47½ Bedworth 15
49½ Longford.......... 13
50½ Foleshill.......... 12
52½ COVENTRY 10
53½ Stivichall 9
57½ KENILWORTH.. 5
61½ Guy's Cliffe 1
62½ WARWICK [*d*].. *

To Leamington 2m.

To Bath, through Cheltenham. See § 65, Warwick to Cheltenham, 41½; thence to Bath, § 42, 40½m.

Through Cirencester. See annexed column, § 155.

Points of Junction.

[*d*] *Through Derby:*

DONCASTER
To Mansfield 20m.

MANSFIELD
To Derby 21½m.—§ 144. Thence, through Birmingham, to Bath, [*d* 2].

DERBY
To Coventry 45m.—§ 85.

COVENTRY
To Warwick 10m. Thence, as in the annexed column.

[*d* 2] DERBY
To Lichfield 24m.—§ 40.

LICHFIELD
To Birmingham 16m. Thence, through Worcester, § 39,150; or through Cheltenham, § 43.

[*e*] BIRMINGHAM
To Stratford on Avon (p. 17) 23m.

STRATFORD ON AVON
To Halford Bridge 10m.; thence to Stow on the Wold, &c. as in the annexed column.

[*f*] *Another Route:*

CIRENCESTER
To Tetbury 10m.; thence to Cross Hands Inn 10½m.—§ 70.

Warwickshire.

2 LEAMINGTON 81½
* WARWICK [*d*] .. 79½
2½ Barford........... 77
6 Wellesburne Hastings............. 73½
10½ Upper Eatington .. 69
12½ HALFORD BRIDGE [*e*] 67

Gloucestershire.

21½ MORTON IN MARSH 58
25½ STOW ON THE WOLD [*e*]..... 54
29 Stow Bridge 50½
31½ Broadwater Bottom 48
34½ L. *to Northleach* ½*m.* 45
37½ Foss Bridge 42½
38½ Foss Cross........ 41
44½ CIRENCESTER.. 35

To Bristol 35½m. § 70.

To Marlborough, § 92.

48 Thames &Sev. Canal 31½

Wiltshire.

56 MALMESBURY . 23½

To Chippenham 9½*m.; thence to Bath* 13*m.*

63 Lackington 16½

Gloucestershire.

64½ Acton Turvil...... 14½
68 CROSS HANDS INN [*f*] 11½
Thence, § 42, to
79½ BATH .... *

G § 156

Lancashire.

	* LANCASTER	66½
5	Caton	61½
7	Claughton..........	59½
9	HORNBY.........	57½
11	Melling	55½
12	Division of the Road	54½

L. *to Kirkby Lonsdale* [*a*]

12¾	Cransfield..........	53¾

Yorkshire.

15	Black Burton	51½
18	Ingleton	48½

To Pateley Bridge, § 157.

33	HAWES..........	33½
37	Bainbridge.........	29½
38½	ASKRIGG [*b*]....	29
43	Carperby	23½
45½	Redmire	21
51½	Halfpenny House..	15
56½	RICHMOND	10

R. *to Catterick Bridge* 3½*m.; thence to Northallerton* 12*m.*

To Stockton on Tees [*c*].

L. *to Greta Bridge* 10*m.; thence to Bernard Castle* 3½*m.*

59½	Gilling	7
64	Stanwick	2½
66½	Pierce Bridge ...	*

Thence to DURHAM (p. 45 A) 20½*m.; and onwards to Newcastle.*

Points of Junction.

[*a*] LANCASTER
To Kirkby Lonsdale 15½m.

KIRKBY LONSDALE
To Sedbergh 11m.

SEDBERGH
To Kirkby Stephen 13m.

[*b*] KENDAL
To Sedbergh 11m.

SEDBERGH
To Askrigg 18½m.

[*c*] RICHMOND
To Enter Common T. G. 11½m.; thence, through Yarm, to Stockton on Tees, 12½m.

STOCKTON
To Sunderland 27m.—P. 48.

[*d*] PATELEY BRIDGE
To Ripon 12½m.

RIPON
To Skipton Bridge 7m.; thence to Thirsk 5m.

THIRSK
To Helmsley, Pickering, and Scarborough, § 157.

[*e*] *At Market Weighton*,
To South Cave 8m.; thence to Brough Ferry ½m.

Ga § 157

	* LANCASTER	81½

As in § 152, to

Yorkshire.

18	Ingleton	63½
22	Clapham...........	59½

To Settle and Skipton, as in opp. col. § 158.

24½	Wharfe	57
28	Great Staniforth ...	53½

Over Malham Moor.

32½	Malham Water	49
37	Calecop	44½
40	Grassington	41½
46½	Greenhough Hill ..	35
49½	PATELEY BRIDGE	32

To Studley Royal 10*m.; thence to Ripon* 2½*m.* [*d*]

54	Brimham Hall.....	27½
56	Burn Yates	25½
59	RIPLEY	22½

To Harrogate 4½*m.*

63½	KNARESBORO'.	18
66½	Flaxby T. G.......	15
68	Thornville Royal..	13½
71½	Green Hammerton.	10
73	Skip Bridge.......	8½
80	Holdgate	1½
81½	YORK	*

To Market Weighton [*e*], *Beverley, and Hull*, § 102.

*	KENDAL [*f*]....	89
	As in page 40, to	
	Yorkshire.	
19½	INGLETON	69½
23½	Clapham..........	65½
	To Pateley Bridge, § 157.	
29¼	Giggleswick.......	59¾
30	SETTLE	59
34	Long-Preston......	55
36	Hellifield Cochins..	53
39	Cold Coniston	50
41	Gargrave	48
44	Sturton Thorlby ...	45
46	SKIPTON........	43
	To Bradford 20m. [*i*]	
51½	Addingham........	37½
54	Ilkley	35
58½	Burley	30½
61	OTLEY..........	28
64	Pool	25
	To Leeds 8m. [*k*]; *thence to Ferry Bridge 15m.*	
66	Arthington........	23
67½	Weardley	21½
69	HAREWOOD....	20
73¾	Collingham........	15¼
75¼	Division of the Road	13¾
	To Wetherby 1½m.; thence to York 13m.	
76¼	Thorp Spa	12¾
80	TADCASTER	9
89	YORK	*

Points of Junction.

[*f*] KESWICK
To Ambleside 16m.

AMBLESIDE
To Kendal 14m.

[*g*] WHITEHAVEN
To Hawkshead 26½m.

HAWKSHEAD
To Kendal 14m.—P. 40.

[*h*] KIRKBY STEPHEN
To Hardrow 14m.

[*i*] SKIPTON
To Keighley 10m.; thence to Bradford 10m.

BRADFORD
To Wakefield 14m.

WAKEFIELD
To Doncaster 20m.
See p. 38 N.

[*k*] SKIPTON
To Otley 15m.; thence to Leeds 11m.

LEEDS
To Peckfield 10m.; thence to Selby 11m.

SELBY
To Snaith 8m.; thence to Howden 9½m.

HOWDEN
To South Cave 12½m.; thence to Hull 12½m.—§ 98.

*	KENDAL [*g*]....	72
8¼	Lincoln's Inn Bridge	63¾
	Yorkshire.	
10½	SEDBERGH	61½
14	Morthwaite Bridge.	58
16	Smorthwaite Bridge	56
17	Little Town	55
22	Thwaite Bridge....	50
25	Hardrow [*h*]......	47
25½	*To Hawes ½m.*	46½
30½	ASKRIGG	41½
35	Carperby	37
37½	Redmire	34½
41	Wensley	31
42	LEYBURN	30
43	Harmby	29
44	Spennythorne	28
45¾	Ulshaw Bridge	26¼
46	Cover Bridge......	26
46½	East Witton	25½
48½	Jervaux Abbey....	23½
51	Low Ellington	21
53½	MASHAM	18½
57	Nosterfield	15
64	York Gate Inn	8
	To Boroughbridge 7m.; thence to York 17m.	
72	THIRSK	*
	Thence to Helmsley, Pickering, & Scarborough, § 161.	

Lancashire.

31½	LIVERPOOL	91
	As in p. 29, to	
*	PRESTON [a]....	59½
1½	Walton le Dale....	58
5½	Samlesbury	54
8½	Mellor............	51
16	Whalley	43½
20	CLITHEROE	39½
21	Chatburn..........	38½
	Yorkshire.	
23	Sawley	36½
27	Gisburn	32½
32	West Marton......	27½
33	Church Marton	26½
35½	Broughton	24
38½	SKIPTON	21
	To Otley, Tadcaster, and York, § 158.	
	At Otley, to Leeds, Howden, and Hull.	
44	Bolton Bridge ...	15½
45½	Hazlewood........	14
49½	Blubber Houses....	10
53½	Kettlesing	6
56½	Division of the Road	3
	L. *to Ripley 3m.; thence to Ripon* 8m. [c].	
59½	HARROGATE ...	*

To Knaresborough 2m.; thence to YORK 18m. § 157.

Points of Junction.

[a] *Another Route from Preston to Skipton:*

PRESTON
To Blackburn 12m.

BLACKBURN
To Burnley 12m.; thence to Colne 6½m.

At Burnley to Halifax, Wakefield, and Doncaster, p. 38.

COLNE
To Skipton 13m.

[b] *Other Routes:*

HARROGATE
To York 20m.

YORK
To New Malton 18m.

NEW MALTON
To Snainton 12m.; thence to Scarborough.

Or,
[b 2] BOROUGH-BRIDGE
To Easingwold 10½m.

EASINGWOLD
To New Malton 19m.

[c] RIPON
To Thirsk 12m.

THIRSK
To Tontine Inn 12m.; thence to Guisborough 17½m. Page 48.

To Stockton on Tees, Sunderland, and Shields. P. 48.

RIPON
To Northallerton 6½m.; thence to Darlington and Durham, p. 43.

Yorkshire.

*	HARROGATE [b]	65
5	Ferrinsby	60
9	BOROUGH-BRIDGE	56
	To New Malton [b 2].	
13	Dishforth	52
15½	Topcliffe	49½
21	THIRSK	44
24½	Sutton under Whitstone Cliffe	40½
29½	Scawton	35½
34	HELMSLEY	31
36½	Nawton	28½
39½	KIRKBY MOORSIDE..........	25½
40	Kelholme	25
43	Sinnington	22
44½	Wrelton	20½
45½	Aislaby	19½
46	Middleton	19
47½	PICKERING.....	17½
50	Thornton	15
51¼	Wilton	13¾
53½	Ebberston.........	11½
55	Snainton	10
57	Brompton	8
58½	Wykeham	6½
60½	East Ayton	4½
64	Falsgrave.........	1
65	SCARBORO' [b].	*

Ge § 162

59	CARLISLE [d] to	
	Yorkshire.	
*	GRETA BRIDGE....	57
2	Smallways........	55
	See opp. col. § 163.	
9½	Scotch Corner.....	47½
13	Citadella	44
	To Catterick Bridge ½m.; thence to York § 164.	
14½	Scorton...........	42½
15	Bolton...........	42
17½	Kiplin...........	39½
18½	Great Langton.....	38½
22¾	Yafforth	34¼
24½	NORTHALLERTON...........	32½
	To Boroughbridge (p. 43) 18½*m.; thence to York* 17*m.*	
30½	Thornton-in-the-Street..........	26½
33½	THIRSK	23½
35½	Stockwell T. G. ...	21½
39¾	Thormanby........	17¼
44	EASINGWOLD ..	13
48	Tollerton Lanes ...	9
52	Skipton	5
53	Skelton...........	4
57	YORK...........	*

To Market Weighton 19*m.* [*g*]*; thence to Beverley and Hull*, § 102.

CROSS ROADS.

Points of Junction.

[d] CARLISLE
To Penrith 18m.—P. 46.

PENRITH
To Appleby 13m.

APPLEBY
To Brough 8½m.; thence to Greta Bridge 19½m.

[d2] BROUGH
To Bowes 13m.; thence to Bernard Castle 4½m.

BERNARD CASTLE
To Staindrop 5½m.; thence to Bishop's Auckland 9m.

BISHOP'S AUCKLAND
To Durham 10m. § 169.

[e] BERNARD CASTLE
To Pierce Bridge 13m.; thence to Darlington 5m.

DARLINGTON
To Stockton on Tees 10½m.; thence to Guisborough, § 170.

DARLINGTON
To Yarm 10m.

[f] *Junction of Road from Harrogate.*

HARROGATE
To York 20m. § 160.

[g] MARKET WEIGHTON
To South Cave 8m.; thence to Brough Ferry ½m. Across the Humber to Wintringham 3m.; thence to Glandford Brigg, Louth, &c.

Gf § 163

*	ALDSTON MOOR	43¼
3½	Carrigillgate	39¾
	Durham.	
8	Harwood	35¼
14	Newbiggin........	29¼
17½	MIDDLETON IN TEASDALE ...	25¾
21	Romaldkirk	22¼
27	BERNARD CASTLE	16¼
	To Staindrop 5½*m.* [*d* 2]	
	To Pierce Bridge 13*m.* [*e*].	
	Yorkshire.	
30	GRETA BRIDGE....	13¼
	Junction of Road from Carlisle by Penrith and Appleby [d].	
32	Smallways........	11¼
	To Richmond 8*m.; thence to Catterick Bridge* 3½*m.*	
39¼	ScotchCorner, 3Tuns	4
43¼	CATTERICK BRIDGE	*

Gf § 164

*	CATTERICK BRIDGE	40
7½	Leeming T. G.	32½
9	Londonderry	31
11	LEEMING LANE....	29
16	York Gate Inn....	24
23	BORO'BRIDGE..	17
30	Gr. Hammerton [f]	10
31½	Skip Bridge	8½
38½	Holdgate	1½
40	YORK	*

Gh § 165

Cumberland.

*	KESWICK [a]	98
4½	Threlkeld	93½
11½	Penruddock	86½
17	PENRITH	81
21½	Longwathby	76½
25½	Melmerby	72½
29	Hartside Cross	69
36	ALDSTON MOOR	62

To St. John's Weardale 13m.; thence to Wolsingham and Durham [d].

To Bernard Castle, § 163.

Northumberland.

42	Green Gate	56
47½	Catten	50½
53	Scotland	45
56	HEXHAM	42

To Newcastle, § 168.

60	Pict's Wall	38

Cross the Military Road.

61	Chollerton	37

L. *to Bellingham* 10*m.*

64	Collell	34
74	Cambo	24

To Morpeth 12*m.*

86	ROTHBURY	12
90	Rimside Moor Guide Post	8

R. *to Rimside House* ½*m.*
L. *to Wooler,* 16½*m.*

98	ALNWICK	*

Points of Junction.

[a] WORKINGTON
To Cockermouth 7½m.

COCKERMOUTH
To Keswick 12m.—P. 40.

[a 2] KESWICK
To Thorney Stone 11½m.

IREBY
To Thorney Stone 2½m.

[b] WORKINGTON
To Little Clifton 8½m.

[c] WORKINGTON
To Maryport 5m.

MARYPORT
To Aspatria 8m.; thence to Wigton 7½m.

WIGTON
To Carlisle 10½m.

ALLONBY
To Wigton 12m.

[d] ALDSTON MOOR
To St. John's Weardale 13m.; thence to Wolsingham 13m.

WOLSINGHAM
To Durham 15m.

Gh § 166

Cumberland.

*	WHITEHAVEN	40
2	Moresby	38
4	Distington	36
6	Winscales	34
8	Crossbarrow	32
8¾	Little Clifton [b]	31¼
11	Brigham	29
14	COCKERMOUTH	26
19	Ouse Bridge	21
23¼	Uldale	16¾
24½	Thorney Stone	15½

Junction of Roads from Keswick and Ireby [a 2].

30½	Warnell	9½
31½	Upper Welton	8½
34	Hawksdale	6
35½	Dalston	4½
40	CARLISLE [c]	*

To Moffatt 45*m.; thence to* GLASGOW 56*m.* [e].

To Hawick 44*m.; thence to Jedburgh* 10½*m.* See page 46.

To EDINBURGH *by Selkirk* 91*m.* [*f*].

——— *by Moffatt and Linton* 94*m.* [e2].

THE MILITARY ROAD.

Cumberland.

- * CARLISLE 56¼
- ¾ Stanwix 55½
- 4¾ High Crosby 51½
- 9¼ BRAMPTON 47
- 11¾ Naworth Castle on the left 44½
- 15¼ Tammon Inn 41

Northumberland.

- 18 GLENWHELT 38¼
- 19 Division of the Road 37¼
  To Hexham, § 168.
- 24¼ Whin Shields 32
- 27¼ Kennel 29
- 31¾ Caraw Brow 24½
- 34¼ Walwick 22
- 35¼ CHOLLERFORD BRIDGE 21

Junction of Road from Bellingham, [g].

- 36¼ Hillhead 20
- 39¾ Wheat Sheaf Inn .. 16½

Junction of Road from Jedburgh.

- 43¼ Wall Houses 13
- 45¾ Harlow Hill 10½
- 49¼ Heddon-on-the-Wall 7
- 52¼ Chapel Hill 4
- 53¼ Denton Bourn 3
- 56¼ NEWCASTLE-ON-TYNE .... *

Points of Junction.

[e] CARLISLE
To Gretna Green 14m.

GRETNA
To Lockerby 15m.; thence to Moffatt 16½m.

MOFFATT
To Glasgow 56m. P. 47.

[e 2] MOFFATT
To Linton 30m.; thence to Edinburgh 16m.

---

[f] CARLISLE
To Langholme 20½m.; thence to Mospaul Inn 10½m.

MOSPAUL INN
To Hawick 13m.; thence to Selkirk 11m.

SELKIRK
To Torsance 12m.; thence to Edinburgh 24½m.

---

[g] BELLINGHAM
To Newcastle 32m.

---

[h] *Another Route:*

NEWCASTLE
By Gateshead to Scot's House T.G. 5m.; thence to Sunderland 6½m.

THE MAIL ROAD.

- * CARLISLE 56

As in the opp. col. to

Northumberland.

- 18 GLENWHELT 38
- 19 Division of the Road 37
- 21 HALTWHISTLE 35
- 23½ Milkridge 32½
- 26 Barden Mills...... 30
- 30 Haydon 26

Cross the South Tyne.

- 33½ Junction of Road from Aldston Moor, § 165 .... 22½
- 36 HEXHAM 20
- 37 Division of the Road 19
  To Riding 3¼m.; thence to Newcastle 16¼m.

Cross the Tyne.

- 39 CORBRIDGE.... 17
- 46 Horsley 10
- 49 Heddon-on-the-Wall 7
- 52 Chapel Hill 4
- 53 Denton Bourn 3
- 56 NEWCASTLE-ON-TYNE......... *

To North Shields 7½m.; thence to Tynemouth 1½m.

At North Shields,

R. *to South Shields ½m.; thence to Sunderland 7¾m.* [h]

Westmorland.

* KENDAL [*a*] .. 71
4½ Grayrigg.......... 66½
11 Division of the Road 60
To Appleby 12½*m.* [*a* 2].
14 Langdale 57
19 Cold Beck......... 52
24 KIRKBY STEPHEN [*b*]. 47
26 Winton............ 45
27½ Brough Sowerby .. 43½
28¾ BROUGH......... 42¼

Yorkshire.

36½ Spittle House 34½
42 Bowes............. 29
To Greta Bridge 6½*m.*

Durham.

46½ BERNARD CASTLE........... 24½
R. *to Pierce Bridge* [*c*].
L. *to Wolsingham* 13*m.*
52 STAINDROP 19
53¼ Raby............. 17¾
57¼ West Auckland ... 13¾
61 BISHOP'S AUCKLAND 10
66½ Holywell House .. 4½
68 Sunderland Bridge 3
69½ Elvet Moor 1½
71 DURHAM .... *
To Sunderland 13*m.; thence to South Shields* 7¼. p. 48.

Points of Junction.

[*a*] DALTON
To Ulverstone 5m.

ULVERSTONE
To Newby Bridge 8½m.; thence to Kendal.

[*a* 2] KENDAL
To Orton 14m.; thence to Appleby 9½m.

[*b*] KENDAL
To Sedbergh 10½m.

SEDBERGH
To Rother Bridge 6m.; thence to Kirkby Stephen, 13½m.

[*c*]
BERNARD CASTLE
To Pierce Bridge 13m.; thence to Darlington 5m.

DARLINGTON
To Stockton-on-Tees 10½m.; thence to Hartlepool 12½m.

STOCKTON-ON-TEES.
To Guisborough 12½m.

[*d*] STOCKTON-ON-TEES
To Castle Eden Inn 14m.; thence to Sunderland 13½m.

SUNDERLAND
To South Shields 7½m.; thence to Tynemouth 2m.

Yorkshire.

* SCARBOROUGH 71½
3½ Burniston......... 68
4½ Cloughton......... 67
7½ Stainton Dale 64
13 Robin Hood's Bay 58½
18¼ WHITBY........ 53¼
22½ Lythe 49
29½ Scaling Dam 42
33½ Lockwood Beck ... 38
38½ GUISBOROUGH. 33
43½ West Upsall 28
44½ Ormsby........... 27

Durham.

51 STOCKTON-ON-TEES......... 20½
To Hartlepool 12½*m.*
52½ Norton Inn 19
To Bishop Wearmouth, Sunderland, and Shields, p. 48 [*d*].
56½ Thorpe 15
59 Layton 12½
60½ SEDGEFIELD .. 11
69½ Shincliffe......... 2
71½ DURHAM .... *
To Shotley Bridge 15*m.*
To Newcastle 14½*m.; thence to Morpeth, Alnwick, and Edinburgh*, p. 43.

	Gn § 171	
*	YORK [e]	89
1¾	Dring Houses	87¼
6½	Street Houses	82½
9½	TADCASTER	79½
13½	Division of the Road	75½
15½	ABBERFORD	73½
19½	Garforth Bridge	69½
22¼	Swillington Bridge	66¾
25	Newmarket	64
28½	WAKEFIELD [f]	60½
	Thence, page 37, to	
52½	SHEFFIELD	36½
	To Shrewsbury, § 172.	
	Derbyshire.	
57	Greenhill Common	32
59	DRONFIELD	30
62½	Whittington Common	26½
65	CHESTERFIELD	24
70½	Clay Cross T. G.	18½
75½	Peacock Inn	13½
79	Heage T. G.	10
82	Bargate	7
84½	Duffield	4½
86½	Allestry	2½
89	DERBY	*

To Coventry; thence to Warwick and Leamington, § 55, 54.
To Lichfield and Birmingham, § 40: *thence*, § 42, 43, *thro' Cheltenham, to*

BATH.

Points of Junction.

[e]
SCARBOROUGH
To Malton 22m.; thence to York 18m.—§ 101.

[f]
HARROGATE
To Leeds 15½m.

LEEDS
To Wakefield 9m.—P. 37.

[g] BUXTON
To Leek 12m.; thence to Stone 15m.

STONE
To Stafford 7½m.

STAFFORD
To Wolverhampton; thence to Kidderminster and Worcester, § 91.

WORCESTER
To Bath, § 150.

[h] BUXTON
To Leek 12m.

LEEK
To Sandon 18¼m.; thence to Lichfield 17½m.

	Go § 172	
*	SHEFFIELD	50
3½	Hill Top	46½
	Derbyshire.	
5	Ringinglow T. G.	45
10	Grindleford Bridge	40
12	Calver	38
14	Hasop	36
17	Ashford	33
20¾	Moneyash	29¼
22¾	Crankston Grange	27¼
24	Crowdy Cote	26
	Staffordshire.	
25	LONGNOR	25
	To Cheadle 16m.; *thence to Stone* 10m.	
26½	Harding's Booth	23½
31½	Upper Hulme	18½
35	LEEK [g]	15
	To Newcastle; thence to Shrewsbury, § 105. *To Lichfield* [h].	
38	Cheadleton	12
40½	Wetley Rocks	9½
41½	Cellar Head	8½
44	Weston Coney	6
48½	Oulton	1½
50	STONE [g]	*

Thence to Shrewsbury § 2.
To Stafford [g]; *thence, through Worcester, to*

BATH.

Dorsetshire.

*	WEYMOUTH....	63
4½	Osmington........	58½
11	Winfrith..........	52
14	Wool Bridge......	49
17	Stoke Green	46
20	WAREHAM	43
25½	Lychett Minster ...	37½
29	Bushels	34
33½	WIMBORN MINSTER........	29½

Hampshire.

38½	New Bridge	24½
	Junction of Road from Poole [c]	
43	RINGWOOD	20
46	Picked Post	17
52	Stoney Cross.....	11
54½	Cadnam	8½
	To Winchester 17m.; thence to Farnham and Guildford [c]	
59	Totton............	4
59½	Redbridge	3½
61	Milbrook	2
63	SOUTHAMPTON	*

To Portsmouth. [b]

To Alton (p 60 B) *28m.; thence to* GUILDFORD *19½m.*

Thence, to Leatherhead, Epsom, Croydon, &c. [f]

Points of Junction.

[a] HEREFORD
To Ross 14½m. page 5.

ROSS
To Gloucester 16½m.

GLOUCESTER
To Cirencester 18m. p. 8.

---

[b]
CHRISTCHURCH
To Lyndhurst 13m; thence to Southampton 9½m.

SOUTHAMPTON
To Portsmouth 20½m. §24; Or, by Gosport and across the Ferry, 17½m.

---

[c] POOLE
To Cadnam 26m.; thence to Romsey 6m.

ROMSEY
To Winchester 11m.

WINCHESTER
To Alton 18m.

[c 2] ALTON
To Farnham 9½m.

FARNHAM
To Guildford 10m.

GUILDFORD
To Dorking 12m.; thence to Reigate 6m.

REIGATE
To River Head 18½m; thence to Maidstone 17½m.

Gloucestershire.

*	CHELTENHAM .	72
2½	Leckhampton Court	69½
6½	Birdlip	65½
20	CIRENCESTER[a]	52
23	Ampney Crucis....	49
25½	Poulton (Wilts) ...	46½
29	FAIRFORD	43
33	LECHLADE	39

Berkshire.

35	Buscot............	37
39	FARRINGDON ..	33
	To Abingdon (p 8) *14m.; thence to Henley on Thames, 21m.*	
42½	Stanford	29½
46½	East Charlow	25½
47½	WANTAGE	24½
	To Wallingford 14m. thence to Henley on Thames 10½m.	
	Over the Downs to	
62	Streatley	10
63½	Basildon..........	8½
66	Pangbourn........	6
68	Purley	4
72	READING	*

Or, through Wallingford, as follows:

Wantage to Wallingford 14m.; thence to Reading (§ 80) 15½m.

He § 175

Berkshire.

* READING 32
3½ Loddon Bridge 28½
4½ Merry Hill Green.. 27½
R. *to Wokingham 3½m.; thence to Ascot Heath 7m.*
6 Bill Hill 26
9 Binfield Common .. 23
To Windsor 9m. [*d*]
See page 1 A.
9½ Junction of Road from Wokingham 23½
11 Bracknell 21
14½ Ascot Heath 17½
15 Sunning Hill Wells 17

Surrey.

18½ Virginia Water.... 13½
21¼ Egham [*d*] 10¾
Or, at Binfield Common, along the Windsor Road, and through the Park, the distance nearly the same.

Middlesex.

22½ STAINES 9½
29½ Hampton 2½
30½ Hampton Court.. 1½

Surrey.

32 KINGSTON ...... *
To Brighton (§ 34) *46m.*
To Worthing 49m.

Points of Junction.

[*d*] WINDSOR
To Egham 5m.; thence to Kingston, 10¾m.

KINGSTON
To Reigate 14m.

REIGATE
To Brighton 32¼m. § 34.

[*e*]
GREAT MARLOW
To Salt Hill 10½m.; thence to Hounslow 11¾m.

HOUNSLOW
To Kingston 5¼m.

[*f*] GUILDFORD
To Leatherhead 12¼m.; thence to Epsom 4m. Page 79.

EPSOM
To Ewell 1¼m.; thence to Croydon 7½m.

CROYDON
To Bromley 6½m.; thence to Dartford 12m.

DARTFORD
To Gravesend 7m.
Thence to Rochester, Chatham, and Canterbury, p. 82.

He § 176

Surrey.

* KINGSTON [*e*].. 59
5 Merton 54
7½ Mitcham.......... 51½
11¼ CROYDON [*f*].. 47¾
To Brighton, p. 78, 79.
15 Sandersted 44
16 Warlingham....... 43
20½ Bottley Hill 38½
22¼ Lympsfield........ 36¾

Kent.

25½ WESTERHAM ... 33½
27½ Brasted 31½
30 Riverhead [*c* 2].. 29
R. *to Tunbridge; thence to Hastings*, p. 80.
33½ Seal.............. 25½
36½ Igtham 22½
39½ Wrotham Heath . 19½
42 Leybourne 17
44 Ditton............ 15
47½ MAIDSTONE.... 11½
To Hythe and Folkestone, p. 81.
48½ Pennenden Heath . 10½
54 Stoctonbury Valley 5
57 Key Street........ 2
59 Sittingbourne ... *
Thence (§ 33) 15½m. to CANTERBURY.

	NORWICH	122
	See pp 52, 55, to	
	Cambridgeshire.	
*	CAMBRIDGE [a]	61
7	Bourn Leyes Common............	54
12	Eltisley	49
	Huntingdonshire.	
18	ST. NEOTS......	43
	Bedfordshire.	
19½	Eaton Socon	41½
	To Kettering 26½m.	
24	Great Barford	37
30	BEDFORD	31
33	Bromhead Bridge..	28
37¾	Turvey	23¼
	Buckinghamshire.	
41¾	OLNEY..........	19¼
46½	NEWPORT PAGNEL	14½
48½	Stanton Bridge....	12½
52½	STONEY STRATFORD	8½
53¾	Calverton	7¼
55½	Beachampton	5½
57	Thornton..........	4
61	BUCKINGHAM..	*

To Oxford, § 77.
To Cheltenham, § 66.

Points of Junction.

[a] YARMOUTH
To Norwich 23½m.
NORWICH
To Thetford 29m.
THETFORD
To Newmarket 19½m; thence to Cambridge 13m.

[b] BOSTON
To Holbeach 17m. (§ 128) thence to Wisbeach 14m.
WISBEACH
To Downham Market 13m. thence to Stoke Ferry 7m.

[c] *Another Route:*
LYNN
To Swaffham 15½m. Thence to Brandon 15m. Page 53.
SWAFFHAM
To Thetford 17½m.

[d] THETFORD
To Bury St. Edmunds 13½m. Page 55 F.
BURY ST. EDMUNDS
To Sudbury 16½m.,—p. 54.
SUDBURY
To Neyland 9½m.; thence to Colchester 6m.

[e] ELY
To Soham 5½m; thence to Bury 19½m.
BURY
To Stowmarket 15m. Another Route from Bury to Ipswich is through Hadleigh: — Bury to Hadleigh 18m. thence to Ipswich 10m.

	Norfolk.	
*	LYNN [c]	62½
4	Setchy	58½
10½	Stradsett..........	52
12	Junction of Road from Downham Market [b]	50½
13	Wereham	49½
15	STOKE FERRY	47½
19	Methwold	43½
	Suffolk.	
25	BRANDON [c]..	37½
	Norfolk.	
31	THETFORD [c]..	31½
	To Bury St. Edmunds; thence to Colchester [d].	
	Suffolk.	
33¾	Euston	28¾
37½	Honington	25
40½	IXWORTH	22
47½	Wetherden........	15
51	STOW MARKET.	11½
	From Bury St. Edm. [e].	
54½	NEEDHAM......	8
56½	Baleham..........	6
58	Blakenham	4½
59½	Caydon	3
62½	IPSWICH........	*

I § 181

Wiltshire.

*	SALISBURY	56
½	Fisherton Ainger	55½
3½	Wilton T. G.	52½
5	Burcombe	51
6¼	Burford	49¾
8¾	Dinton	47¼
10¾	Teffont	45¼
12	Chilmark	44
14¼	Fonthill	41¾
15¾	HINDON	40¼
18½	Willoughby Hedge T. G.	37½

To Mere 4m.; thence to Wincanton and Ilchester, p. 65.

Somersetshire.

24	Kilmington	32
28	Hardway	28
34	Ainsford Inn	22
39	Lydford	17

To Somerton 5m.; thence to Taunton, p 70.

45¾	Piper's Inn	10¼
46¾	Ashcot	9¼
52	Bawdrip	4
56	BRIDGEWATER	*

To Dulverton [*h*].

To Minehead; thence to Ilfracombe [*g*].

Points of Junction.

[*f*] WINCHESTER
To Salisbury 22½m.—§ 29.

SOUTHAMPTON
To Romsey 12m.; thence to Salisbury 16m.

PORTSMOUTH
To Salisbury, § 14 *d*.

[*g*]
BRIDGEWATER
To Nether Stowey 9m.; thence to Watchet 9m.

WATCHET
To Dunster 3m.; thence to Minehead 2½m.

MINEHEAD
To Porlock 6m.

PORLOCK
To Linton 13m.; thence to Ilfracombe 15m.

[*h*]
BRIDGEWATER
To Raleigh's Cross 16½m.; thence to Dulverton 10½m.

DULVERTON
To South Molton 13m.; thence to Barnstaple 11½m.

BARNSTAPLE
To Ilfracombe 10m.

Ia § 182

*	SALISBURY	44½
	See § 15, to	
10¾	Deptford Inn	33¾
	And thence to	
21¾	WARMINSTER	22¾

To Westbury 4m.; thence to Trowbridge & Bradford, § 183.

23	Bugley	21½
25½	Corsley Heath	19

Somersetshire.

29	FROME	15½

To Bath, § 151.

31½	Whatley	13
33	Little Elm	11½
	Over Mendip Hills.	
36½	Long Cross	8

To Shepton Mallet 2m.

42½	East Horrington	2
44½	WELLS	*

Ia § 183

*	WARMINSTER	18
4	Westbury	14
6	Division of the Road	12

R. *to Melksham; thence to Chippenham*, § 47.

6¾	Bradley	11¼
8	Studley	10

R. *to Trowbridge* ½*m.*

9½	BRADFORD	8½

Somersetshire.

14¾	Bathford	3¼
15½	Bath Easton	2½
18	BATH	*

Ic § 184

Somersetshire.

*	BRIDGEWATER [b]	29
3½	North Petherton	25½
6	Thurloxton	23
7½	Walford Bridge	21½
11	TAUNTON	18
13½	Trull	15½
14½	Pondiford	14½
16	Blagdon	13
	Devonshire.	
24	Up-Ottery	5
27	Monkton	2
29	HONITON	*

To Sidmouth and Exmouth, § 45.

Id § 185

Somersetshire.

*	TAUNTON	22¾
2	Orchard Portman	20¾
4½	Staple Fitzpain	18¼
9½	Combe St. Nicholas	13¼
11½	CHARD [c]	11¼
	Dorsetshire.	
14½	Titherley Cross	8¼
	Devonshire.	
18½	AXMINSTER	4¼
20¼	Hunter's Lodge Inn	2½
	To Bridport 10½m.; thence to Weymouth 23m. p. 68.	
	Dorsetshire.	
22¾	LYME REGIS	*

Points of Junction.

[a] MINEHEAD
To Bridgewater (p. 71) 25½m.

BRIDGEWATER
To Piper's Inn 10¼m.

[b] BRISTOL
To Cross 17½m.; thence to Bridgewater 17½m. § 36.

[c] WELLS
To Glastonbury 5½m.; thence to Somerton 8m.

SOMERTON
To Ilminster 13½m.; thence to Chard 4m.

[d] ILCHESTER
To Bruton 15m.

BRUTON
To Frome 11½m.

[e] DEVIZES
To Swindon 19m.

SWINDON
To Farringdon 12½m.

FARRINGDON
To Oxford 18m.—§ 72.

Ie § 186

*	TAUNTON	60½
5	Durston	55½
9	Alfred's Pillar	51½
10	Burrowbridge	50½
14	Sedgmoor T. G.	46½
16	Pedwell	44½
17¼	PIPER'S INN [a]	43¼
18½	Walton	42
20¼	Street	40¼
22	GLASTONBURY.	38½
	L. *to Wells 5½m.; thence to Bath and Bristol.*	
23	Edgarly	37½
25	West Pennard	35½
28	Pilton	32½
30½	SHEPTON MALT.	30
32½	Doulting	28
36	Layton	24½
38	Holiwell	22½
41½	FROME [d]	19
44½	Beckington	16
45¾	Road	14¾
	Wiltshire.	
48	Southwick	12½
49½	Studley	11
50½	TROWBRIDGE	10
	L. *to Bradford 2m.*	
51½	Hilperton	9
54½	Littleton	6
56½	Seend	4
60½	DEVIZES	*

To Beckhampton Inn 7½m.; thence to Swindon & Oxford [e].

Devonshire.

*	EXETER	60½
1¼	Heavitree	59¼
4	Honiton Clyst	56½
10¾	Fair Mile Inn	49¾
12¾	Fenny Bridge	47¾
16	HONITON [g]	44½
17	Mount Pleasant	43½
20¼	Wilmington	40¼
24½	Kilmington	36
26	AXMINSTER	34½
28	Hunter's Lodge Inn	32½

Dorsetshire.

31¾	Charmouth	28¾
35¾	Chidiock	24¾
38½	BRIDPORT [h]	22
42	Traveller's Rest	18½
	Over Arkeswell Down.	
45½	Longbredy	15
48½	Winterborne Abbas	12
	L. to Dorchester 5m.; thence to Blandford and Salisbury, p. 62.	
51½	Winterborne St. M.	9
54	Upway	6½
55½	Broadway	5
59¾	MELCOMB REGIS	¾
60½	WEYMOUTH	*

To Wareham (§ 173) *20m.; thence to Corfe Castle 5m.*

At Wareham, to Christchurch 18m.—To Poole 11½m.

Points of Junction.

[f] WEYMOUTH
To Ringwood, as below, 43m.

RINGWOOD
To Cadnam 11½m.; thence to Southampton 8½m.

WEYMOUTH
To Wareham (§ 173) 20m.; thence to Wimborn Minster 13½m.

WIMBORN
To Ringwood 9½m.; thence to Romsey 17½m.

ROMSEY
To Winchester 11m.

[g] BARNSTAPLE
To South Molton 11½m.; thence to Tiverton 18½m.

TIVERTON
To Collumpton 5½m.; thence to Honiton 10½m.

[h] EXMOUTH
To Sidmouth 10m.

SIDMOUTH
To Lyme Regis 15½m.; thence to Bridport 8½m.

[i] PORTSMOUTH
To Petersfield 18½m.; thence to Alton 13m.

ALTON
To Reading 22½m.—§ 81.

Hampshire.

*	SOUTHAMPTON [f]	45¼
5½	Chandler's Ford	39¾
7½	Otterborne	37¾
9½	Compton	35¾
11	St. Croix	34¼
12	WINCHESTER [f]	33¼
	To Whitchurch and Newbury; thence to Oxford, § 52.	
14¼	King's Worthy	31
17¼	Lunway's Inn	28
20¾	East Stratton Park	24½
22¾	Popham	22½
23¾	POPHAM LANE	21½
29¾	BASINGSTOKE	15½
	To Oxford, § 83. *To Hartford Bridge, Bagshot, & Egham,* p. 61 r.	
32¾	Basing T. G.	12½
33¾	Sherfield	11½
38	Strathfield Say	7¼

Wiltshire.

39	Riseley	6¼
40	Swallowfield	5¼
42	Three Miles Cross	3¼

Berkshire.

43¼	Whitby	2
45¼	READING [i]	*

To Windsor, § 175.
To Henley and High Wycombe, § 180.
To Maidenhead (p. 72) *13m.; thence to Beaconsfield.*

Ii § 189

Dorsetshire.

*	POOLE..........	27
6½	WIMBORN MINSTER..........	20½
9	Stanbridge........	18
12	Horton Inn........	15
16	CRANBOURN ...	11

Wiltshire.

19½	Tilpit	7½
24½	Combe Bisset......	2½
27	SALISBURY	*

Ik § 190

Hampshire.

*	CHRISTCHURCH	27½
1	Staples Cross......	26½
3½	Sopley............	24
5	Avon..............	22½
7	Lower Kingston ...	20½
9	RINGWOOD	18½
10¼	Blasford Green....	17¼
12	Ibberley..........	15½
15	FORDINGBRIDG.	12½
16½	Upper Burgate....	11
18½	South Chardford ...	9

Wiltshire.

20½	Downton Wick....	7
22½	Charlton Street	5
24½	Bodenham	3
27½	SALISBURY.....	*

Points of Junction.

[a]
SOUTHAMPTON
T Romsey 12m.; thence to Salisbury 16m.

PORTSMOUTH
To Cosham 4½m.; thence to Romsey 24m.

ROMSEY
To Salisbury 16m.—§ 14.

[b] **SALISBURY**
To Old Sarum 2m.; thence to Amesbury 6m.

[c] **DEVIZES**
To Beckhampton Inn 7½m.; thence to Swindon 11m.

SWINDON
To Highworth 6½m.; thence to Oxford, § 72.

Another Route from Salisbury to Swindon:
Over the Plain to East Everley 15½m.; thence to Marlborough 11½m.

MARLBOROUGH
To Swindon 11m.

[c 2]
EAST EVERLEY
To Great Bedwin 9m.; thence to Hungerford 7½m.

Il § 191

*	SALISBURY [a].	68¼
	To Old Sarum 2m. [b]	
6	Woodford Hut.....	62¼
7¾	Long Barrow Cross	60½
13	*L. over the Downs to Market Lavington 5m.; thence to Melksham 10m.—To Chippenham, § 47.*	
16½	Red Horn T. G. ...	51¾
19	Lide..............	49¼
21	Nursteed	47¼
22	DEVIZES........	46¼
	R. to Swindon; thence to Oxford [c].	
24	Rowde	44¼
26¾	Chitway Heath	41½
28	Sandy Lane	40¼
29¾	Red Hill..........	38½
30¼	Derry Hill........	38
32¾	CHIPPENHAM..	35½
37¾	Lower Stanton St. Quintin.........	30½
39¾	Corston Bridge	28½
42	MALMESBURY .	26¼

Thence, see § 48, to

Gloucestershire.

57¼	STROUD	11
61¼	Painswick	7
	To Cheltenham and Worcester, § 48, 49.	
68¼	GLOUCESTER...	*

To Worcester and Birmingham, § 38, 39.—At Worcester, to Kidderminster, § 91; thence, thro' Wolverhampton and Stafford, to MANCHESTER.

Wiltshire.

* SALISBURY [f]. 49
6¾ Winterslow Hut.... 42¼
7½ Lobcombe Corner.. 41½

Hampshire.

10 Middle Wallop.... 39
13 Down Farm 36
15½ Little Ann 33½
17½ ANDOVER 31½
19½ Down House 29½
22½ Hurstborne........ 26½
24½ WHITCHURCH.. 22½

To Basingstoke (p. 61) 11½*m.; thence to Reading* 14½*m.*

31½ KINGSCLERE... 17½
34 Fair Oak 15

Berkshire.

38 Wasing 11
39½ ALDERMASTON 9½
41 Junction of Road from Bath and Bristol [g]..... 8
44½ THEAL............ 4½
49 READING ...... *

To St. Albans, § 180.
To Maidenhead Bridge (p. 72) 13½*m.; thence to Beaconsfield* 7*m.*
To Windsor, Kingston, &c. § 174.

Points of Junction.

[f] WEYMOUTH
To Dorchester 8m.

DORCHESTER
To Blandford 16m.

BLANDFORD
To Salisbury 22½m. Page 62.

POOLE
To Cranbourn 17m.

CRANBOURN
To Salisbury 11m. Page 62 G.

[g] BATH
To Devizes 18½m.

DEVIZES
To Marlborough 14½m. thence to Reading 35m.

BRISTOL
To Chippenham 20½m.

CHIPPENHAM
To Calne 5¾m.; thence to Marlborough 13m.

MARLBOROUGH
To Reading 35m. See pp. 72, 73.

* READING....... 46

Oxfordshire.

1 Caversham........ 45
5¼ Shiplake.......... 40¾
8 HENLEY ON THAMES...... 38
9¼ Fawley Court..... 36¾
11 Mill End.......... 35

Buckinghamshire.

12¼ Medenham 33¾
15 GREAT MARLOW 31
17¾ Handy Cross...... 28¼
20 HIGH WYCOMBE 26
27 AMERSHAM..... 19
31½ Cheynies.......... 14½

Hertfordshire.

32½ Chorley Wood 13½
34½ RICKMANSWORTH 11½
36½ Cashio Bridge 9½
38 WATFORD...... 8
40½ Garstons.......... 5½
42½ Waterdale........ 3½
44½ St. Stephens....... 1½
46 ST. ALBANS .... *

To Hatfield 5*m.; thence to Hertford* 7½*m. Thence to Dunmow, Braintree, and Colchester*, § 69.

REFERENCES TO THE

MAPS,

The Counties being Geographically arranged, and their Contiguity shown by the Index Map on the opposite page.

ENGLAND & WALES
An INDEX MAP, shewing the contiguity of the Counties.
Explanation of the County Maps
SCOTLAND
IRELAND
IRISH SEA
ST. GEORGE'S CHANNEL
Cardigan Bay
BRISTOL CHANNEL
ENGLISH CHANNEL
GERMAN OCEAN
FRANCE
Northumberland
Cumberland
Durham
Westmoreland
North Riding
York Shire
East Riding
West Riding
Lancashire
Isle of Man
Cheshire
Derby Shire
Lincoln Shire
Norfolk
Suffolk
Essex
Kent
Sussex
Surry
Hamp Shire
Wilt Shire
Somerset Shire
Dorset Shire
Devon Shire
Cornwall
Shrop Shire
Stafford Shire
Leicester Shire
Warwick Shire
Hereford Shire
Oxford Sh.
Berk Shire
Gloucester Shire
Monmouth Shire
Glamorgan Shire
Carmarthen Shire
Cardigan Sh.
Radnor Shire
Montgomery Shire
Merioneth Shire
Carnarvon Shire
Denbigh Sh.
Flint
Bedford Sh.
Northampton Shire
Lundy
Mouth of the Humber
Straits of Dover
The Cities and County Towns are denoted by red, & the respective Rapes, Lathes & Hundreds, of each County by different Colours, which distinctions are peculiar to the Superior Edition.
Longitude West fr. London.

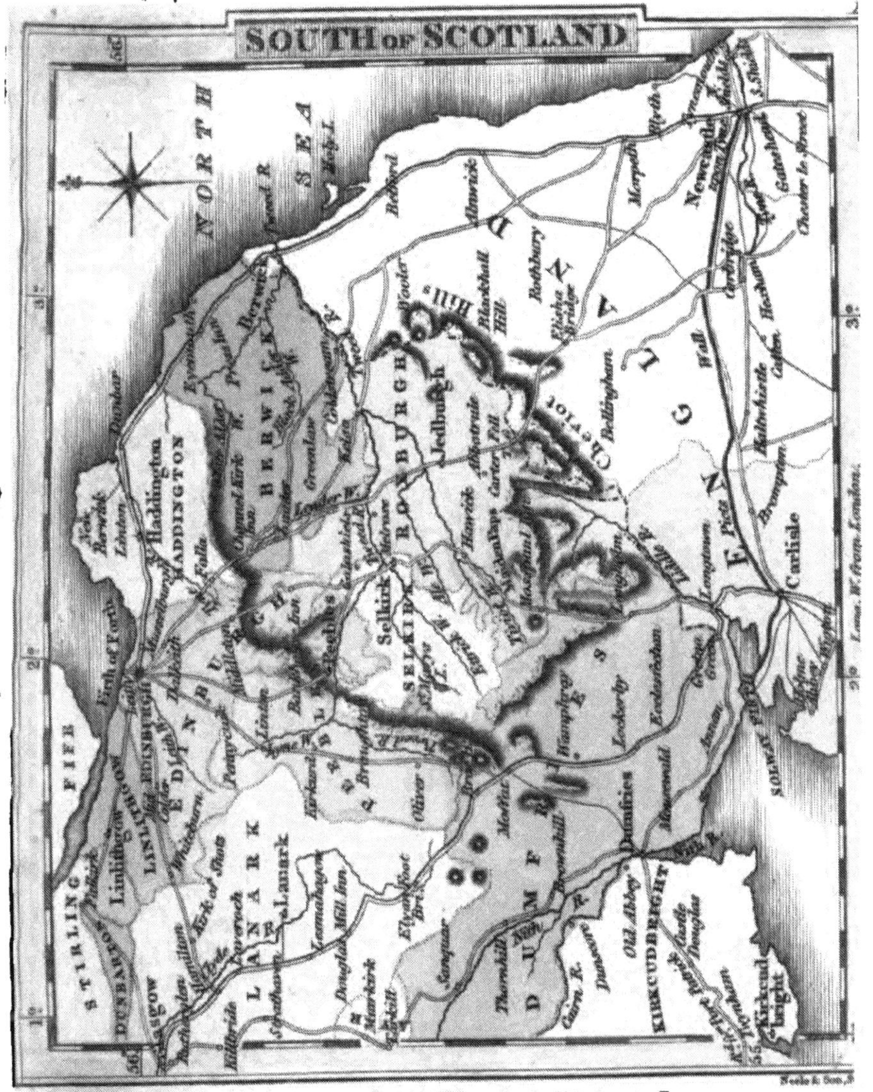

London Pub.^d Sepr 8. 1823, by Sherwood Jones & Co Paternoster Row.

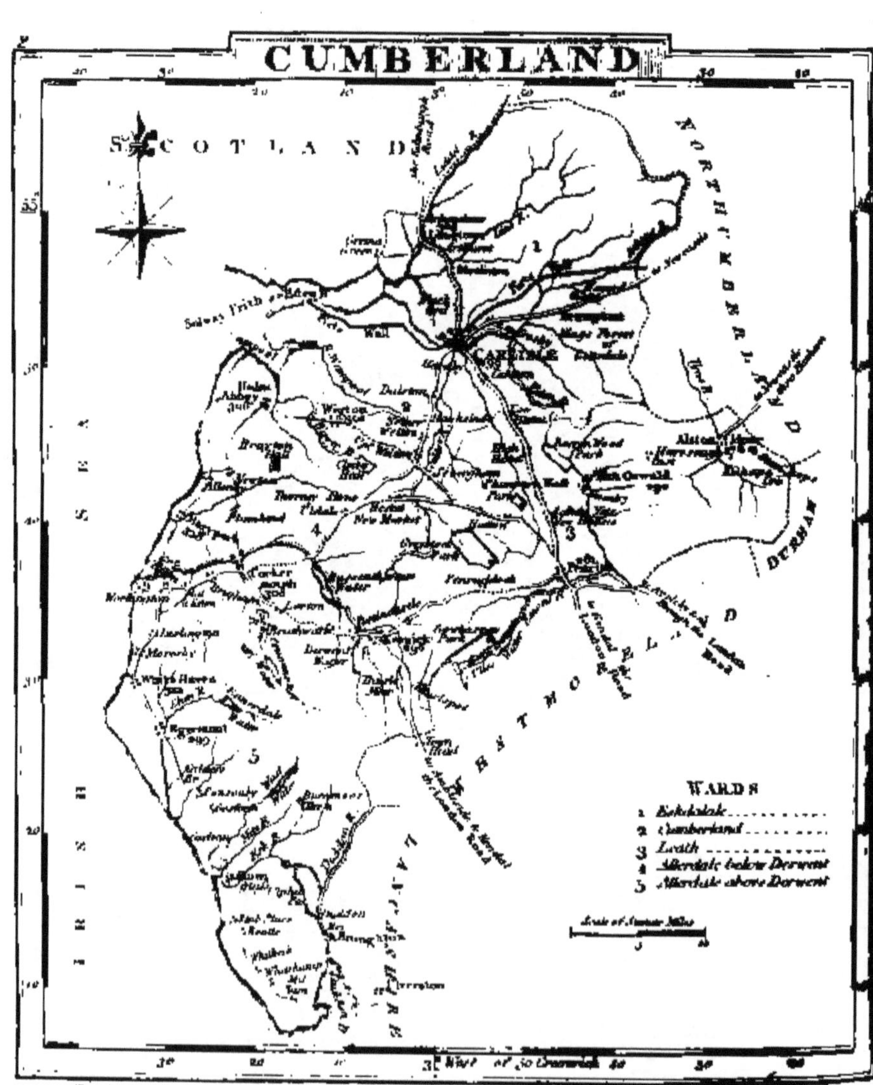

The City and County Town is denoted by red and the respective Hundreds of the County by different Colours which distinctions are peculiar to the superior Edition.

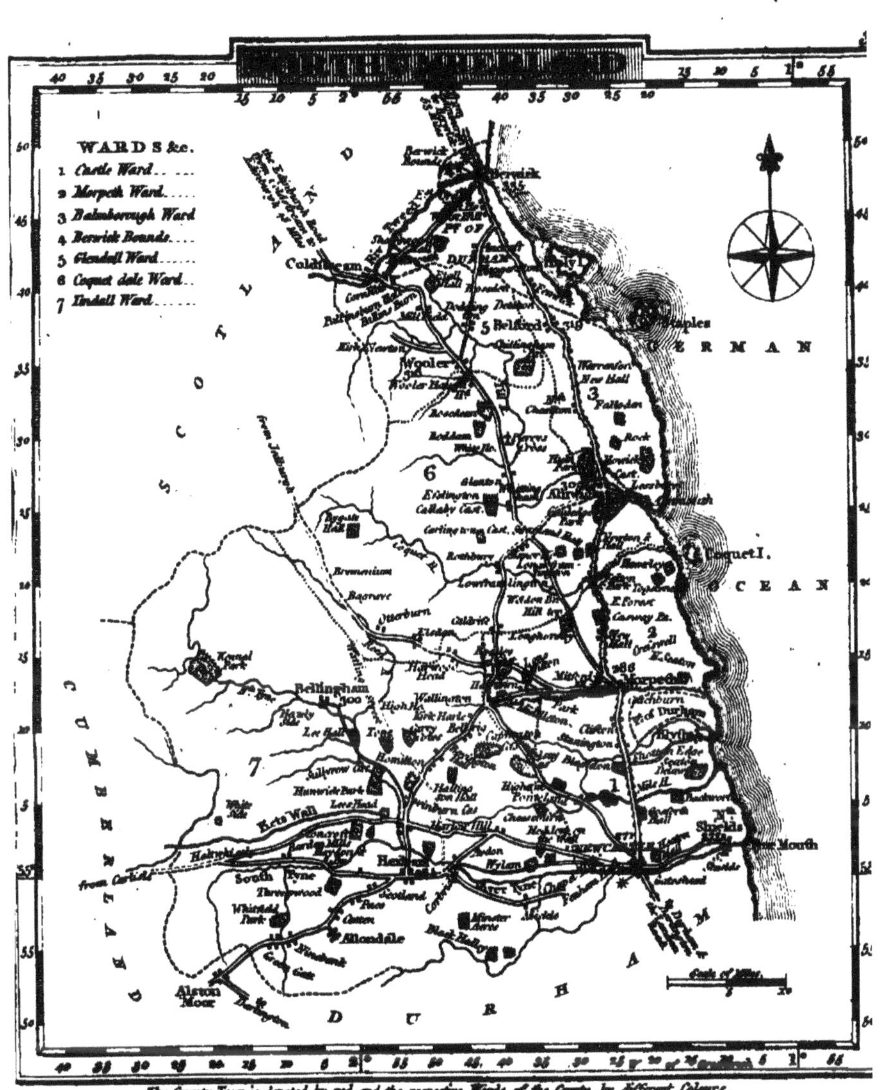

The County Town is denoted by red and the respective Wards of the County by different Colours, which distinctions are peculiar to the superior Edition.

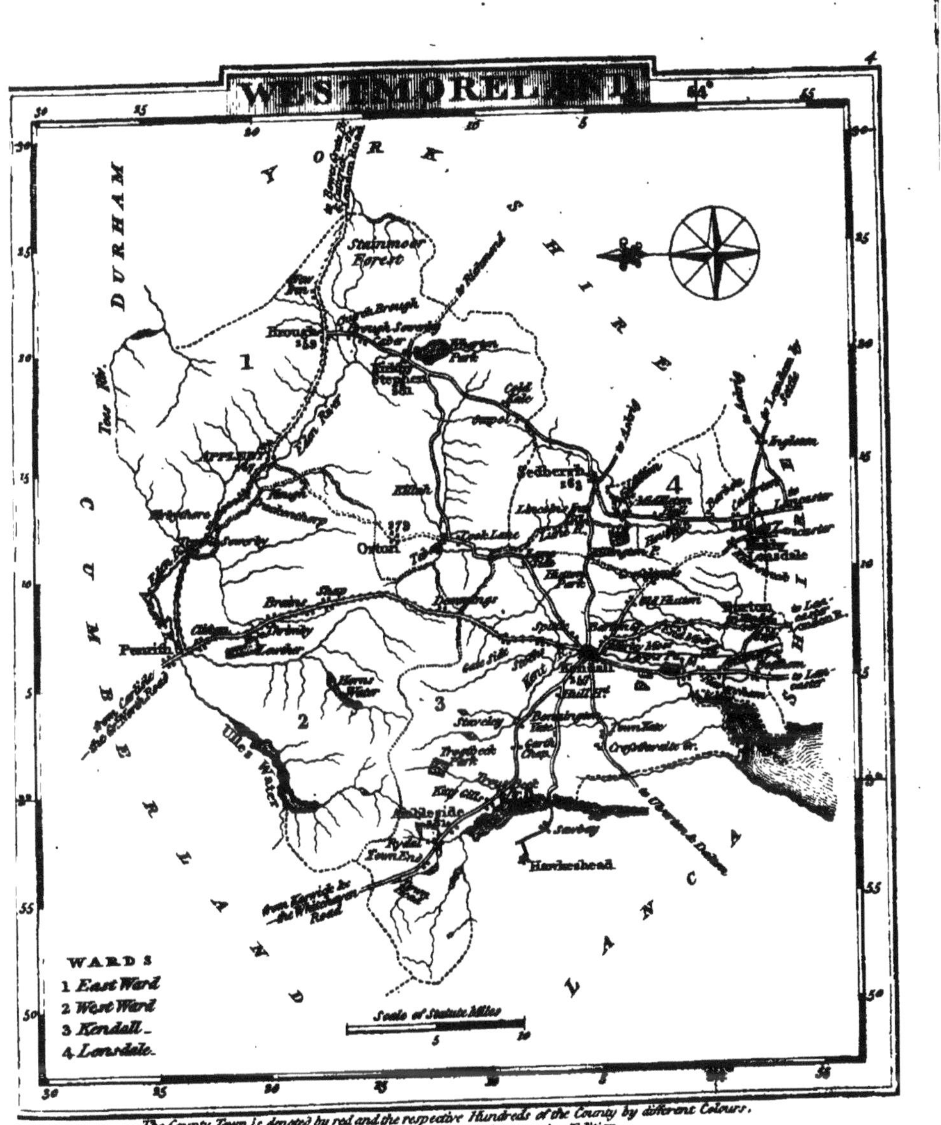

The County Town is denoted by red and the respective Hundreds of the County by different Colours, which distinctions are peculiar to the superior Edition.

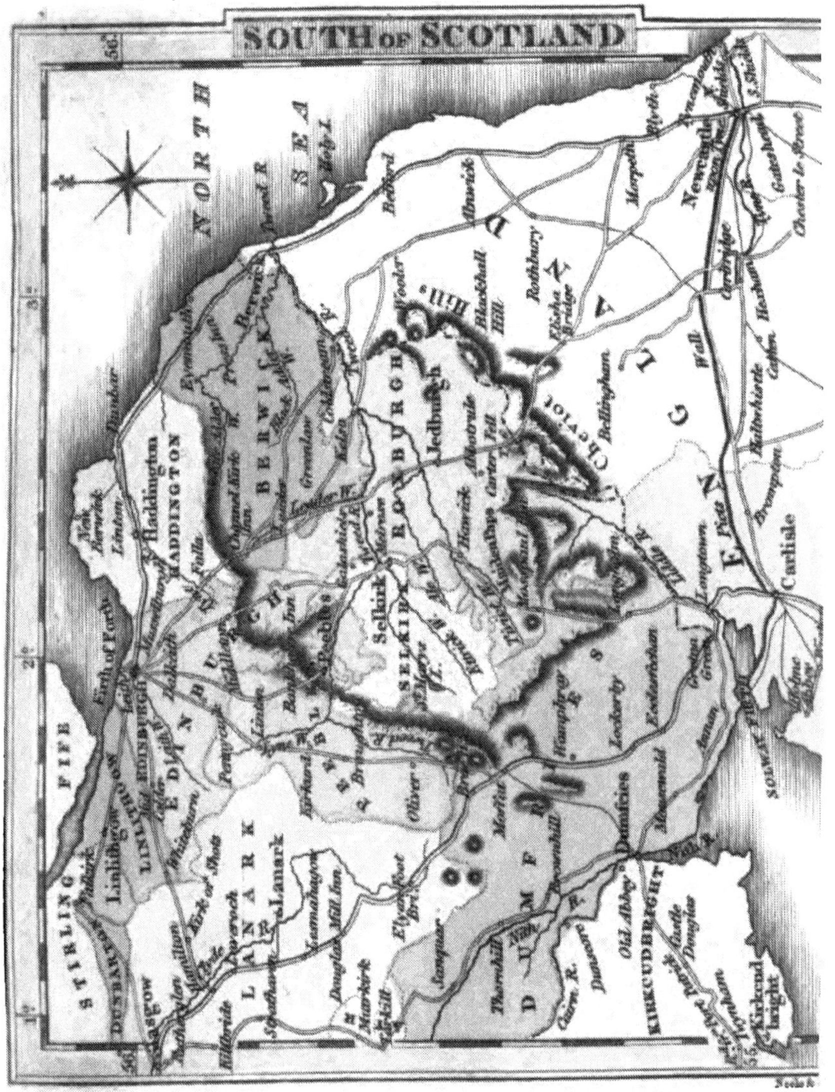

London Pub^d Sepr 8. 1823, by Sherwood Jones & Co Paternoster Row.

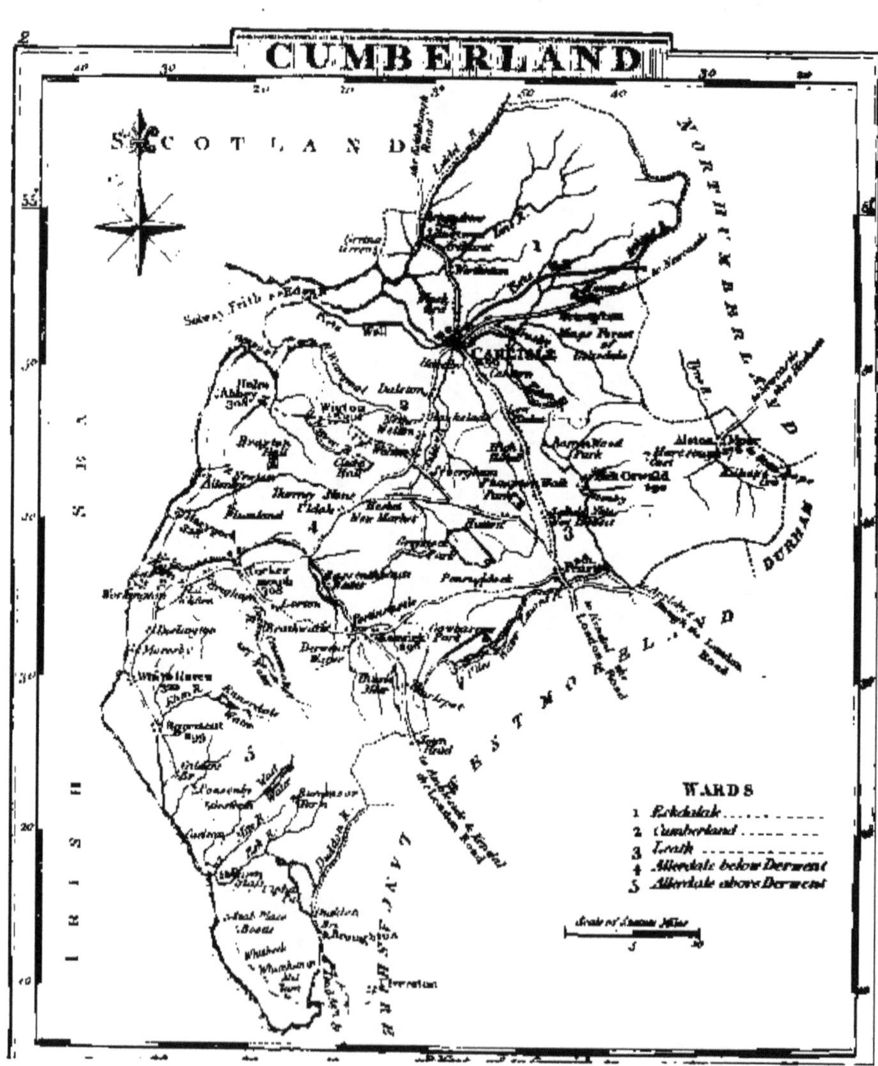

CUMBERLAND
SCOTLAND
CARLISLE
Solway Frith
Wigton
Dalston
Penrith
Keswick
Cockermouth
Workington
Whitehaven
Egremont
Brampton
Alston
NORTHUMBERLAND
DURHAM
WESTMORLAND
LANCASHIRE
IRISH SEA
WARDS
1 Eskdale
2 Cumberland
3 Leath
4 Allerdale below Derwent
5 Allerdale above Derwent

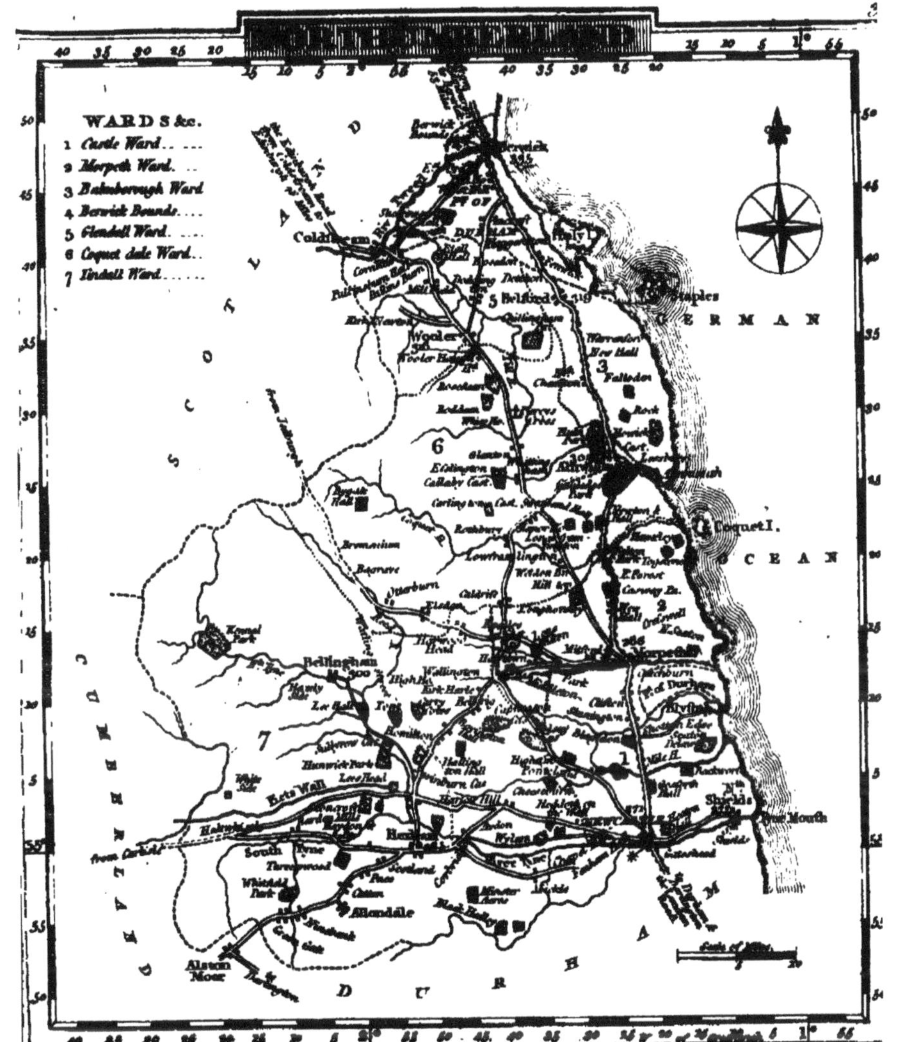

The County Town is denoted by red and the respective Wards of the County by different Colours, which distinctions are peculiar to the superior Edition.

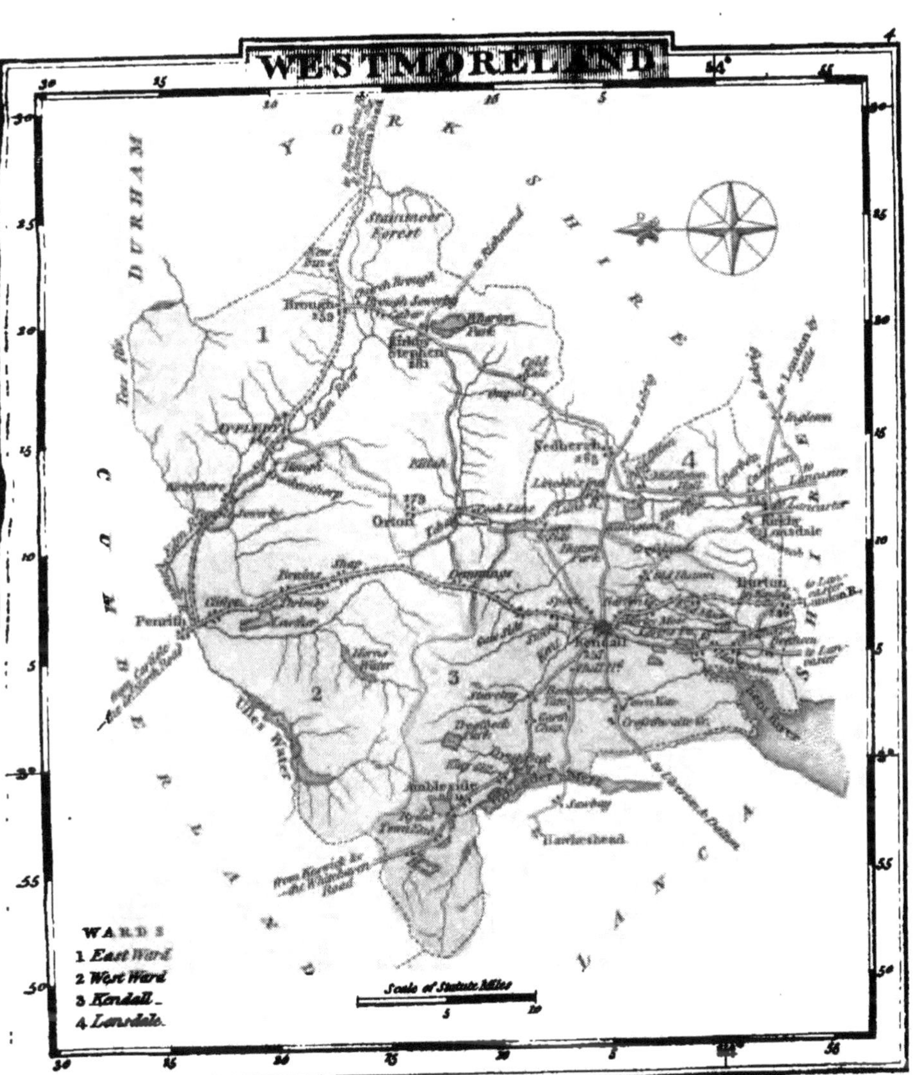

The County Town is denoted by red and the respective Hundreds of the County by different Colours, which distinctions are peculiar to the superior Edition.

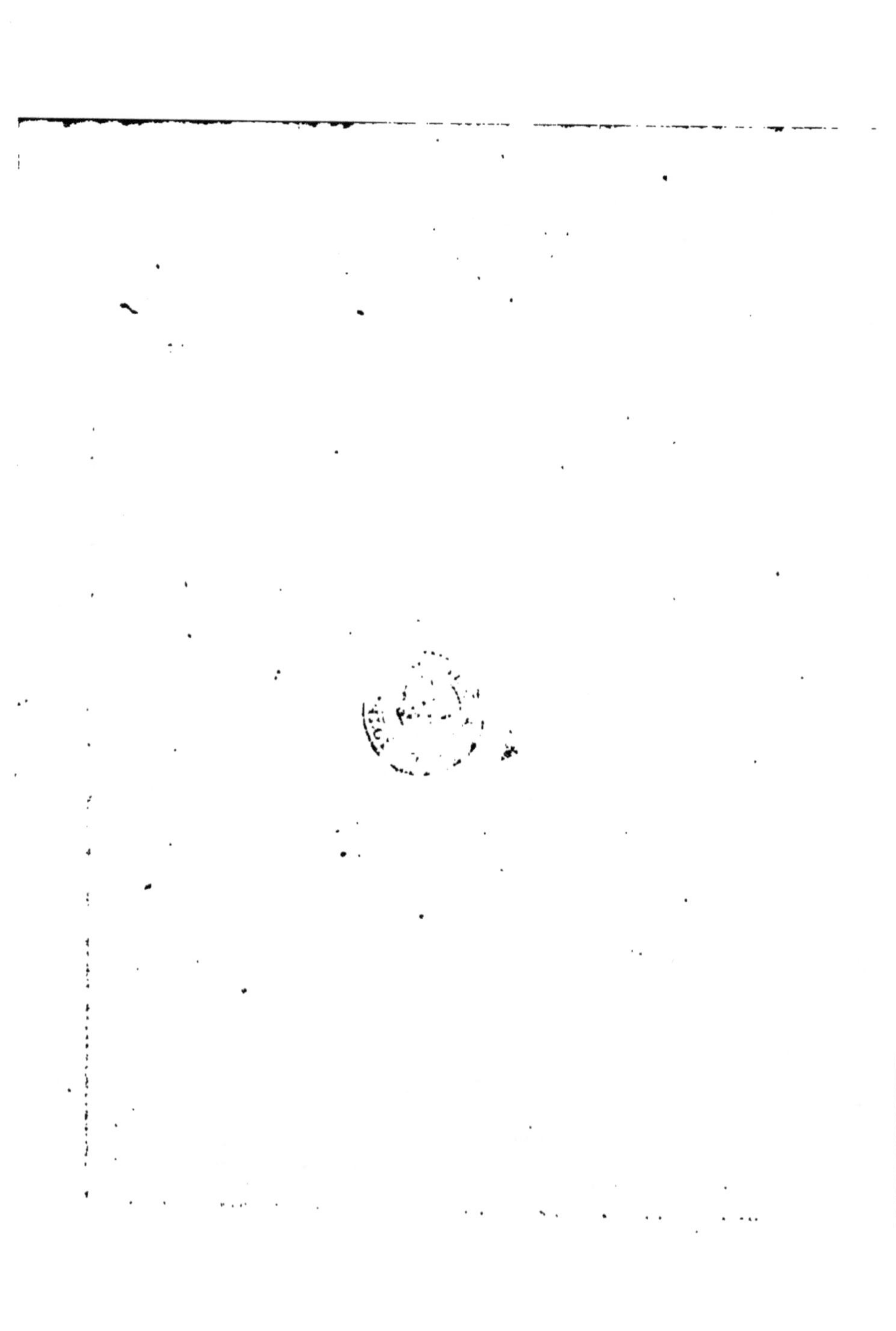

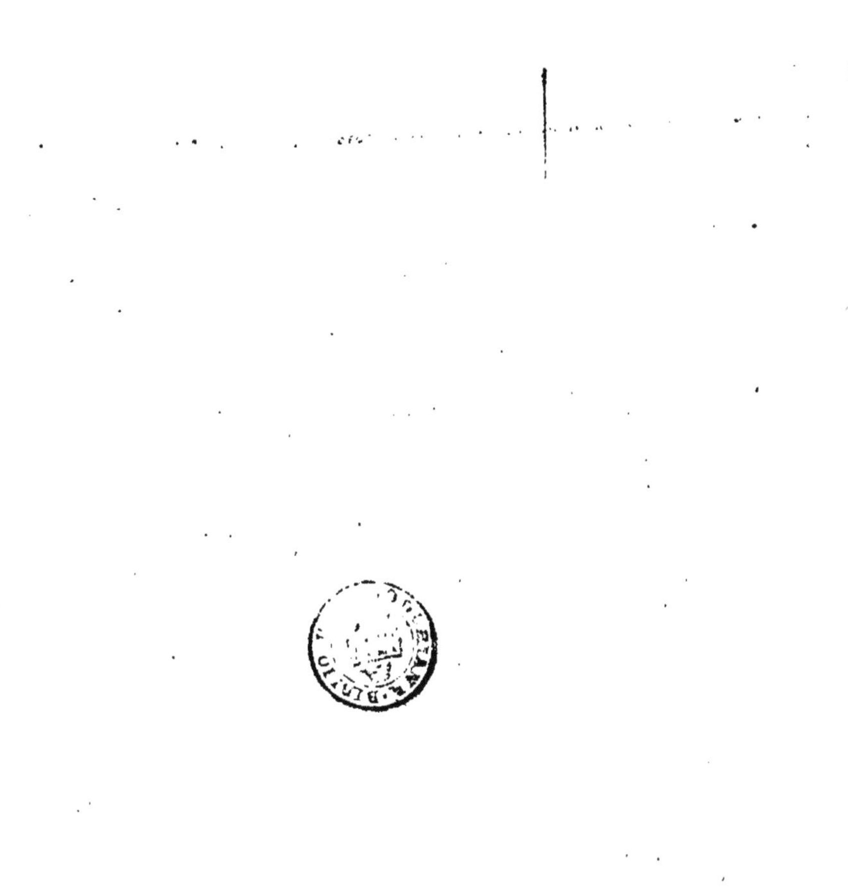

THE
LAKES.

Allonby
Wigton
CARLISLE
Maryport
Cockbridge
Ellen R.
Ireby
Workington
Derwent R.
Cockermouth
Over Water
Hesket Newmarket
High Hesket
High Pike
Clifton
Distington
Whitehaven
Lowes W.
Lorton
Skiddow
Saddle Back
Hutton
Caldew R.
Graystock
Penrith
St. Bees Heads
St. Bees
Ehen R.
Ennerdale
Crummock Water
Keswick
Egremont
Derwent W.
Grange
Low Dore
Buttermere
Newchurch
Ulles Water
Beckermont
Wastedale Head
Eagle Craggs
Borrowdale Fells
Dunmel Raise Stones
Brampton
Wastedale
Waste Water
Langdale Pikes
Hard Knot
Wrynose
Burnmoor Tarn
Mite R.
Irt R.
Broad W.
High Street
Haws Water
Grassmere
Rydal
Kentmere Tarn
Ravenglass
Eskdale
Esk R.
Ambleside
Lever Water
Water Head
Goats Tarn
Hawkshead
Devock Lake
Duddon R.
Bootle
Coniston W.
Wests Station
Esthwaite W.
Bowness
Kendal
Black Comb
Broughton
Scale of Miles
CUMBERLAND
WESTMORELAND
LANCASHIRE

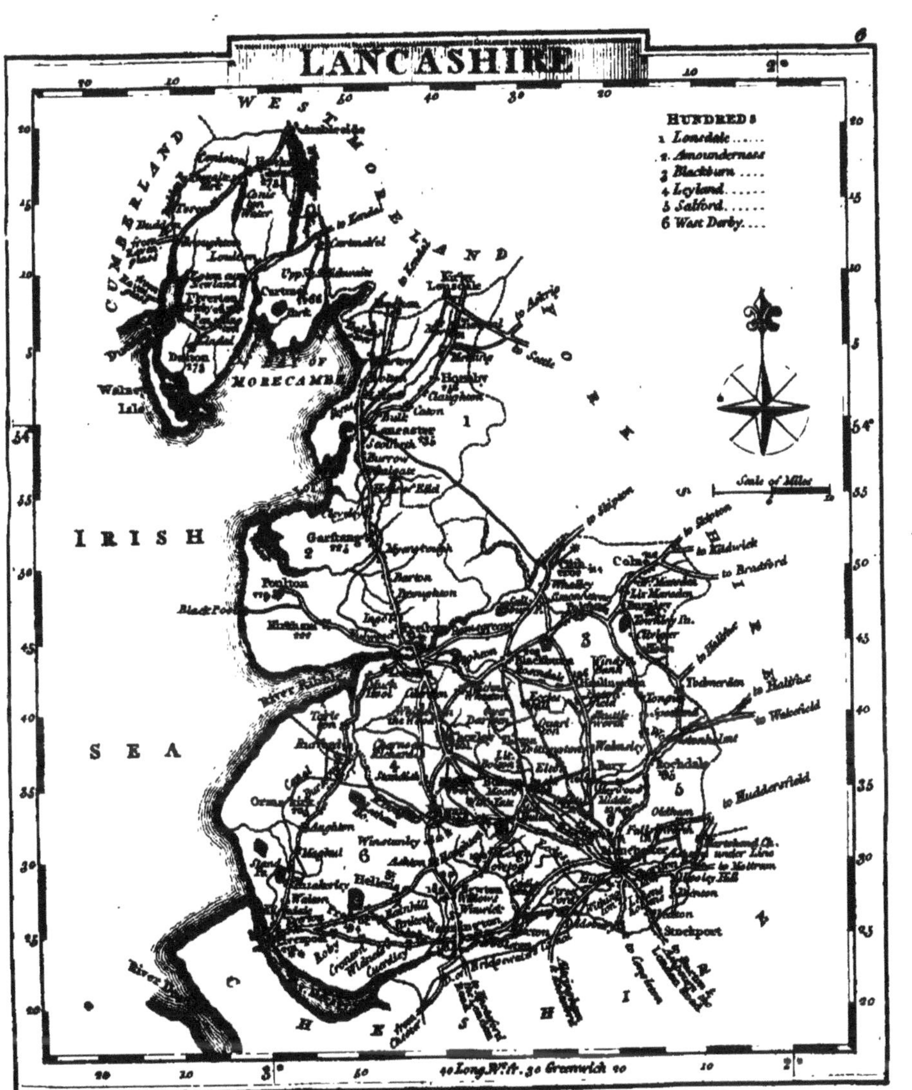

The Cities and County Towns are denoted by red, and the respective Hundreds of the County by different Colours which distinctions are peculiar to the Superior Edition.

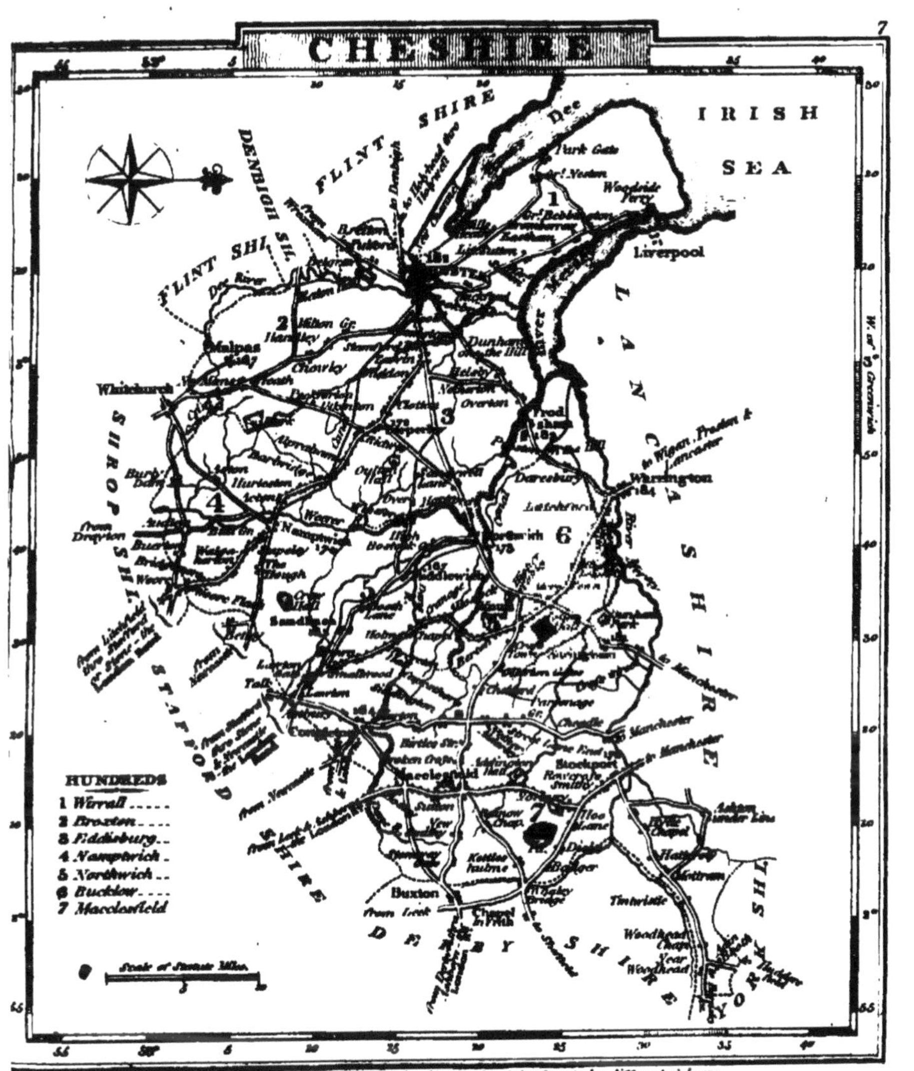

The City is denoted by red, and the respective Hundreds of the County by different Colours, which distinctions are peculiar to the superior Edition.

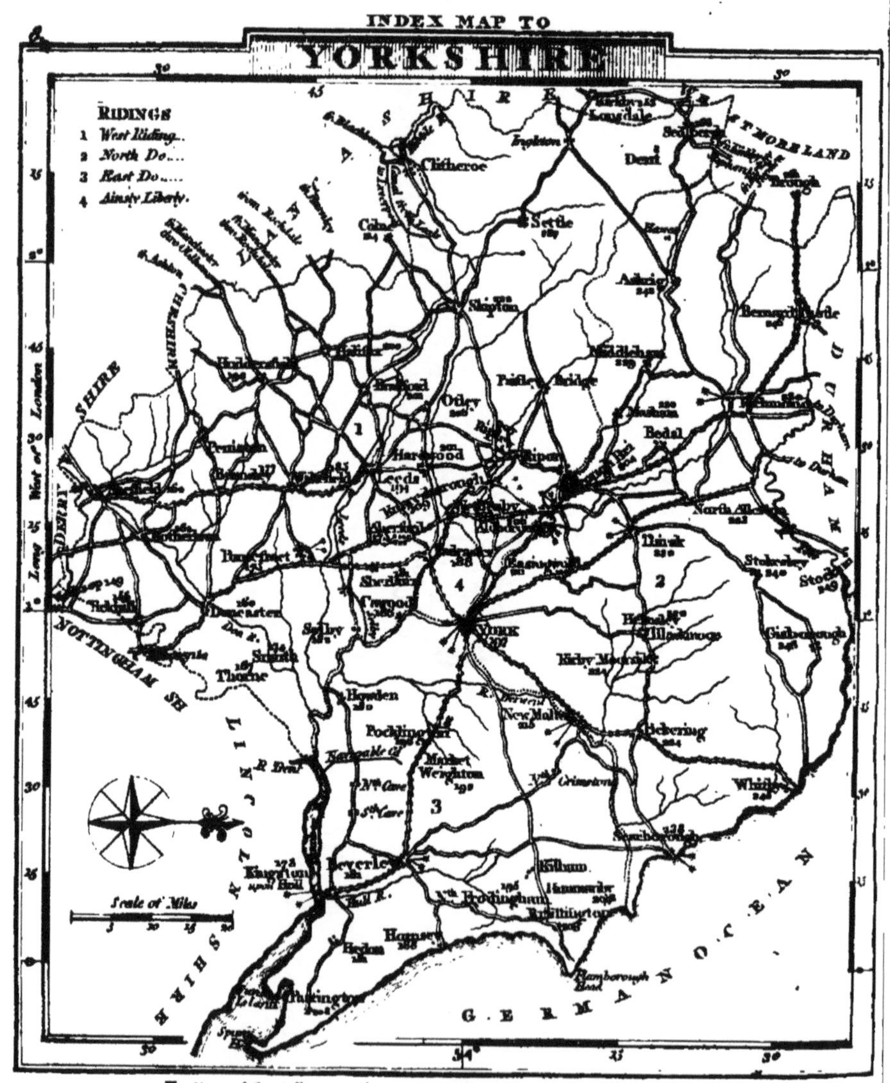

The City and County Town, are denoted by red, and the respective Ridings of the County, by different Colors, which distinctions, are peculiar to the Superior Edition.

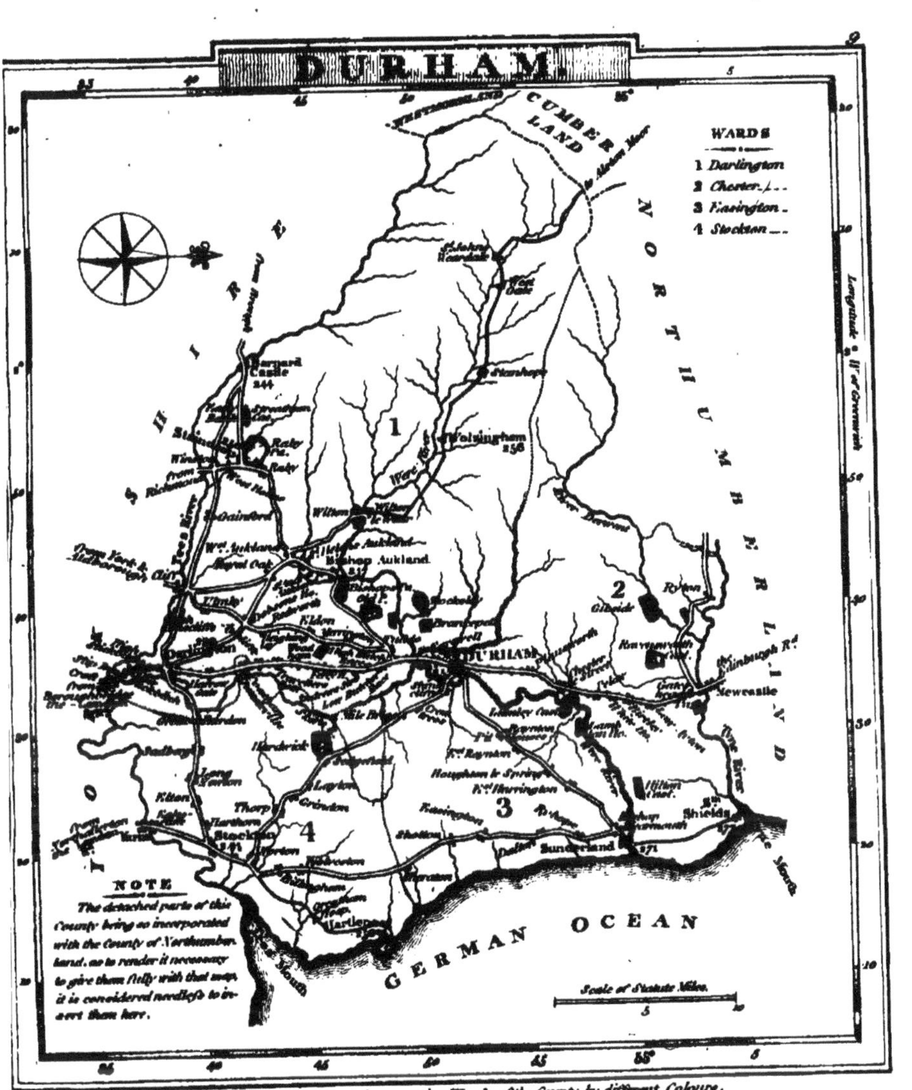

The City is denoted by red, and the respective Wards of the County, by different Colours, which distinctions are peculiar to the Superior Edition.

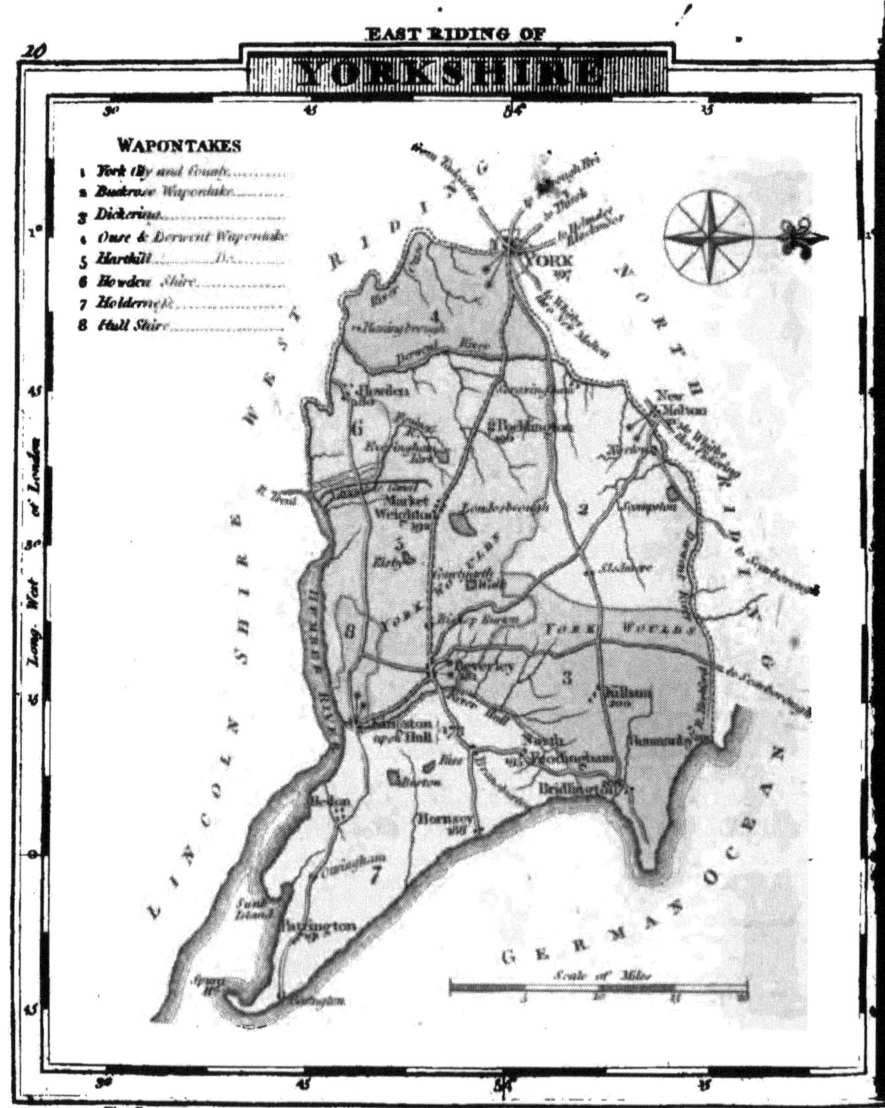

The City and County town are denoted by red, and the respective Wapontakes of the Riding by different colours, which distinctions are peculiar to the Superior Edition.

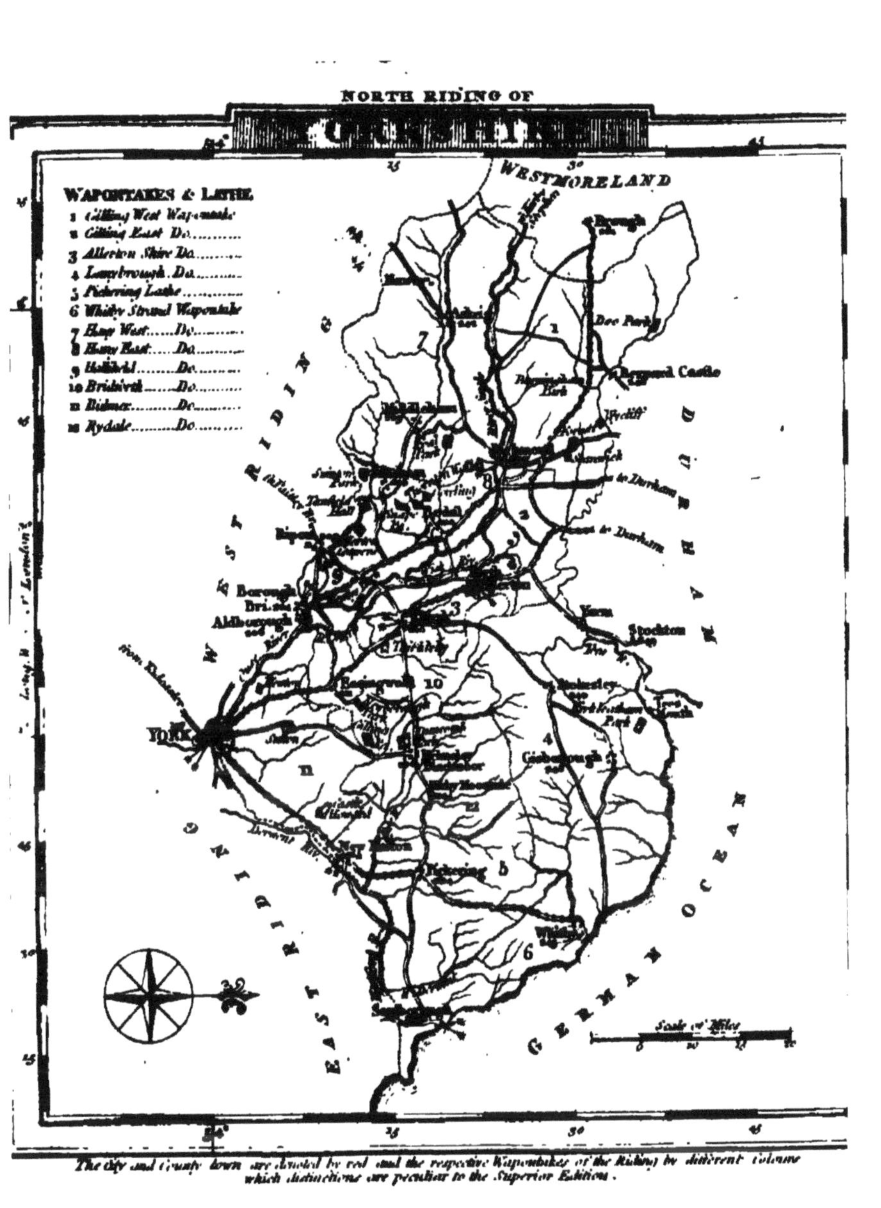

The City and County town are denoted by red and the respective Wapontakes of the Riding by different colours which distinctions are peculiar to the Superior Edition.

The City, and County towns, are denoted by red, and the respective Wapontakes, of the ridings, by different Colours, which distinctions are peculiar to the Superior Edition

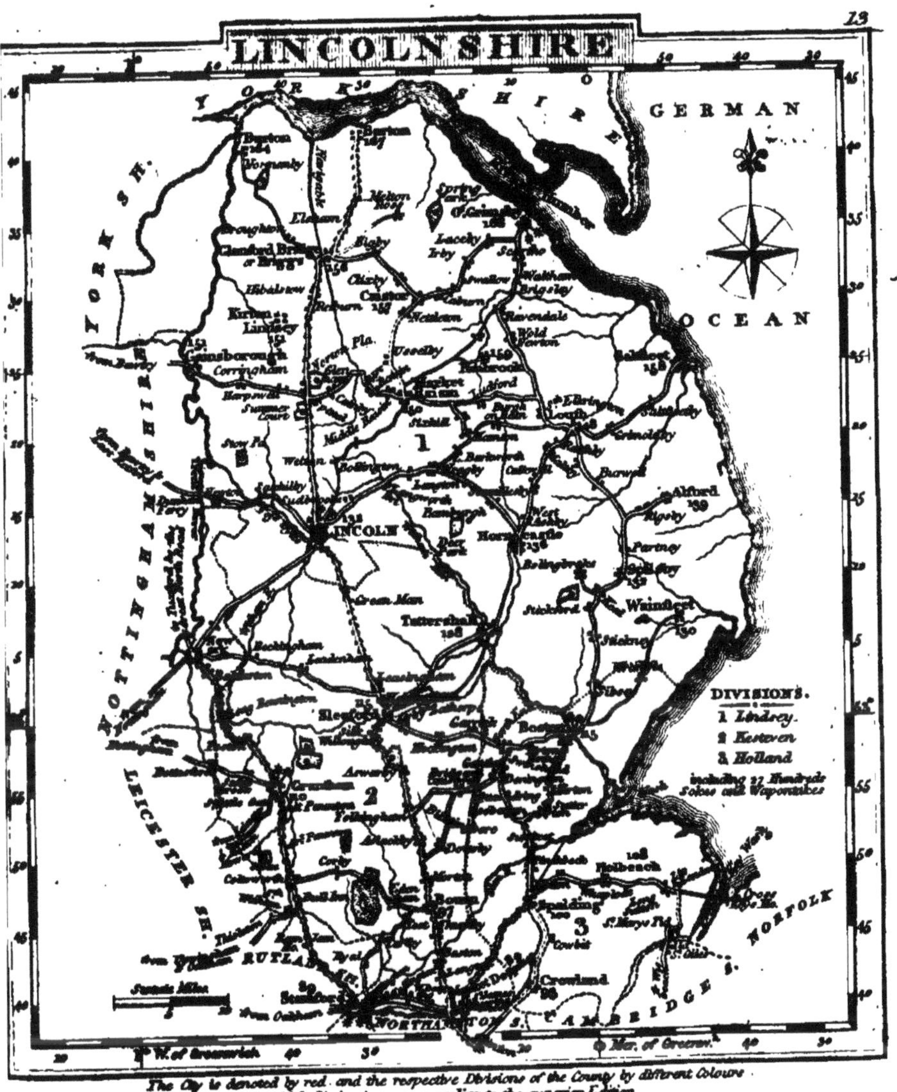

The City is denoted by red. and the respective Divisions of the County by different Colours which distinctions are peculiar to the superior Edition.

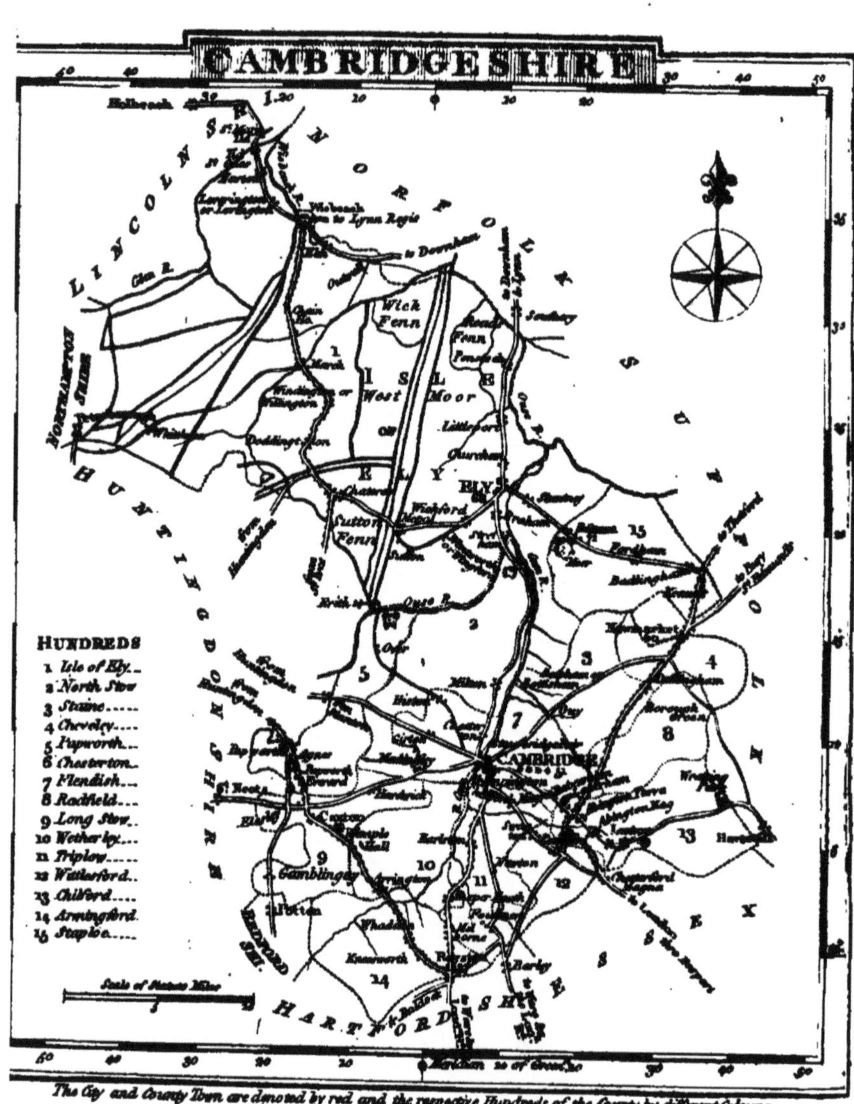

The City and County Town are denoted by red and the respective Hundreds of the County by different Colours which distinctions are peculiar to the Superior Edition

The City is denoted by Red, and the respective Hundreds of the County by different Colours, which distinctions are peculiar to the superior Edition.

The County Town is denoted by red and the respective Hundreds of the County by different Colours which distinctions are peculiar to the superior Edition.

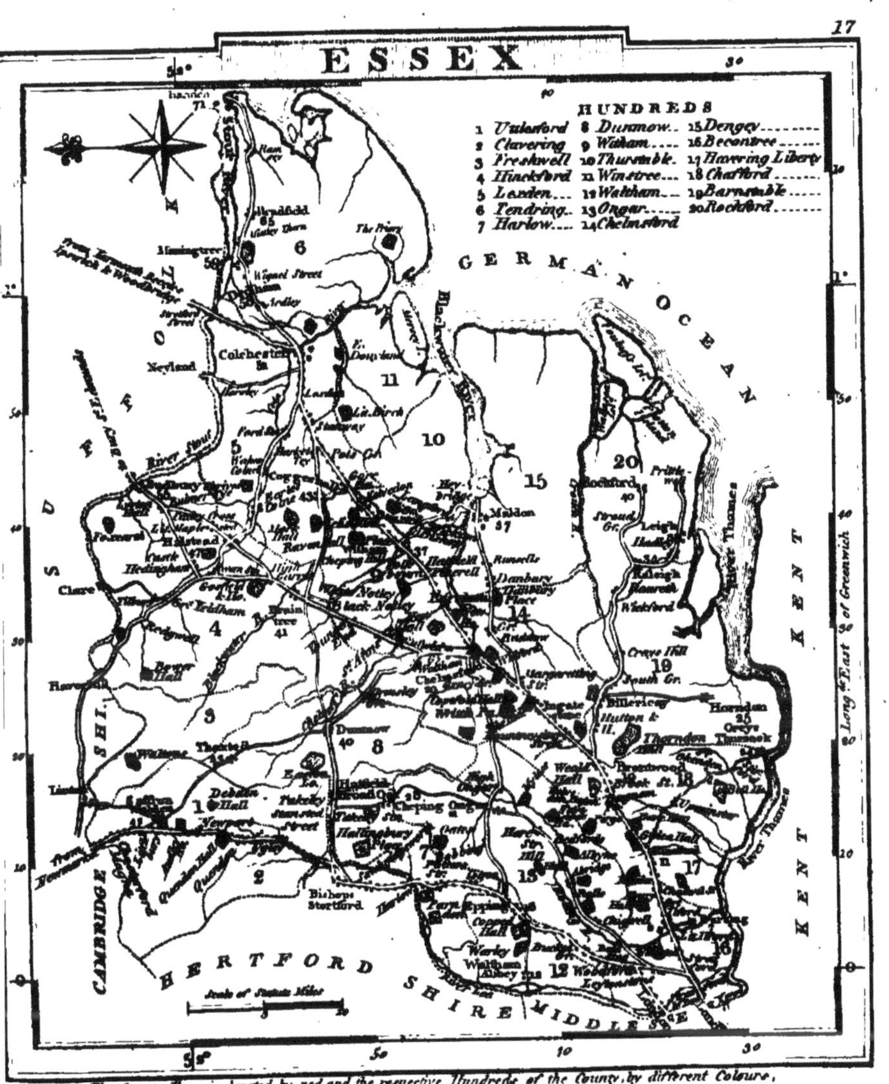

The County Town is denoted by red and the respective Hundreds of the County by different Colours, which distinctions are peculiar to the superior Edition.

The City, and County Town, are denoted by red, and the respective Hundreds of the County by different Colours which distinctions are peculiar to the Superior Edition.

The County Town is denoted by red, and the respective Hundreds of the County, by different Colours; which distinctions are peculiar to the superior Edition.

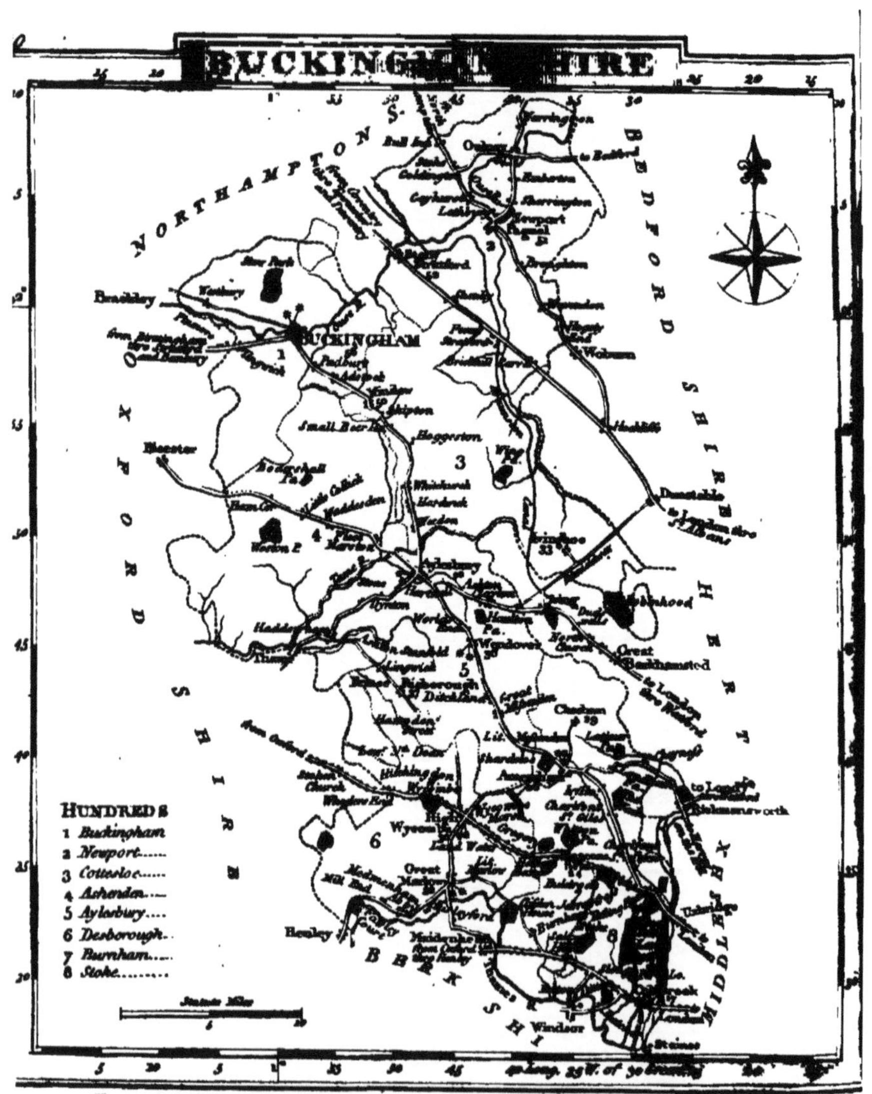

The County Town is denoted by red and the respective Hundreds of the County by different Colours which distinctions are peculiar to the Superior Edition.

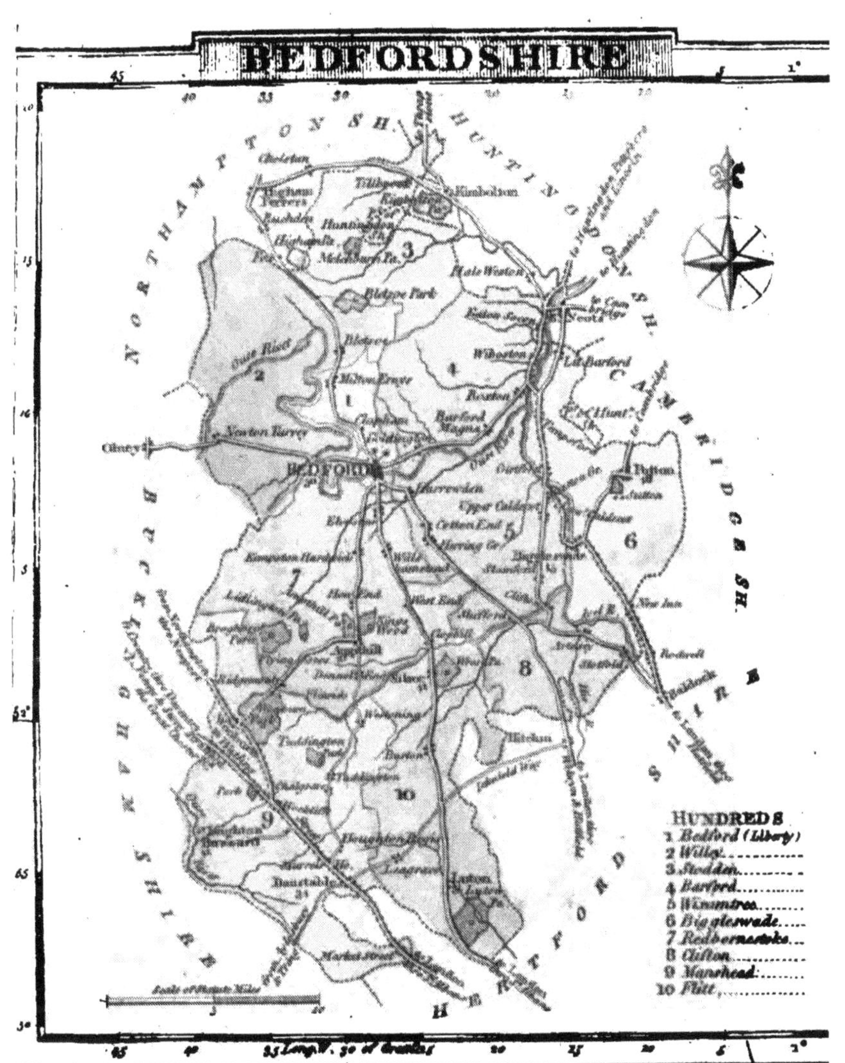

The County Town is denoted by red and the respective Hundreds of the County by different Colours which distinctions are peculiar to the Superior Edition

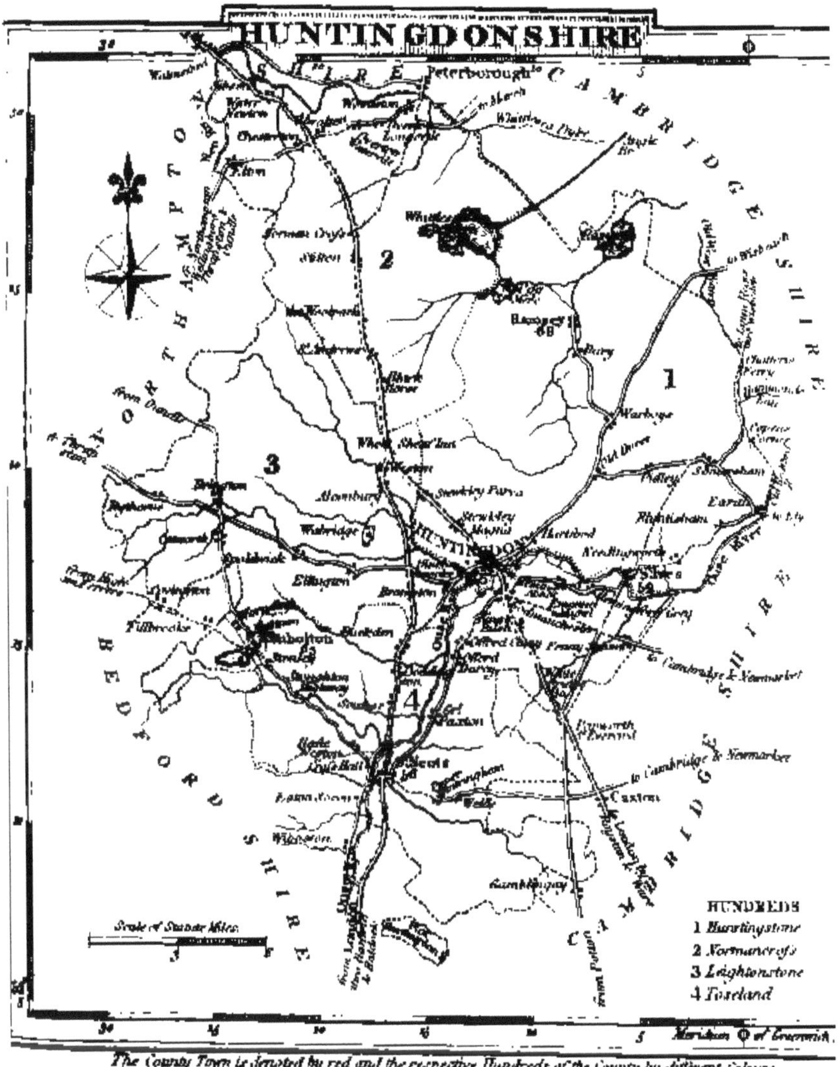

HUNTINGDONSHIRE

HUNDREDS
1 *Hurstingstone*
2 *Normancross*
3 *Leightonstone*
4 *Toseland*

Scale of Statute Miles.

Meridian of Greenwich.

The County Town is denoted by red and the respective Hundreds of the County by different Colours, which distinctions are peculiar to the superior Edition.

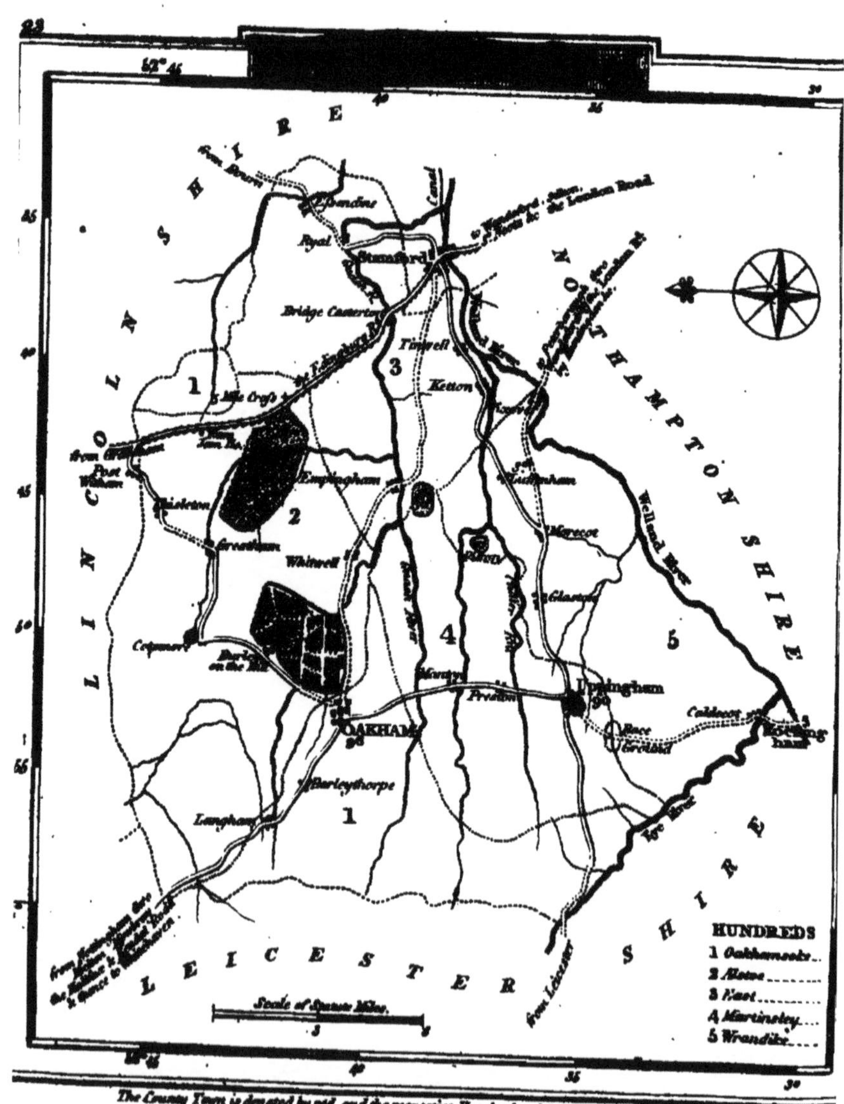

The County Town is denoted by red, and the respective Hundreds of the County by different Colours, which distinctions are peculiar to the superior Edition.

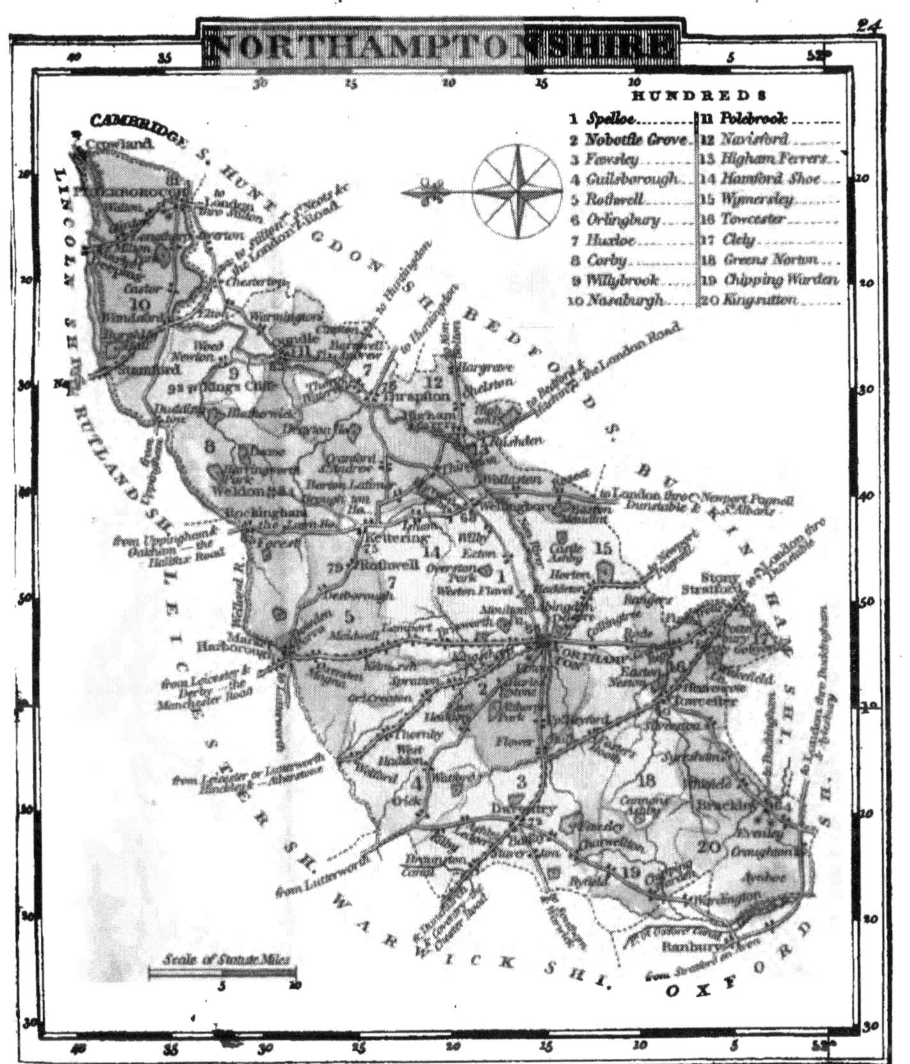

The City & County Town, are denoted by red and the respective Hundreds of the County by different Colours which distinctions are peculiar to the superior Edition.

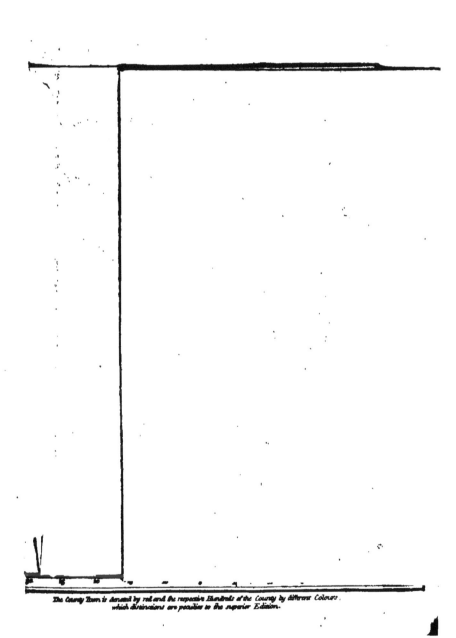

The County Town is denoted by red and the respective Hundreds of the County by different Colours, which distinctions are peculiar to the superior Edition.

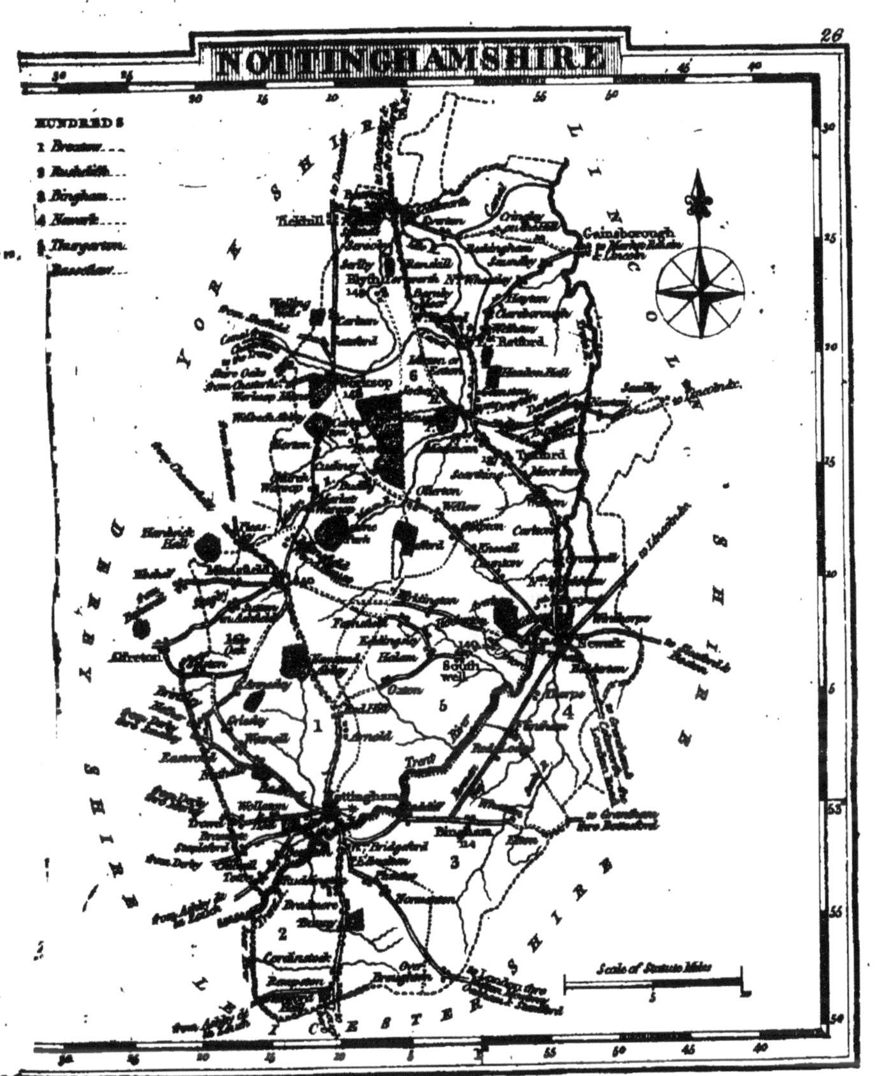

The County Town is denoted by red and the respective Hundreds of the County by different Colours, which distinctions are peculiar to the superior Edition.

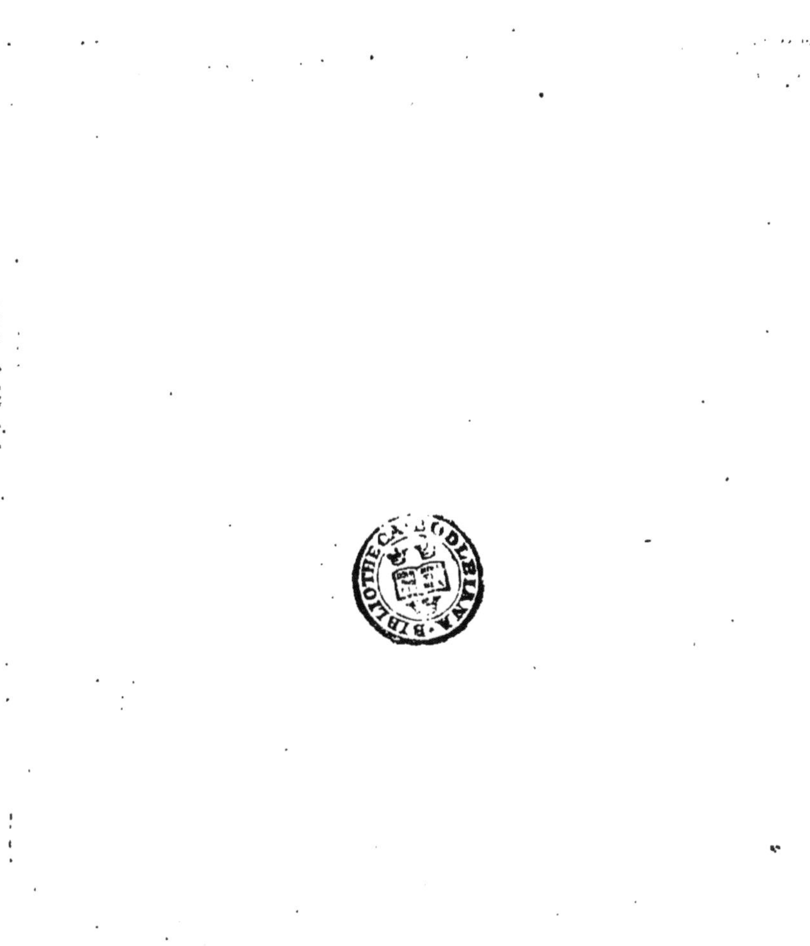

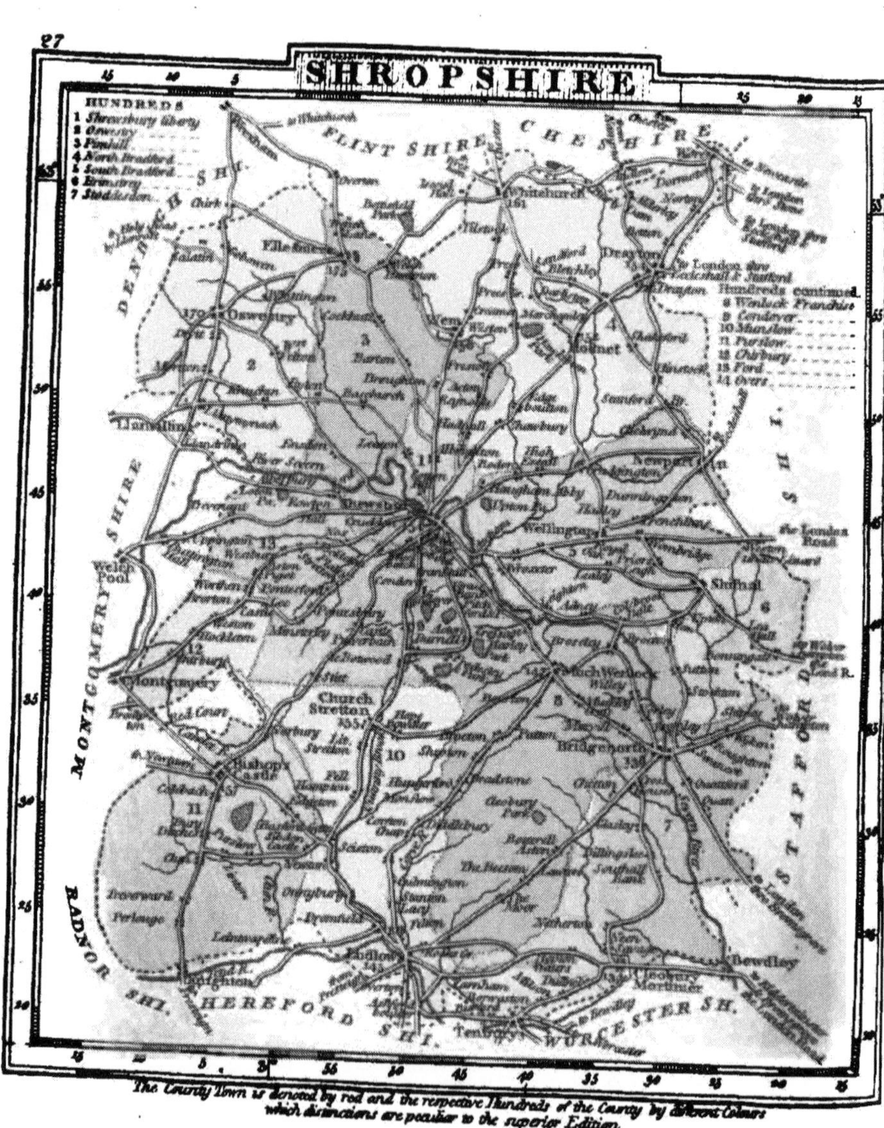

The County Town is denoted by red and the respective Hundreds of the County by different Colours which distinctions are peculiar to the superior Edition.

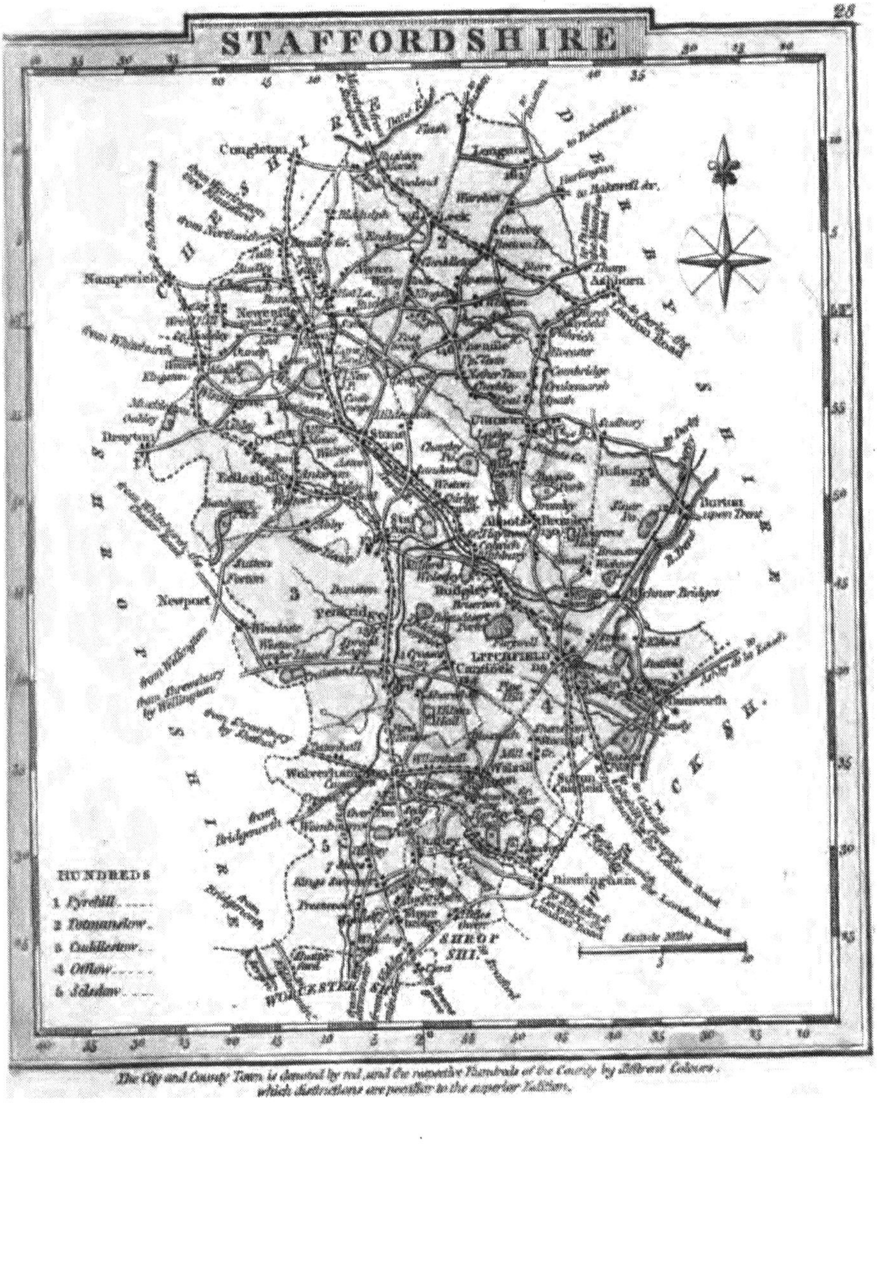

STAFFORDSHIRE

HUNDREDS

1. *Pyrehill*
2. *Totmanslow*
3. *Cuddlestow*
4. *Offlow*
5. *Seisdon*

The City and County Town is denoted by red, and the respective Hundreds of the County by different Colours, which distinctions are peculiar to the superior Edition.

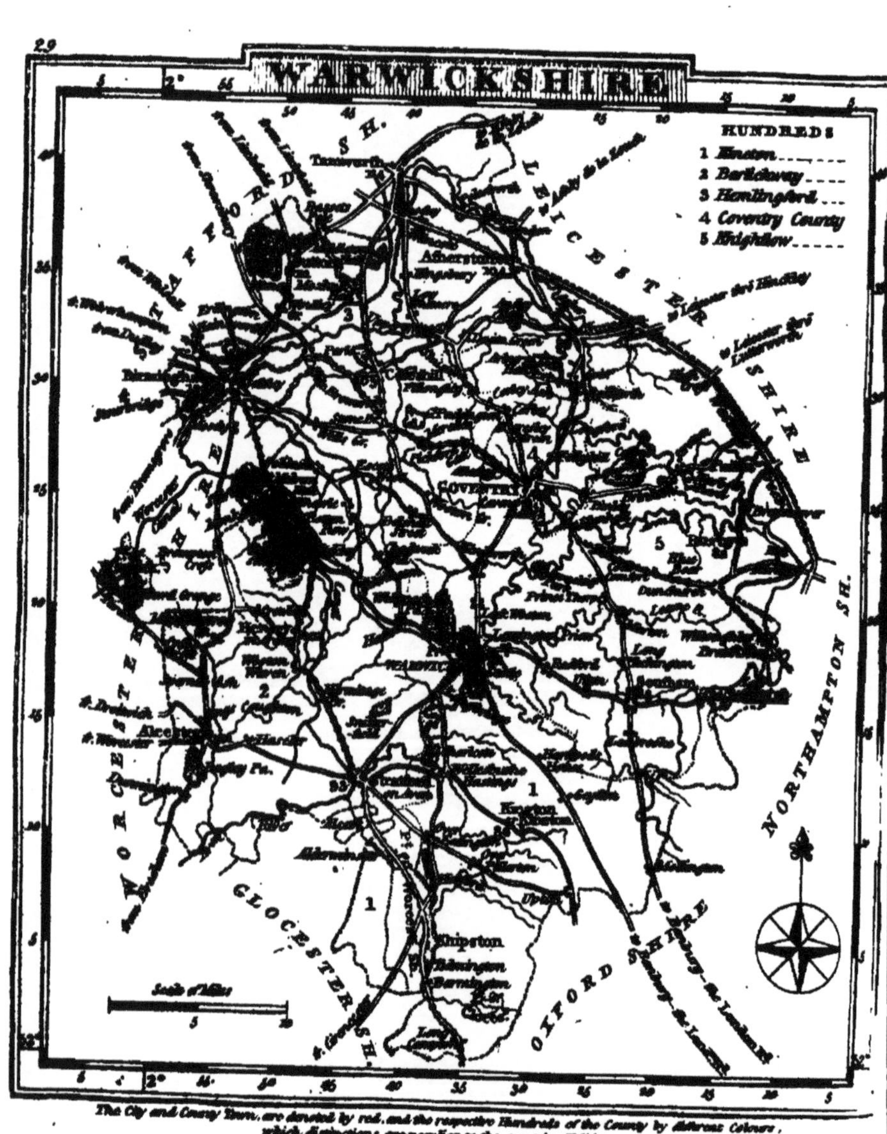

The City and County Town, are denoted by red, and the respective Hundreds of the County by different Colours, which distinctions are peculiar to the superior Edition.

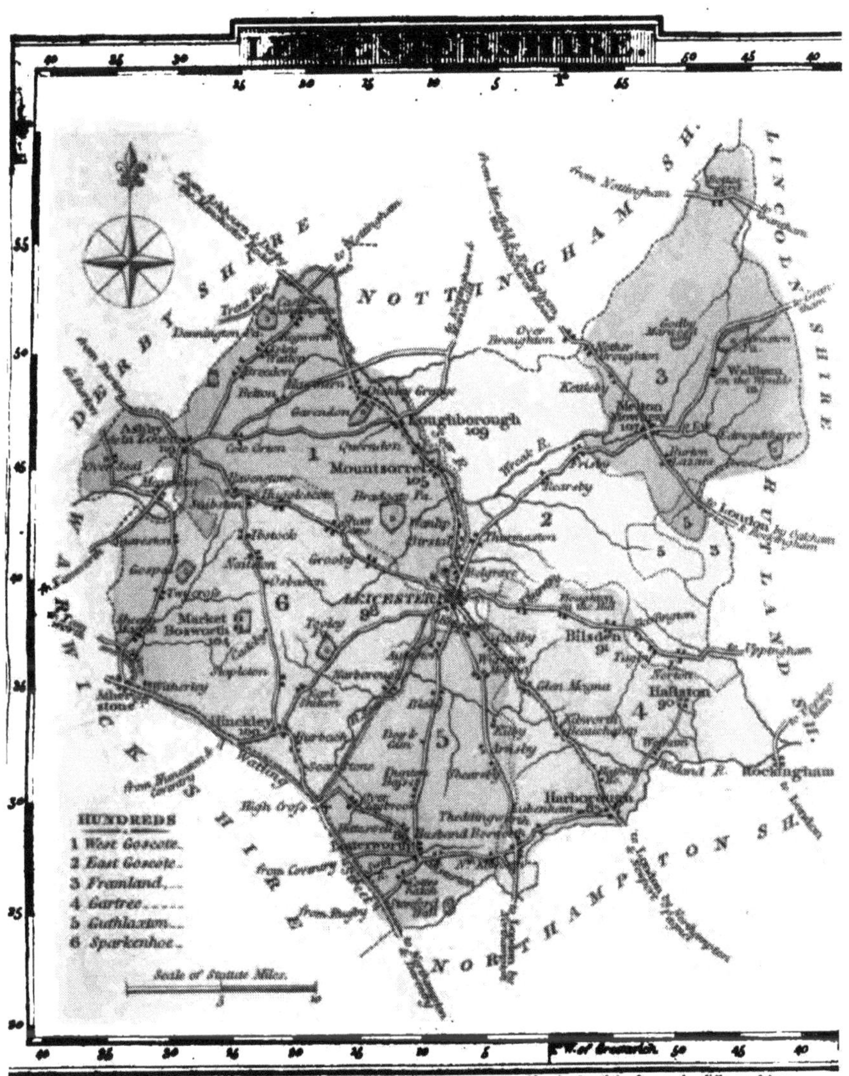

The County Town is denoted by red, and the respective Hundreds of the County by different Colors which distinctions are peculiar to the superior Edition.

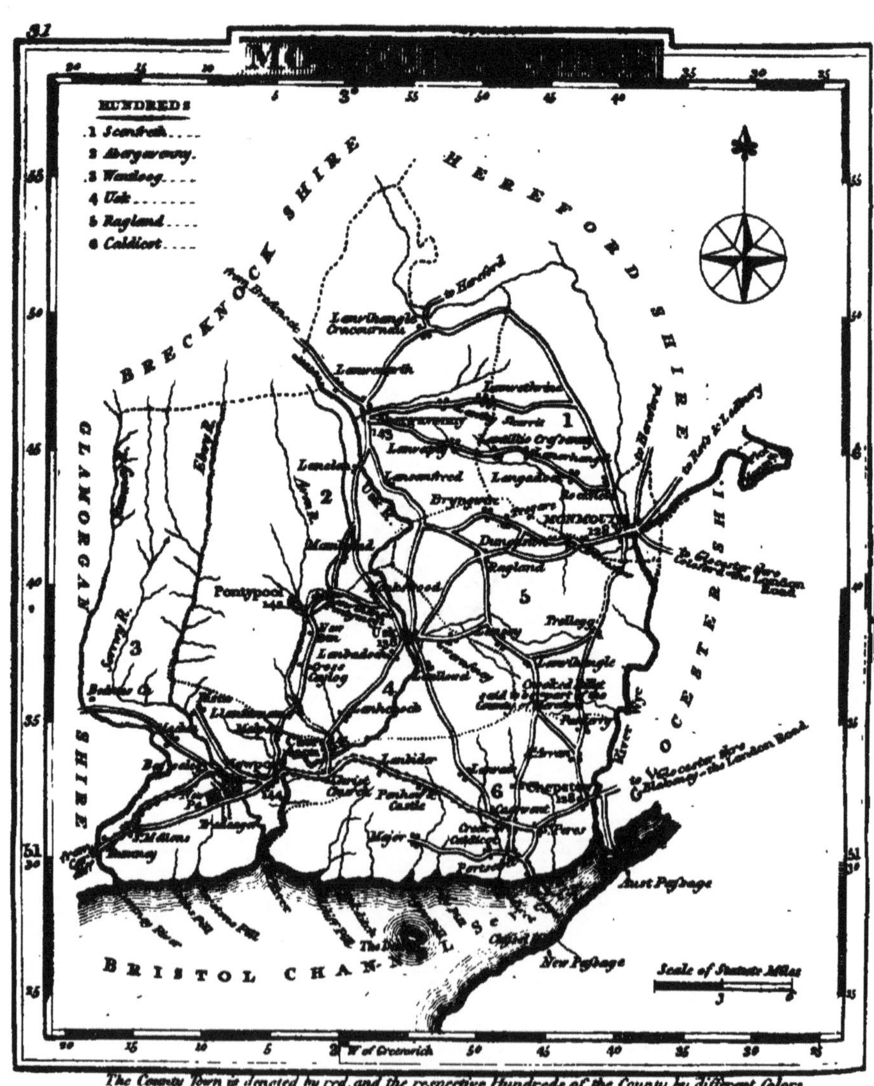

81
HUNDREDS
1 Scenfreth
2 Abergavenny
3 Wentloog
4 Usk
5 Ragland
6 Caldicot
BRECKNOCK SHIRE
HEREFORD SHIRE
GLAMORGAN SHIRE
BRISTOL CHAN
Pontypool
Raglan
Chepstow
Lanwenarth
Llanvihangle Crucorneu
Trelleck
to Hereford
from Brecknock
New Passage
Aust Passage
Scale of Statute Miles
W of Greenwich
The County Town is denoted by red, and the respective Hundreds of the County by different Colors which distinctions are peculiar to the superior Edition.

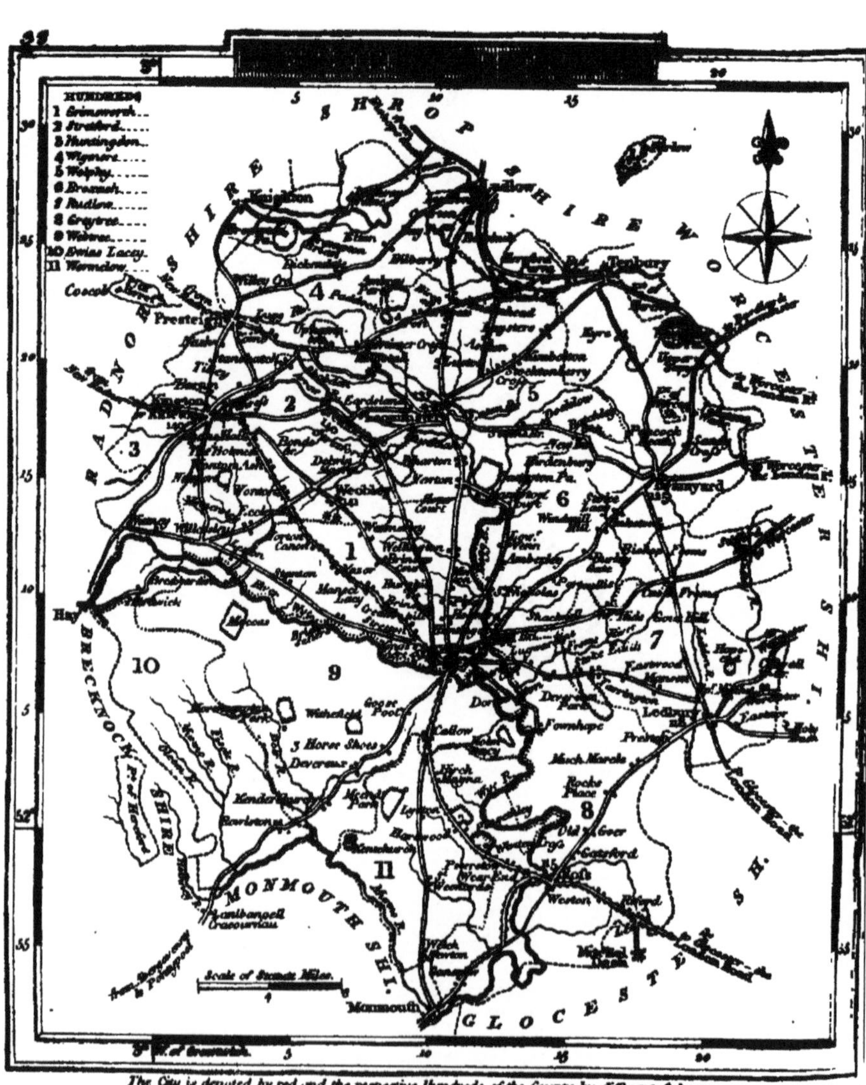

The City is denoted by red and the respective Hundreds of the County by different Colours, which distinctions are peculiar to the superior Edition.

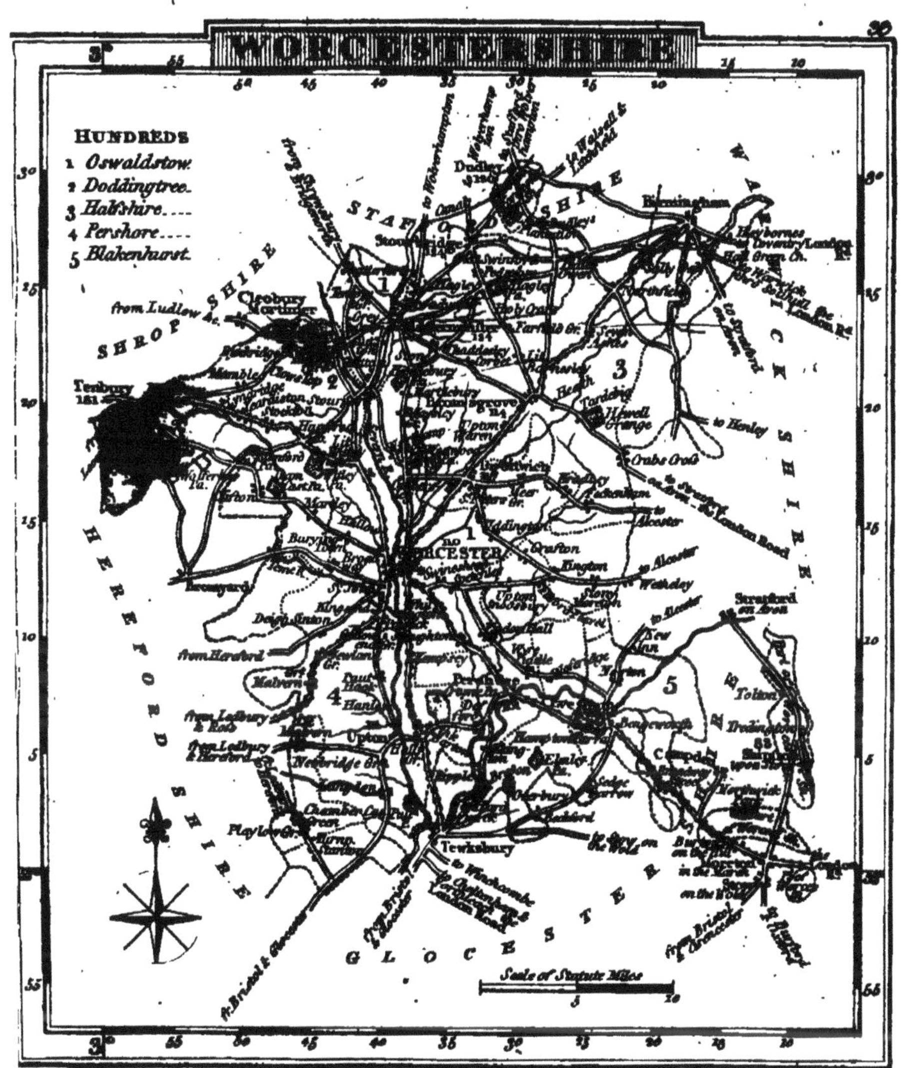

The City is denoted by red, and the respective Hundreds of the County, by different Colours, which distinctions are peculiar to the Superior Edition.

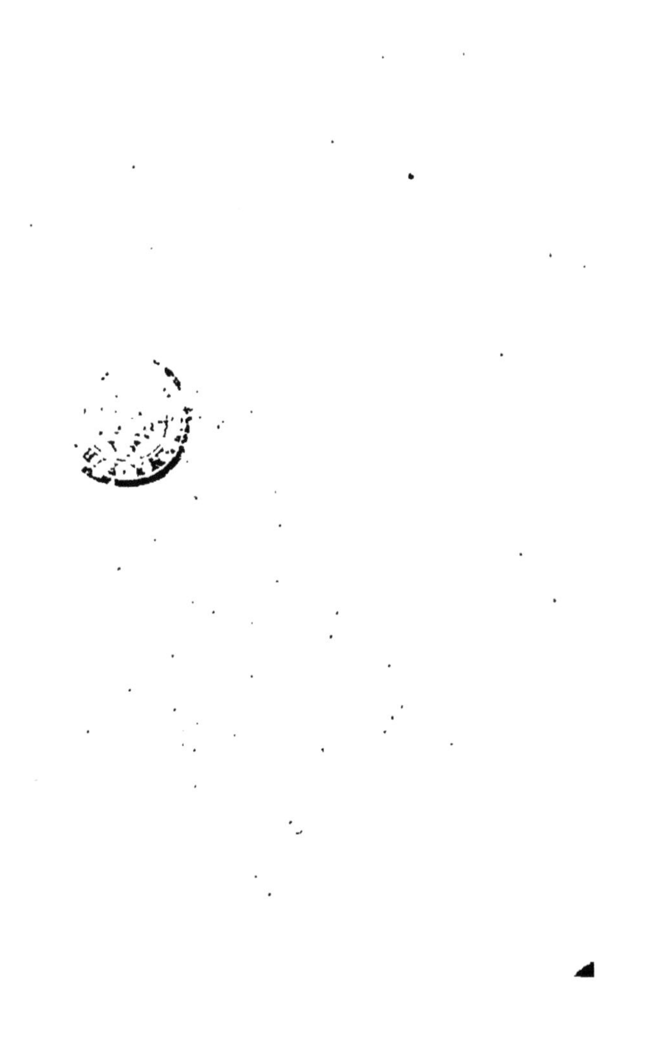

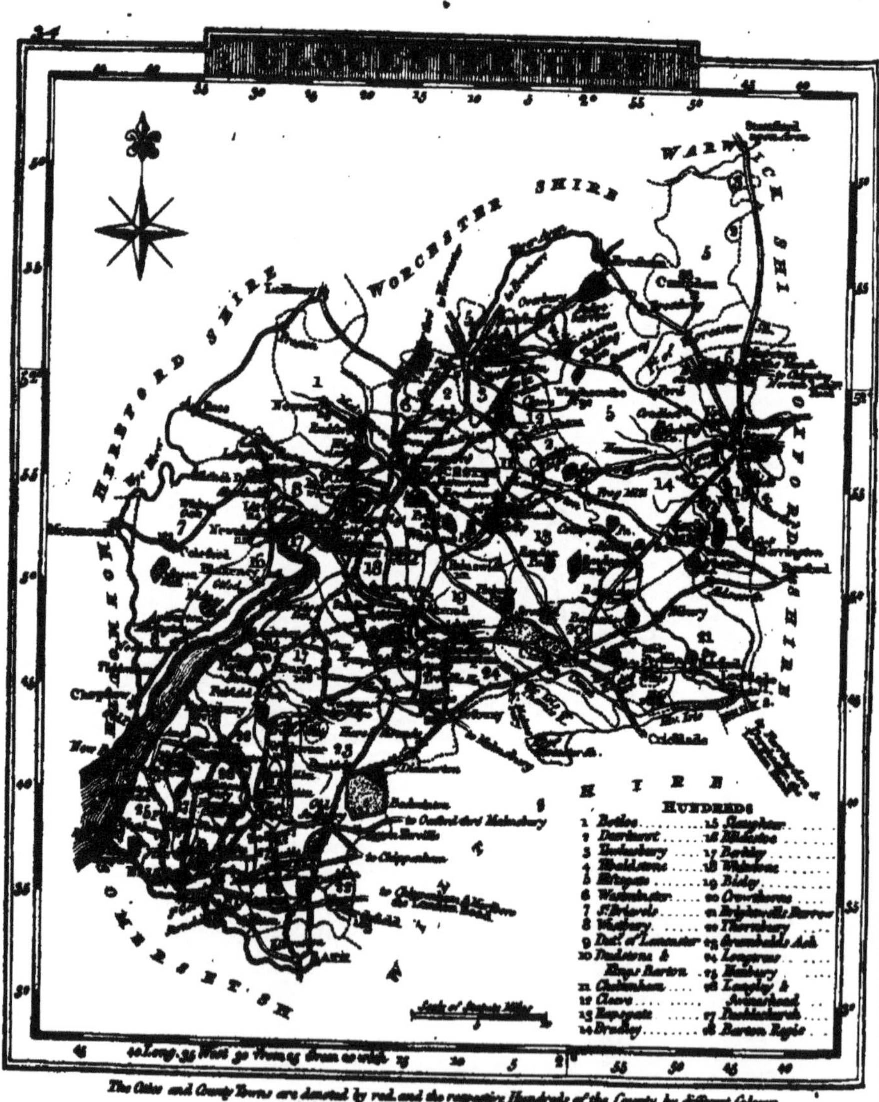

The Cities and County Towns are denoted by red and the respective Hundreds of the County by different Colours which distinctions are peculiar to the Superior Edition.

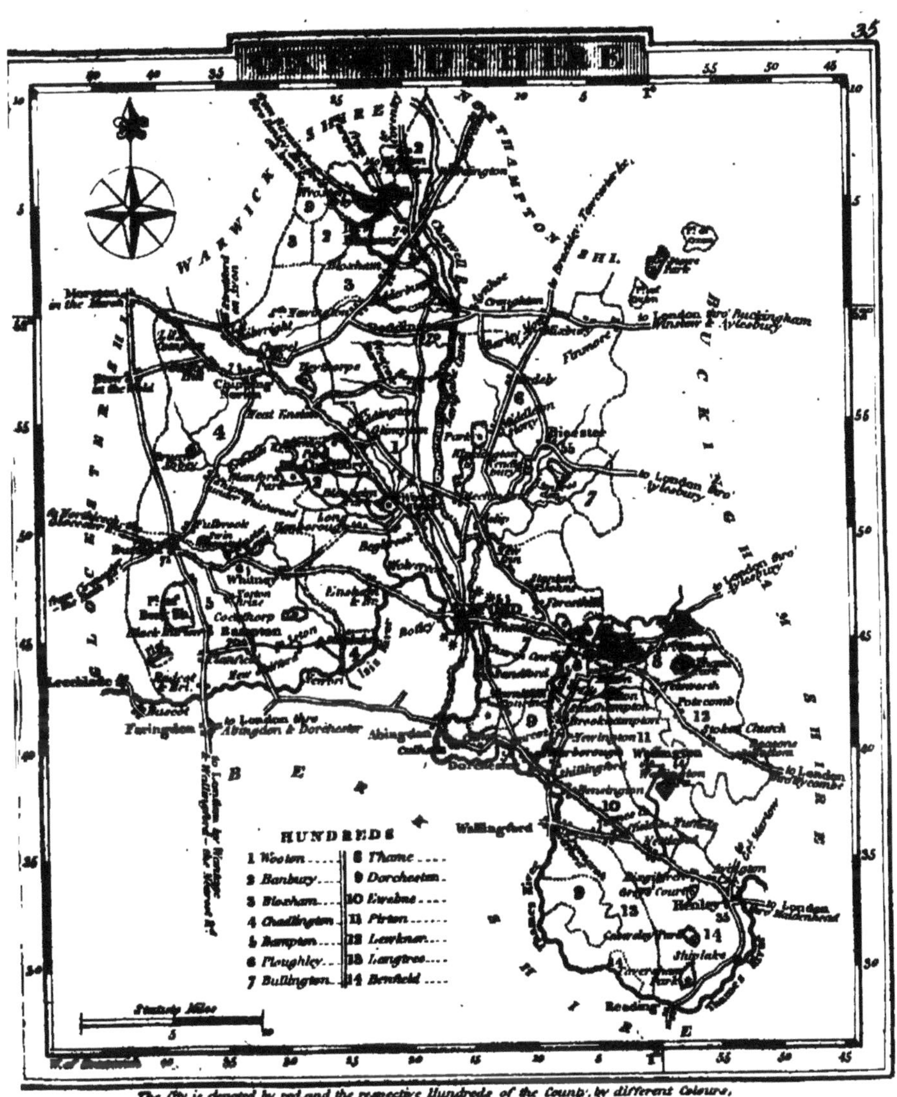

The City is denoted by red, and the respective Hundreds of the County, by different Colours, which distinctions are peculiar to the superior Edition.

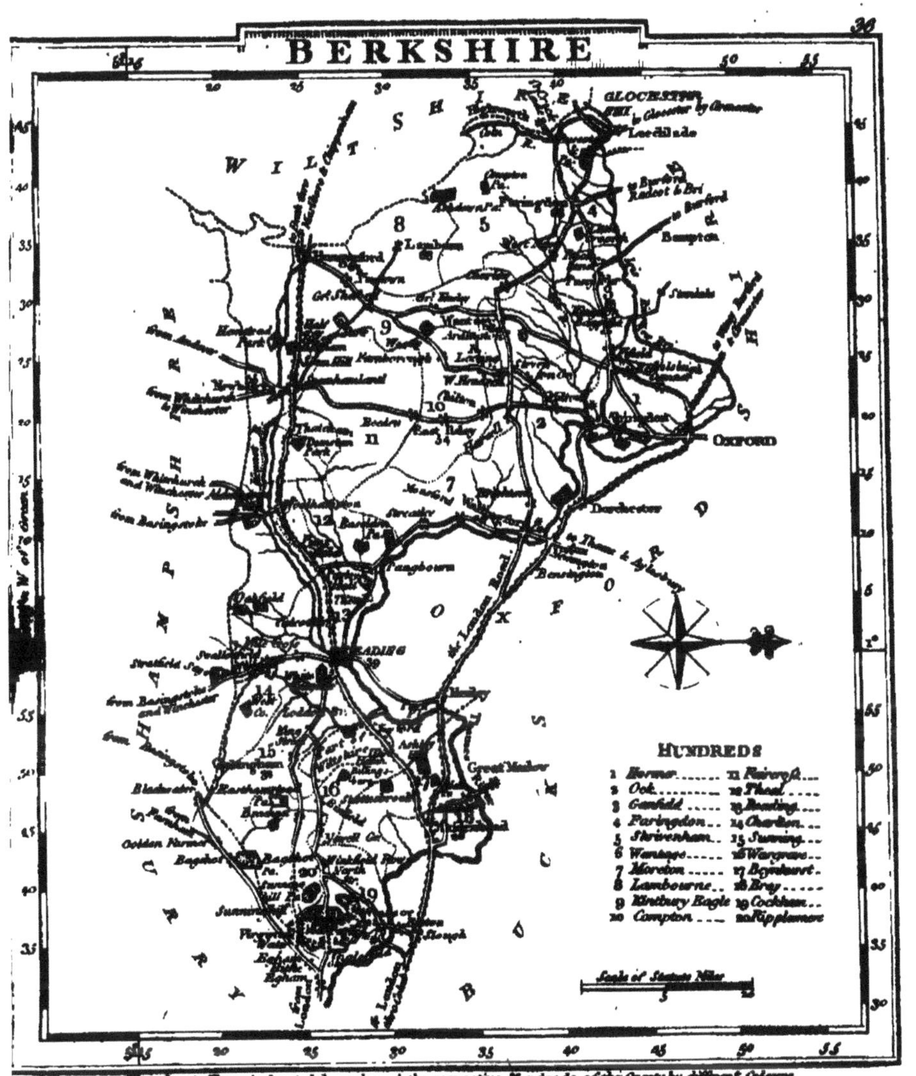

The County Town is denoted by red and the respective Hundreds of the County by different Colours which distinctions are peculiar to the Superior Edition.

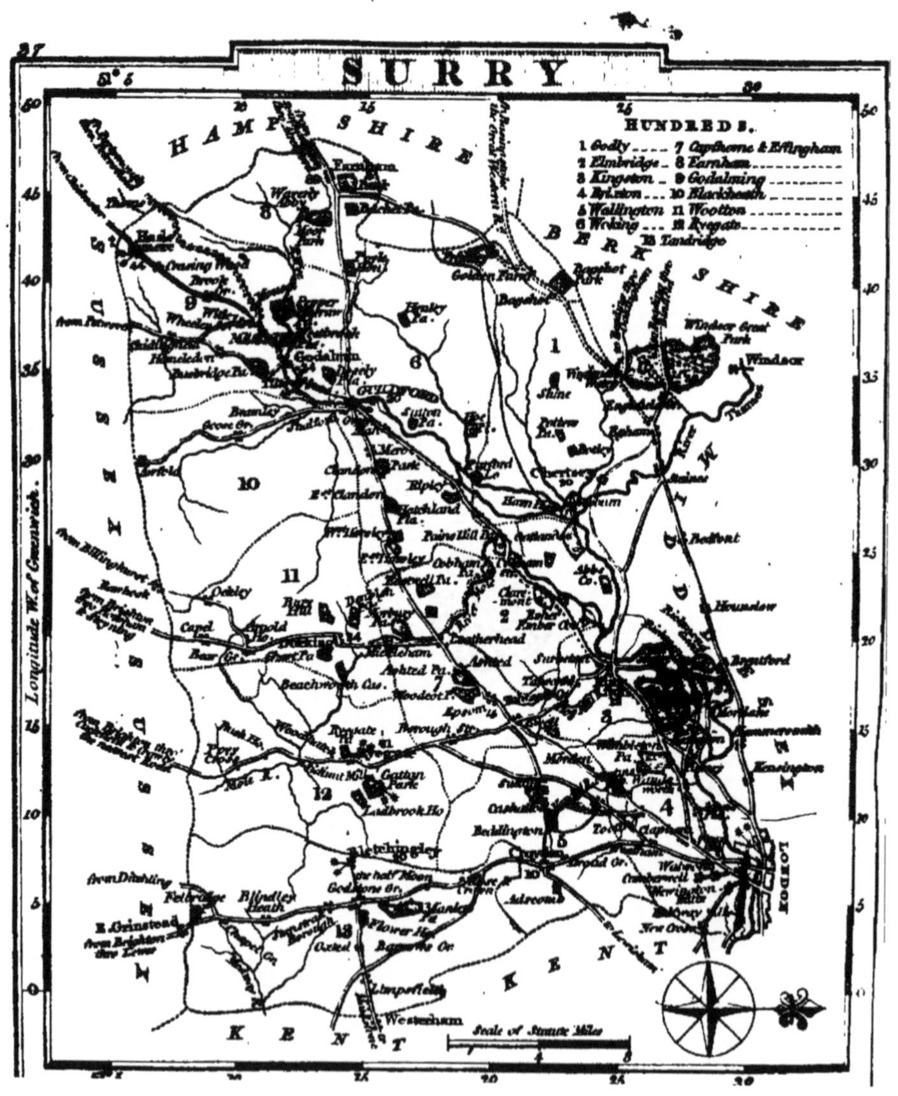

SURRY
HUNDREDS.
1 Godly
2 Elmbridge
3 Kingston
4 Brixton
5 Wallington
6 Woking
7 Copthorne & Effingham
8 Farnham
9 Godalming
10 Blackheath
11 Wootton
12 Reigate
13 Tandridge
HAMPSHIRE
BERKSHIRE
KENT
LONDON
Longitude W. of Greenwich
Scale of Statute Miles
Farnham
Bagshot
Windsor
Godalming
Guildford
Dorking
Leatherhead
Epsom
Kingston
Croydon
Wimbledon
Clapham
Camberwell
Kensington
Hammersmith
Hounslow
Westerham
Limpsfield
E. Grinstead
Beddington
Addington

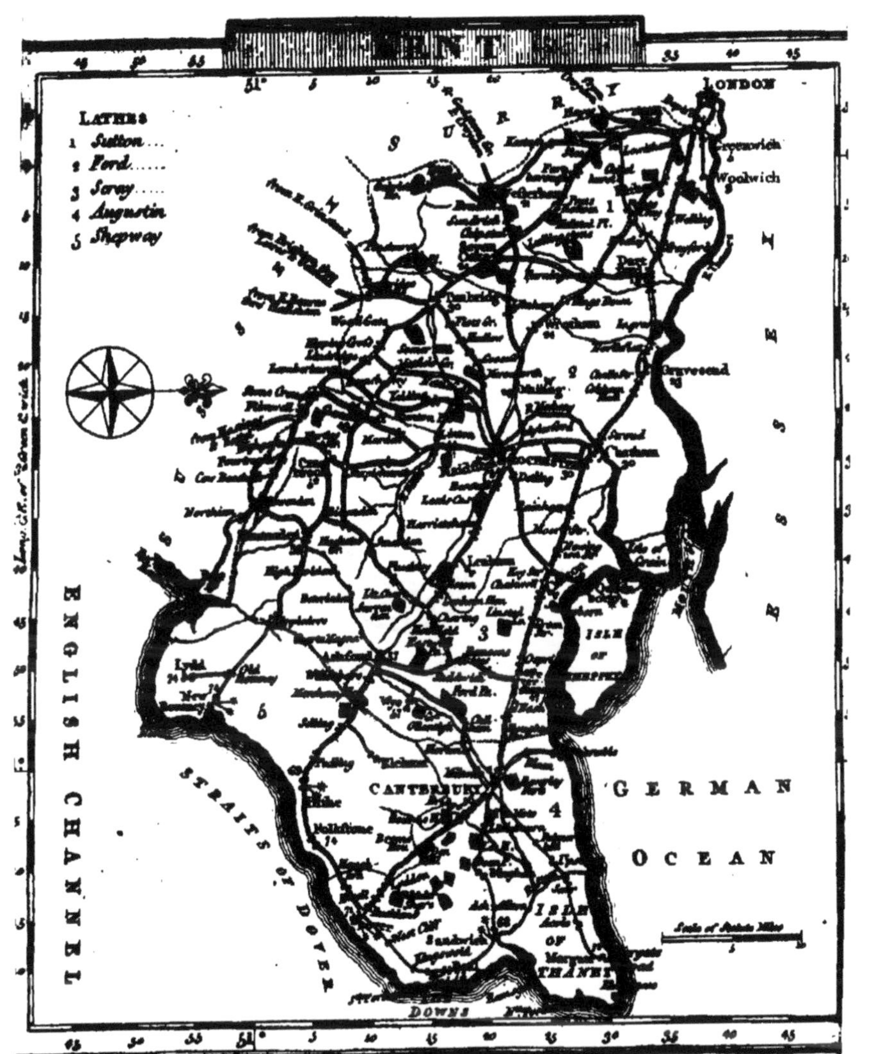

The Cities and County Towns are denoted by red, and the respective Lathes of the County by different Colours which distinctions are peculiar to the superior Edition.

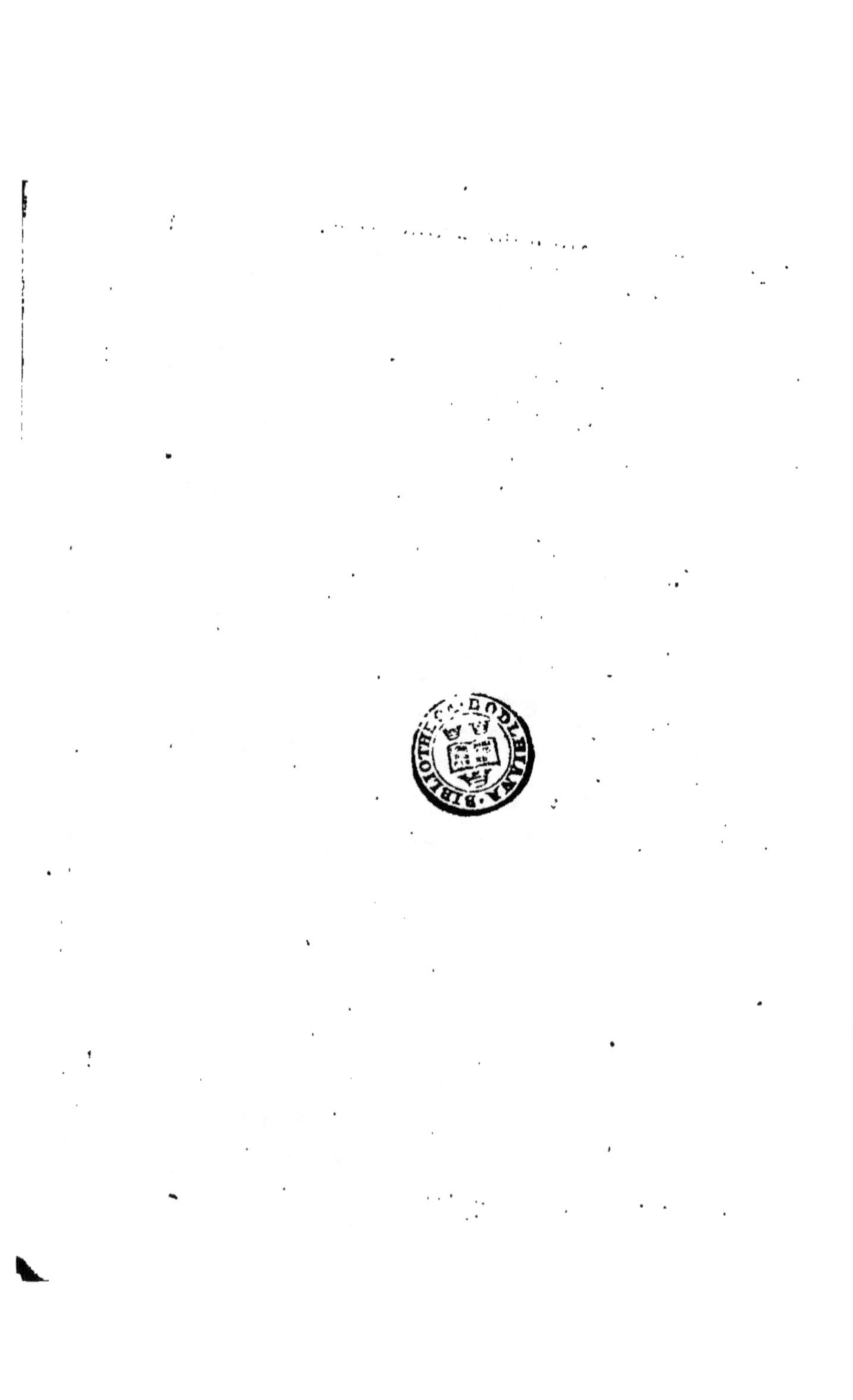

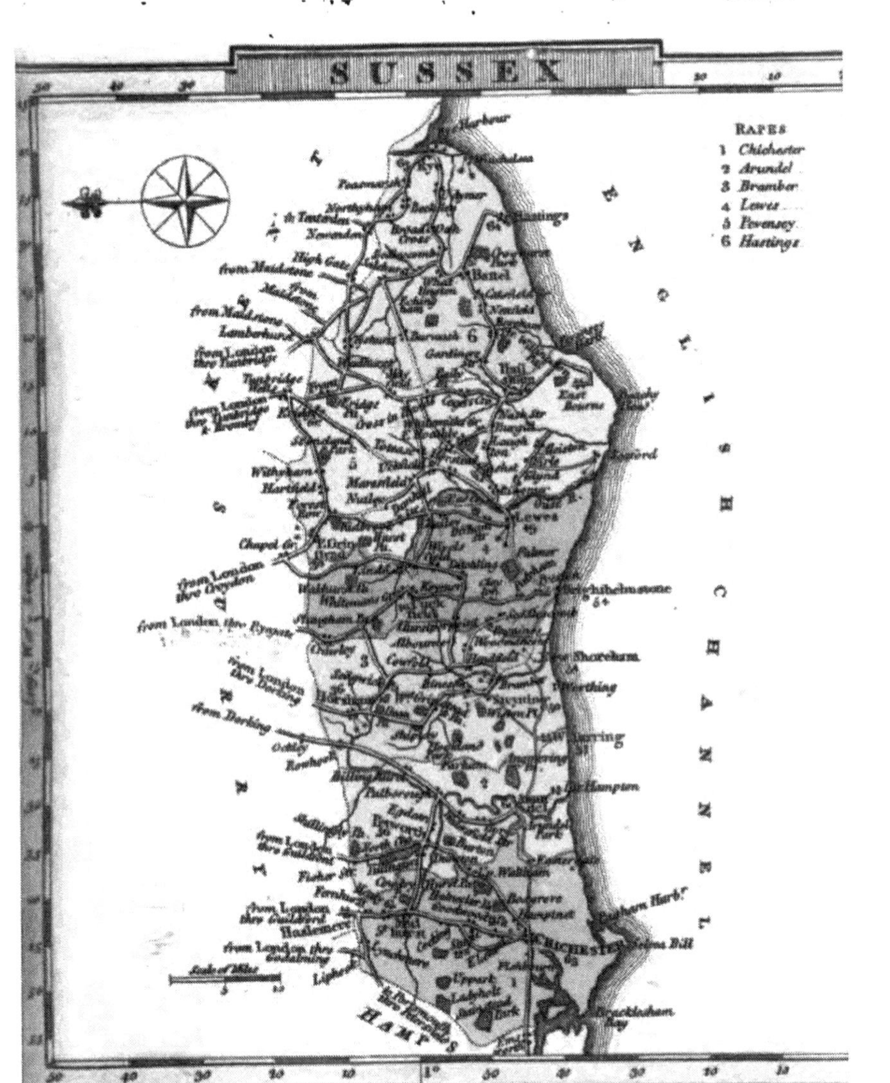

The City and County Town is denoted by red and the respective Rapes of the County by different Colours which distinctions are peculiar to the Superior Edition.

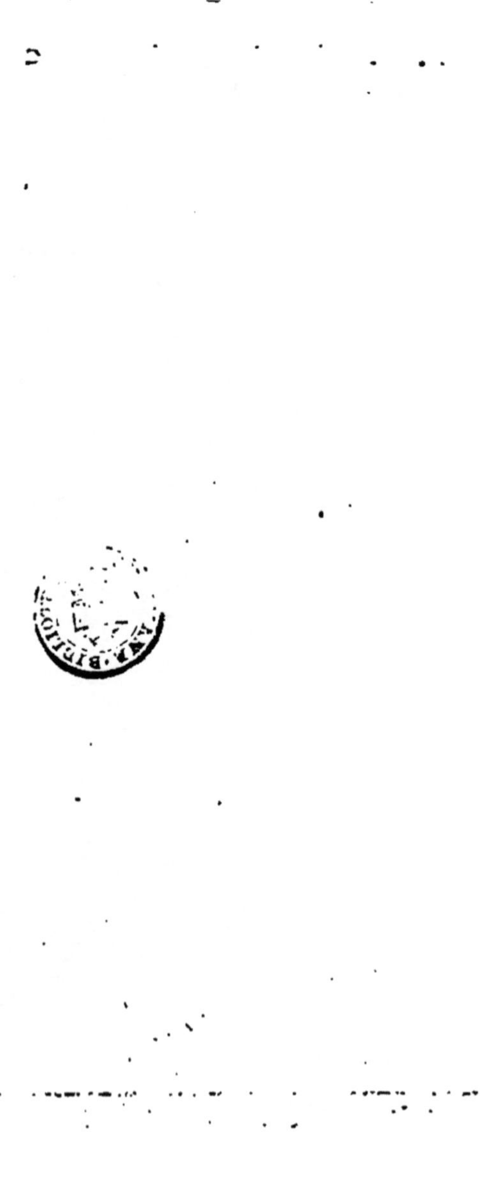

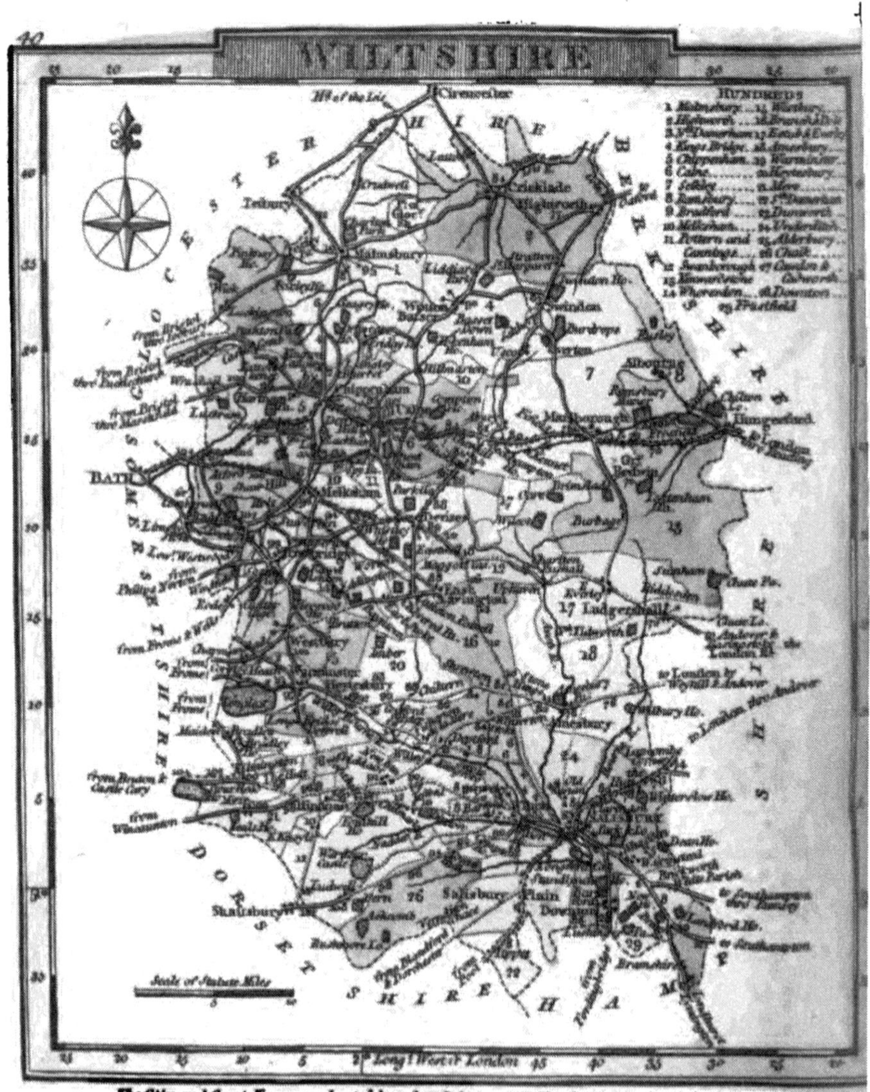

The Cities and County Towns are denoted by red, and the respective Hundreds of the County by different Colours which distinctions are peculiar to the Superior Edition.

The Cities & County Towns are denoted by red & the respective Hundreds of the County by different Colours, which distinctions are peculiar to the Superior Edition.

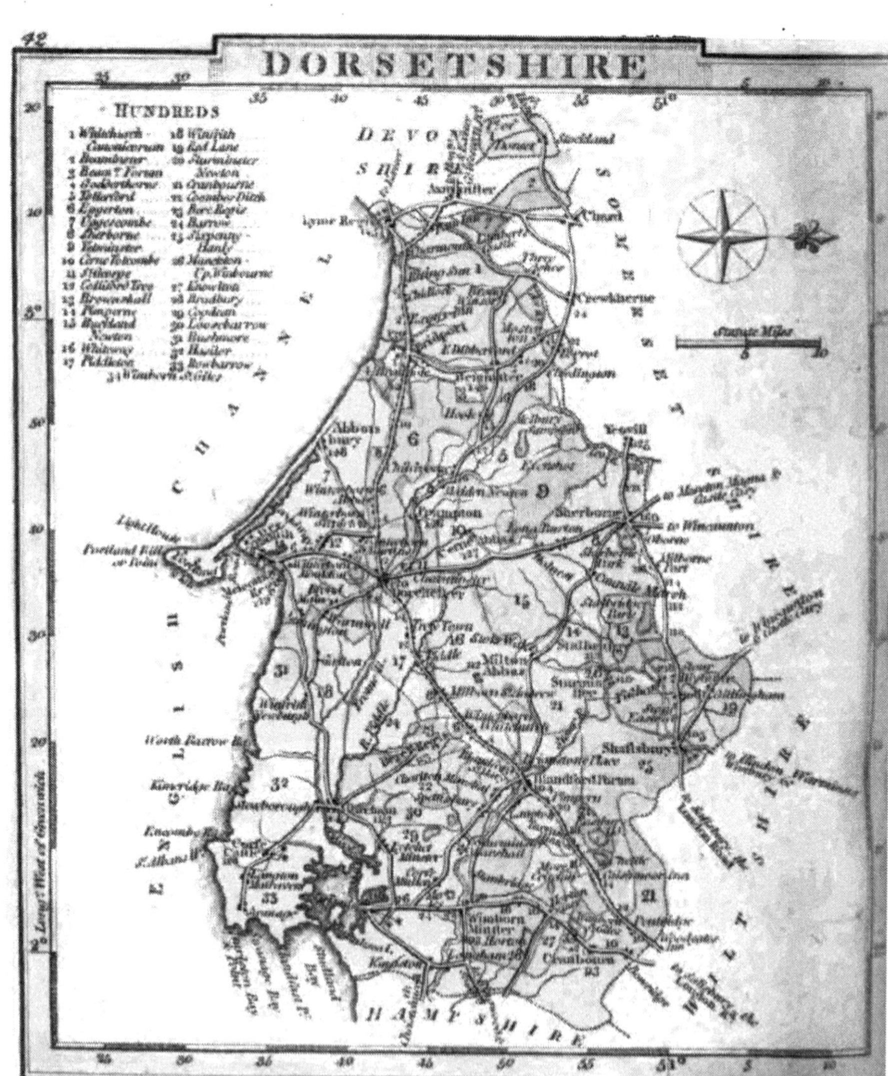

The Cities and County Towns are denoted by red, and the respective Hundreds of the County by different Colours which distinctions are peculiar to the Superior Edition.

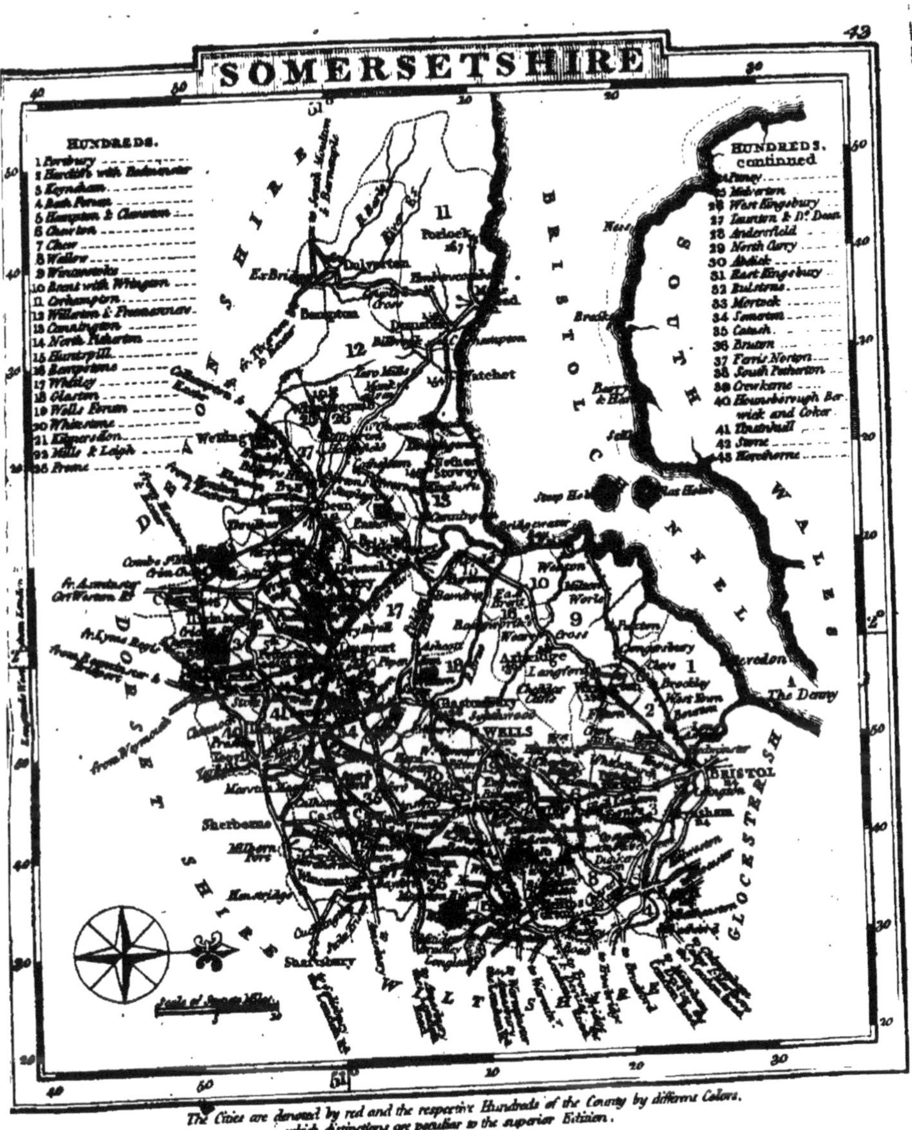

The Cities are denoted by red and the respective Hundreds of the County by different Colors, which distinctions are peculiar to the superior Edition.

The Cities and County Towns are denoted by red, and the respective Hundreds of the County by different Colours which distinctions are peculiar to the Superior Edition.

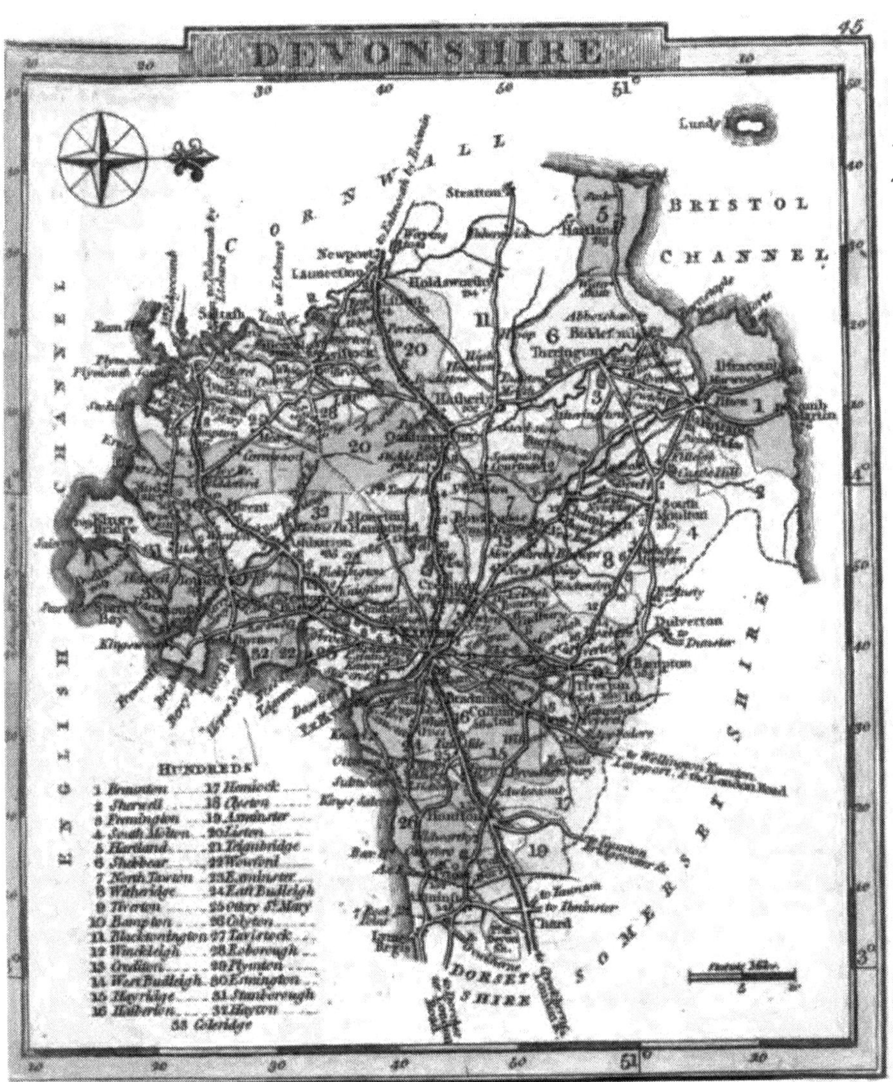

The Cities and County Towns are denoted by red, and the respective Hundreds of the County by different Colours, which distinctions are peculiar to the Superior Edition.

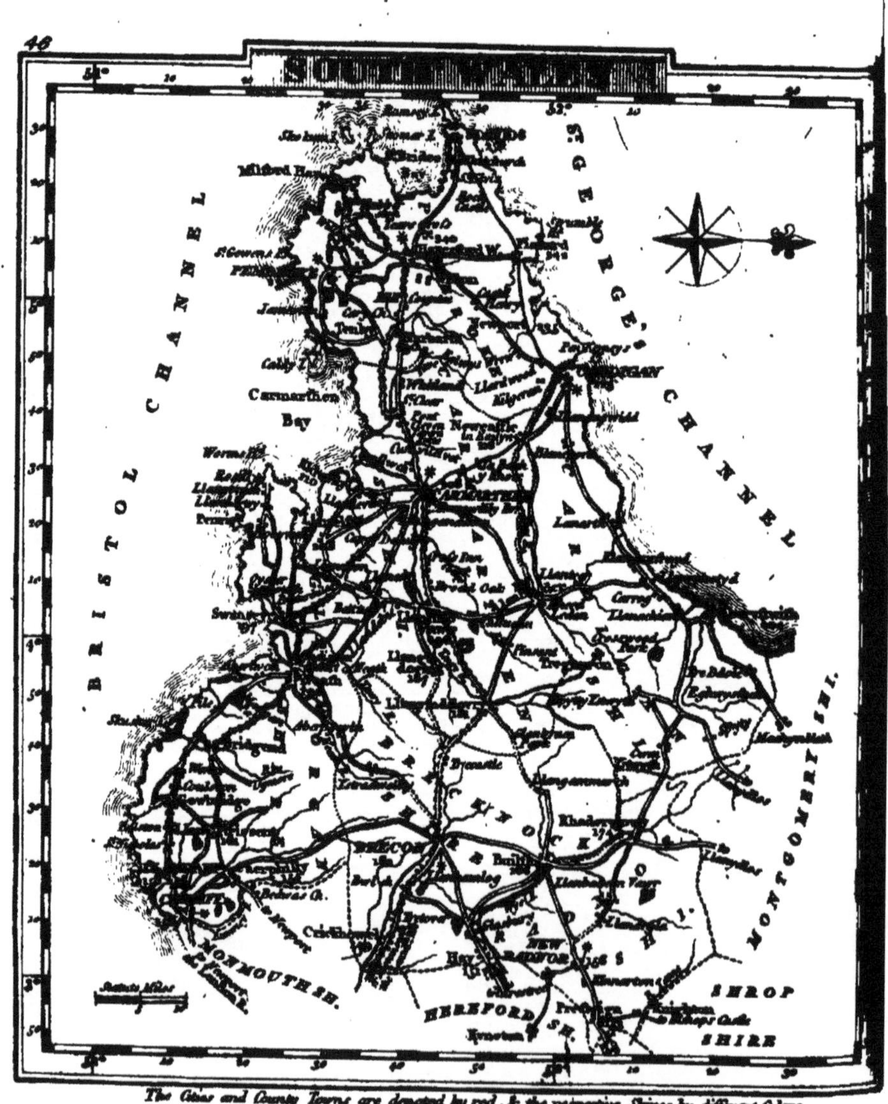

The Cities and County Towns are denoted by red, & the respective Shires by different Colors, which distinctions are peculiar to the superior Edition.

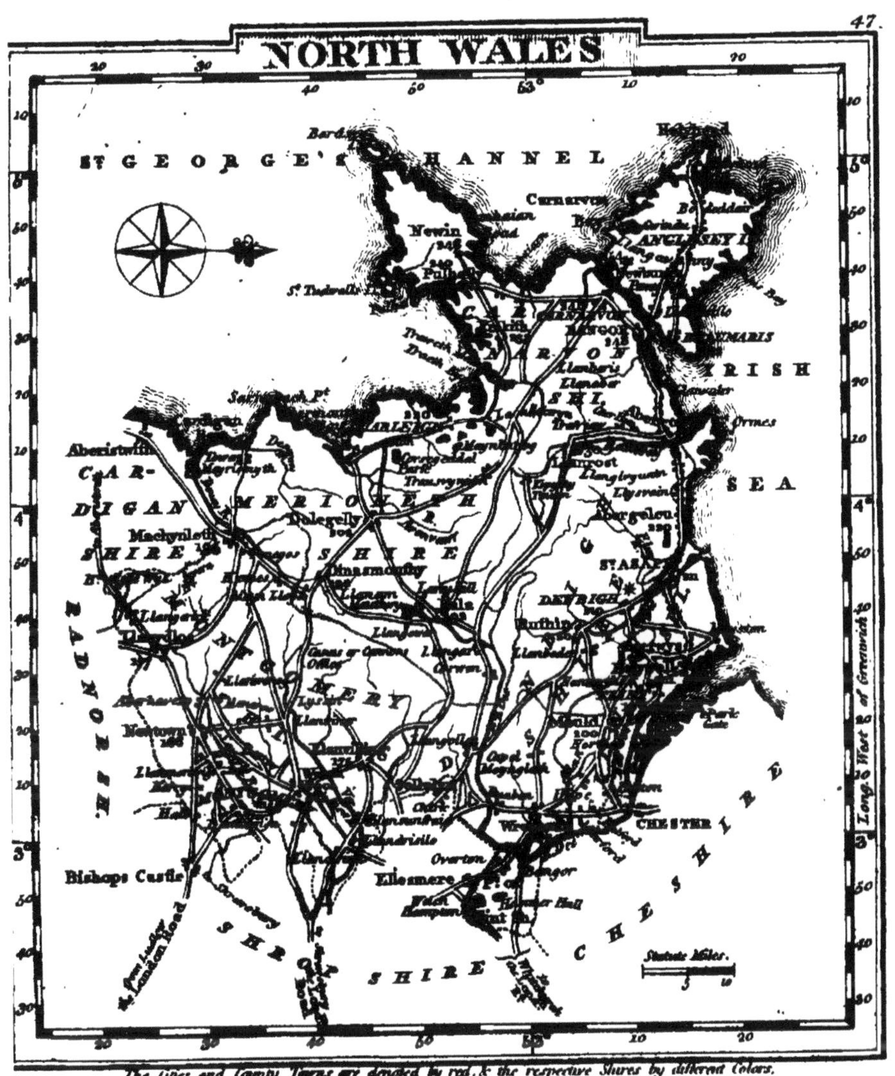

The Cities and County Towns are denoted by red, & the respective Shires by different Colors, which distinctions are peculiar to the superior Edition.

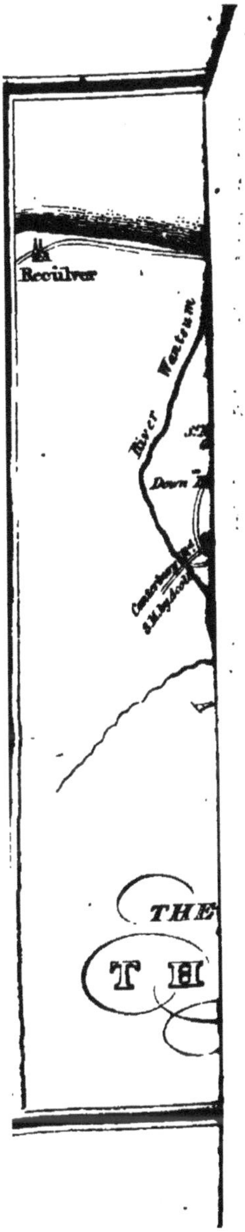

Reculver

River Wantsum

Down

THE

T H

Roman Capital
and those at t
to, in the lin

print. The le
the order of t
the route co

ion, the place

M

borough, through
nchester, § 4 *f*
wsbury, § 1
ampton, [§ 17 *d*]
, § 1 *f*
sea, [§ 12 *g*]
r, § 12
§ 17 *r*
ll, § 111
ington, § 4 *f*
pool, § 1
hester, [§ 17 *e*] *r*
erhampton, § 111
ester, p 11 *r*
ling, [§ 17 *a*] *r*
ham, § 4 *f*
through Man-
ster, § 4 *f*

.... 56

.... 13
70 114

.... 97

. p 41... 68
.... 94
bridge... 207
.... 48
3 I...... 307

.... 136

INDEX.

EXPLAINED.—The Roads from London are distinguished by Italic type, and by Roman Capitals; the figures immediately following the places referring to the page of the route, and those at the end of the line shewing the distance from London.—The Cross Roads are referred to, in the lines underneath, by the number of the section, with this character prefixed §.

The LOCAL INDICES, as at Aberystwith, below, are distinguished by small Roman print. The letters *f* signify 'forward,' and *r* 'reverse.' Thus, Aberystwith to Bristol, § 17 *r*, the order of the route being reversed and ending at § 16. Again, Aberystwith to Atherstone, § 7 *f*: the route continuing forward along the line A i, as explained page 87.

β implies branch from the direct line of road. The distance being given from London, the place is easily referred to, on the line whence it branches.

M

INDEX.

INDEX.

INDEX.

INDEX.

INDEX.

INDEX.

INDEX.

INDEX.

INDEX.

INDEX.

INDEX.

INDEX.

INDEX.

INDEX.

INDEX.

INDEX.

INDEX.

INDEX.

INDEX.

INDEX.

INDEX.

INDEX.

INDEX.

INDEX.

ERRATA.

The Reader is requested to correct the following Errata with a Pen:

Page 16,	at AYLESBURY, the reference should be to p. 14.			
27,	col. 3, *erase the line* Cave *after* Wolseley Bridge.			
33,	at LEICESTER, the reference should be to p. 30.			
51,	LINCOLN,	do.	do.	p. 50.
57,	IPSWICH,	do.	do.	p. 56.
64,	BATH,	do.	do.	p. 72.

J. G. Barnard, Printer, Skinner Street, London.

Lightning Source UK Ltd.
Milton Keynes UK
UKHW021253200120
357276UK00008B/2194